HUNTERS, FARMERS, AND CIVILIZATIONS

Readings from
**SCIENTIFIC
AMERICAN**

HUNTERS, FARMERS, AND CIVILIZATIONS: Old World Archaeology

With Introductions by
C. C. Lamberg-Karlovsky
Harvard University

W. H. Freeman and Company
San Francisco

To the memory of Dame Kathleen Kenyon, Sir Max
Mallowan, Sir Mortimer Wheeler, and Professor
Fuad Safar

Some of the SCIENTIFIC AMERICAN articles in *Hunters,
Farmers, and Civilizations: Old World Archaeology* are
available as separate Offprints. For a complete list of articles now available as Offprints, write to W. H. Freeman and
Company, 660 Market Street, San Francisco, California
94104.

Library of Congress Cataloging in Publication Data

Main entry under title:

Hunters, farmers, and civilizations, old world
  archaeology.

  Includes bibliographies and index.
  1. Paleolithic period—Addresses, essays, lectures.
2. Neolithic period—Addresses, essays, lectures.
3. Bronze age—Addresses, essays, lectures.   I. Lamberg-
Karlovsky, C. C., 1937–   II. Scientific American.
GN768.H86   1979   930′.1   78–27049
ISBN 0-7167-1073-0
ISBN 0-7167-1074-9 pbk.

Printed in the United States of America

9 8 7 6 5 4 3 2 1

PREFACE

This volume of selected readings from SCIENTIFIC AMERICAN replaces the earlier one entitled *Old World Archaeology: Foundations of Civilization.* In the Preface to that volume, I indicated the growing interest in archaeology both in this country and abroad. This interest has not abated; it has intensified.

It was only a century ago that archaeology was perceived as an antiquarian concern. Its principal purpose was to uncover impressive monuments, remove their most outstanding art objects, and display them in the great museums, which were predominantly in the Western world. Today, the archaeological resources of a country are of major significance in an understanding of its past. Hardly a nation does not have laws protecting its archaeological monuments and a national museum in which to display them.

The quickened pace of industrial development, however, threatens the very existence of archaeological sites. Large-scale irrigation systems, the development of roads, and industries have caused the destruction of archaeological sites in developing countries. Recognizing that archaeological sites, like an unpolluted environment, are limited resources that must be protected, nations throughout the world have instituted programs to salvage and preserve their archaeological past, to protect the national heritage represented by these sites.

Today it is not sufficient to excavate archaeological sites merely to obtain objects for display in a museum. Archaeologists now are not content merely to recover and describe the treasures of the past. Archaeology has come of age in addressing itself to some of the most provocative questions in human history. Today archaeologists ask of their data how and why past circumstances evolved as they did. What were the circumstances that led us to depart from hunting and gathering (an economic subsistence pattern that lasted for 99 percent of our evolutionary past) and to develop agriculture some 10,000 years ago? What were the conditions and causal factors, some 5000 years ago, that led to that most precarious of inventions, the city? These questions and others are addressed in the collected essays of this volume.

The quickened pace of archaeological research in previously little known areas, such as Southeast Asia, Africa, and the islands of the Pacific, has greatly expanded our knowledge and appreciation of the complex societies of the past. Entire avenues of research into and wholly new understandings of proto-human and human life and behavior, which were unknown at the time the earlier book of SCIENTIFIC AMERICAN papers was published, are presented in this volume. The articles by Isaac, Solheim, and Schmandt-Besserat, to name but three, incorporate new insights and understandings of our complex past.

The articles gathered in this volume provide us with a view of over 1 million years of our cultural evolution. The great time scale of archaeology not only provides us with an appreciation and understanding of the almost infinite diversity of our past but also allows us to guide our decisions today by considering past circumstances that led to success or failure.

In a rapidly changing world, an archaeological perspective reminds us that such concerns as overpopulation and environmental abuses are not new and that our own civilization is but one of many over the course of human history. A deepened understanding of our past leads to a universal understanding of our shared humanity, so fundamental to coexistence in the world today.

October 1978   C. C. Lamberg-Karlovsky

CONTENTS

IV   EUROPEAN COMMUNITIES: NEOLITHIC TO MEDIEVAL

Note on cross-references to SCIENTIFIC AMERICAN *articles:* Articles included in this book are referred to by title and page number; articles not included in this book but available as Offprints are referred to by title and offprint number; articles not included in this book and not available as Offprints are referred to by title and date of publication.

HUNTERS, FARMERS, AND CIVILIZATIONS

I

PALEOLITHIC HUNTERS AND GATHERERS

I PALEOLITHIC HUNTERS AND GATHERERS

INTRODUCTION

When Glyn Daniel wrote the essay that begins this section, the antiquity and evolution of human beings was thought not to exceed a million years. In the same year that Professor Daniel wrote (1959), Louis and Mary Leakey discovered at Olduvai Gorge, Tanzania, the first living floors with an almost complete skull of a robust man-ape called *Australopithecus*. Continued excavations at Olduvai have distinguished two species of this primate: *Australopithecus robustus,* having a heavy jaw and adapted to a herbivorous diet, and *Australopithecus africanus,* rather closer to humans and having a lighter jaw perhaps related to an omnivorous diet. The latter species, a more gracile hominid, was referred to by its discoverers as *Homo habilis* ("handy person") because of its *inferred* ability to make stone tools. The reconstruction of hand bones revealed an opposable thumb, which could have afforded a precise manipulation for making tools to standard patterns. Fragments of lava were found on the Olduvai floors associated with *Australopithecus robustus*, which allowed for potassium-argon dating. The dates derived from this technique place both australopithecine species within the range of 1.75–2.0 million years ago.

Human Origins: The Lower Pleistocene

The exact relationship between these two species of australopithecines still needs clarification. Earlier hominid specimens of *Homo*, associated with tools, were subsequently discovered in the Omo Valley on the Kenya-Ethopia border and in East Turkana. The oldest specimen of an australopithecine comes from Lothagam, Kenya, where a solitary jaw fragment has been potassium-argon dated to 5.5 million years ago. Within the past decade extensive paleoanthropological work has been undertaken in East Africa in search of our earliest ancestors.

In 1974 Maurice Taieb and Don C. Johanson found a near-complete skeleton of a primate at Hadar in northern Ethiopia. This hominid, known as "Lucy," is dated to about 3 million years ago. "Lucy" stood short of 4 feet tall and died at about age 20. It may be that the Hadar finds are from a time when both *Australopithecus* and *Homo* coexisted—when one type of fossil hominid was evolving into another. In recent years Richard Leakey has been working in northern Kenya in the rich, fossil-bearing area along the eastern shores of Lake Turkana. He has located numerous hominid remains, including one complete skull, the so-called 1470 cranium thought to be *Homo* and dated to 2.9 million years ago.

With the increasing evidence derived from fieldwork, we may ask anew how the earliest human beings evolved some 5 million years ago. The question has been answered in about as many different fashions as there are specialists who have addressed themselves to it. An increasingly popular hypothesis, incorporating the most recent evidence, has *Homo* represented by skull 1470 and other East Turkana finds, branching off from the australopithecines some time before 3 million years ago. Eventually the australopithecines were to become extinct.

An increasingly accepted view of human evolution separates *Homo* from *Australopithecus* around 3.5 million years ago. However, the relationship between *Homo habilis* and earlier *Homo* remains unclear, as does the relationship among the different australopithecines (see figure).

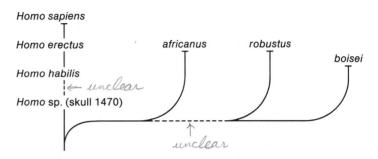

The Archaeology of Early Hominids

Our present knowledge about the life of Lower Pleistocene hominids comes almost entirely from the Olduvai Gorge.

The archaeology at Olduvai Gorge remains unique, for only here have extensive living floors of *Australopithecus* been uncovered. In the Omo Valley only one campsite has been located where bones and tools have been found together. No traces of campsites or tools were discovered with the more recent finds of skull 1470 at Lothagam or with "Lucy" at Hadar. At Olduvai, tools, bones, and crude shelters are found on the camp floor in almost exactly the same positions in which they were dropped over 2 million years ago.

Olduvan tools are the earliest tools fabricated by hominids. They consist of broken pebbles and flakes and are not standardized in the manner of later Stone Age tools, which served as weapons, scrapers, and cutting tools. Recent experiments have shown how versatile these tools can be. Glynn Isaac has recorded how a modern-day pastoralist near Lake Turkana skinned an antelope with a flake he struck from a cobble of lava and removed the limb bone with the tool to get at the marrow.

The articles in this volume by Sally Binford and Lewis Binford and by Glynn Isaac represent excellent hypothetical models detailing the adaptation of the early hominids to their environmental conditions. Isaac's article is the only contribution here that attempts to understand the evolution of the earliest hominids by defining the cultural criteria of humanity in terms of environment, subsistence, food sharing, the home base, tool making, and speech.

The Middle Pleistocene

If we accept the latest results from potassium-argon dating, the transition from Lower to Middle Pleistocene occurred around 700,000 years ago. Although the most crucial progress in the process of hominization occurred in the earlier Lower Pleistocene, we know least about that epoch. The Middle Pleistocene is dated from around 700,000 to 100,000 B.C., which marks the beginning of the Upper Pleistocene. These geological epochs are correlated with particular glaciations, climatic regimes, and characteristic faunas that identify them. Culturally, the Lower Pleistocene refers to the Lower Paleolithic--the Olduvan culture of the australopithecines and early *Homo*. The Middle Pleistocene coincides with the Middle Paleolithic and is characterized by Mousterian stone tools of *Homo erectus*. The articles by de Lumley, Solecki, and

Howell review the evidence from the Middle Paleolithic on three different continents.

The two most striking aspects of the Middle Pleistocene are the wide geographical distribution of *Homo erectus* and the technical innovation of the hand-axe—a tool of standardized manufacture that was flaked over part or all of both faces in such a way as to produce a working edge around the perimeter.

Homo erectus was first discovered in 1831 in central Java by Eugène Dubois, who named this hominid *Pithecanthropus erectus.* Related hominid finds were made throughout the 1920's in the limestone quarries at Choukoutien, 25 miles from Peking, and named there *Sinanthropus pekinensis*; we would now classify both hominids as *Homo erectus.* In subsequent years *Homo erectus* fossils were found in river sands at Mauer, Germany; Vértesszölös, Hungary; Sidi Abderrahman, Morocco; and Ternifine, Algeria. A near-complete skull has been recovered from Bed II at Olduvai and dated by the potassium-argon technique to 600,000 years ago. In addition to these sites yielding human fossils, there are extensive archaeological sites that inform us of human culture. It is not necessary for us to review the cultural accomplishments of *Homo erectus*—these are discussed in the articles. However, it is important to say a few words about the species *Homo erectus*, for the sites discussed in this section deal with the cultural remains in the absence of their producer.

The skull bones of *Homo erectus* indicate a brain capacity of 775 to 1300 cubic centimeters (cc). In its upper limits, this overlaps our modern cranial capacity. The skull was more rounded than that of earlier hominids, having conspicuous brow ridges and a sloping forehead. The skull bones are thicker and the jawbone is more massive than their modern counterparts, but the teeth are more similar to those of modern humans. *Homo erectus* has limbs and hips fully adapted to an upright posture, standing to an average height of 5 feet. By 500,000 B.C. it had successfully adapted to a variety of climates and populated the continents of Africa, Asia, and Europe. The new cultural and social adaptations simulating the challenges of surviving in new environments are discussed by Howell for Africa, by de Lumley for Europe, and by Solecki for Asia.

The Upper Pleistocene

The first half of the Late Pleistocene (100,000–50,000 B.C.) saw the physical evolution of Neanderthal man and the evolution of an ever-increasing cultural complexity. Physical anthropologists have long argued over whether Neanderthals belong to the modern human family, *Homo sapiens*, and the controversy continues today. Most physical anthropologists would classify them as *Homo sapiens neanderthalensis*.

The Neanderthal tool kit became more varied and complex, particularly throughout southern Europe, North Africa, and southwestern Asia. Several distinct stone tool traditions appear throughout this area—testimony to the increasing rate of regional development and specialization. One such industry takes its name from Levallois, a site near Paris, where tools were manufactured from a block of flint prepared in such a way that flakes could be struck from one face, ready to use as they were chipped from the core. Another widespread tradition, first identified in the cave of Le Moustier (Dordogne, France), involved striking flakes from disc cores and producing points or side scrapers from the flakes. Both of these techniques of stone tool manufacture have been recorded, with variations, over a large area (see the articles of Solecki and of Howell), most notably North Africa, southwestern Asia, and particularly Palestine, where they are referred to conveniently as Levalloiso-Mousterian tool industries.

Neanderthal man was advancing not only in the production of material culture but also in biological capacity as a "thinker"—a carrier of a distinctive and unique culture that he was capable of transmitting to subsequent generations. Pekin man cracked open human skulls in order to extract their brains. (Of course, we don't know whether he was merely satisfying a physical appetite or perhaps, by analogy with Melanesian practice, engaging in ritual cannibalism.)

Neanderthal man was surely of a different nature than his possible evolutionary progenitor, *Homo erectus*. For instance, Neanderthals initiated the practice of careful burial and concern for the dead. Ralph Solecki, in his excavations at Shanidar Cave, had the good fortune to excavate a number of Neanderthal skeletons. One burial was obviously an intentional interment: An unusual percentage of pollen from a variety of flowers around the grave suggested that Neanderthals, in burying their dead, placed or planted quantities of flowers around the body! On the terrace in front of the Mount Carmel cave in Palestine, a cemetery of ten Neanderthals was uncovered. One of the dead was wounded in the thigh, apparently by a wooden spear; we are left to speculate about the cause of the wound. The Mount Carmel burials all had their legs drawn up to the body. A female Neanderthal at La Ferraissie, France, was so tightly flexed that she may have been bound by thongs, a practice that might reflect the desire of the living to keep the dead permanently immovable and away. Throughout this long period we have little information on Neanderthal adaptive responses to the changing environment, which was characterized by periodic retreats and advances of the European ice sheets, which in turn affected the climate over even wider areas.

Articles in this section also detail the latter half of the Late Pleistocene, beginning around 50,000 years ago. Developments throughout this period were of prime importance to human history. It is difficult for us to appreciate the enormous time scale on which these advances were made. If we take a generation to be 25 years, then it was 80 generations ago that Jesus walked the earth, 160 generations ago that the Sumerians thrived in Mesopotamia (see the article by S. N. Kramer in Section III), and over 1300 generations ago that Neanderthals inhabited Shanidar Cave. Thus the final emergence of modern humans, their expansion over virtually the entire earth (all except Australia, the Arctic, and Antarctica), and their differentiation into the varied races of our species occurred well over a thousand generations ago. Neanderthals achieved the cranial capacity of modern humans (ca. 1200 B.C.), which is more than double that of the earlier australopithecines. Modern humans differ from Neanderthals only in their lighter jaw, more pointed chin, smaller teeth, and less prominent brow ridges.

Geographically, the Late Pleistocene was marked by a great expansion in the area of human settlement. Radiocarbon dates attest to the fact that 12,000 years ago both the New World and Australasia were occupied; in fact, the New World was inhabited as much as 5000 years prior to that. It is interesting to note that the world as a whole was colonized while people were still hunters and gatherers. By their invasion of the New World, the Stone Age hunters opened a new and exciting chapter in human cultural history. Over the whole world new flint industries appeared, based on the production, by specialized techniques, of blades with parallel flakes. Understanding of the expansion in the Late Pleistocene is further enhanced by P. Smith's article summarizing the new evidence for Egypt.

By contrasting the different articles in this section, we can realize the great degree of cultural and biological variation over the long range of human evolution. Some papers discuss the tangible remains of Paleolithic technology; the marvelous aesthetic accomplishments seen in the caves of France are presented in the article by André Leroi-Gourhan. We can see, in the superb reconstruction of what is clearly the earliest house (some 300,000 years old) yet excavated, at Terra Amata, France, that human tools and homes had already separated this creature from the rest of the animal kingdom. How unfortunate for archaeologists that actual physical remains of the builders were not found in association with this cultural complex; however, we may assume that they were advanced *Homo erectus* or perhaps even Neanderthal. It is an inescapable fact that archaeologists rarely find the association they would like; and even when they do, there is still room to speculate about religious beliefs, kinship systems, and so on. Neanderthals' survival depended, no doubt, on their greatest biological asset, that which separated them from the rest of the animal kingdom: their brain.

Today we are faced with a revolution in our understanding and appreciation of the accomplishments of Paleolithic humans. Evidence that their thought processes were already complex tens of thousands of years ago has recently been advanced by Alexander Marshack. Not content to accept as random the intentionally produced marks and patterns incised on Paleolithic bone and stone artifacts, Marshack undertook a microscopic analysis. He found them to have a mathematical replication in certain sets and classes. An intensive analysis led him to conclude that they were systematic notations, intended to record a calendrical system. Thus we can today appreciate in our ancestors of some 1000 generations ago their great intellectual conquest of time by means of their ability to predict the calendrical cycle of seasons. In recognizing this, we come closer to appreciating and identifying with this previously misunderstood "savage brute" of the past who, in one way or another, remains with us to the present.

1

The Idea of Man's Antiquity

by Glyn E. Daniel
November 1959

When Father MacEnery found flint implements in the same stratum with the fossils of extinct animals, he pushed human history far beyond 4004 B.C., the date most people took as man's beginning

Digging near the Bavarian city of Bayreuth in 1771, Johann Friedrich Esper found human bones at the same level as the remains of extinct animals. He was more startled than elated by his find, because it confronted him with a disturbing anachronism in the then-accepted timetable of the world's history. In the preceding century Archbishop Ussher had worked out this chronology from the complicated genealogies of *Genesis;* he concluded that the world and man had been created in 4004 B.C. Six millennia took in everything, and man was only a trifle younger than time itself. In this view of human history there was no inkling that sources other than written ones existed. The antiquaries of the time were concerned with describing monuments and cataloguing portable relics; they had no idea that history lay in the soil, much less any notion of how to wrest it from its grave. Samuel Johnson spoke for the pre-archaeological scholar when he declared: "All that is really known of the ancient state of Britain is contained in a few pages. . . . We can know no more than what old writers have told us."

Except for a few pagan myths, the old writers did not suggest that there were men before Man. Geology in Esper's and Johnson's time was little more than an elaboration of the Biblical story of Creation and the Flood. In accordance with that tradition it was easy, and not without logic, to explain fossils and river gravels in terms of the Flood, or sometimes of several floods. This was catastrophist or diluvialist geology. There was, to be sure, some talk of animals antedating 4004 B.C., but their fossils were believed to be the remains of creatures discarded by the Creator before his culminating creation: the world of Genesis. But with the creation of Adam, according to the doctrine, further creation ceased. Opposed to this account were the antediluvians—the near-heretics who held that man may have lived before Adam. This was the danger apprehended by Esper, and it caused him to ask: "Did [the bones] belong to a Druid or to an Antediluvian or to a mortal man of more recent time? I dare not presume without sufficient reason these members to be of the same age as the other animal petrifactions. They must have got there by chance."

The "sufficient reason" Esper asked

FLINT TOOL FROM HOXNE IN SUFFOLK is typical of the discoveries that caused speculation about man's antiquity. This hand-axe, dated according to the stratum in which it was found and the workmanship it displays, belongs to the Lower Paleolithic of about half a million years ago. The illustration appeared in 1800 in *Archeologia*, a publication of the Society of Antiquaries of London.

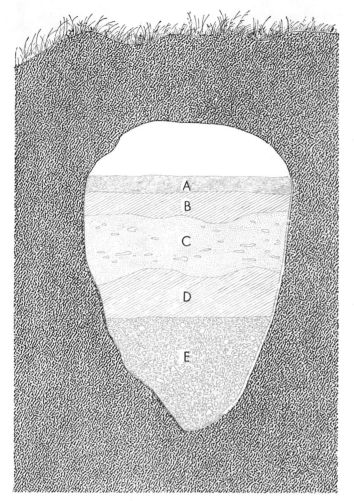

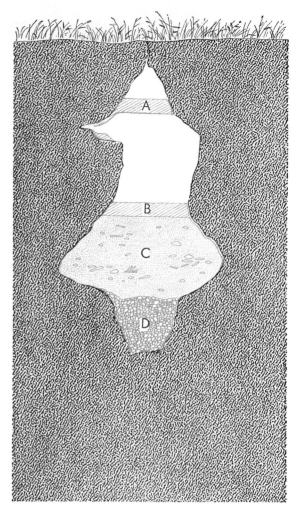

DEVON CAVES IN ENGLAND figured prominently in establishing the antiquity of man. Kent's Cavern (*left*) was the earlier find. Under surface layer (A) lay a stalagmite stratum (B) which sealed the cave earth (C) containing human artifacts amid the remains of extinct animals. Layers D and E are stalagmite and breccia. The floor of the 600-foot long Brixham Cave (*right*) had once been at A, but when excavated in 1858 the stalagmite at B was the cave floor. In the six feet of cave earth (C) were remains similar to those found in Kent's Cavern. Level D is gravel bed. Both the caves measure more than 20 feet from roof to gravel-bed bottom.

for was soon to be forthcoming. James Hutton, in his *Theory of the Earth*, published in 1785, offered the first persuasive alternative to cataclysmic geology. He suggested that the stratification of rocks was due not to floods and other supernatural calamities but to processes still going on in seas and rivers and lakes. He wrote: "No processes are to be employed that are not natural to the globe, no action to be admitted except those of which we know the principle." Hutton's reasoning was carried forward by William Smith—"Strata" Smith as he was called—who assigned relative ages to rocks according to their fossil contents, and who argued for an orderly, noncatastrophic deposition of strata over a long period of time—much longer than 6,000 years.

But the climate of opinion was still catastrophist. In 1797, just 26 years after Esper's discovery, John Frere, a gentleman of Suffolk, sent to the Secretary of the Society of Antiquaries of London some hand-axes and other implements of flint found at Hoxne, near Diss. In his accompanying letter he wrote: "If [these] weapons of war, fabricated and used by a people who had not the use of metals . . . are not particularly objects of curiosity in themselves, they must, I think, be considered in that light from the situation in which they are found, [which] may tempt us to refer them to a very remote period indeed; even beyond that of the present world."

They were indeed to be referred "to a very remote period": modern archaeologists would place them in the Lower Paleolithic of perhaps half a million years ago. But at the time no one took Frere's speculations seriously.

William Buckland, Reader in Geology at Oxford and later Dean of Westminster, perhaps typified catastrophist thinking. In 1823 he published his great book *Reliquiae Diluvianae, or Observations on the Organic Remains contained in Caves, Fissures and Diluvial Gravel, and on Other Geological Phenomena attesting the Action of an Universal Deluge.* Buckland himself had found evidence of the antiquity of man, but he refused to believe it. He had excavated Goat's Hole Cave near Paviland in South Wales and amid Upper Paleolithic implements had found the skeleton of a young man. (He believed it to be that of a young woman, and it is still referred to as the Red Lady of Paviland.) But he insisted that the skeleton was "clearly not coeval with the antediluvian bones of the extinct species" of animals. He made similar discoveries in the caves of the Mendip Hills of southwestern England but again refused to believe they were antediluvian. He argued instead that the caves had "been used either as a place of sepulture in early times or resorted to for refuge by the wretches that perished in it, when the country was suffering under one of our numerous military operations. . . . The state of the bones affords indication of very high antiquity but there is no reason for not considering them post-Diluvian."

When a Roman Catholic priest, Father MacEnery, discovered some flint implements at Kent's Cavern near Torquay in Devon, he wrote of them to Buckland. Buckland reacted characteristically. The flints had been found amid the stratified remains of rhinoceros and other animals under the unbroken, stalagmite-sealed floor of the cave. Buckland avoided the implications of this sealed evidence and offered another ingenious and tortured explanation that preserved catastrophist doctrine. He told MacEnery that ancient Britons must have camped in the cave; they had probably scooped out ovens in the stalagmite and in that way the flint implements had got below. Thus, according to Buckland, the association of the flints with the skeletal remains of extinct animals was only apparent. It was all very reasonable, except that, as MacEnery noted, there were no such ovens in the

cave. But Buckland was insistent, and out of deference to his views MacEnery did not publish his evidence.

At about this time, however, the National Museum in Copenhagen had been opened to the public with its antiquities arranged in three ages: Stone, Bronze and Iron. This classification was the work of Christian Jurgenson Thomsen, director of the Museum, and he set forth its underlying idea in a treatise that served as a guidebook to the display. His three-age system has been described very properly as "the cornerstone of modern archaeology"; it helped to secure recognition for the view that the human species had come through a long prehistory. (The word "prehistory" did not appear in print until 1851, when Daniel Wilson used it in *The Archaeology and Prehistoric Annals of Scotland*.)

The 1830's were eventful for the emerging new science of archaeology. In 1833 Sir Charles Lyell published his *Principles of Geology*, a powerful contribution to the cause of the fluvialists, as the supporters of Hutton and Smith were called. This book was in its

way as important as Darwin's *Origin of Species*. Lyell took the many fragmentary observations and insights of the fluvialists and organized them into a coherent system. He stated the principle of uniformitarianism: the central geological idea that strata could only be interpreted correctly by assuming that the agencies that formed them had operated at a uniform rate and in a uniform way, just as they work in the present. Lyell's great book was a staggering blow to catastrophist geology. But though the discoveries of Esper and Frere were thus rationalized, and the work of Hutton and Smith endorsed, this was not yet sufficient to swing general opinion behind belief in the true antiquity of man. More evidence was needed to shatter the old view and establish the new one; it soon came from Devon and northern France.

Boucher de Perthes was a customs official at Abbeville in the north of France. He had become interested in archaeology when he encountered neolithic artifacts and bones—"Celtic" remains as they were called—brought up by the dredging of the Somme Canal. His interest grew as more remains of "diluvial" man and animals were found in the quarries of nearby Manchecourt and Moulin-Quignon. By 1838, some five or six years after Lyell's *Principles* had appeared, de Perthes set forth his views in a five-volume work entitled *De la création: essai sur l'origine et la progression des êtres*. At about the same time he was exhibiting *haches diluviennes*, roughly chipped hand-axes, before the Société Imperiale d'Emulation de la Somme in Abbeville and at the Institut de Paris.

He was received with the same coldness suffered by his fellows in England, and like them he was regarded as a crank. "At the very mention of the words 'axe' and 'diluvium,'" he once remarked, "I observe a smile on the face of those to whom I speak. It is the workmen who help me, not the geologists." But de Perthes worked on and accumulated more evidence. The association he observed of human artifacts and extinct animals in the Somme gravels was compelling and no longer to be explained by the diluvial theory. In 1847 he published the first part of a three-volume work entitled *Antiquités celtiques et antédiluviennes*. The very title of the work indicates the effect his researches had on his thinking: the *haches diluviennes* were now *haches antédiluviennes*.

In England, meanwhile, the new archaeology had found other champions. William Pengelly, a schoolmaster, reworked MacEnery's cavern in Kent and,

SKULL OF NEANDERTHAL WOMAN was found in Forbes Quarry at Gibraltar in 1848. First believed to be a new species, Neanderthal was later seen to be a human variant. Missing portions of skull are outlined in this drawing from Hugo Obermaier's *Fossil Man in Spain*.

viewing the evidence there in terms of Lyell's uniformitarianism, saw it as proof of man's antiquity. But he realized that objections could be raised because the cavern had been disturbed by other workers. He found an entirely new site in an undisturbed cave across the bay in Devon above Brixham Harbour—Windmill Hill Cave. To supervise his excavations here he enlisted a committee of distinguished geologists in London. Pengelly, carrying out the actual digging, worked from July, 1858, to the next summer. It was a successful year. On the floor of the cave "lay a sheet of stalagmite from three to eight inches thick having within it and on it relics of lion, hyena, bear, mammoth, rhinoceros and reindeer." Below the floor Pengelly found flint tools.

The Brixham discoveries were compelling. Sir Charles Lyell said of them: "The facts recently brought to light during the systematic investigation of the Brixham Cave must, I think, have prepared you to admit that scepticism in regard to the cave evidence in favour of the antiquity of man had previously been pushed to an extreme."

The revolution was nearing a crisis: within the immediately foreseeable future man's history was to reach back beyond Archbishop Ussher's 6,000 years. The catastrophist theory was once and for all to be discarded and with it the Biblical notion that the world and man represented unalterable acts of special creation.

In 1858, while Pengelly was digging in the Brixham cave, the Scottish geologist Hugh Falconer visited Boucher de Perthes at Abbeville. De Perthes' evidence of man's antiquity immediately convinced Falconer. When he returned to London, he persuaded the geologist Joseph Prestwich and the antiquary John Evans to go and see the finds of Abbeville for themselves. As Evans was leaving for France, he wrote of the widely separated events that were revising men's beliefs: "Think of their finding flint axes and arrowheads at Abbeville in conjunction with the bones of elephants and rhinoceroses 40 feet below the surface in a bed of drift. In this bone cave in Devon now being excavated . . . they say they have found flint arrowheads among the bones and the same is reported of a cave in Sicily. I can hardly believe it. It will make my ancient Britons quite modern if man is carried back in England to the days when elephants, rhinoceroses, hippopotamuses and tigers were also inhabitants of the country."

Evans then records what happened when they got to France. De Perthes showed them his collection of flint axes and implements "found among the beds of gravel, . . . the remains of a race of men who existed at the time when the deluge or whatever was the origin of these gravel beds took place. One of the most remarkable features of the case is that nearly all . . . of the animals whose bones are found in the same beds as the axes are extinct. There is the mammoth, the rhinoceros, the urus, . . . etc." Then they arrive at the actual gravel pits: "Sure enough, the edge of an axe was visible in an entirely undisturbed bed of gravel and eleven feet from the surface. We had a photographer with us to take a view of it so as to corroborate our testimony."

The evidence at Abbeville convinced Evans and Prestwich as it had convinced Falconer, and this, with Pengelly's work at Windmill Hill Cave, brought the whole matter to a head. When they got back to London, Prestwich read a paper to the Royal Society in which he said: "It was not until I had myself witnessed the conditions under which these flint implements had been found at Brixham that I became fully impressed with the validity of the doubts thrown upon the previously prevailing opinions with respect to such remains in caves." That famous meeting of the Royal Society was on May 26, 1859, and of it John Evans wrote: "There were a good many geological nobs there: Sir Charles Lyell, Murchison, Huxley, Morris, Dr. Perry, Faraday, Wheatstone, Babbage, etc. . . . Our assertions as to the finding of the weapons seemed to be believed."

A week later Evans read a paper on the same subject to the Society of Antiquaries of London. In his account of this meeting he remarked: "I think I was generally believed in."

In August Sir Charles Lyell himself went to see the evidence of the Abbeville pits. He too was convinced, and a month later, in his presidential address to Section C of the British Association for the Advancement of Science, with Prince Albert presiding, he said: "I am fully prepared to corroborate the conclusions recently laid before the Royal Society by Mr. Prestwich." The battle was over; the great antiquity of man was an established fact. Victorian thought had to adjust itself not only to organic evolution but also to the antiquity of man; 4004 B.C. was forgotten.

It is perhaps strange that Charles Darwin himself was not at first impressed by the findings of de Perthes. Later in life he confessed: "I am ashamed to think that I concluded the whole was rubbish. Yet [de Perthes] has done for man something like what Agassiz did for glaciers." Perhaps Darwin held back because he did not want to involve his theory of evolution, at least at the outset, in anything so controversial as the ancestry of man. In the first edition of the *Origin of Species* he refused to discuss the relationship of evolution to man, and made only one cryptic statement on the general thesis of his book: "Light will be thrown on the origin of man and his history." In later editions this sentence was modified to: "Much light will be thrown. . . ."

But Darwin threw no light, not at any rate until 1871, when he published his views on the relation between man and general evolutionary theory in his *Descent of Man*. But this was eight years after T. H. Huxley's *Evidence as to Man's Place in Nature* had been published, and a dozen years after the climactic events of 1859. Thus whatever contribution Darwin made to the discovery of the antiquity of man, it was indirect and unwitting. It consisted entirely in the new way of thinking that he exemplified: uniformitarianism and evolution. The doctrine of evolution had man evolving from a prehuman ancestor; obviously there must somewhere be evidence of his passage from savagery through barbarism to civilization. The roughly chipped tools from Devon and the Somme now were more than credible, they were essential. People now had to accept the discoveries of de Perthes and Pengelly, where only a generation or two before, when the immutability of the species and catastrophist diluvialism were the dominant ideas, such discoveries had been scorned or ignored. Thus though Darwinism did not create prehistoric archaeology, it did give a great impetus to its acceptance and study; it helped set the stage for the acceptance of the idea of man's antiquity.

But even after the idea seemed well established, many students of the mid-century discoveries had misgivings about them. There was one particularly troublesome point: Men had left their axes but no trace of their physical selves, no bones. "Find us human remains in the diluvium," some of de Perthes' countrymen said to him, "and we will believe you." For de Perthes it was a sad challenge; this was 1863 and he was an old man of 75. Unable to dig for himself, he offered a 200-franc reward to the first quarryman to find human remains. With four months' wages as the prize, the quarrymen could not leave it to honest luck. Soon after the offer was made, they "found" human remains; first a human tooth; five days later a human jaw.

Boucher de Perthes was vindicated, and his French colleagues were at last satisfied. But the drama had not played out. Some British archaeologists had long suspected that de Perthes' gravel pits were being salted, and they proved that the jaw and several hand-axes had been inserted into the gravel faces by some of his workmen. It was a cruel blow.

Fortunately the case did not hang by so meager a thread. There was genuine skeletal evidence of man's antiquity. Two years before the 1859 pronouncements about the antiquity of man, the long bones and skullcap of a manlike being had been discovered in a limestone cave in the ravine of Neanderthal near the Rhenish city of Düsseldorf.

Hermann Schaaffhausen, who first described these remains, noted the large size, low forehead and enormous browridges of the skullcap. He believed that the Neanderthal skeleton belonged to "a barbarous and savage race," and he regarded it "as the most ancient memorial of the early inhabitants of Europe."

There was still more evidence. A female cranium had been found nine years before that, in 1848, during blasting operations in the Forbes Quarry at Gibraltar. The significance of the relic was not realized at the time, but at this juncture, in 1859, George Busk read a paper on it before a meeting of the British Association. The ebullient Falconer, who had persuaded Evans and Prestwich to visit de Perthes six years before, again apprehended the importance of a crucial find. He perceived

that here was a new species of man; he proposed to name it *Homo calpicus*, after Calpe, the ancient name for Gibraltar. He wrote his suggestion to Busk, referring somewhat redundantly to his "Grand, Priscan, Pithecoid, Agrioblematous, Platycnemic, wild *Homo calpicus* of Gibraltar." It was only later realized that this "grand, primitive, manlike, wild-eyed, flat-headed, wild Calpic man of Gibraltar" was not one of a new species but a member of that curious human variant, Neanderthal man.

And so by 1859 all the evidence for proper recognition of the antiquity of man was available: artifacts from the Somme and south Devon and fossils from Neanderthal and Gibraltar. The century since then has been given to building on that premise, to filling in its outlines with new evidence of man's physical and cultural evolution.

2

Stone Tools and Human Behavior

by Sally R. Binford and Lewis R. Binford
April 1969

Statistical analysis of the implements found at Paleolithic sites can identify the groups of tools that were used for various kinds of jobs. These groupings suggest how early man's life was organized.

The main evidence for almost the entire span of human prehistory consists of stone tools. Over the more than three million years of the Pleistocene epoch hunting and gathering peoples left behind them millions of such tools, ranging from crudely fractured pebbles to delicately flaked pieces of flint. Modern students of these objects are attempting to understand their various functions, and much of current prehistoric research is concerned with developing methods for achieving this understanding.

For many years prehistorians devoted almost all their efforts to establishing cultural sequences in order to determine what happened when. Chronologies have been established for many parts of the Old World, both on the basis of stratigraphy and with the aid of more modern techniques such as radioisotope dating and pollen analysis. Although many details of cultural sequences remain to be worked out, the broad outlines are known well enough for prehistoric archaeologists to address themselves to a different range of questions, not so much what happened when as what differences in stone tools made at the same time mean.

Traditionally differences in assemblages of stone tools from the same general period were thought to signify different cultures. Whereas the term "culture" was never very clearly defined, it most often meant distinct groups of people with characteristic ways of doing things, and frequently it was also taken to mean different ethnic affiliations for the men responsible for the tools. Such formulations cannot readily be tested and so are scientifically unsatisfactory. If we were to examine the debris left behind by people living today, we would find that differences in such material could most often be explained by dif-

ferences in human activities. For example, the kinds of archaeological remains that would be left by a modern kitchen would differ markedly from those left by miners. This variation in archaeological remains is to be understood in terms of function—what activities were carried out at functionally different locations—and not in terms of "kitchen cultures" or "mining cultures."

The example is extreme, but it serves to illustrate a basic difference between the assumptions underlying our research and those on which the more traditional prehistory is based. The obvious fact that human beings can put different locations to different uses leads us to the concept of settlement type and settlement system, the framework that seems most appropriate for interpreting prehistoric stone-tool assemblages. In what follows we are restating, and in some respects slightly modifying, some useful formulations put forward by Philip L. Wagner of Simon Fraser University in British Columbia.

All known groups of hunter-gatherers live in societies composed of local groups that can be internally organized in various ways; invariably the local group is partitioned into subgroups that function to carry out different tasks. Sex and age are the characteristics that most frequently apply in the formation of subgroups: the subgroups are generally composed of individuals of the same age or sex who cooperate in a work force. For example, young male adults often cooperate in hunting, and women work together in collecting plant material and preparing food. At times a larger local group breaks up along different lines to form reproductive-residence units, and these family subgroups tend to be more permanent and self-sustaining than the work groups.

Although we have no idea how prehistoric human groups were socially partitioned, it seems reasonable to assume that these societies were organized flexibly and included both family and work groups. If the assumption is correct, we would expect this organization to be reflected in differences both between stone-tool assemblages at a given site and between assemblages at different sites.

Geographical variations would arise because not all the activities of a given society are conducted in one place. The ways that game, useful plants, appropriate living sites and the raw materials for tool manufacture are distributed in the environment will directly affect where subgroups of a society perform different activities. One site might be a favorable place for young male hunters to kill and partly butcher animals; another might be a more appropriate place for women and children to gather and process plants. Both work locations might be some distance from the group's main living site. One would expect the composition of the tool assemblages at various locations to be determined by the kinds of tasks performed and by the size and composition of the group performing them.

Temporal variations can also be expected between assemblages of stone tools, for several reasons. The availability of plants and animals in the course of the year is a primary factor; it varies as a result of the reproductive cycles of the plants and animals. The society itself varies in an annual cycle; the ways the members of a society are organized and how they cooperate at different times of the year change with their activities at different seasons. Moreover, any society must solve integrative problems as a result of the maturation of the young, the death of some members, relations with other groups and so on. The behavioral modifications prompted by such considerations will be reflected in the society's use of a territory.

In addition to these factors that can affect the archaeological material left behind by a society, there are other determinants that profoundly modify site utilization. It is the kinds of site used for different activities and the way these specialized locations are related that are respectively termed settlement type and settlement system.

In technologically simple societies we can distinguish two broad classes of activities: extraction and maintenance. Extraction involves the direct procurement of foods, fuels and raw materials for tools. Maintenance activities consist in the preparation and distribution of foods and fuels already on hand and in the processing of raw materials into tools. Since the distribution of resources in the environment is not necessarily related to the distribution of sites providing adequate living space and safety, we would not expect extraction and maintenance activities to be conducted in the same places.

Base camps are chosen primarily for living space, protection from the elements and central location with respect to resources. We would expect the archaeological assemblages of base camps to reflect maintenance activities: the preparation and consumption of food and the manufacture of tools for use in other less permanent sites.

Another settlement type would be a work camp, a site occupied while smaller social units were carrying out extractive tasks. Archaeologically these would appear as kill sites, collecting stations and quarries for extracting flint to be used in toolmaking. The archaeological assemblages from these sites should be dominated by the tools used in the specific extractive tasks. If a work camp were occupied for a rather long period and by a fairly large subgroup, we would anticipate that some maintenance activities would also be reflected in the archaeological remains.

It is the way these two general classes of camps are used by any society that defines the settlement system. If a hunting-gathering society were relatively sedentary, we would expect the tools at the base camp to exhibit little seasonal variation because the base camp would have been occupied for most of the year. Under some conditions, however, we would expect to find more than one kind of base camp for a society. If the organization of

TYPICAL BORER

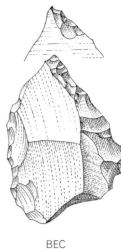

BEC

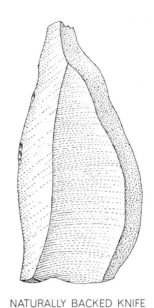

NATURALLY BACKED KNIFE

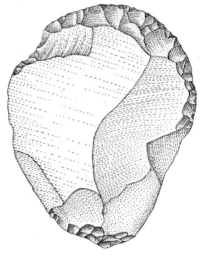

TYPICAL END SCRAPER

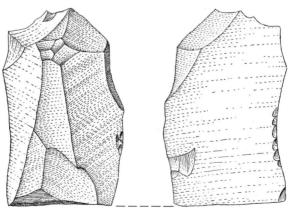

ATYPICAL BURIN

FIVE CLASSES OF STONE TOOLS predominate in the largest of the five groups, or factors, revealed by the authors' analyses. Of the 40 classes of tools subjected to multivariate analysis, 16 appear in this cluster, named Factor I. Few of the classes seem suited to hunting or heavy work; they were probably base-camp items for making other tools of wood or bone.

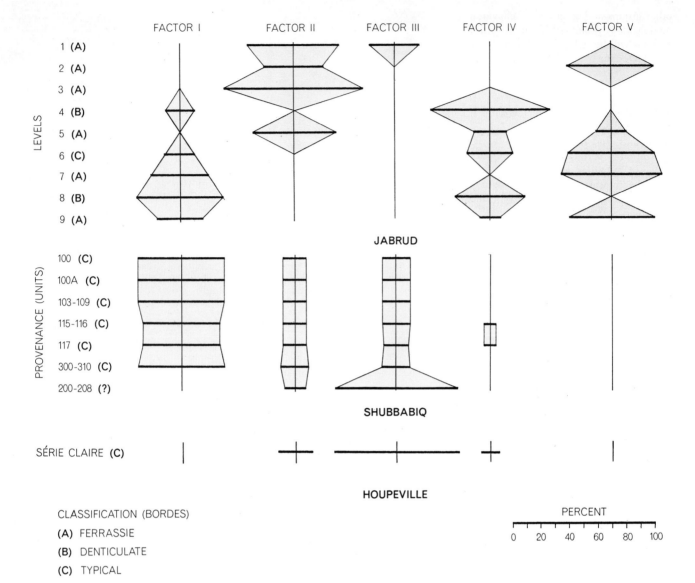

FACTOR I FACTOR II FACTOR III FACTOR IV FACTOR V

LEVELS

1 (A)
2 (A)
3 (A)
4 (B)
5 (A)
6 (C)
7 (A)
8 (B)
9 (A)

JABRUD

PROVENANCE (UNITS)

100 (C)
100A (C)
103-109 (C)
115-116 (C)
117 (C)
300-310 (C)
200-208 (?)

SHUBBABIQ

SÉRIE CLAIRE (C)

HOUPEVILLE

CLASSIFICATION (BORDES)

(A) FERRASSIE
(B) DENTICULATE
(C) TYPICAL

PERCENT

0   20   40   60   80   100

RELATIVE SIGNIFICANCE of the five factors identified in the tool assemblages from three Mousterian sites is indicated by the percentage of total variation attributable to each factor in each sample analyzed. Every sample but one bears the name (*key, bottom left*) by which the French archaeologist François Bordes characterizes the entire assemblage. The homogeneity of the samples from the Mugharet es-Shubbabiq cave site in Israel (*center*) is in sharp contrast to the heterogeneity of the samples from the Jabrud rock-shelter in Syria (*top*). The authors suggest that the cave was a base camp but that the rock-shelter was only a work camp, occupied at different times by work parties with different objectives. The Houpeville assemblage (*bottom*) is not like either of the others.

the society changes during the year, perhaps consisting of larger groups during the summer months and dispersing into smaller family units during the lean winter months, there would be more than one kind of base camp, and each would have its distinct seasonal characteristics.

The work camps would display even greater variation; each camp would be occupied for a shorter time, and the activities conducted there would be more specifically related to the resources being exploited. One must also consider how easy or how difficult it was to transport the exploited resource. If a party of hunters killed some big animals or a large number of smaller animals, the entire group might assemble at the kill site

not only to eat but also to process the large quantities of game for future consumption. In such a work camp we would expect to find many of the kinds of tools used for food processing, even though the tasks undertaken would be less diverse than those at a base camp.

The extent to which maintenance tasks are undertaken at work camps will also be directly related to the distance between work camp and base camp. If the two are close together, we would not find much evidence of maintenance activities at the work camp. As the distance between work camp and base camp increases, however, the work-camp assemblage of tools would reflect an increase in maintenance activities. This leads us to

suggest a third type of settlement: the transient camp. At such a location we would find only the most minimal evidence of maintenance activities, such as might be undertaken by a traveling group in the course of an overnight stay.

We have outlined here the settlement system of technologically simple hunter-gatherers. Although the system is not taken directly from any one specific living group, it does describe the generalized kind of settlement system that ethnographers have documented for people at this level of sociocultural complexity. In order to assess the relevance of such a settlement system for hunter-gatherers in the Paleolithic period it was necessary first to relate stone tools to human activities and then to determine how these tools were distributed at different types of site.

The kind of analysis we carried out might well have been impossible without the basic work on the classification of stone tools done by François Bordes of the University of Bordeaux. The archaeological taxonomy devised by Bordes for the Middle Paleolithic has become a widely accepted standard, so that it is now possible for prehistorians working with Middle Paleolithic materials from different parts of the world to describe the stone tools they excavate in identical and repeatable terms.

In addition to compiling a type list of Mousterian, or Middle Paleolithic, tools, Bordes has offered convincing arguments against the "index fossil" approach to the analysis of stone tools. This approach, borrowed from paleontology, assigns a high diagnostic value to the disappearance of an old tool form or the appearance of a new one; such changes are assumed to indicate key cultural events. Bordes has insisted on describing assemblages of tools in their entirety without any a priori assumption that some tools have greater cultural significance than others. This radical departure in classification, combined with highly refined excavation techniques, provides a sound scientific basis on which much current prehistoric research rests.

According to what has become known as *la méthode Bordes*, stone artifacts are classified according to explicitly stated attributes of morphology and technique of manufacture. The population of stone tools from a site (the assemblage) is then described graphically, and the relative frequencies of different kinds of stone tools from various sites can be compared. Such a statistical technique, which deals with a single class of variables, is quite appropriate for the description of assemblages of stone tools. The explanation of multiple similarities and differences, however, requires different statistical techniques.

The factors determining the range and form of activities conducted by any group at any site may vary in terms of many possible "causes" in various combinations. The more obvious among these might be seasonally regulated phenomena affecting the distribution of game, environmental conditions, the ethnic composition of the group, the size and structure of the group regardless of ethnic affiliation and so on. Other determinants of activities might be the particular situation of the group with respect to

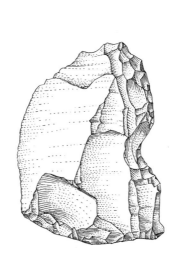

NOTCHED PIECE

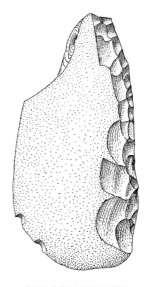

SIDE SCRAPER WITH
ABRUPT RETOUCH

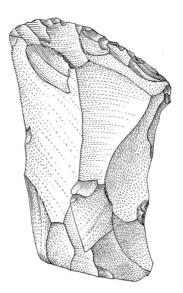

TRUNCATED FLAKE

DENTICULATE

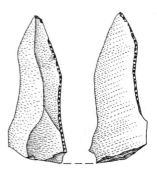

RACLETTE

UNIDENTIFIED TOOL KIT, with five predominant classes of artifacts, comprises Factor IV. The tasks for which it was intended are not known. Bordes has suggested, however, that denticulates (*bottom left*) may have been utilized for the processing of plant materials.

food, shelter, the supply of tools or the availability of raw materials. In short, the "causes" of assemblage variation are separate activities, each of which is related to the physical and social environment and to the others.

Given this frame of reference, the summary description of frequencies of tool types in an assemblage, which is the end product of Bordes's method, represents a blending of activity units and their determinants. We needed to partition assemblages into groups of tools that reflect activities. To use a chemical analogy, the end product of Bordes's method of describing the entire assemblage is a compound; we hoped to isolate smaller units, analogous to the constituent elements of a compound, that would represent activities. In our view variation in assemblage composition is directly related to the form, nature and spatial arrangement of the activities in which the tools were used.

Since the settlement-system model we had in mind is based on ethnographic

examples, we wanted to ensure that the archaeological materials we analyzed were made by men whose psychological capacities were not radically different from our own. The Mousterian, a culture complex named after the site of Le Moustier in the Dordogne, dates from about 100,000 to 35,000 B.C. Mousterian tools are known from western Europe, the Near East, North Africa and even central China. Where human remains have been discovered in association with Mousterian tools they are the remains of Neanderthal man. Once considered to be a species separate from ourselves, Neanderthal man is generally accepted today as a historical subspecies of fully modern man. A great deal of archaeological evidence collected in recent years strongly suggests that the behavioral capacities of Neanderthal man were not markedly different from our own.

The Mousterian assemblages we chose for our analysis came from two sites in the Near East and one in northern

France. One of us had excavated a cave site in Israel (Mugharet es-Shubbabiq, near Lake Tiberias) and had analyzed the stone tools found there in Bordes's laboratory and under his supervision. We also used assemblages that had been excavated in the 1930's by Alfred Rust at Jabrud, a rock-shelter near Damascus in Syria; this material had been studied and reclassified by Bordes. The French material came from the open-air site of Houpeville and had been excavated and analyzed by Bordes. We chose these samples because they represented three kinds of site, but more important because they had all been classified by Bordes. This meant that extraneous variation due to the vagaries of classification was eliminated.

To describe the two Near Eastern sites briefly, Shubbabiq is a large cave located in a narrow, deep valley that is dry for most of the year. The cave mouth faces east and its floor covers nearly 350 square meters, with slightly less than 300 meters well exposed to natural light. Un-

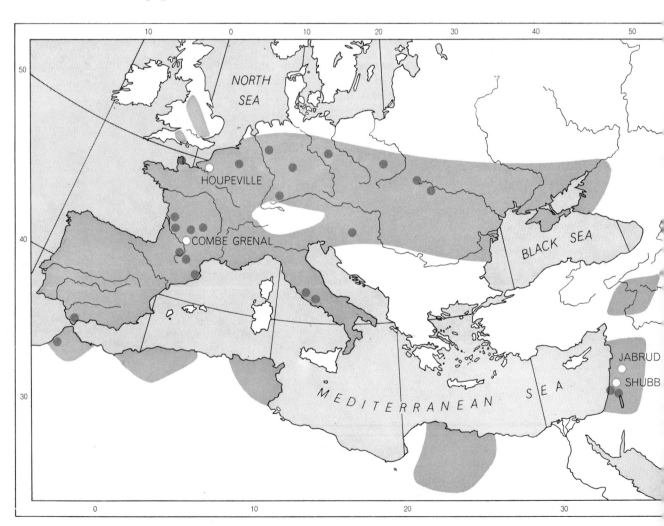

STONE TOOLS of the Mousterian tradition are found throughout Europe and also in the Near East. They were made from 100,000 to 35,000 years ago and are associated in many instances with the remains of Neanderthal man (*colored dots*). The authors' statistical

fortunately the Mousterian deposits in the main part of the cave had been destroyed by more recent inhabitants. Five of the samples from Shubbabiq used in our study came from deposits in the rear of the cave. The sixth, Unit 200–208, was a small deposit outside the cave entrance. The Syrian site, Jabrud Shelter I, is long and narrow. Like Shubbabiq, it faces east, and because it is more open it is much more exposed to the elements. Located on the edge of the Anti-Lebanon range, it looks down on the floor of a valley. At the time of the occupations that interested us the shelter had about 178 square meters of floor space. Rust excavated a trench some 23 meters long and three meters wide along the shelter's back wall. The shelter yielded many layers of Mousterian tools, but only the upper nine strata contained assemblages that could be compared with those from Shubbabiq.

Our study sought to answer three questions. First, does the composition of the total assemblage from any occupa-

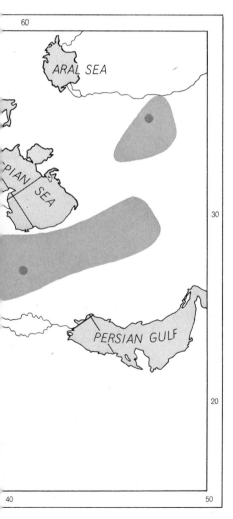

tion level correspond to any single human activity, or does information summarized in a single class of variables obscure the fact that each assemblage represents an assortment of activities? Second, is there any regularity in the composition of assemblages at a single location that can be interpreted in terms of regular patterns of human behavior? Third, is there some kind of directional change over a period of time in assemblages from a single location that suggests evolutionary changes in human behavior?

The statistical analysis of a single class of variables is termed univariate analysis. Multivariate statistical analysis allows one to calculate the measure of dependence among many classes of variables in several ways. Because we needed to determine the measure of dependence relating every one of some 40 classes of tools found in varying percentages in 17 different assemblages from three sites to every one of the remaining 39 classes, we faced a staggering burden of calculations. Such a job could not have been undertaken before the advent of high-speed computers. Factor analysis, which has been applied in areas as unrelated as geology and sociology, seemed the most appropriate method. Our analysis was run at the University of Chicago's Institute for Computer Research, with the aid of a modification of a University of California program for factor analysis (Mesa 83) and an IBM 7090 computer.

The factor analysis showed that in our samples the different classes of Mousterian artifacts formed five distinct clusters. The most inclusive of the five—Factor I—consists of 16 types of tools. Within this grouping the tools showing the highest measure of mutual dependence are, to use Bordes's taxonomic terminology, the "typical borer," the "typical end scraper," the "bec" (a small, beaked flake), the "atypical burin" (an incising tool) and the "naturally backed knife" [see illustration on page 13]. None of these tools is well suited to hunting or to heavy-duty butchering, but most are well designed for cutting and incising wood or bone. (The end scraper seems best adapted to working hides.) On these grounds we interpret Factor I as representing activities conducted at a base camp.

The next grouping produced by the factor analysis we interpret as a kit of related tools for hunting and butchering. The tools in this group—Factor II—are of 12 types. Three varieties of spear point are dominant; in Bordes's terminology they are the "plain Levallois point," the

"retouched Levallois point" and the "Mousterian point." Side scrapers of four classes are the other tools that show the highest measure of mutual dependence: the "simple straight," the "simple convex," the "convergent" and the "double" side scraper [see illustration on page 18].

In Factor III the main diagnostic tools are cutting implements. They include the "typical backed knife," the "naturally backed knife" (also found in Factor I), "typical" and "atypical" Levallois flakes, "unretouched blades" and "end-notched pieces" [see illustration on page 19]. With the exception of the end-notched pieces all these tools appear to be implements for fine cutting. Their stratigraphic association with evidence of fire suggests that Factor III is a tool kit for the preparation of food.

Factor IV is distinctive. Its characteristic tools are "denticulates" (flakes with at least one toothed edge), "notched pieces," "side scrapers with abrupt retouch," "raclettes" (small flakes with at least one delicately retouched edge) and "truncated flakes." We find it difficult even to guess at the function of this factor. Bordes has suggested that some of these tools were employed in the processing of plant materials.

The tools with the highest measure of mutual dependence in Factor V are "elongated Mousterian points," "disks," "scrapers made on the ventral surfaces of flakes," "typical burins" (as opposed to the atypical burin in Factor I) and "unretouched blades" (which are also found in Factor III). The fact that there is only one kind of point and one kind of scraper among the diagnostic implements suggests that Factor V is a hunting and butchering tool kit that is more specialized than the one represented by Factor II.

What answers does the existence of five groups of statistically interdependent artifacts among Mousterian assemblages give to the three questions we raised? In response to the first question we can show that neither at Shubbabiq nor at Jabrud does the total assemblage correspond to any single human activity. The degree to which individual factors account for the variation between assemblages can be expressed in percentages [see illustration on page 14]. To consider the Shubbabiq findings first, the percentages make it plain that, with the exception of a group of tools in Unit 200–208, the assemblages as a whole are internally quite consistent. The major part of the variation is accounted for by

analyses utilized tools from two sites in the Near East and two in Europe (*open circles*).

18

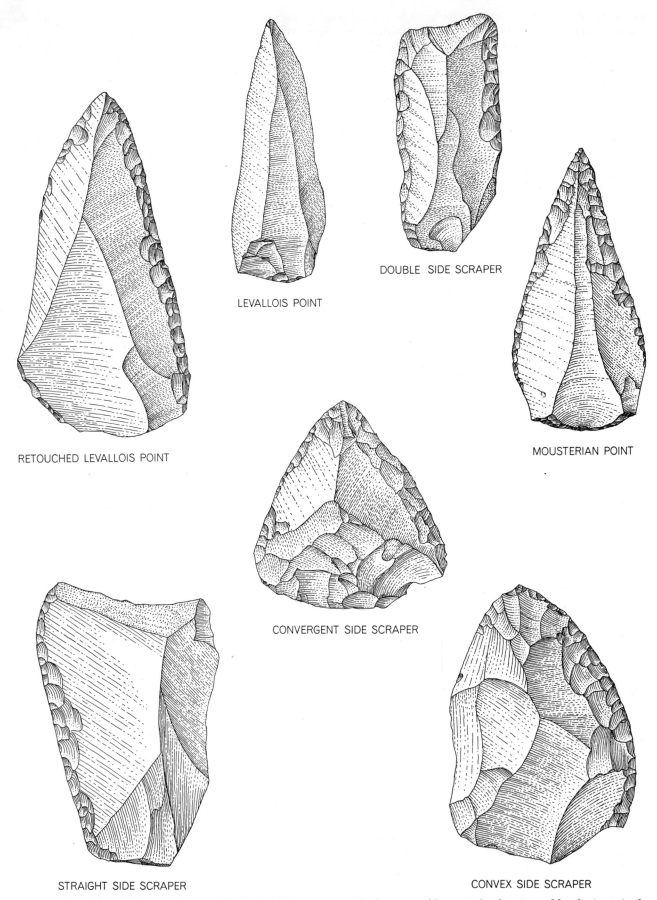

RETOUCHED LEVALLOIS POINT

LEVALLOIS POINT

DOUBLE SIDE SCRAPER

MOUSTERIAN POINT

CONVERGENT SIDE SCRAPER

STRAIGHT SIDE SCRAPER

CONVEX SIDE SCRAPER

POINTS AND SCRAPERS outnumber other kinds of tools among the 12 classes comprising the second-largest factor. The seven predominant classes in the assemblage are illustrated. Factor II is evidently an assemblage suited to hunting and butchering animals. This illustration and the others of Mousterian tools are based on original drawings by Pierre Laurent of the University of Bordeaux.

Factor I, the base-camp grouping; the remainder is shared between Factor II, the all-purpose hunting and butchering tool kit, and Factor III, the food-preparation cluster. The distinctive denticulate factor—Factor IV—appears in only two samples and represents less than 10 percent of the variability in each.

As we have mentioned, Unit 200–208 consists of tools from the deposit outside the cave mouth. Three small accumulations of ash—evidence of fires—were also found in the deposits. It seems more than coincidence that the tool grouping dominating this unit is the one associated with food preparation. In any event, the consistent homogeneity of the other excavation units at Shubbabiq suggests that the cave served the same purpose throughout its occupancy, a finding that also answers our second question. Although the occupation of the cave may have spanned a considerable period of time, the regularity of the factors suggests a similar regularity in the behavior of the occupants.

The percentages of variability accounted for at the Jabrud rock-shelter suggest in turn that Jabrud served repeatedly as a work camp where hunting was the principal activity. Evidently the valley the shelter overlooks was rich in game. The animal bones collected during the original excavation of the site have been lost, but recent work at the same site by Ralph S. Solecki of Columbia University indicates that the valley once abounded in horses—herd animals that were frequently killed by Paleolithic hunters.

The Jabrud findings also provide an answer to our third question. The decreasing importance of Factor V—the specialized hunting tool kit—and its replacement by the more generalized hunting equipment of Factor II suggests directional changes in the behavior of Jabrud's inhabitants. The same is true of the steady decline and eventual disappearance of the base-camp maintenance tools represented by Factor I.

Some of the data from Jabrud even provide a hint of a division of labor by sex in the Middle Paleolithic. The tools characteristic of Factor IV are quite consistently made of kinds of flint that are available in the immediate vicinity of the site, whereas the hunting tools tend to be made of flint from sources farther away. If, in accordance with Bordes's suggestion, the denticulates were used primarily to process plant materials, the expedient fashioning of denticulates out of raw materials on the spot coincides nicely with the fact that

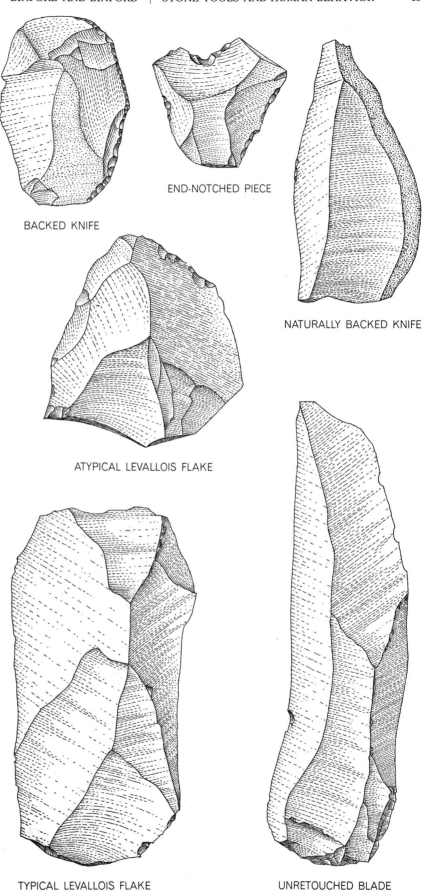

BACKED KNIFE

END-NOTCHED PIECE

NATURALLY BACKED KNIFE

ATYPICAL LEVALLOIS FLAKE

TYPICAL LEVALLOIS FLAKE

UNRETOUCHED BLADE

TOOLS FOR FINE CUTTING are the predominant implements of Factor III. An exception (*top middle*) belongs to the class of end-notched pieces. Their association with hearths suggests that the knives, blades and flakes of Factor III were used for food preparation.

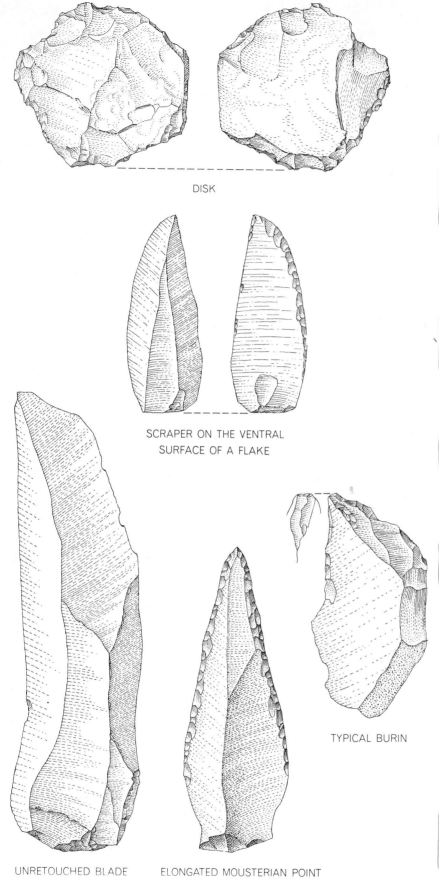

DISK

SCRAPER ON THE VENTRAL
SURFACE OF A FLAKE

TYPICAL BURIN

UNRETOUCHED BLADE   ELONGATED MOUSTERIAN POINT

MORE HUNTING TOOLS are found in Factor V; the five predominant classes are illustrated. The presence of only one class of points and one of scrapers suggests, however, that Factor V reflects specialized hunting rather than the general hunting implied by Factor II.

among living hunter-gatherers women are responsible for the collecting and processing of plant materials.

Recent advances in understanding of the minimum number of persons needed to maintain a self-sustaining human social unit provides additional evidence in favor of our view that Jabrud served as a work camp and that Shubbabiq was a base camp. William W. Howells of Harvard University has suggested that a self-sustaining group must number between 20 and 24 individuals. (He does not imply that the group would necessarily remain together during the entire year.) Taking Howells' estimate as a starting point, we can propose that any base camp where a group could live at full strength must include enough space for the daily activities of 20 to 24 people over a period of several months. Raoul Naroll of the State University of New York at Buffalo suggests that the minimum amount of sheltered space required by an individual is some 10 square meters. On this basis the 178 square meters of floor space in the Jabrud shelter could not have accommodated more than 18 individuals. Shubbabiq cave has enough sheltered floor space for 25 to 30 individuals. Taken together with the differences in the composition of the tool assemblages at the two sites, this leads us to conclude that the sites are basically different types of settlement within a differentiated settlement system.

The tools from Houpeville, called the *Série Claire,* has a totally different geographical context. Since Houpeville is an open-air site and the only one in the study, we feel that an attempt to draw conclusions about its function would be almost meaningless. The *Série Claire* sample nonetheless offers a further demonstration of the power of multivariate analysis. When calculated by univariate statistics, the total configuration of the Houpeville assemblage strongly resembles that of Shubbabiq, that is, the summarized statistics of frequencies of tool types are very similar. When subjected to factor analysis, however, the assemblages from the two sites look quite different. Factors I and V are missing altogether at Houpeville; Factor III, the cluster of food-preparation implements that constitutes a minor percentage of the variability at Shubbabiq, is the major component of the *Série Claire.*

Although we found the results of this factor analysis provocative, it was quite clear that many of our specific interpretations of the factors could not be tested on the basis of such limited data. We felt it essential to add other classes of information to the analysis: animal bones, pollen counts (as checks on climatic inferences) and the distribution of other traces of man (such as hearths) within each occupation level. Such data were available from the site of Combe Grenal, a deeply stratified rock-shelter in the Dordogne region of France excavated by Bordes. They are undoubtedly the finest and most complete Mousterian data in the world. Soil analysis has been done of all the deposits; animal bones are well preserved; pollen profiles have been made for all the 55 Mousterian occupation levels. The sophisticated excavation techniques used at Combe Grenal make it possible to reconstruct the relation of each tool at the site to other tools, to hearths and to clusters of animal bones. We were thus delighted when Bordes graciously volunteered to allow us to analyze his findings.

Our analysis of the Combe Grenal data has occupied the past eight months. (It has been made possible by a grant from the National Science Foundation.) While the work is far from complete, results of a preliminary factor analysis can be summarized here. First, the larger and more complete sample has shown a far wider range of variability than the smaller samples from the Near East have. The tool assemblages in all the Mousterian levels thus far analyzed—41 in number—consist of two or more factors. The factor analysis produced a total of 14 distinct tool groupings, in contrast to the five factors in the Near Eastern sites. In comparing the Combe Grenal analysis with that of the material from the Near East we note some gratifying consistencies. Such a replication of results with independent data from another region suggests that we have managed to isolate tool groupings that have genuine behavioral significance.

In attempting to relate clusters of tool types to environmental variables such as climate (measured by pollen and sediment studies) and game (as shown by animal bones) we have found no simple, direct form of correlation. There is, however, a nonrandom distribution of the frequency with which a given factor appears in levels that are representative of different environments. It appears that major shifts in climate, sufficient to cause shifts in the distribution of plants and animals, did precipitate a series of adaptive readjustments among the inhabitants of Combe Grenal.

Our present work on the material from Combe Grenal has led us to propose a series of refinements in interpretation. It is clear, for example, that the portability of game played a significant role in determining whether an animal was butchered where it was killed or after it was carried back to the site. We are now reclassifying the bones from that site by categories based on size, as well as by anatomical parts represented, and this should provide information that is not currently discernible. Whether an animal is an upland or a valley form and whether it occurs as one of a herd or as an individual is also evidently significant. We suggest that the behavior of the animals hunted had a profound effect on the degree of preparation for the hunt and on the size and composition of the hunting groups.

It should be stressed that the findings presented here are our own and not Bordes's. As a matter of fact, discussions of our interpretations with Bordes are usually lively and sometimes heated, although they are always useful. We all agree that Combe Grenal contains so much information in terms of so many different and independent classes of data that many kinds of hypothesis can be tested. Indeed, a procedure that requires the testing and retesting of every interpretation against independent classes of data could be the most significant outcome of our work.

If one goal of prehistory is the accurate description of past patterns of life, certainly it is the job of the archaeologist to explain the variability he observes. Explanation, however, involves the formulation and testing of hypotheses rather than the mere assertion of the meaning of differences and similarities. Many traditionalists speak of "reading the archaeological record," asserting that facts speak for themselves and expressing a deep mistrust of theory. Facts never speak for themselves, and archaeological facts are no more articulate than those of physics or chemistry. It is time for prehistory to deal with the data according to sound scientific procedure. Migrations and invasions, man's innate desire to improve himself, the relation of leisure time to fine arts and philosophy—these and other unilluminating clichés continue to appear in the literature of prehistory with appalling frequency. Prehistory will surely prove a more fruitful field of study when man is considered as one component of an ecosystem—a culture-bearing component, to be sure, but one whose behavior is rationally determined.

3

The Food-Sharing Behavior of Protohuman Hominids

by Glynn Isaac
April 1978

*Excavations at two-million-year-old sites in East Africa
offer new insights into human evolutionary progress
by showing that early erect-standing hominids made
tools and carried food to a home base*

Over the past decade investigators of fossil man have discovered the remains of many ancient protohumans in East Africa. Findings at Olduvai, Laetolil, Koobi Fora, the Omo Valley and Hadar, to name some prominent locations, make it clear that between two and three million years ago a number of two-legged hominids, essentially human in form, inhabited this part of Africa. The paleontologists who have unearthed the fossils report that they differ from modern mankind primarily in being small, in having relatively large jaws and teeth and in having brains that, although they are larger than those of apes of comparable body size, are rarely more than half the size of modern man's.

The African discoveries have many implications for the student of human evolution. For example, one wonders to what extent the advanced hominids of two million years ago were "human" in their behavior. Which of modern man's special capabilities did they share? What pressures of natural selection, in the time since they lived, led to the evolutionary elaboration of man's mind and culture? These are questions that paleontologists find difficult to answer because the evidence that bears on them is not anatomical. Archaeologists, by virtue of their experience in studying prehistoric behavior patterns in general, can help to supply the answers.

It has long been realized that the human species is set apart from its closest living primate relatives far more by differences in behavior than by differences in anatomy. Paradoxically, however, the study of human evolution has traditionally been dominated by work on the skeletal and comparative anatomy of fossil primates. Several new research movements in recent years, however, have begun to broaden the scope of direct evolutionary inquiry. One such movement involves investigations of the behavior and ecology of living primates and of other mammals. The results of these observations can now be compared with quantitative data from another new area of study, namely the cultural ecology of human societies that support themselves without raising plants or animals: the few surviving hunter-gatherers of today. Another important new movement has involved the direct study of the ecological circumstances surrounding human evolutionary developments. Investigations of this kind have become possible because the stratified sedimentary rocks of East Africa preserve, in addition to fossil hominid remains, an invaluable store of data: a coherent, ordered record of the environments inhabited by these protohumans.

The work of the archaeologist in drawing inferences from such data is made possible by the fact that at a certain stage in evolution the ancestors of modern man became makers and users of equipment. Among other things, they shaped, used and discarded numerous stone tools. These virtually indestructible artifacts form a kind of fossil record of aspects of behavior, a record that is complementary to the anatomical record provided by the fossil bones of the toolmakers themselves. Students of the Old Stone Age once concentrated almost exclusively on what could be learned from the form of such tools. Today the emphasis in archaeology is increasingly on the context of the artifacts: for example the distribution pattern of the discarded tools in different settings and the association of tools with various kinds of food refuse. A study of the contexts of the early African artifacts yields unique clues both to the ecological circumstances of the protohuman toolmakers and to aspects of their socioeconomic organization.

Comparing Men and Apes

What are the patterns of behavior that set the species *Homo sapiens* apart from its closest living primate relatives? It is not hard to draw up a list of such differences by comparing human and ape behavior and focusing attention not on the many features the two have in common but on the contrasting features. In the list that follows I have drawn on recent field studies of the great apes (particularly the chimpanzee, *Pan troglodytes*) and on similar studies of the organization of living hunter-gatherer societies. The list tends to emphasize the contrasts relating to the primary subsistence adaptation, that is, the quest for food.

First, *Homo sapiens* is a two-legged primate who in moving from place to place habitually carries tools, food and other possessions either with his arms or in containers. This is not true of the great apes with regard to either posture or possessions.

Second, members of *Homo sapiens* so-

PAST AND PRESENT LANDSCAPES in the Rift Valley region of East Africa, shown schematically on the opposite page, summarize the geological activity that first preserved and later exposed evidence of protohuman life. Two million years ago (*top*) the bones of hominids (*1–4, color*) and other animals (*x's, color*) were distributed across hills and a floodplain (*foreground*) adjacent to a Rift Valley lake. Also lying on the surface were stone tools (*black dots*) made, used and discarded by the protohumans. Layers of sediments then covered the bones and tools lying on the floodplain; burial preserved them, whereas the bones and tools in the hills were eventually washed away. Today (*bottom*), after a fault has raised a block of sediments, erosion is exposing some of the long-buried bones and clusters of tools, including the three types of site shown on the surface in the top block diagram (*A–C*). Sites of Type A contain clusters of stone tools together with the leftover stone cores that provided the raw material for the tools and waste flakes from the toolmaking process, but little or no bone is present. Sites of Type B contain similar clusters of tools in association with the bones of a single large animal. Sites of Type C also contain similar clusters of tools, but the bones are from many different animal species.

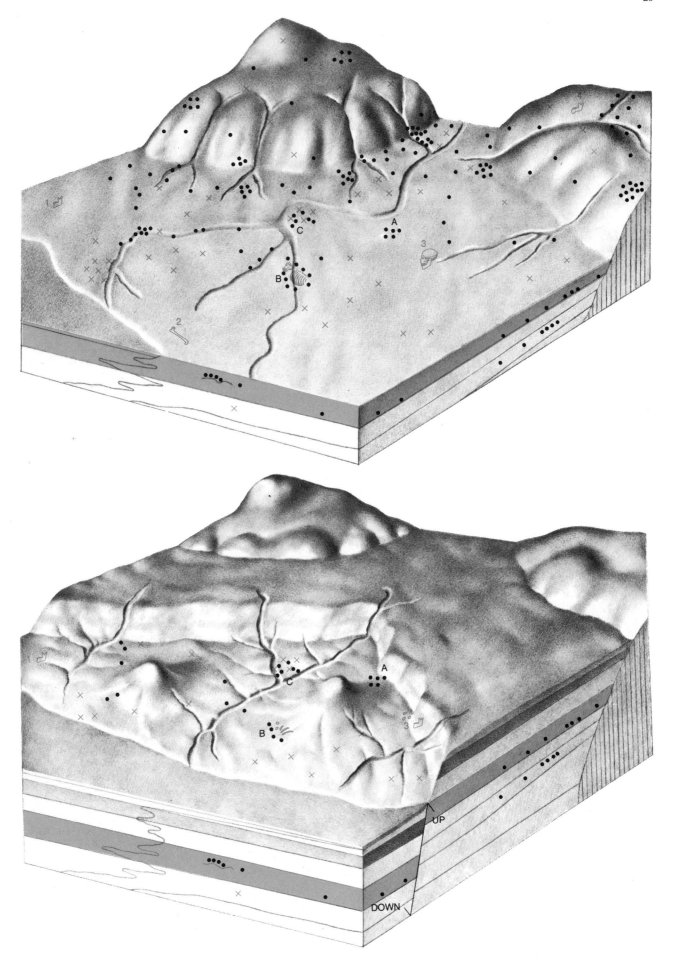

cieties communicate by means of spoken language; such verbal communication serves for the exchange of information about the past and the future and also for the regulation of many aspects of social relations. Apes communicate but they do not have language.

Third, in *Homo sapiens* societies the acquisition of food is a corporate responsibility, at least in part. Among members of human social groupings of various sizes the active sharing of food is a characteristic form of behavior; most commonly family groups are the crucial nodes in a network of food exchange. Food is exchanged between adults, and it is shared between adults and juveniles. The only similar behavior observed among the great apes is seen when chimpanzees occasionally feed on meat. The chimpanzees' behavior, however, falls far short of active sharing; I suggest it might better be termed tolerated scrounging. Vegetable foods, which are the great apes' principal diet, are not shared and are almost invariably consumed by each individual on the spot.

Fourth, in human social groupings there exists at any given time what can be called a focus in space, or "home base," such that individuals can move independently over the surrounding terrain and yet join up again. No such home base is evident in the social arrangements of the great apes.

Fifth, human hunter-gatherers tend to devote more time than other living primates to the acquisition of high-protein foodstuffs by hunting or fishing for animal prey. It should be noted that the distinction is one not of kind but of degree. Mounting evidence of predatory behavior among great apes and monkeys suggests that the principal contrast between human beings and other living primates with respect to predation is that only human beings habitually feed on prey weighing more than about 15 kilograms.

The gathering activities of human hunter-gatherers include the collection of edible plants and small items of animal food (for example lizards, turtles, frogs, nestling birds and eggs). Characteristically a proportion of these foodstuffs is not consumed until the return to the home base. This behavior is in marked contrast to what is observed among foraging great apes, which almost invariably feed at the spot where the food is acquired.

Still another contrast with great-ape feeding behavior is human hunter-gatherers' practice of subjecting many foodstuffs to preparation for consumption, by crushing, grinding, cutting and heating. Such practices are not observed among the great apes.

Human hunter-gatherers also make use of various kinds of equipment in the quest for food. The human society with perhaps the simplest equipment ever observed was the aboriginal society of Tasmania, a population of hunter-gatherers that was exterminated in the 19th century. The inventory of the Tasmanians' equipment included wood clubs, spears and digging sticks, cutting tools made of chipped stone that were used to shape the wood objects, and a variety of containers: trays, baskets and bags. The Tasmanians also had fire. Although such equipment is simple by our standards, it is far more complex than the kind of rudimentary tools that we now know living chimpanzees may collect and use in the wild, for example twigs and grass stems.

In addition to this lengthy list of subsistence-related behavioral contrasts between human hunter-gatherers and living primates there is an entire realm of other contrasts with respect to social organization. Although these important additional features fall largely outside the range of evidence to be considered here, they are vital in defining human patterns of behavior. Among them is the propensity for the formation of long-

DESOLATE LANDSCAPE in the arid Koobi Fora district of Kenya is typical of the kind of eroded terrain where gullying exposes both bones and stone tools that were buried beneath sediments and volcanic ash more than a million years ago. Excavation in progress (*center*) is exposing the hippopotamus bones and clusters of artifacts that had been partially bared by recent erosion and were found by Richard Leakey in 1969. The site is typical of the kind that includes the remains of a single animal and many tools manufactured on the spot.

term mating bonds between a male and one or more females. The bonds we call "marriage" involve reciprocal economic ties, joint responsibility for aspects of child-rearing and restrictions on sexual access. Another such social contrast is evident in the distinctively human propensity to categorize fellow members of a group according to kinship and metaphors of kinship. Human beings regulate many social relations, mating included, according to complex rules involving kinship categories. Perhaps family ties of a kind exist among apes, but explicit categories and rules do not. These differences are emphasized by the virtual absence from observed ape behavior of those distinctively human activities that are categorized somewhat vaguely as "symbolic" and "ritual."

Listing the contrasts between human and nonhuman subsistence strategies is inevitably an exercise in oversimplification. As has been shown by contemporary field studies of various great apes and of human beings who, like the San (formerly miscalled Bushmen) of the Kalahari Desert, still support themselves without farming, there is a far greater degree of similarity between the two subsistence strategies than had previously been recognized. For example, with regard to the behavioral repertories involving meat-eating and tool-using the differences between ape and man are differences of degree rather than of kind. Some scholars have even used the data to deny the existence of any fundamental differences between the human strategies and the nonhuman ones.

It is my view that significant differences remain. Let me cite what seem to me to be the two most important. First, whereas humans may feed as they forage just as apes do, apes do not regularly postpone food-consumption until they have returned to a home base, as human beings do. Second, human beings actively share some of the food they acquire. Apes do not, even though chimpanzees of the Gombe National Park in Tanzania have been observed to tolerate scrounging when meat is available.

From Hominid to Human

Two complementary puzzles face anyone who undertakes to examine the question of human origins. The first relates to evolutionary divergence. When did the primate stock ancestral to the living apes diverge from the stock ancestral to man? What were the circumstances of the divergence? Over what geographical range did it take place? It is not yet established beyond doubt whether the divergence occurred a mere five to six million years ago, as Vincent M. Sarich of the University of California at Berkeley and others argue on biochemical grounds, or 15 to 20 million years ago, as many paleontologists believe on the grounds of fossil evidence.

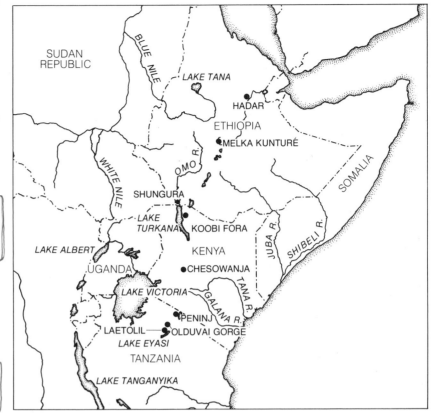

PROMINENT SITES in East Africa include (from north to south) Hadar, Melka Kunturé and Shungura in Ethiopia, the Koobi Fora district to the east of Lake Turkana in Kenya, Chesowanja in Kenya and Peninj, Olduvai Gorge and Laetolil in Tanzania. Dates for clusters of stone tools, some associated with animal bones, uncovered at these sites range from one million years ago (Olduvai Upper Bed II) to 2.5 million (Hadar upper beds). Some sites may be even older.

	OLDUVAI	KOOBI FORA	OMO VALLEY	OTHER
1.0	UPPER BED II			
1.2	MIDDLE BED II			PENINJ MELKA KUNTURÉ CHESOWANJA
1.4	LOWER BED II	KARARI SITES		
1.6	BED I	KBS, HAS		
1.8				
2.0				
2.2			SHUNGURA MEMBER F	
2.4		?	SHUNGURA MEMBER E	
2.6				HADAR UPPER BEDS
2.8				
3.0				
3.2				HADAR LOWER BEDS
3.4				
3.6				LAETOLIL

YEARS BEFORE PRESENT (MILLIONS)

RELATIVE ANTIQUITY of selected sites in East Africa is indicated in this table. Olduvai Gorge beds I and II range from 1.8 to 1.0 million years in age. The Shungura sites in the Omo Valley are more than two million years old. Two Koobi Fora locales, the hippopotamus/artifact site (HAS) and the Kay Behrensmeyer site (KBS), are at least 1.6 million years old. Initial geological studies of the Koobi Fora sites suggested that they might be 2.5 million years old (*colored line*). Only hominid fossils have been found in the lower beds at Hadar and at Laetolil.

At least one fact is clear. The divergence took place long before the period when the oldest archaeological remains thus far discovered first appear. Archaeology, at least for the present, can make no contribution toward solving the puzzle of the split between ancestral ape and ancestral man.

As for the second puzzle, fossil evidence from East Africa shows that the divergence, regardless of when it took place, had given rise two to three million years ago to populations of smallish two-legged hominids. The puzzle is how to identify the patterns of natural selection that transformed these protohumans into humans. Archaeology has a major contribution to make in elucidating the second puzzle. Excavation of these protohuman sites has revealed evidence suggesting that two million years ago some elements that now distinguish man from apes were already part of a novel adaptive strategy. The indications are that a particularly important part of that strategy was food-sharing.

The archaeological research that has inspired the formulation of new hypotheses concerning human evolution began nearly 20 years ago when Mary Leakey and her husband Louis discovered the fossil skull he named "Zinjanthropus" at Olduvai Gorge in Tanzania. The excavations the Leakeys undertook at the site showed not only that stone tools were present in the same strata that held this fossil and other hominid fossils but also that the discarded artifacts were associated with numerous broken-up animal bones. The Leakeys termed these concentrations of tools and bones "living sites." The work has continued at Olduvai under Mary Leakey's direction, and in 1971 a major monograph was published that has made the Olduvai results available for comparative studies.

Other important opportunities for archaeological research of this kind have come to light in the Gregory Rift Valley, at places such as the Koobi Fora (formerly East Rudolf) region of northern Kenya, at Shungara in the Omo Valley

of southwestern Ethiopia and in the Hadar region of eastern Ethiopia. Current estimates of the age of these sites cover a span of time from about 3.2 million years ago to about 1.2 million.

Since 1970 I have been co-leader with Richard Leakey (the son of Mary and Louis Leakey) of a team working at Koobi Fora, a district that includes the northeastern shore of Lake Turkana (the former Lake Rudolf). Our research on the geology, paleontology and paleoanthropology of the district involves the collaboration of colleagues from the National Museum of Kenya and from many other parts of the world. Work began in 1968 and has had the help and encouragement of the Government of Kenya, the National Science Foundation and the National Geographic Society. Our investigations have yielded archaeological evidence that corroborates and complements the earlier evidence from Olduvai Gorge. The combined data make it possible to see just how helpful archaeology can be in answering

a

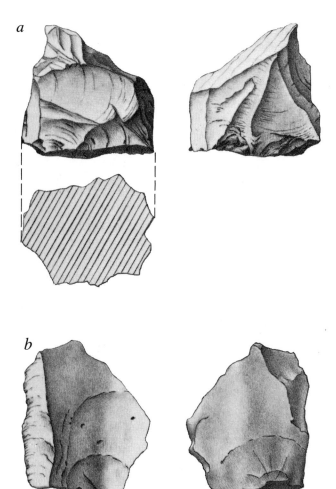

b

c

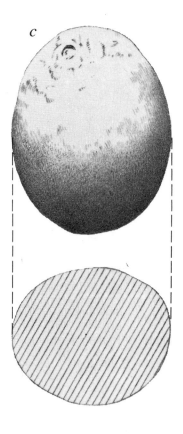

d

KOOBI FORA ARTIFACTS include four from the HAS assemblage (*left*) and four from the KBS assemblage (*right*). All are shown actual size; the stone is basalt. The HAS core (*a*) shows what is left of a piece of stone after a number of flakes have been struck from it by percussion. The jagged edges produced by flake removal give the core po- tential usefulness as a tool. The flakes were detached from the core by blows with a hammerstone like the one shown here (*c*). The sharp edges of the flakes, such as the example illustrated (*b*), allow their use as cutting tools. The tiny flake (*d*) is probably an accidental product of the percussion process; the presence of many stone splinters such

questions concerning human evolution.

At Koobi Fora, as at all the other East African sites, deposits of layered sediments, which accumulated long ago in the basins of Rift Valley lakes, are now being eroded by desert rainstorms and transient streams. As the sedimentary beds erode, a sample of the ancient artifacts and fossil bones they contain is exposed at the surface. For a while the exposed material lies on the ground. Eventually, however, the fossil bones are destroyed by weathering or a storm washes away stone and bone alike.

All field reconnaissance in East Africa progresses along essentially similar lines. The field teams search through eroded terrain looking for exposed fossils and artifacts. In places where concentrations of fossil bone or promising archaeological indications appear on the surface the next step is excavation. The digging is done in part to uncover further specimens that are still in place in the layers of sediments and in part to gather exact information about the original stratigraphic location of the surface material. Most important of all, excavation allows the investigators to plot in detail the relative locations of the material that is unearthed. For example, if there are associations among bones and between bones and stones, excavation will reveal these characteristics of the site.

The Types of Sites

The archaeological traces of protohuman life uncovered in this way may exhibit several different configurations. In some ancient layers we have found scatterings of sharp-edged broken stones even though there are no other stones in the sediments. The broken stones come in a range of forms but all are of the kind produced by deliberate percussion, so that we can classify them as undoubted artifacts. Such scatterings of artifacts are often found without bone being present in significant amounts. These I propose to designate sites of Type A.

In some instances a layer of sediment may include both artifacts and animal bones. Such bone-and-artifact occurrences fall into two categories. The first consists of artifacts associated with bones that represent the carcass of a single large animal; these sites are designated Type B. The second consists of artifacts associated with bones representing the remains of several different animal species; these sites are designated Type C.

The discovery of sites with these varied configurations in the sediments at Koobi Fora and Olduvai provides evidence that when the sediments containing them were being deposited some 2.5 to 1.5 million years ago, there was at least one kind of hominid in East Africa that habitually carried objects such as stones from one place to another and made sharp-edged tools by deliberately fracturing the stones it carried with it. How does this archaeological evidence match up with the hominid fossil record? The fossil evidence indicates that

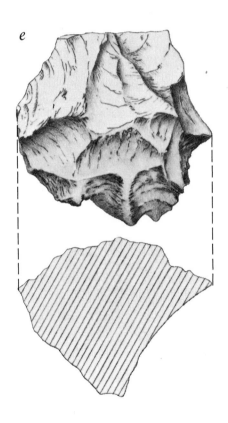

as this one in the HAS tool clusters indicates that the stone tools were made on the spot. At the same time the absence of local unworked stone as potential raw material for tools suggests that the cores were carried to the site by the toolmakers. The artifacts from the second assemblage also include a core (e) that has had many flakes removed by percussion and another small splinter of stone (h). The edges of the two flakes (f, g) are sharp enough to cut meat, hide, sinew or wood. As at the hippopotamus/artifact site, the absence of local raw material for stone tools at the Kay Behrensmeyer site suggests that suitable lumps of lava must have been transported there by the toolmakers.

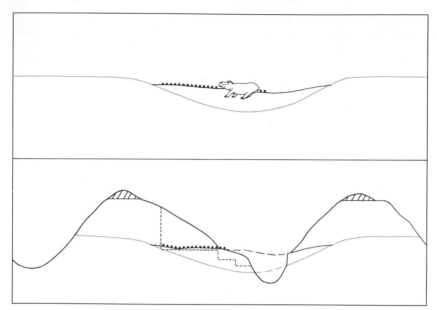

KOOBI FORA LANDSCAPE in the vicinity of the hippopotamus/artifact site consisted of a level floodplain near the margin of a lake (*top section*). Protohuman foragers apparently found the carcass of a hippopotamus lying in a stream-bed hollow and made tools on the spot in order to butcher the carcass. Their actions left a scatter of stone tools among the bones and on the ground nearby. The floodplain was buried under layers of silt and ash and was subsequently eroded (*bottom section*), exposing some bones and tools. Their discovery led to excavation.

two and perhaps three species of bipedal hominids inhabited the area at this time, so that the question arises: Can the species responsible for the archaeological evidence be identified?

· For the moment the best working hypothesis seems to be that those hominids that were directly ancestral to modern man were making the stone tools. These are the fossil forms, of early Pleistocene age, classified by most paleontologists as an early species of the genus *Homo*. The question of whether or not contemporaneous hominid species of the genus *Australopithecus* also made tools must be set aside as a challenge to the ingenuity

of future investigators. Here I shall simply discuss what we can discover about the activities of early toolmaking hominids without attempting to identify their taxonomic position (or positions).

Reading the Evidence

As examples of the archaeological evidence indicative of early hominid patterns of subsistence and behavior, consider our findings at two Koobi Fora excavations. The first is a locality catalogued as the hippopotamus/artifact site (HAS) because of the presence of fossilized hippopotamus bones and stone tools.

The site is 15 miles east of Lake Turkana. There in 1969 Richard Leakey discovered an erosion gully cutting into an ancient layer of volcanic ash known as the KBS tuff. (KBS stands for Kay Behrensmeyer site; she, the geologist-paleoecologist of our Koobi Fora research team, first identified the ash layer at a nearby outcrop.) The ash layer is the uppermost part of a sedimentary deposit known to geologists as the Lower Member of the Koobi Fora Formation; here the ash had filled in one of the many dry channels of an ancient delta. Leakey found many bones of a single hippopotamus carcass weathering out of the eroded ash surface, and stone artifacts lay among the bones.

J. W. K. Harris, J. Onyango-Abuje and I supervised an excavation that cut into an outcrop where the adjacent delta sediments had not yet been disturbed by erosion. Our digging revealed that the hippopotamus carcass had originally lain in a depression or puddle within an ancient delta channel. Among the hippopotamus bones and in the adjacent stream bank we recovered 119 chipped stones; most of them were small sharp flakes that, when they are held between the thumb and the fingers, make effective cutting implements. We also recovered chunks of stone with scars showing that flakes had been struck from them by percussion. In Paleolithic tool classification these larger stones fall into the category of core tool or chopper. In addition our digging exposed a rounded river pebble that was battered at both ends; evidently it had been used as a hammer to strike flakes from the stone cores.

The sediments where we found these artifacts contain no stones larger than a pea. Thus it seems clear that the makers of the tools had carried the stones here from somewhere else. The association between the patch of artifacts and the hippopotamus bones further suggests that toolmakers came to the site carrying stones and hammered off the small sharp-edged flakes on the spot in order to cut meat from the hippopotamus carcass. We have no way of telling at present whether the toolmakers themselves killed the animal or only came on it

HAMMERSTONE unearthed at the hippopotamus/artifact site is a six-centimeter basalt pebble; it is shown here being lifted from its position on the ancient ground surface adjacent to the hippopotamus bones. Worn smooth by water action before it caught the eye of a toolmaker some 1.7 million years ago, the pebble is battered at both ends as a result of use as a hammer.

dead. Given the low level of stone technology in evidence, I am inclined to suspect scavenging rather than hunting.

The HAS deposit was formed at least 1.6 million years ago. The archaeological evidence demonstrates that the behavior of some hominids at that time differed from the behavior of modern great apes in that these protohumans not only made cutting tools but also ate meat from the carcasses of large animals. The hippopotamus/artifact site thus provides corroboration for evidence of similar behavior just as long ago obtained from Mary Leakey's excavations at Olduvai Gorge.

This finding does not answer all our questions. Were these protohumans roaming the landscape, foraging and hunting, in the way that a troop of baboons does today? Were they instead hunting like a pride of lions? Or did some other behavioral pattern prevail? Excavation of another bone-and-arti-

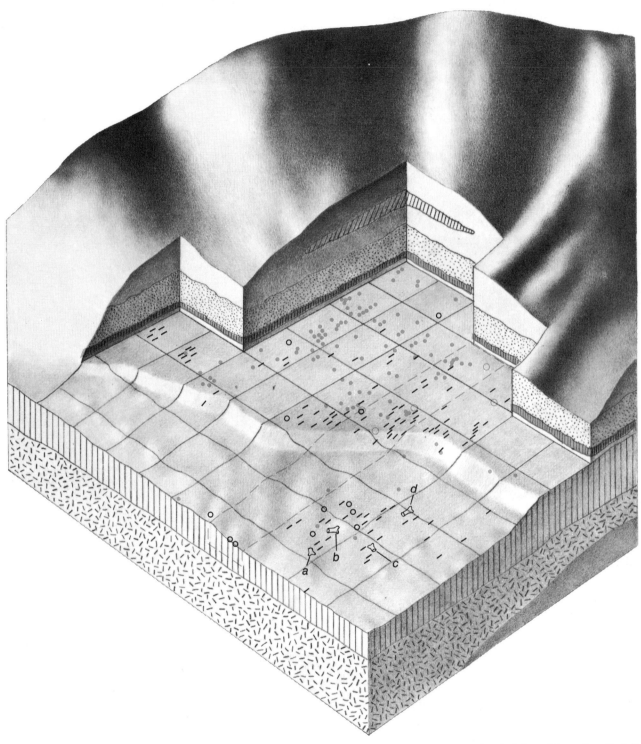

FINDINGS at the hippopotamus/artifact site are shown schematically in this block diagram; squares are one meter to a side. In the foreground are the objects that had been exposed by weathering: hippopotamus limb bones (*a–d*) and teeth (*small open circles*), many fragments of bone (*short dashes*) and a few stone artifacts (*colored dots*). Trenching (*dashed line, color*) and hillside excavation over a wide **area exposed an ancient soil surface (*color*) overlying a deposit of silty tuff. Lying on the ancient surface were stone cores (*open circles, color*) from which sharp-edged flakes had been struck, more than 100 other stone artifacts and more than 60 additional fragments of teeth and bones. The scatter of tools and broken bones suggests the hypothesis that the toolmakers fed on meat from the hippopotamus.**

fact association, only a kilometer away from the hippopotamus/artifact site, has allowed us to carry our inquiries further.

The second site had been located by Behrensmeyer in 1969. Erosion was uncovering artifacts, together with pieces of broken-up bone, at another outcrop of the same volcanic ash layer that contained the HAS artifacts and bones. With the assistance of John Barthelme of the University of California at Berkeley and others I began to excavate the site. The work soon revealed a scatter of several hundred stone tools in an area 16 meters in diameter. They rested on an ancient ground surface that had been covered by layers of sand and silt. The concentration of artifacts exactly coincided with a scatter of fragmented bones. Enough of them, teeth in particular, were identifiable to demonstrate that parts of the remains of several animal species were present. John M. Harris of the Louis Leakey Memorial Institute in Nairobi recognized, among other

species, hippopotamus, giraffe, pig, porcupine and such bovids as waterbuck, gazelle and what may be either hartebeest or wildebeest. It was this site that was designated KBS. The site obviously represented the second category of bone-and-artifact associations: tools in association with the remains of many different animal species.

Geological evidence collected by A. K. Behrensmeyer of Yale University and others shows that the KBS deposit had accumulated on the sandy bed of a stream that formed part of a small delta. At the time when the toolmakers used the stream bed, water had largely ceased to flow. Such a site was probably favored as a focus of hominid activity for a number of reasons. First, as every beachgoer knows, sand is comfortable to sit and lie on. Second, by scooping a hole of no great depth in the sand of a stream bed one can usually find water. Third, the growth of trees and bushes in the sun-parched floodplains of East Africa is often densest along watercour-

ses, so that shade and plant foods are available in these locations. It may also be that the protohuman toolmakers who left their discards here took shelter from predators by climbing trees and also spent their nights protected in this way.

Much of this is speculative, of course, but we have positive evidence that the objects at the KBS site did accumulate in the shade. The sandy silts that came to cover the discarded implements and fractured bones were deposited so gently that chips of stone small enough to be blown away by the wind were not disturbed. In the same silts are the impressions of many tree leaves. The species of tree has not yet been formally identified, but Jan Gilette of the Kenya National Herbarium notes that the impressions closely resemble the leaves of African wild fig trees.

Carrying Stones and Meat

As at the hippopotamus/artifact site, we have established the fact that stones

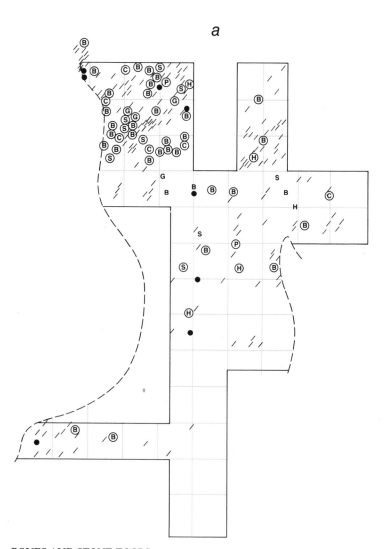 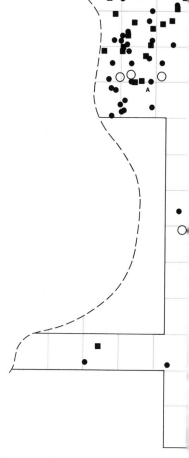

a

BONES AND STONE TOOLS were also found in abundance at the Kay Behrensmeyer site. As the plot of bone distribution (*a*) shows, the animal remains represent many different species. These are identified by capital letters; if the find was a tooth the letter is circled. Most are small to medium-sized bovids, such as gazelle, waterbuck and hartebeest (*B*). The remains of crocodile (*C*), giraffe (*G*), hippopotamus (*H*), porcupine (*P*) and extinct species of pig (*S*) were also present. Dots and dashes locate unidentified teeth and bone fragments respectively.

larger than the size of a pea do not occur naturally closer to the Kay Behrensmeyer site than a distance of three kilometers. Thus we know that the stones we found at the site must have been carried at least that far. With the help of Frank Fitch and Ron Watkins of the University of London we are searching for the specific sources.

It does not seem likely that all the animals of the different species represented among the KBS bones could have been killed in a short interval of time at this one place. Both considerations encourage the advancement of a tentative hypothesis: Like the stones, the bones were carried in, presumably while there was still meat on them.

If this hypothesis can be accepted, the Kay Behrensmeyer site provides very early evidence for the transport of food as a protohuman attribute. Today the carrying of food strikes us as being commonplace, but as Sherwood Washburn of the University of California at Berkeley observed some years ago such an

action would strike a living ape as being novel and peculiar behavior indeed. In short, if the hypothesis can be accepted, it suggests that by the time the KBS deposit was laid down various fundamental shifts had begun to take place in hominid social and ecological arrangements.

It should be noted that other early sites in this category are known in East Africa, so that the Kay Behrensmeyer site is by no means unique. A number of such sites have been excavated at Olduvai Gorge and reported by Mary Leakey. Of these the best preserved is the "Zinjanthropus" site of Olduvai Bed I, which is about 1.7 million years old. Here too a dense patch of discarded artifacts coincides with a concentration of broken-up bones.

There is an even larger number of Type A sites (where concentrations of artifacts are found but bones are virtually or entirely absent). Some are at Koobi Fora; others are in the Omo Valley, where Harry V. Merrick of Yale Uni-

versity and Jean Chavaillon of the French National Center for Scientific Research (CNRS) have recently uncovered sites of this kind in members E and F of the Shungura Formation. The Omo sites represent the oldest securely dated artifact concentrations so far reported anywhere in the world; the tools were deposited some two million years ago.

One of the Olduvai sites in this category seems to have been a "factory": a quarry where chert, an excellent tool material, was readily available for flaking. The other tool concentrations, with very few associated bones or none at all, may conceivably be interpreted as foci of hominid activity where for one reason or another large quantities of meat were not carried in. Until it is possible to distinguish between sites where bone was never present and sites where the bones have simply vanished because of such factors as decay, however, these deposits will remain difficult to interpret in terms of subsistence ecology.

What, in summary, do these East Af-

b

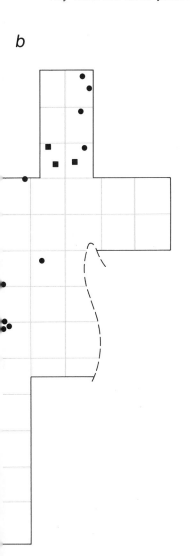

c

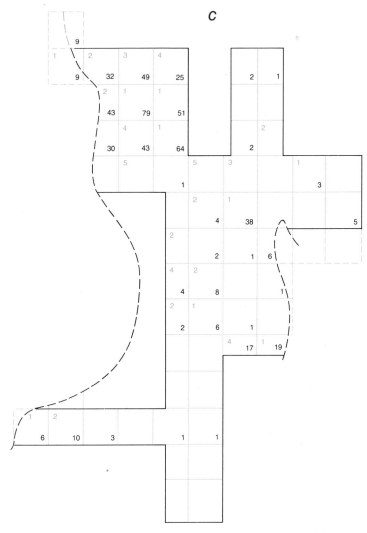

The plot of artifact distribution (*b*) shows that three of four stone cores (*open circles*), most waste stone (*squares*) and flakes and fragments of flakes (*dots*) were found in 12 adjacent squares. Also found here was an unworked stone (*A*) that, like the cores, must have been carried to the site from a distance. Plotting of all tools and bones unearthed at the site was not attempted. Numbers in grid squares (*c*) show how many flakes and bits of waste stone (*color*) and fragments of bone (*black*) were recorded without exact plotting in each square.

rican archaeological studies teach us about the evolution of human behavior? For one thing they provide unambiguous evidence that two million years ago some hominids in this part of Africa were carrying things around, for example stones. The same hominids were also making simple but effective cutting tools of stone and were at times active in the vicinity of large animal carcasses, presumably in order to get meat. The studies strongly suggest that the hominids carried animal bones (and meat) around and concentrated this portable food supply at certain places.

Model Strategies

These archaeological facts and indications allow the construction of a theoretical model that shows how at least some aspects of early hominid social existence may have been organized. Critical to the validity of the model is the inference that the various clusters of remains we have uncovered reflect social and economic nodes in the lives of the toolmakers who left behind these ancient patches of litter. Because of the evidence suggestive of the transport of food to certain focal points, the first question that the model must confront is why early hominid social groups departed from the norm among living subhuman primates, whose social groups feed as they range. To put it another way, what ecological and evolutionary advantages are there in postponing some food consumption and transporting the food?

Several possible answers to this question have been advanced. For example, Adrienne Zihlman and Nancy Tanner of the University of California at Santa Cruz suggest that when the protohumans acquired edible plants out on the open grasslands, away from the shelter of trees, it would have been advantageous for them to seize the plant products quickly and withdraw to places sheltered from menacing predators. Others have proposed that when the early hominids foraged, they left their young behind at "nest" or "den" sites (in the manner of birds, wild dogs and hyenas) and returned to these locales at intervals, bringing food with them to help feed and wean the young.

If we look to the recorded data concerning primitive human societies, a third possibility arises. Among extant and recently extinct primitive human societies the transport of food is associated with a division of labor. The society is divided by age and sex into classes that characteristically make different contributions to the total food supply. One significant result of such a division is an increase in the variety of foodstuffs consumed by the group. To generalize on the basis of many different ethnographic reports, the adult females of the society contribute the majority of the "gathered" foods; such foods are mainly plant products but may include shellfish, amphibians and small reptiles, eggs, insects and the like. The adult males usually, although not invariably, contribute most of the "hunted" foodstuffs: the flesh of mammals, fishes, birds and so forth. Characteristically the males and females range in separate groups and each sex eventually brings back to a home base at least the surplus of its foraging.

Could this simple mechanism, a division of the subsistence effort, have initiated food-carrying by early hominids? One cannot dismiss out of hand the models that suggest safety from competitors or the feeding of nesting young as the initiating mechanisms for food-carrying. Nevertheless, neither model seems to me as plausible as one that has division of labor as the primary initiating mechanism. Even if no other argument favored the model, we know for a fact that somewhere along the line in the evolution of human behavior two patterns became established: food-sharing and a division of labor. If we include both patterns in our model of early hominid society, we will at least be parsimonious.

Other arguments can be advanced in favor of an early development of a division of labor. For example, the East African evidence shows that the protohuman toolmakers consumed meat from a far greater range of species and sizes of animals than are eaten by such living primates as the chimpanzee and the baboon. Among recent human hunter-gatherers the existence of a division of labor seems clearly related to the females being encumbered with children, a handicap that bars them from hunting or scavenging, activities that require speed afoot or long-range mobility. For the protohumans too the incorporation of meat in the diet in significant quantities may well have been a key factor in the development not only of a division

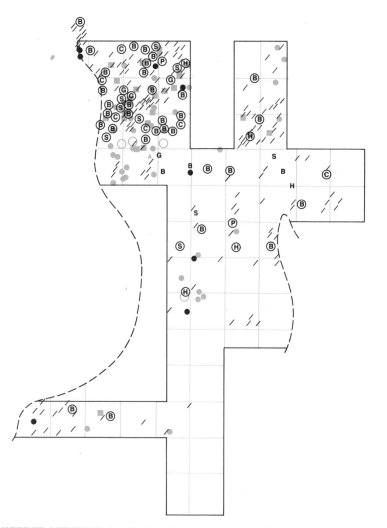

CLUSTERED MIXTURE of artifacts and animal bones at the Kay Behrensmeyer site is evident when the stone (*color*) and bone (*black*) plots are superposed. Combinations of this kind are sometimes produced by stream action, but such is not likely to be the case here, as is attested by the preservation of leaf impressions and other readily washed-away debris such as fine splinters of stone. It appears instead that the protohumans who made and discarded their tools here were also responsible for the bone accumulation because they met here to share their food.

of labor but also of the organization of movements around a home base and the transport and sharing of food.

The model I propose for testing visualizes food-sharing as the behavior central to a novel complex of adaptations that included as critical components hunting and/or scavenging, gathering and carrying. Speaking metaphorically, food-sharing provides the model with a kind of central platform. The adaptive system I visualize, however, could only have functioned through the use of tools and other equipment. For example, without the aid of a carrying device primates such as ourselves or our ancestors could not have transported from the field to the home base a sufficient amount of plant food to be worth sharing. An object as uncomplicated as a bark tray would have served the purpose, but some such item of equipment would have been mandatory. In fact, Richard Borshay Lee of the University of Toronto has suggested that a carrying device was the basic invention that made human evolution possible.

What about stone tools? Our ancestors, like ourselves, could probably break up the body of a small animal, as chimpanzees do, with nothing but their hands and teeth. It is hard to visualize them or us, however, eating the meat of an elephant, a hippopotamus or some other large mammal without the aid of a cutting implement. As the archaeological evidence demonstrates abundantly,

the protohumans of East Africa not only knew how to produce such stone flakes by percussion but also found them so useful that they carried the raw materials needed to make the implements with them from place to place. Thus whereas the existence of a carrying device required by the model remains hypothetical as far as archaeological evidence is concerned, the fact that tools were used and carried about is amply attested to.

In this connection it should be stressed that the archaeological evidence is also silent with regard to protohuman consumption of plant foods. Both the morphology and the patterns of wear observable on hominid teeth suggest such a plant component in the diet, and so does the weight of comparative data on subsistence patterns among living nonhuman primates and among nonfarming human societies. Nevertheless, if positive evidence is to be found, we shall have to sharpen our ingenuity, perhaps by turning to organic geochemical analyses. It is clear that as long as we do not correct for the imbalance created by the durability of bone as compared with that of plant residues, studies of human evolution will tend to have a male bias!

As far as the model is concerned the key question is not whether collectable foods—fruits, nuts, tubers, greens and even insects—were eaten. It is whether these protohumans carried such foods about. Lacking any evidence for the

consumption of plant foods, I shall fall back on the argument that the system I visualize would have worked best if the mobile hunter-scavenger contribution of meat to the social group was balanced by the gatherer-carrier collection of high-grade plant foods. What is certain is that at some time during the past several million years just such a division of labor came to be a standard kind of behavior among the ancestors of modern man.

A final cautionary word about the model: The reader may have noted that I have been careful about the use of the words "hunter" and "hunting." This is because we cannot judge how much of the meat taken by the protohumans of East Africa came from opportunistic scavenging and how much was obtained by hunting. It is reasonable to assume that the carcasses of animals killed by carnivores and those of animals that had otherwise died or been disabled would always have provided active scavengers a certain amount of meat. For the present it seems less reasonable to assume that protohumans, armed primitively if at all, would be particularly effective hunters. Attempts are now under way, notably by Elizabeth Vrba of South Africa, to distinguish between assemblages of bones attributable to scavenging and assemblages attributable to hunting, but no findings from East Africa are yet available. For the present I am inclined to accept the verdict of J. Desmond

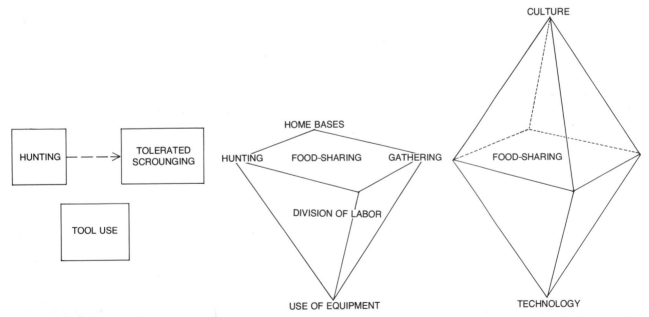

BEHAVIOR PATTERNS that differ in degree of organization are contrasted in these diagrams. Living great apes, exemplified here by the chimpanzee, exhibit behavior patterns that became important in human evolution but the patterns (*left*) exist largely as isolated elements. Hunting occurs on a small scale but leads only to "tolerated scrounging" rather than active food-sharing; similarly, tools are used but tool use is not integrated with hunting or scrounging. The author's model (*center*) integrates these three behavior patterns and others into a coherent structure. Food-sharing is seen as a central structural element, incorporating the provision of both animal and plant foods, the organization of a home base and a division of labor. Supporting the integrated structure is a necessary infrastructure of tool and equipment manufacture; for example, without devices for carrying foodstuffs there could not be a division of labor and organized food-sharing. In modern human societies (*right*) the food-sharing structure has undergone socioeconomic elaboration. Its infrastructure now incorporates all of technology, and a matching superstructure has arisen to incorporate other elements of what is collectively called culture.

Clark of the University of California at Berkeley and Lewis R. Binford of the University of New Mexico. In their view the earliest meat-eaters might have obtained the flesh of animals weighing up to 30 kilograms by deliberate hunting, but the flesh of larger animals was probably available only through scavenging.

Tools as Testimony

Of course, the adaptive model I have advanced here reflects only a working hypothesis and not established fact. Nevertheless, there is sufficient evidence in its favor to justify looking further at its possible implications for the course of human evolution. For example, the model clearly implies that early toolmaking hominids displayed certain patterns of behavior that, among the patterns of behavior of all primates, uniquely characterize our own species and set it apart from its closest living relatives, the great apes. Does this mean that the toolmaking hominids of 1.5 to two million years ago were in fact "human"?

I would surmise that it does not, and I have been at pains to characterize these East African pioneers as protohumans. In summarizing the contrasts between living men and living apes I put high on the list language and the cultural phenomena that are dependent on it. We have no direct means of learning whether or not any of these early hominids had language. It is my suspicion, however, that the principal evolutionary change in the hominid line leading to full humanity over the past two million years has been the great expansion of language and communication abilities, together with the cognitive and cultural capabilities integrally related to language. What is the evidence in support of this surmise?

One humble indicator of expanding mental capacities is the series of changes that appears in the most durable material record available to us: the stone tools. The earlier tools from the period under consideration here seem to me to show a simple and opportunistic range of forms that reflect no more than an uncomplicated empirical grasp of one skill: how to fracture stone by percussion in such a way as to obtain fragments with sharp edges. At that stage of toolmaking the maker imposed a minimum of culturally dictated forms on his artifacts. Stone tools as simple as these perform perfectly well the basic functions that support progress in the direction of becoming human, for example the shaping of a digging stick, a spear and a bark tray, or the butchering of an animal carcass.

The fact is that exactly such simple stone tools have been made and used ever since their first invention, right down to the present day. Archaeology also shows, however, that over the past several hundred thousand years some assemblages of stone tools began to reflect a greater cultural complexity on the part of their makers. The complexity is first shown in the imposition of more arbitrary tool forms; these changes were followed by increases in the number of such forms. There is a marked contrast between the pure opportunism apparent in the shapes of the earliest stone tools and the orderly array of forms that appear later in the Old Stone Age when each form is represented by numerous standardized examples in each assemblage of tools. The contrast strongly suggests that the first toolmakers lacked the highly developed mental and cultural abilities of more recent humans.

The evidence of the hominid fossils and the evidence of the artifacts together suggest that these early artisans were nonhuman hominids. I imagine that if we had a time machine and could visit a place such as the Kay Behrensmeyer site at the time of its original occupation, we would find hominids that were living in social groups much like those of other higher primates. The differences would be apparent only after prolonged observation. Perhaps at the start of each day we would observe a group splitting up as some of its members went off in one direction and some in another. All these subgroups would very probably feed intermittently as they moved about and encountered ubiquitous low-grade plant foods such as berries, but we might well observe that some of the higher-grade materials—large tubers or the haunch of a scavenged carcass—were being reserved for group consumption when the foraging parties reconvened at their starting point.

To the observer in the time machine behavior of this kind, taken in context with the early hominids' practice of making tools and equipment, would seem familiarly "human." If, as I suppose, the hominids under observation communicated only as chimpanzees do or perhaps by means of very rudimentary protolinguistic signals, then the observer might feel he was witnessing the activities of some kind of fascinating bipedal ape. When one is relying on archaeology to reconstruct protohuman life, one must strongly resist the temptation to project too much of ourselves into the past. As Jane B. Lancaster of the University of Oklahoma has pointed out, the hominid life systems of two million years ago have no living counterparts.

Social Advances

My model of early hominid adaptation can do more than indicate that the first toolmakers were culturally protohuman. It can also help to explain the dynamics of certain significant advances in the long course of mankind's development. For example, one can imagine that a hominid social organization involving some division of labor and a degree of food-sharing might well have been able to function even if it had communicative abilities little more advanced than those of living chimpanzees. In such a simple subsistence system, however, any group with members that were able not only to exchange food but also to exchange information would have gained a critical selective advantage over all the rest. Such a group's gatherers could report on scavenging or hunting opportunities they had observed, and its hunters could tell the gatherers about any plant foods they had encountered.

By the same token the fine adjustment of social relations, always a matter of importance among primates, becomes doubly important in a social system that involves food exchange. Language serves in modern human societies not only for the exchange of information but also as an instrument for social adjustment and even for the exchange of misinformation.

Food-sharing and the kinds of behavior associated with it probably played an important part in the development of systems of reciprocal social obligations that characterize all human societies we know about. Anthropological research shows that each human being in a group is ordinarily linked to many other members of the group by ties that are both social and economic. The French anthropologist Marcel Mauss, in a classic essay, "The Gift," published in 1925, showed that social ties are usually reciprocal in the sense that whereas benefits from a relationship may initially pass in only one direction, there is an expectation of a future return of help in time of need. The formation and management of such ties calls for an ability to calculate complex chains of contingencies that reach far into the future. After food-sharing had become a part of protohuman behavior the need for such an ability to plan and calculate must have provided an important part of the biological basis for the evolution of the human intellect.

The model may also help explain the development of human marriage arrangements. It assumes that in early protohuman populations the males and females divided subsistence labor between them so that each sex was preferentially tapping a different kind of food resource and then sharing within a social group some of what had been obtained. In such circumstances a mating system that involved at least one male in "family" food procurement on behalf of each child-rearing female in the group would have a clear selective advantage over, for example, the chimpanzees' pattern of opportunistic relations between the sexes.

I have emphasized food-sharing as a principle that is central to an understanding of human evolution over the past two million years or so. I have also set forth archaeological evidence that food-sharing was an established kind of behavior among early protohumans. The notion is far from novel; it is implicit in many philosophical speculations and in many writings on paleoanthropology. What is novel is that I have undertaken to make the hypothesis explicit so that it can be tested and revised.

Accounting for Evolution

Thus the food-sharing hypothesis now joins other hypotheses that have been put forward to account for the course of human evolution. Each of these hypotheses tends to maintain that one or another innovation in protohuman behavior was the critical driving force of change. For example, the argument has been advanced that tools were the "prime movers." Here the underlying implication is that in each successive generation the more capable individuals made better tools and thereby gained advantages that favored the transmission of their genes through natural selection; it is supposed that these greater capabilities would later be applied in aspects of life other than technology. Another hypothesis regards hunting as being the driving force. Here the argument is that hunting requires intelligence, cunning, skilled neuromuscular coordination and, in the case of group hunting, cooperation. Among other suggested prime movers are such practices as carrying and gathering.

If we compare the food-sharing explanation with these alternative explanations we see that in fact food-sharing incorporates many aspects of each of the others. It will also be seen that in the food-sharing model the isolated elements are treated as being integral parts of a complex, flexible system. The model itself is probably an oversimplified version of what actually happened, but it seems sufficiently realistic to be worthy of testing through further archaeological and paleontological research.

Lastly, the food-sharing model can be seen to have interconnections with the physical implications of fossil hominid anatomy. For example, a prerequisite of food-sharing is the ability to carry things. This ability in turn is greatly facilitated by a habitual two-legged posture. As Gordon W. Hewes of the University of Colorado has pointed out, an important part of the initial evolutionary divergence of hominids from their primate relatives may have been the propensity and the ability to carry things about. To me it seems equally plausible that the physical selection pressures that promoted an increase in the size of the protohuman brain, thereby surely enhancing the hominid capacity for communication, are a consequence of the shift from individual foraging to food-sharing some two million years ago.

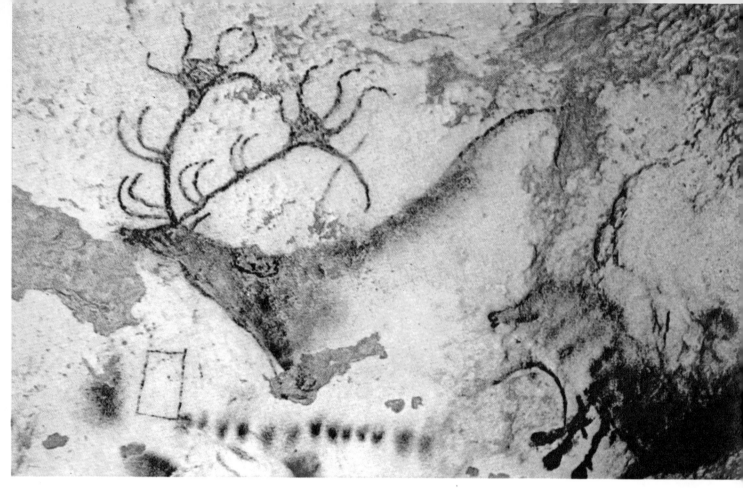

RED DEER STAG (*above*) appears on a cave wall at Lascaux, a French Paleolithic site discovered in 1940. Both the stag and the two abstract signs below it, a rectangle and a row of dots, were painted on the rock surface with a manganese pigment; the stag is about five feet high. The painting was made some 15,000 years ago.

SPOTTED HORSE (*below*) dominates a cave wall at Pech-Merle, another French Paleolithic site. A hand seen in negative outline indicates the scale of the painting, which, like the stag, belongs to the early Magdalenian period of European prehistory. Abstract signs include many dots and a grill-like red rectangle by the hand.

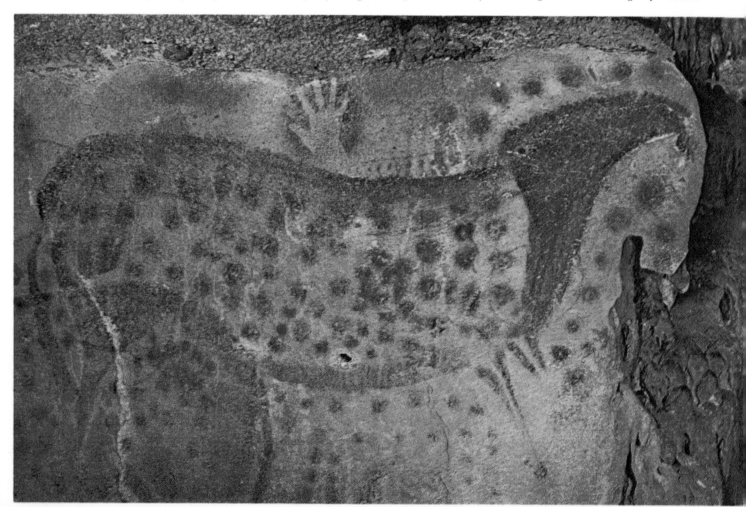

The Evolution of Paleolithic Art

by André Leroi-Gourhan
February 1968

The first artistic tradition occupied two-thirds of the period spanned by the entire history of art. How it evolved is studied by the classification of its works in terms of time and space

The earliest forms of art, at least among those art forms that can be dated with any certainty, were created in Europe between 30,000 and 10,000 B.C. They belong to a time before the oldest civilizations and the earliest agriculture—the Upper Paleolithic period at the end of the last continental glaciation. Paleolithic art has manifested itself in two principal forms: engraved or sculptured objects found by the thousands in excavations from the Urals to the Atlantic, and the awe-inspiring decorations of more than 100 caves in France and Spain. It has now been studied for nearly a century, and such caves as Lascaux and Altamira have become as well known as the most famous art works of historic times.

Until recently studies of Paleolithic art were focused largely on its aesthetic and magico-religious significance. Today attention has turned to the relations among such art forms—to their classification in terms of time and space. As a result we can now begin to perceive how Paleolithic art evolved from its appearance in Aurignacian times to its inexplicable disappearance in Magdalenian times 20,000 years later.

Can an art that embraced all Europe for such a mighty span truly be considered a single art? Should we perhaps speak of prehistoric arts, as we speak of the arts of Africa? The analogy provides the answer to our question: The living arts of Africa south of the Sahara, with all their nuances, are clearly subdivisions of one wholly African art. They cannot be confused with the art of any other region. In the same sense Paleolithic art also constitutes a single episode in art history. Such is the unanimous opinion of its students. This view is based on the continuity that Paleolithic art exhibits in region after region over a span of 20

millenniums. Greek art or Christian art is so identified because its images continuously translate its ideologies. In the same way the term "Paleolithic art" serves to relate various techniques of representation that have undergone changes over a long period of time to a body of figurative themes that has remained remarkably constant. Indeed, consistency is one of the first facts that strikes the student of Paleolithic art. In painting, engraving and sculpture on rock walls or in ivory, reindeer antler, bone and stone, and in the most diverse styles, Paleolithic artists repeatedly depict the same inventory of animals in comparable attitudes. Once this unity is recognized, it only remains for the student to seek ways of arranging the art's temporal and spatial subdivisions in a systematic manner.

The Problem of Chronology

The task of temporal subdivision is by no means an easy one. To understand its difficulties, let us imagine an art historian who must arrange in their correct chronological order 1,000 statues belonging to every epoch from 500 B.C. to A.D. 1900. Imagine further that his only points of reference are five or six of the statues that are by chance correctly dated. The prehistorian's position is the same—or worse. The large majority of the Paleolithic period's small sculptures (which we classify as "portable art" to distinguish them from "wall art," the paintings, engravings and sculptures of the caves and rock-shelters) were discovered at the beginning of this century, a time when precision in the excavation of stratified sites was far from absolute. As a result there are very few instances in which associations are established between excavated works of art and imple-

ments such as scrapers and projectile points that have been firmly dated on the basis of stratigraphy. Even in the few cases where such dating is possible, the style of the object is not always so clear-cut as to allow strong conclusions. Finally, the thousands of wall paintings and engravings created during the period are not stratified at all. If the earth floors of their caves contain the remains of more than one Paleolithic culture, it is difficult to decide to which of these culture periods the art should be assigned. For all these reasons classifying Paleolithic art is a task considerably harder than the classification of prehistoric man's other material remains.

The work of the Abbé Breuil over more than half a century provides the principal source of traditional views concerning the evolution of Paleolithic art. This pioneer prehistorian undertook a prodigious labor of inventory and classification with the limited means available in his day. Except for a few instances in which specific dating was possible, his method of establishing the relative chronology of wall art rested on three assumptions. The first was simply that when two wall paintings are superimposed, the one underneath must be the older. The second, based on the probability that the caves where wall art is found were inhabited continuously for many centuries, was that one should find examples of work from many periods among the decorations. The third assumption was that, since the animal and human forms depicted in the caves were executed individually for magical purposes, there is no order in their arrangement. It follows from this last assumption that such works are not necessarily contemporaneous and that they are not, when taken together, evidence of any organized body of thought.

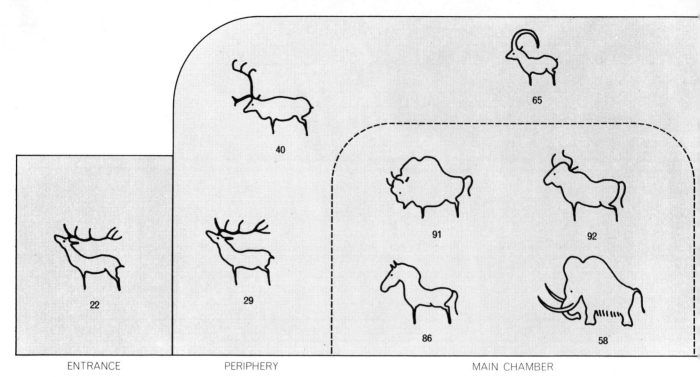

ENTRANCE   PERIPHERY   MAIN CHAMBER

METHODICAL ARRANGEMENT of the animal depictions at various Paleolithic sites was revealed by the author's survey of 62 caves. The diagram shows an idealized cave with an entrance, a main chamber and its periphery and, finally, a back passage to a deep inner area. Numbers below each animal figure show the percent of depictions of that animal present in that part of all the

From this viewpoint (which is still held by some prehistorians) wall art represents the gradual accumulation of isolated pictures, each created by the need of the moment. When one stands before the great wall paintings of Lascaux in France or Altamira in Spain, however, it is hard to imagine how the random accumulation of isolated subjects could possibly have led to an assemblage that impresses the most naïve viewer with its overall balance. Doubts on this score are what inspired Annette Laming-Emperaire to publish her important study of 1962: *The Meaning of Paleolithic Wall Art*. There she vigorously challenges the traditional theories. My own work has been motivated by a similar conviction and is based on the following postulate. If, rather than working haphazardly, the men of the Paleolithic consciously—or

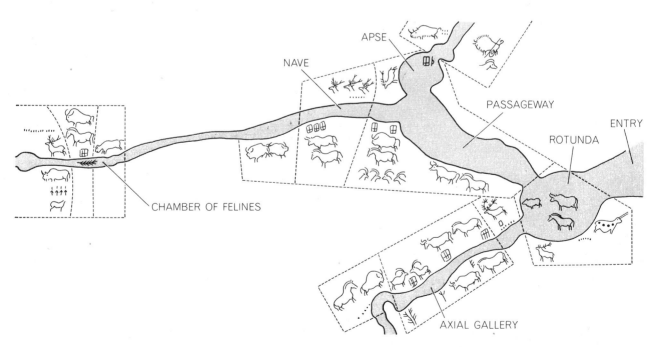

LASCAUX CAVE, a famous Paleolithic site in France, is shown in plan view; more than 300 feet separate the cave's deepest recess (*left*) from the entrance (*right*). The broken lines enclosing the groups of depictions suggest how the cave's many decorated areas were originally subdivided. The stag and the two abstract signs just inside the Axial Gallery are reproduced in color on page 36.

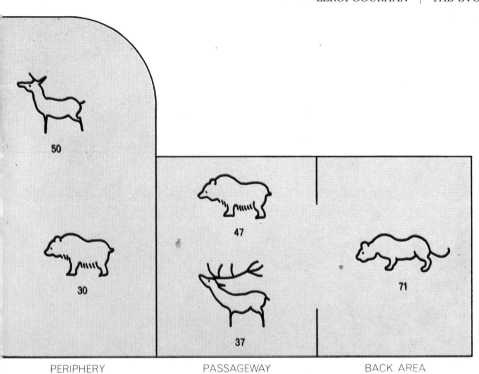

PERIPHERY   PASSAGEWAY   BACK AREA

caves surveyed. More than 90 percent of all bison and wild-ox paintings appear in main chambers, as do most horse paintings. Most stag paintings are located elsewhere: nearly 40 percent are in inner areas, 22 percent are in entrances and 29 percent are in peripheral areas.

even unconsciously—introduced order into the way their pictures are positioned, then an analysis of where various animal paintings are located in a sizable number of caves (say 50 or more out of the 100-odd sites) should reveal what general scheme, if any, the artists had in mind.

To test this postulate I have reviewed the topography of some 60 caves, established the position of more than 2,000 individual animal pictures in them and tabulated the results. The following related facts can be perceived: (1) If one defines "central position" either as the middle of a painted panel or as the most prominent chamber within a cave, it is in this position that more than 85 percent of all pictures of bison, wild oxen and horses are found. (2) The next most prominent animals—deer, ibex and mammoth—appear in positions other than a central one. (3) Three other species—rhinoceros, lion and bear—are found only in the deepest parts of the cave, or far from the central position [see bottom illustration on page 43].

A similar analysis can be made of the subjects other than animals that are depicted in Paleolithic art: representations of humans, male and female, and signs that are more or less abstract. More than 80 percent of all the female figures—and of the symbols that I call "wide" abstract signs, which are evidently related to fe-

male figures—are found in the same central places where bison and wild oxen are depicted. Other symbols designated "narrow" signs are in the same areas where the remaining animal figures are found; that is to say, nearly 70 percent of them are in positions that are peripheral.

This is not the place to consider what such patterns may be able to tell us about the religious beliefs of Paleolithic man. For anyone who is trying to establish a chronology of Paleolithic art, however, the orderliness of these arrays has its own significance. First, one is led to the conclusion that in most of the wall art in most of the caves the separate elements belong to a single period, and that later works were executed in other parts of the cave. Even in those caves where the wall art clearly represents the accumulation of several periods, the later works repeat the elements and order of the earlier ones. Second, in any single assemblage of pictures the wide abstract signs are all much the same, whereas in caves that contain a number of separate picture groups the wide signs differ from group to group. The existence of these differences suggests that the wide signs can serve as chronological guideposts, or at the very least as guides to the relations between the various styles in which the animal figures are executed. Thus, regardless of any hypotheses concerning

prehistoric religion, the fact that there is order in Paleolithic man's art provides a basis for investigating its evolution.

Discovering Points in Time

All such problems of chronology would have vanished long ago if only one of two things had happened. Each Paleolithic site could have yielded stratified sequences of buried sculptures and the style of the material from each stratum could have shown it to be unmistakably contemporaneous with one after another of the cave's displays of wall art. Alternatively, the examples of the wall art in a number of caves could all have been executed in a single style, and the artifacts excavated from the floors of the same caves could all have been attributed to a single interval of time. In actuality very few examples of wall art can be firmly attributed to a specific period during the many millenniums in which prehistoric art flourished. Still, the few examples that do exist provide us with some degree of chronological framework.

As a starting point, there are no known examples of representational art before the Aurignacian period, beginning about 30,000 B.C. There are, however, firmly dated pieces of Aurignacian sculpture. They are found, for example, in the Aurignacian strata of two sites in the Dordogne valley of France: the Cellier rock-shelter and La Ferassie. They are crudely engraved figures of animals and wide and narrow signs.

Our next bench mark in time is found in strata of Solutrean age (about 15,000 B.C.) at the Roc de Sers site in the Charente valley of France: a low-relief frieze rendered in a vigorous style. It depicts horses, bison, ibexes and men. The date is firmly established because the rock of the frieze had fallen from its original position and was discovered lying face down between two strata containing Solutrean artifacts.

A third bench mark is provided by a number of engraved stone plaques discovered in strata of Upper Magdalenian age (about 10,000 B.C.) in the caves of Teyjat in the Dordogne. The animals depicted on the plaques are the same as those in the Roc de Sers frieze, but they are executed in a more detailed, almost photographic style. The final bench mark, denoting the end of Paleolithic art, is also found in the Dordogne. At Villepin engraved pebbles from strata dating to the very end of the Magdalenian period (about 8000 B.C.) display sketchy, often barely identifiable animal figures.

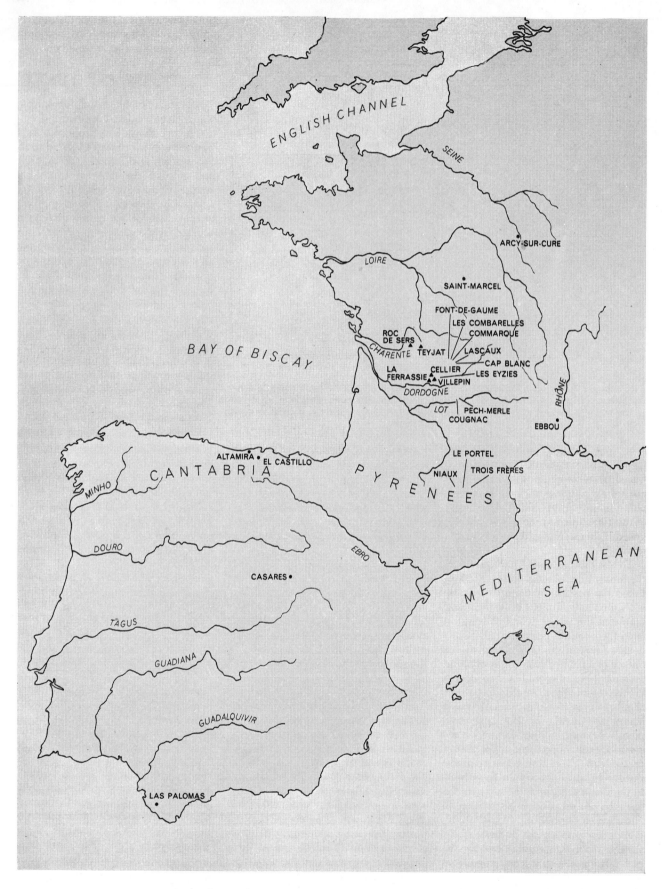

HEARTLAND of Paleolithic cave art was western Europe south of the Loire River. Sites mentioned by the author in the valleys of the Charente, the Dordogne and the Lot and in the foothills of the French Pyrenees are shown, as are some with cave art in Canta-brian, central and southern Spain, in France north of the Charente and in the Rhône valley. Cave art has also been found at three sites in Italy and Sicily. Five Charente-Dordogne sites marked with triangles contained sculpture in strata with well-established dates.

Four points in time, all found in the same Dordogne-Charente region, scarcely suffice to establish a chronology for all Europe. Fortunately a number of less exact bench marks are available in France, Spain and Italy. Although these bench marks can be fixed no more exactly than around the start, the middle and the end of the Upper Paleolithic, they are in general accord with the Dordogne-Charente reference points and allow us not only to recognize the entire period's major chronological subdivisions but also to perceive a new and very important fact. Up to now it has been thought that the portable art and the wall art of the Upper Paleolithic evolved in a strictly parallel manner, and that one could find pictures characteristic of each of the period's subdivisions in the caves. It is now apparent that, on the contrary, wall art was extremely rare or even nonexistent early in the Upper Paleolithic, that most of it belongs to a middle phase during which the portable art becomes less abundant, and that portable art catches up with wall art once more in the period's final phase.

The Evolution of Abstract Signs

Students of Paleolithic art have always been intrigued by certain abstract signs that appear in wall art almost from its beginning to its end, although not so commonly as pictures of animals. In the opinion of some investigators some of the signs represent huts or tents; other signs are interpreted as representing weapons and traps, shields and even primitive heraldic designs. It would seem, however, that only a few signs out of the hundreds known can be explained by their resemblance to actual objects. If instead of selecting a few such examples one makes an inclusive inventory of all the things found in wall art that do not obviously portray animals, a rather different picture emerges. One can even group such representations into general categories. One category is men and women, sometimes pictured whole and sometimes reduced to a head or torso. To this category can be added numerous realistic representations of the male and female sexual organs, which evidently have the same significance as the fuller figures. The existence of these drawings has suggested to some scholars that a fertility cult existed in Paleolithic times. This is hard to disprove, but given the fact that the male and female representations are as often separate as they are together, they would appear to be at best quite abstract fertility symbols.

YEARS B.C.	CULTURE	PERIOD	EXAMPLE
5,000			
10,000	LATE MAGDALENIAN V–VI	CLASSIC (STYLE IV)	
	MIDDLE MAGDALENIAN III–IV		
	EARLY MAGDALENIAN I–II	ARCHAIC (STYLE III)	
15,000	SOLUTREAN		
	INTER-GRAVETTIAN-SOLUTREAN	PRIMITIVE (STYLE II)	
20,000			
	GRAVETTIAN		
25,000		PRIMITIVE (STYLE I)	
	AURIGNACIAN		
30,000			

EVOLUTION of Paleolithic art took place during the era's final 20,000 years, a period known as the Upper Paleolithic. The first examples are dated around 30,000 B.C., when the Aurignacian culture makes its appearance. They were crude outlines cut into rock (*bottom figure is unidentified; the others portray horses*). This Style I work, as it is classified by the author, and later work in Style II comprise the primitive period. The best-known cave art was produced during the archaic (Style III) and the classic (Style IV) periods.

By far the largest number of signs belong to one or the other of the two groups I have mentioned: the wide and narrow signs. The wide signs include rectangles, triangles, ovals and shield shapes. Most of them clearly belong to the category of human representations; they are quite realistic depictions of the female sexual organ. The narrow signs include short strokes, rows of dots and barbed lines. Some of them clearly suggest male sexual organs, although they are extremely stylized. For that matter, the entire inventory of abstract signs could well be nothing but animal and human figures rendered symbolically.

These abstract signs are strikingly diverse in both time and space. One kind of rectangle, for example, accompanies animal figures that themselves have a number of stylistic features in common: the rectangle appears in the Dordogne, in the nearby Lot valley and in Cantabria, beyond the Pyrenees in Spain. This enables us to assign all the cave art in which the rectangle appears to the same time period. At the same time how abstract decoration is used to embellish each rectangle varies sufficiently from cave to cave to establish the fact that the art of Lascaux in the Dordogne, of Pech-Merle in the Lot valley and of Altamira in Spain each belongs to a distinct ancient province. Such a distinction

FOUR QUADRUPEDS, three of them bison, show how styles evolved. Work in Style I (*bottom engraving, cross section at right*) seldom depicted entire animals as here; both line and workmanship are rough. Style II technique (*second from bottom, cross section at left*) remains primitive but forms are more powerful. In Style III (*painting second from top*) line and color have been mastered although anatomical details are unperfected. The work in Style IV (*top painting*) shows both anatomical fidelity and a sense of movement.

cannot be made with equal precision when one must base one's judgment on the style in which the animals are depicted. As a matter of fact, signs remote from realism are a better mirror of local influences than animal portraits are. I have therefore based my use of abstract signs on a twofold principle: first, that as generalized forms they are contemporaneous and, second, that in their details they reveal regional influences.

As in the pictures of animals, the abstract signs do not establish much in the way of precise chronology. Most of the sites where they are found contain nothing that can be rigorously dated. Nonetheless, they make it possible to establish a sequence that is about as reliable as the one based on animal figures. For example, the oldest known abstract signs appear about 30,000 B.C., in Aurignacian times. The wide signs are realistically feminine; the narrow ones are either realistically masculine or are stylized into a series of strokes or dots. In Solutrean times, roughly from 20,000 to 15,000 B.C., full figures of men and women seem to predominate; the style of the latter is familiar to us from the numerous "Venus figurines" that have been found in both western and eastern Europe. The transition between Solutrean and early Magdalenian times (between 15,000 and 13,000 B.C.) is a period of rectangular signs, followed closely by bracket-shaped ones. At this point regional differences in abstract signs make their classification difficult, although a revival in the popularity of small sculptures provides a precise means of determining the chronological position of other animal representations. During the Magdalenian proper, from 13,000 to 9000 B.C., the most important group of abstract signs are "key-shaped" ones, derived from the representation of a woman in profile [*see illustration on page 44*]. In the Dordogne and the Lot Valley it is possible to trace the evolution from early to middle Magdalenian by means of the key-shaped signs. Thereafter these signs become increasingly stylized, both in space (as one moves south) and in time (as the end of the Magdalenian approaches).

Key-shaped signs are by no means the only abstractions of this period. Here a variety of influences appear to have crisscrossed in space and time. At Les Eyzies in the Dordogne, for example, roof-shaped signs (which apparently evolved out of the bracket-shaped ones) seem to take the place of the key shapes. Another trend in symbolism is marked by the appearance of what some scholars have assumed are representations of

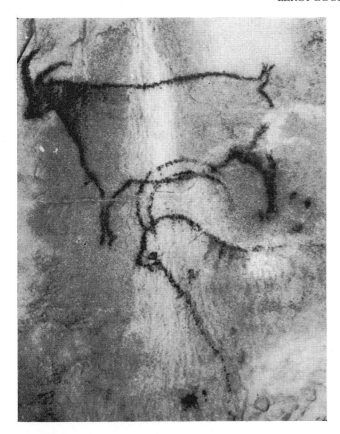

PAINTED IBEXES of the archaic period, a female (*top*) and a male, were done in red ocher at Cougnac, a Lot valley site in France. Painting, engraving and combinations of both are known.

ENGRAVED IBEX, also executed during the archaic period, is one of scores of animal figures cut into the cave walls at Ebbou, a Rhône valley site in France that contains engravings exclusively.

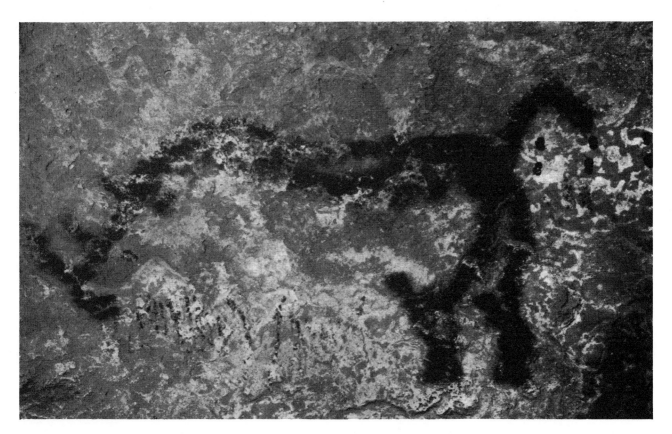

PAINTED RHINOCEROS, one of the animals typically found in the back areas of caves, occupies a niche opening off the main chamber at Lascaux. The work, in manganese, is transitional between Style III and Style IV. Dots by the tail form an abstract sign.

wounds on the bodies of animals. Both symbolic wounds and realistic representations of the female sexual organ are found in a comparable setting in a large number of caves. Since the realistic female representations of the Magdalenian are executed differently from the earliest female representations, it seems likely that the "wounds" are a different kind of female symbol.

The Time Scale

By putting together all three classes of evidence—from excavations, from the study of reasonably well-dated wall art and from the evolution of human figures and abstract signs—a chronological framework can be erected that begins to approximate reality. The most attractive of all Paleolithic art works, the animal pictures, remain the most difficult to interpret directly. The reason is that any analysis of their evolution is founded on criteria of style, and judgments of style are primarily subjective. When details that allow objective evaluation are scanty, only the most general conclusions are possible. What appears to be an important criterion may reflect nothing more than a regional characteristic or the relative skill of the artist.

In spite of such qualifications, it can be said that the evidence in general allows us to discern the emergence of three great periods of Paleolithic art during the 20,000 years from the Aurignacian to the end of the Magdalenian.

They are, first, a primitive period, then an archaic period (in the same sense that one speaks of archaic Greek art: a well-developed body of art rapidly approaching maturity) and finally a classic period. Where the conditions are most favorable, as in the Dordogne-Charente region, we can point to the succession of four styles in the course of the three major periods. These I have designated Styles I and II (in the primitive period), Style III (in the archaic) and Style IV (in the classic). Even finer subdivisions are possible: the wall art of Lascaux and Pech-Merle, for example, is divisible into early and late Style III, and elsewhere Style IV shows similar early and late stages.

What are the characteristics of each period and style? Style I embraces history's oldest examples of representational art, examples that are precisely dated to the Aurignacian period by virtue of the fact that they are found in association with Aurignacian tools. The Aurignacian sculptures of Cellier and La Ferassie are Style I. As I noted earlier, the representations of animals from this time are very crude; sometimes the whole body is shown but more often the rendering is limited to a head or a forequarter. The inventory of animals includes the horse, the bison, the wild ox, the ibex and the rhinoceros—in other words, the main cast of characters found throughout Paleolithic art. The representations include realistic depictions of the female sexual organ as well as such male symbols as lines and rows of dots.

A long interval, extending from 25,000 to 18,000 B.C. and thus from the late Aurignacian through Gravettian times to early Solutrean ones, is the setting for Style II. In a chronology based on the evolution of techniques this 7,000-year interval is a confused period. One can assume that a number of cultures succeeded one another, but it is hard to equate the changes in one region with those in another. In any case, this was the period in which Paleolithic art attained its greatest geographical range, from the Atlantic coast on the west to the valley of the Don on the east. It is also the period in which the first wall art appears: paintings and engravings executed on the walls of open rock-shelters or on those cave walls that were illuminated by daylight.

The animal forms of Style II are powerful, but the technique of rendering remains quite primitive. The stereotyped curved line representing the neck and back and the line representing the belly are drawn first; the details characteristic of each animal species are then roughly connected to the generalized torsos and are often left unfinished. The abstract signs that are included in the wall art remain close to realism and generally consist of ovals and series of strokes. In the realm of small sculptures the numerous female figurines of this period, usually made of stone or of mammoth ivory, all have much the same shape. The trunk is corpulent and rendered in some detail but the extremities and the

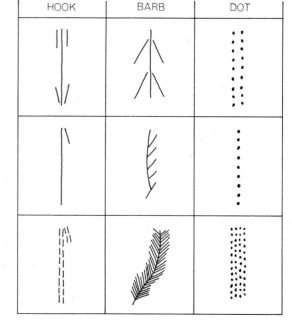

	OVAL	RECTANGLE	KEY SHAPE		HOOK	BARB	DOT
NORMAL							
SIMPLIFIED							
DERIVED							

"WIDE" AND "NARROW" SIGNS are considered by the author to be symbolic of the sexes and to have evolved from earlier depictions of female and male figures or sexual organs. Three groups of symbols are shown for each sex, in normal and more abstract forms.

head are stylized and often quite reduced in size.

Style III, which is typical of the entire archaic period, finds its most eloquent expression in the great frieze of the Roc de Sers in Charente, in the equally impressive murals at Lascaux and in some of the Spanish cave paintings. The representations of animals retain a primitive flavor: the bodies are bulky and the small heads and hooves are joined to the bodies without much care for detail or proportion. Line, however, is now handled with great sensitivity, and the control of painting and sculptural technique is complete. The interplay of manganese blacks and ocher reds and yellows in the paintings and the use of color accents on the low reliefs reflect a mastery of both mediums. Representations of humans are scarce and do not compare in quality with the animal pictures. On the other hand, the abstract signs characteristic of Style III, which are rectangular or bracket-shaped, show such a diversity of embellishment that they have been compared to heraldic coats of arms.

Chronologically the style of the archaic period occupies the interval between 18,000 and 13,000 B.C., thus including the late Solutrean and the early Magdalenian. The evolution of animal portrayal can be traced through all five millenniums. At Lascaux and at Pech-Merle, for example, one can differentiate between early Style III animal paintings that are still close to Style II and late Style III paintings that already verge on Style IV.

In western Europe small sculptures are notably rare during the archaic period; of the few works in the category of portable art most are engraved plaques. In eastern Europe, on the other hand, there is no Style III wall art at all but there is a trove of animal and human figurines. Such regional differences probably correspond to ethnic ones. Thus one can readily distinguish between an eastern domain (from what is now Czechoslovakia to the U.S.S.R. west of the Urals) and a western one. Although we are a long way from knowing all the schools of Style III in the western domain, variations in rectangular signs and associated animal figures enable us to detect shades of difference between works from the Dordogne, the Lot valley, the central Pyrenees, Cantabria and the Rhône valley.

The whole of the Magdalenian proper, from 13,000 to 9000 B.C., provides the stage for the classic period of Paleolithic art and Style IV. Outside of western

THE TWO SEXES are represented by this array of wide and narrow signs painted on the wall of a cave at El Castillo in Cantabrian Spain during the archaic period. The embellished rectangles belong to one of five groups of female symbols recognized by the author and the rows of dots to one of four male groups (see *illustration on opposite page*).

"WOUNDED" BISON, painted during the classic period at Niaux in the French Pyrenees, is interpreted by the author as neither a hunting scene nor a sorcerer's spell but instead as a combination of animal figure and abstract female sign found only in Style IV. Female signs are usually found with bison and wild-ox pictures in the caves' central chambers.

CRUDELY OUTLINED HEAD of an animal from the earliest Aurignacian stratum at the Cellier rock-shelter in the Dordogne valley is typical of the art of the primitive period.

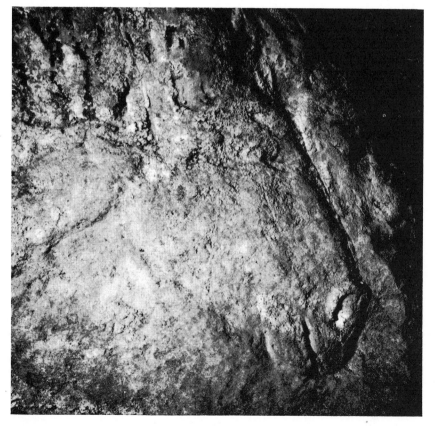

LOW-RELIEF SCULPTURE of a horse's head from Commarque, a Middle Magdalenian cave site in the Dordogne, shows the sophistication of classic period art, 15,000 years later.

Europe, Style IV is not particularly well represented at present, but within that area it is rich in wall art and especially rich in portable art. Small sculptures were widely disseminated in western Europe during the classic period. Toward the end of the period, when an increasingly mild climate allowed occupation of the northern and mountainous areas of Europe, examples of portable art reached the areas of Switzerland, Germany and even Britain. Wall art also extended its boundaries, appearing in Italy for the first time.

The wealth of classic small sculptures makes possible many comparisons between them and Style IV wall paintings that illuminate the main features of the period's art evolution. One result is that a distinction can be made between early and late Style IV animal pictures. In the early period faint traces of the archaic models still remain; regardless of the correctness of their proportions, the animals give the appearance of being suspended in midair. Body contours are filled in with incised lines or splashes of color that convey the texture of the coat. This surface modeling is present in figures found from Spain to the Loire valley in France; each animal species— horse, bison, ibex, reindeer and the like —is rendered by means of the same conventions from one end of this region to the other. In late Style IV representations the rendering of texture is less clear and many animals are presented in simple outline. It is now that anatomical fidelity and a sense of movement reach their peak. If the final art of the Paleolithic lacks the rather solemn grandeur of Lascaux, it nonetheless possesses an extraordinary vitality.

Most of the best-known examples of cave art are either early or late Style IV. These include the wall paintings at Font-de-Gaume, Les Combarelles and Cap Blanc in the Dordogne, the paintings at Le Portel, Trois-Frères and Niaux in the Pyrenees, the great painted ceiling at Altamira and paintings in several other cave sites in Biscay, Cantabria and Asturias. Because Style IV animal pictures are handled in a remarkably uniform manner all the way from Spain to central Europe, regional subdivisions are much harder to establish in the classic period than in the archaic one. Indeed, the uniformity of the classic period suggests not only the existence of contacts between various regional populations but also the existence of a firmly based cosmopolitan artistic tradition. One subdivision that can be detected is a single cohesive Franco-Cantabrian body of early Style IV art; it extends from the Loire valley to the Pyrenees and Asturias and is reflected in the rendering of females in profile and in associated abstract key-shaped signs. The distribution of small Style IV sculptures demonstrates a connection between the Pyrenees-Loire region and areas to the north and east as far as Germany.

What are the main developments during the huge span in which Paleolithic art flourished? At the foot of the evolutionary path a master plan already existed even though techniques were virtually unformed; this was the primitive period. In the extended period of refinement in technique that followed, the key developments involve the delineation of those characteristics that distinguish one species of animal from another; this was the archaic period. Finally both technique and delineation were progressively united in a more and more realistic portrayal of shape and movement; this was the classic period. Then it is all gone, much as the mammoth and the woolly rhinoceros disappeared from the same region. The ideological line uniting an artistic tradition of 20,000 years comes to an end.

Obviously both the long lifetime of Paleolithic art and its disappearance are topics that will occupy generations of investigators. Today, although we know only a fraction of what remains to be learned, we have made some progress. It might be said that historians of Paleolithic art have reached a level of precision comparable to the level achieved by historians of Christian art when they were at last able to fix the date of some object within a century or two. They could be justly criticized for a lack of precision, but they had achieved a clear view of the path along which Christian art had evolved.

ANATOMICAL FIDELITY is characteristic of Style IV work, produced during the classic period of Paleolithic art. The deftly rendered outline of a wild-ox cow's head is one of the animal engravings in the cave at Teyjat, an Upper Magdalenian site in the Dordogne valley.

5   Stone-Age Man on the Nile

by Philip E. L. Smith
August 1976

*Thousands of years before the first pharaohs,
hunters and gatherers lived along the great river.
Their adaptations to their environment underlay the
later development of agriculture and high civilization*

In Egypt today the annual rainfall south of Cairo, if any, is measured in millimeters. This has been true since the days of the pharaohs. In earlier times, however, the level of the Nile was much higher. The great river and its seasonal tributaries watered a countryside that was fertile and temperate in climate even though it was surrounded by inhospitable desert. This combination of circumstances makes prehistoric Egypt virtually a laboratory microcosm for the study of human adaptations.

When did men first inhabit the Nile Valley? Only in recent years has much been learned about Nilotic prehistory; even today knowledge is spotty. We do have proof that people representative of two general stages of human techno-cultural development, the Lower and Middle Paleolithic periods, were present in Lower (or northern) Egypt from about a million to 30,000 years ago. Apart from the evidence to be gleaned from stone tools, however, little is known about those early inhabitants of Egypt. For example, not a single human fossil from these periods has been found.

As we come to within some 22,000 years of the present, in the latter part of the Upper Paleolithic, a more detailed picture of Egyptian prehistory comes into view. We can begin to speak with some conviction of the way people lived, of their settlement patterns, economic activities and technological proficiencies, and of the environmental and climatic conditions that prevailed. It is of more than passing interest because the Old World during the Upper Paleolithic has traditionally been seen against the background of the harsh glacial environment of Europe at that time, when small groups of hunters pursued such cold-climate animals as the woolly mammoth and the reindeer. A greater contrast in settings can scarcely be imagined than that between the chill, art-rich caves of the Pyrenees and the Dordogne on the one hand and the lush green sloughs and side channels of the Nile on the other, where the hippopota-

mus, the hartebeest and the gazelle took the place of the reindeer, the bison and the wild horse.

Most of our new knowledge about prehistoric Egypt is a by-product of the dam construction at Aswan in Upper (or southern) Egypt in the 1960's. The Egyptian and Sudanese governments, in association with the United Nations Educational, Scientific and Cultural Organization, invited many foreign archaeologists to salvage monuments and sample as many as possible of the sites that would eventually be submerged by the enlarged Nile reservoir. Some of those who responded, mainly prehistorians from Canada, the U.S. and the U.S.S.R., concentrated their efforts on sites that had been inhabited by early man. Their work, undertaken in collaboration with colleagues in such related fields as geology and paleontology, has greatly enhanced our understanding of the preagricultural populations of the Nile Valley at the time when the last glaciers were beginning to retreat in Europe.

Not all the early-man sites investigated during the 1960's were in danger of flooding. The area where my group from the National Museum of Canada conducted excavations in 1962 and 1963 was threatened in a different way. The Kom Ombo Plain ("kom" is the Egyptian equivalent of the Near Eastern "tell" or "tepe," mound), about 50 kilometers north of Aswan, is an extensive area of ancient alluvial silts, which, although they are now desiccated, need only water pumped from the Nile to transform them into fertile farmland. Reclamation of this kind had begun at the turn of the century, when European promoters established pumping stations and developed sugar plantations on the plain. Now the Egyptian government decided to follow suit and resettle most of the population that would be flooded out of Egyptian Nubia in the remainder of the plain.

Many valuable Paleolithic sites at Kom Ombo had already been planted

with sugarcane. My group, sponsored by the Canadian government, and a group from Yale University undertook to salvage or sample a fair number of those that were still undisturbed. In so doing we were following in the footsteps of a French engineer and amateur archaeologist, Edmond Vignard, who worked in a Kom Ombo sugar refinery in the early 1920's and made many useful observations at a time when the early-man sites of the plain were still relatively intact.

Other advantages in addition to Vignard's reconnaissance were available to us at Kom Ombo. One was that the

KOM OMBO PLAIN, on the east bank of the Nile some 500 kilometers south of Cairo, is where the author and his colleagues inves-

stratigraphy, and thus the chronology, of the geological formations there has been worked out in considerable detail by Karl W. Butzer of the University of Chicago (together with his student Carl L. Hansen) and also by R. J. Fulton of the Geological Survey of Canada. These studies made it possible to match the various prehistoric sites with the geological record of fluctuations in the level and course of the Nile and also with changes in the local tributary streams that reflect past changes in local rainfall. The second major advantage was that whereas animal remains from the Paleolithic are both scarce and poorly preserved in most of Egypt, large quantities of bones are present at the Kom Ombo sites. The bones, of course, provide the investigator with invaluable clues to the early inhabitants' subsistence activities.

The environment in late Paleolithic times at Kom Ombo was the product of a complex interplay of factors. The behavior of the Nile itself—its long-term cyclical fluctuations, annual inundations, volume and velocity—was determined by climatic events far off in East Africa. Moreover, the local rainfall, the temperature and the behavior of the tributary streams flowing across the plain from their headwaters in the Red Sea Hills some 150 kilometers away were products of patterns of atmospheric circulation in the Northern Hemi-

sphere, where the European glaciers were still influential. Both factors interacted further with the geomorphology of the plain and of adjoining areas. The result was a mosaic of microenvironments and habitats in a restricted geographical zone. In such an unstable ecosystem rapid shifts in the inventory of plants and animals, and in the exploitative methods of the human cultures subsisting on them, might be expected to occur as one or another variable was altered.

In the Nile Valley immediately north and south of Kom Ombo the river and its floodplain have long been confined to a narrow corridor that runs between sandstone cliffs and high terraces. At Kom Ombo, however, a series of geological faults has caused the cliffs to retreat eastward, so that a wide depression, extending over 500 square kilometers, lies along the east bank. From the prehistorian's viewpoint the most interesting features of the local geology are the sediments—silts, sands and pebbles—that were deposited between 15,000 and 10,000 B.C. by the Nile and its tributary streams. The Nilotic silts, the products of soil erosion far to the south in Ethiopia, were laid down when the river was considerably higher and more vigorous than it is today. They stand some 15 meters above the modern floodplain. It is in and on these silts,

known as the Gebel Silsila Formation, that the late Paleolithic sites are found, in some places buried deep and revealed only by erosion or artificial cuts and in others lying exposed on the surface where the desert wind has blown away the concealing silt.

The plain today, with miles of green sugarcane plantations, vegetable fields and irrigation canals surrounding the new town of Kom Ombo, is very different from the arid, dusty wasteland of less than a century ago. It is also very unlike the plain of the late Paleolithic period. Archaeologists no longer accept the notion that before agriculturists transformed the Nile Valley in Neolithic times it was hostile jungle and swamp, difficult to reach, inhabited by dangerous animals and holding little attraction for man. We now know that on the contrary the valley was a zone of fairly open terrain where hunters, gatherers and fishermen had access to a biomass of aquatic and terrestrial resources that could support a considerable population. Moreover, the Kom Ombo Plain was a better than average segment of the Nile Valley, and its inhabitants must have been among the best-nourished people in the late Paleolithic world.

The climate in Upper Egypt at that time was only slightly less arid than it is today. We may guess at an annual

tigated a series of Stone Age living sites dating back to between 15,-000 and 10,000 B.C. The site being excavated here belongs to cultures designated Sebekian and Silsilian, dating back to between 13,-000 and 12,000 B.C. In it the investigators found stone tools characteristic of the cultures and bones of animals hunted by inhabitants. Cliff in the background is part of the northern boundary of the plain.

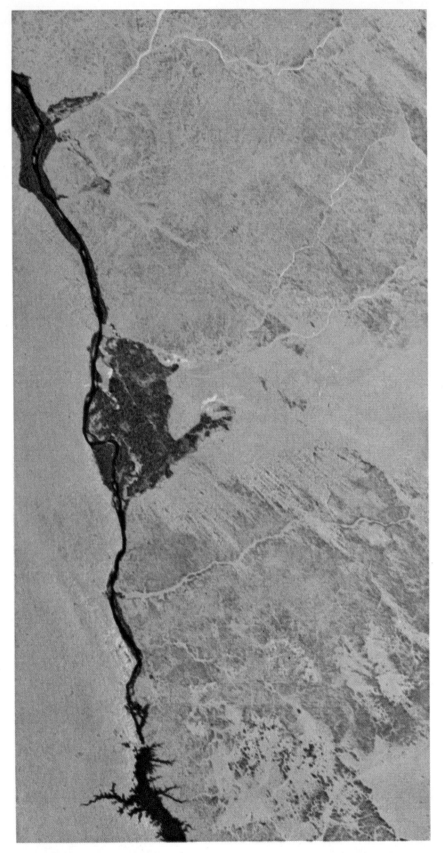

LANDSAT SATELLITE PHOTOGRAPH shows the valley of the Nile as the colorful streak running at the left through the desert. The now intensively cultivated Kom Ombo Plain is the bulge to the right of the river. In this false-color photograph the green of the cultivated areas is translated into red. The widening of the river at the lower left is Lake Nasser, which is backed up behind the Aswan High Dam. At the right are the uplands leading to the Red Sea Hills. The valleys leading down to the Nile are wadis that were once seasonal tributaries of the river. They are now dry except on the rare occasions when there is a cloudburst in the Red Sea Hills.

precipitation of 10 or 20 millimeters, falling mainly in the Red Sea Hills during the winter months. The permanent river and the seasonal tributaries flowing westward from the Red Sea uplands, however, largely canceled out the effects of inadequate rainfall at Kom Ombo. The range of temperatures was lower than it is today by perhaps 10 degrees Celsius, and in winter there could be frost.

By that time the Nile had long established its modern regime of summer flooding, induced by the monsoon rains in East Africa. From August to October the river rose to inundate areas that today lie far beyond its shrunken floodplain. At its height the swollen Nile cut long, meandering side channels across the Kom Ombo Plain, creating what were in effect islands until the waters ebbed late in the fall. The floodplain was probably about five kilometers wide. The human settlements were concentrated along the levees of the seasonal overflow channels when the Nile was high and were shifted to the lower floodplain as the river receded. The banks of the tributaries, now dry wadis, have yielded few campsites; perhaps they were less attractive for settlement.

Little concrete paleobotanical evidence has been recovered at Kom Ombo, but it is possible to gain an overall impression of the vegetation, generally subtropical, that grew on the plain. In the low floodplain, in addition to a grassy mat that covered much of the area, a gallery forest of acacia, tamarisk, sycamore and Egyptian willow probably stood beside the main stream. Less dense growths of the same trees would have occupied the channel levees. Thorn trees probably grew in the larger tributary valleys, and the higher water table outside the zone of annual flooding probably supported a semidesert vegetation of low scrub or brush with dry grassland on the hills and scattered desert shrubs farther east. We can also assume a rich growth of aquatic flora—reeds, sedges, lotuses and papyrus plants—along the river, the side channels and the sloughs.

C. S. Churcher of the University of Toronto has analyzed the animal remains from our excavations. His work has revealed a surprisingly wide range of vertebrates: at least a dozen taxa of mammals, 22 of birds, three of fishes and one taxon of reptiles. Prominent among the mammals are a now extinct large wild ox (*Bos primigenius*), the bubal hartebeest (*Alcelaphus buselaphus,* a species still living in the Sudan) and several species of gazelle. These and the hippopotamus were the most important game animals. There were in addition hares, hyenas, a species of canine, bandicoot rats and possibly the so-called Barbary sheep (the aoudad, *Ammotragus lervia,* still found in North Africa).

In the streams and pools lived the

large Nile catfish, the Nile perch and the African barbel, as well as clams, the Nile oyster and a species of soft-shelled turtle. Many of the bird bones are representative of migratory species; the Nile Valley was probably then, as it is now, an important flyway between Europe and Africa. Wading and diving birds included numerous goose and duck species, the cormorant, the heron, the flamingo, the spoonbill, the crane and the curlew. Apparently the elephant, the giraffe, the rhinoceros and large carnivores such as the lion and the leopard were not present. The ostrich, the wild pig, the zebra and the crocodile may well have existed there, but we found no trace of them among the animal bones.

Such an abundant concentration of plant and animal resources must have made Kom Ombo one of the most attractive human habitats available anywhere in late Paleolithic times. An economy at once river-oriented and diversified was to emerge at Kom Ombo and flourish for at least 5,000 years. Even though much archaeological evidence has been destroyed and precise information on the vegetation is meager, we can to some extent plot the seasonal flow of food energy through the plain and attempt to show how human activities were accommodated to long- and short-term fluctuations in the energy flow.

The earliest of the Upper Paleolithic sites at Kom Ombo are about 17,000 years old. There were probably people on the plain before that time, but either their sites have not been preserved or they remain undiscovered. In any event in the centuries immediately preceding 15,000 B.C. rainfall at Kom Ombo was minimal, there was little seasonal runoff in the tributaries and vegetation and game were probably sparse away from the Nile. From about 15,000 to 10,000 B.C., however, rain was generally more plentiful and tributary runoff was greater. The climatic change evidently contributed to rich and varied cultural developments. The same general phenomenon, although differing in detail, has been reported by other excavators who have worked recently in Lower Nubia and Upper Egypt. Evidence of a cultural flowering up and down the Nile Valley has caused prehistorians to revise the traditional view that the later Paleolithic of the area was impoverished. At Kom Ombo alone during this 5,000-year interval we find emerging a series of styles in the manufacture of stone tools (which prehistorians call industries or sometimes, as a convenient fiction, cultures); they vary considerably in the form of the tools, the methods of manufacture and the kinds of stone the toolmakers preferred. We are still not entirely certain how this unexpected and seemingly anarchic diversity in tool production should be interpreted, but it is surely one of the most intriguing new aspects of the prehistory of Egypt.

The majority of the stone tools are small and light. Small flakes and blades were struck from a stone "core" and then chipped into tools. We find no implements that can be interpreted as axes or adzes, and only a small number of heavy tools (usually roughly split or chipped pebbles) appear to have been used for smashing or chopping. Some of the tools are only a few centimeters in length, small enough to be characterized as microliths. One can only assume that most of the stone artifacts were associated in one way or another with the subsistence activities of their makers; unfortunately, as is usually the case in Paleolithic studies, it is hard to ascertain the precise function or functions of an artifact with any degree of certainty.

The first late Paleolithic stone-tool industry recognized on the Kom Ombo Plain is called the Halfan. Carbon-14 determinations at several small campsites place the Halfan industry around 15,000 B.C. It is a curious industry combining relatively archaic and relatively advanced technological features. The archaic feature is what prehistorians call the Levallois method of removing large flakes from a specially prepared core. The method was known in Egypt, in Europe and elsewhere for hundreds of thousands of years before the Upper Paleolithic period. The advanced feature is the fabrication of small flakes with lightly retouched edges.

Only a few Halfan sites have been found. Perhaps the Kom Ombo Plain was not densely occupied at the time. Indeed, it is not until about 13,000 B.C., following a phase when the volume of the Nile had decreased somewhat and its annual inundations were lower, that sites on the plain become fairly abundant.

A second industry, which we have called the Silsilian, and a third, known as the Sebekian, appear roughly between 13,000 and 12,000 B.C. The Silsilian industry specialized in microlithic tools: many small "backed" blades (that is, blades blunted on one edge) and even tiny triangles and trapezoids made on blades of such exotic multicolored stone as agate, jasper and quartz. The Sebekian industry featured longer, narrower blades with the edges lightly retouched by "nibbling," usually near the base; the makers showed a preference for gray or buff-colored flint. Beginning about 11,000 B.C. and continuing for several

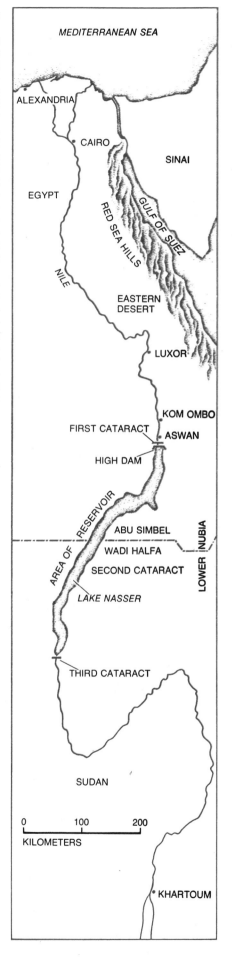

MAP OF THE NILE shows the course of the river from the Sudan (*bottom*) to the Mediterranean (*top*). Some 15 years ago the Egyptian and the Sudanese governments invited many foreign scholars to investigate archaeological sites, actual or potential, along the river that later were flooded by the new reservoir or were destroyed by land reclamation.

millenniums thereafter, a fourth industry, the Sebilian (identified and named by Vignard half a century ago), is found at Kom Ombo. Here the old Levallois technique of core preparation reappears: many of the flakes struck from the core were broad and thin. They were then chipped into geometric shapes, including large triangles and trapezoids as well as microliths. More or less contemporaneous with the Sebilian, and sharing certain of its traits, is a fifth group of artifacts we have named the Menchian

industry. Many of the Menchian tools are made on rather thick, heavy flakes and blades; they may have been used for scraping. Both the Sebilian and the Menchian artifacts seem to be associated with sandstone slabs and handstones that were evidently used for grinding or pulverizing.

To what extent these variations in stone-tool industries reflect distinct sociocultural groupings, or specialized subsistence activities, or the evolution

of one or more traditions over a period of time, it is still difficult to say. The long-term cyclical oscillations of the Nile may well have had some impact on the cultural situation. When the level of the river dropped, as it periodically did for centuries or millenniums, many of the valley zones outside the Kom Ombo Plain where the floodplains were narrower would have been adversely affected as the annual inundations were more restricted. The total biomass of the plants and animals in such areas would have been reduced for long periods, and under such conditions there might have been a tendency for the human groups living in them to move into larger and stabler zones such as the Kom Ombo Plain. The migrations, whether temporary or permanent, of outside groups to the Kom Ombo Plain may help to explain some of the rapid cultural changes and replacements the stone-tool industries seem to reflect between 15,000 and 10,000 B.C.

The exploitable part of the Kom Ombo Plain, which includes the former Nile floodplain, the wadis and the groundwater zones but excludes the modern floodplain (then largely submerged) and isolated rocky outcrops, was probably about 400 square kilometers, or about 150 square miles. It is not easy to calculate the density of Paleolithic populations, but a very approximate figure, based on recorded populations of recent and still living nonagricultural peoples with diversified patterns of subsistence, is about one person per square mile. Thus it is likely that the Kom Ombo Plain could have supported at least 150 people and perhaps as many as 300 under optimum conditions. It is of course unlikely that the population density was constant over the 5,000-year period.

Analyses of the animal remains, together with what we can infer of the river regime and the vegetation patterns, strongly suggest that the plain was capable of supporting human life not just seasonally but all year round. It is nonetheless highly unlikely that the population of the plain could have remained together as a single group throughout the year, or could have remained permanently in a single locality. Probably at any one time the population was split into a number of small bands, perhaps composed of related families who tended to hang together in a loose kind of organization. Each band probably moved in an annual cycle related to the seasonal availability of different food resources. Each of the bands may even have been identified with a certain territory on the plain, although these territories were probably not exclusive. Whether the entire population, or only those who recognized themselves as being culturally related, periodically came together for economic or social purposes we do not know, but judging by

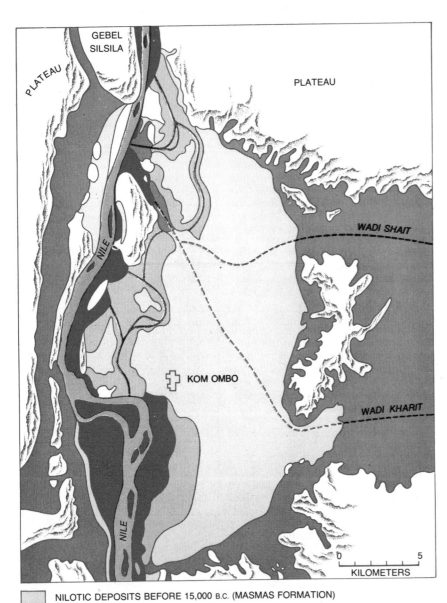

NILOTIC DEPOSITS BEFORE 15,000 B.C. (MASMAS FORMATION)

NILOTIC DEPOSITS 15,000–10,000 B.C. (GEBEL SILSILA FORMATION)

POST-10,000 B.C. NILE AND WADI DEPOSITS

MODERN NILE FLOODPLAIN ALLUVIUM   ROCK OUTCROPS AND HILLS

PREHISTORIC NILE CHANNELS

PREHISTORIC WADI TRIBUTARIES

MAP OF THE KOM OMBO PLAIN shows the prehistoric Nile channels, wadi streams and geological deposits. In the period between 15,000 and 10,000 B.C. the river was considerably higher and more vigorous and the climate somewhat less arid than today. Map is based on studies undertaken by Karl W. Butzer of the University of Chicago and his student Carl L. Hansen.

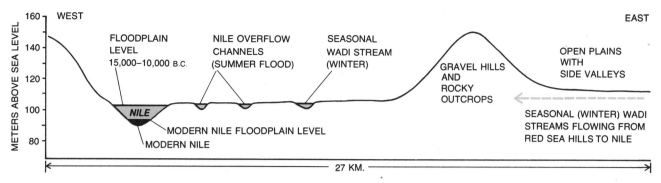

SCHEMATIC CROSS SECTION OF THE PLAIN on a line running east and west in the period between 15,000 and 10,000 B.C. shows height of the Nile, overflow channels and wadi streams. Annual flood of river covered a much greater area than it does today.

the behavior of living hunting peoples it is not unlikely.

The settlement system and subsistence strategy that prevailed were undoubtedly fluid, since they would have had to be correlated with seasonal variations in the abundance of food, just as biomass output itself was linked to short- and long-term pulsations in rainfall and river height. The output was probably spread fairly evenly over most or all of the year, although winter and spring (approximately from November through April) would have been the seasons of abundance. Much of the aquatic biomass, including fish, clams, oysters, waterfowl, turtles and hippopotamus, and such edible plants as water lily, water chestnut, water lettuce, water plantain, papyrus and other reeds, was probably available in all seasons. These foods would have been exploited along the side channels during the flood period from August through October and along the main stream at other seasons. Dry-land provender, including fruits, berries, nuts and edible gums from the acacia, the palm, the sycamore and other trees, and perhaps melons, cucumbers, the "Abyssinian banana" (*Ensete edula*) and various wild grass seeds, would have been most abundant in winter and spring, during and just after the rains. These plants would have been most common along the wadis but would also have grown on the desert steppe beyond them. Roots and bulbs should have been available throughout the year.

Most of the large mammals, particularly the wild ox and the hartebeest (the principal sources of meat), would also have been hunted in winter and spring. One hunting area was the marshy floodplain with its natural pastures beside the lowered river. The wadis and the grassy hills and plains to the east of Kom Ombo were a second area. The herds of wild cattle, unable to go for long periods without water, were almost certainly never far from the channels, pools and pastures of the floodplain and might even have been systematically culled by the hunters all year long. The hartebeests would have ranged more widely, and in the winter, when the tributary streams were flowing, they were probably found along the wadis. Remains of gazelles and asses and perhaps Barbary sheep suggest hunting forays into the drier open grasslands, hills and the fringes of the desert. Fowling was probably in the main a winter activity; many of the birds identified by the bones unearthed at Kom Ombo (for example the crane, smew, goosander and several other species of duck and goose) are migratory.

Late spring and early summer (from April through June) was probably a more difficult period of subsistence. As the heat and aridity increased, the Nile shrank to its lowest level, the grassy vegetation diminished and some of the game dispersed. At this time of year the hunting bands may have been forced to split up into smaller units, each perhaps consisting of a few nuclear families, and to spread out more widely in order to exploit the less abundant food resources of the plain until the summer floods resumed.

In terms of reconstructing seasonal activities on the Kom Ombo Plain, one of the most informative sites we excavated was Gebel Silsila III, near the northern end of the plain about four kilometers east of the present Nile. The site stands near a side channel of the Nile that 15,000 years ago ran a few hundred meters from a range of sandstone cliffs. When we found the site in 1962, it was almost entirely buried under an accumulation of hard, carbonate-rich Nilotic silt as much as a meter thick, deposited by river floods soon after the site was abandoned. Only a scatter of flints and bones exposed on the wind-eroded surface betrayed the site's existence. With the aid of Robert Fulton, my assistant Morgan Tamplin and I spent several months excavating there in the winter of 1962–1963. The site proved to be stratified in two main levels: a rich Sebekian occupation, containing many stone tools and animal remains, overlay a somewhat poorer Silsilian one.

Between 13,000 and 12,000 B.C. the prehistoric inhabitants of the plain had settled near a small depression, some 10 meters in diameter, that held water during at least part of the year. Here they lived and ate, built their fires and made their stone artifacts. The large quantity of flint tools manufactured and discarded on the spot, the great number of broken animal bones and the overall size of the area occupied indicate that, at least for the Sebekian people who lived there last, this may have been an important base camp. They hunted cattle, hartebeest and gazelle (a variety of game that reflects the exploitation of several distinct microenvironments), ate an occasional hippopotamus, caught turtles, catfish and perch and killed at least 14 different kinds of birds. It is possible that the Sebekian group occupied the site during more than one season of the year, although not necessarily the year round or even for very long at any one time. For example, the bones of migratory birds suggest that the Sebekian group was at the site at some time between September and April. The bones of immature gazelles, which presumably, like their modern counterparts, were born either in January or in late July and August, show that the group was present at one or both of these times. The bones of immature hartebeests, born at any time between May and December, also point to summer and/or fall occupancy.

In addition to stone tools and animal bones two more intimate relics of human presence have come from the Gebel Silsila III site. One, found in the lower level, is a milk tooth from a Silsilian child less than seven years old. This evidence that children were among the early occupants of the site lends weight to the view that we are dealing here with a family group rather than, say, a temporary encampment of adult hunters. The other relic is a lump of hardened mud from the upper, Sebekian level. It clearly shows impressions from the palm of a human hand, probably an adult's, and is one of the rare examples of a skin impression from the Paleolithic.

Putting together the data from all the sites at Kom Ombo, we are able to reach certain tentative conclusions about other aspects of the inhabitants' lives. First, there are no caves or sheltering rock overhangs in the surrounding cliffs, and

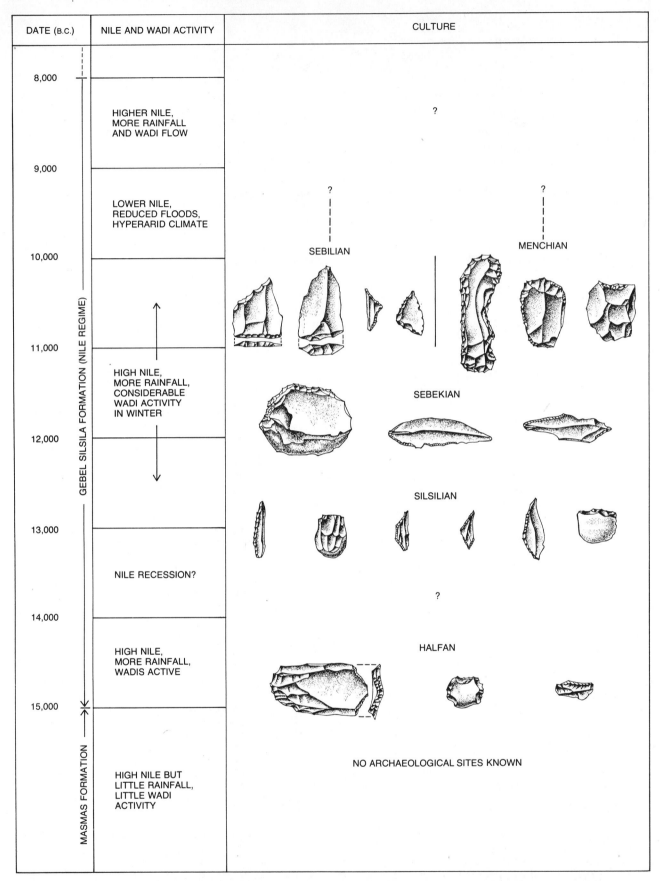

DATE (B.C.)	NILE AND WADI ACTIVITY	CULTURE
8,000		
	HIGHER NILE, MORE RAINFALL AND WADI FLOW	?
9,000		
	LOWER NILE, REDUCED FLOODS, HYPERARID CLIMATE	? ?
10,000		SEBILIAN MENCHIAN
11,000	HIGH NILE, MORE RAINFALL, CONSIDERABLE WADI ACTIVITY IN WINTER	SEBEKIAN
12,000		
13,000		SILSILIAN
	NILE RECESSION?	?
14,000		
	HIGH NILE, MORE RAINFALL, WADIS ACTIVE	HALFAN
15,000		
	HIGH NILE BUT LITTLE RAINFALL, LITTLE WADI ACTIVITY	NO ARCHAEOLOGICAL SITES KNOWN

(Left vertical labels: GEBEL SILSILA FORMATION (NILE REGIME); MASMAS FORMATION)

CHRONOLOGY OF CLIMATES AND CULTURES on the Kom Ombo Plain shows the relations between the two. The stone tools of the Halfan culture are characterized by flakes struck from a specially prepared core and by small blades with lightly retouched edges. The Silsilian culture specialized in microlithic tools, many of which are "backed," or blunted on one edge. The Sebekian culture featured long, narrow blades with edges lightly retouched by "nibbling." The Sebilian flakes, like the Halfan, were struck from a specially prepared core and were then often chipped into geometric shapes. The Menchian tools are heavy; many may have been used for scraping.

so all the living sites on the plain were in the open. At none of the sites have we found traces of permanent dwellings: stone or mud construction or postholes that would indicate substantial wood shelters. We can assume that the inhabitants built brush huts, windbreaks or light tents, shelters that would have left few traces, much as the modern Bushmen and Australian aborigines do.

Second, tools made of bone or horn are rare. Wood was probably used more generally, but no trace of wood implements has survived. The inhabitants of the plain did not have pottery, so that it also seems likely that they used containers made of skin, basketry, bark or wood. They probably made nets and lines for fishing and perhaps fowling. Again, however, none of these artifacts have survived. Whether the bow and arrow were present is not known, but the small stone points of several industries may well have served as arrowheads. Small flint blades may have been set into wood knife handles or fish spears. Dugout or reed canoes and rafts would have been useful during the flood season, and perhaps for crossing to the west bank of the Nile, but again no evidence of such craft has survived.

Like most of the other Paleolithic peoples of the Nile Valley (but unlike many contemporaneous groups elsewhere), the inhabitants of Kom Ombo seem to have shown no interest in beads, pendants, bracelets or other personal adornments. Perhaps the red and yellow ocher found in some of the sites was used for body decoration. It is also possible that the spectacular plumage of such birds as the golden eagle, the osprey and the black kite, whose bones are found at the sites, were used for decorative purposes. We have no good evidence that any of the inhabitants engraved or sculptured bone and stone, as their Magdalenian contemporaries in Europe did. Their art, if they had any, may have been expressed in more perishable materials. Interesting scenes of wild animals, including cattle and hippopotamus, are engraved on the cliffs near our Gebel Silsila sites, but no one can prove they were the work of a late Paleolithic group. Physically the Paleolithic inhabitants of the Kom Ombo Plain were fully modern representatives of *Homo sapiens* and were apparently rather robust in build.

With the benefit of hindsight we can now see that many late Paleolithic peoples in the Old World were poised on the brink of plant cultivation and animal husbandry as an alternative to the hunter-gatherer's way of life. The new livelihood had its formal beginnings around the start of postglacial times in southwestern Asia and perhaps elsewhere as well. One current hypothesis about the origins of agriculture is that it was related to late Pleistocene population growth and increased pressure on food

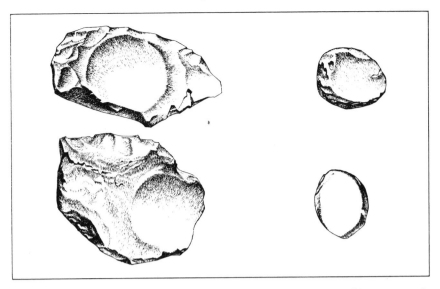

GRINDING STONES are associated with Sebilian and Menchian artifacts. Some were possibly used to process wild plant foods. Stones at left are grinding slabs; those at right are rubbers.

resources. This, the hypothesis contends, led in some cases to the greater exploitation of foods that up to that time had been comparatively neglected, particularly plants, smaller animals, birds, fish and mollusks.

J. Desmond Clark of the University of California at Berkeley and others have recently argued that some evidence for this trend may be seen at Kom Ombo and elsewhere in the lower Nile Valley. Between 13,000 and 10,000 B.C. there appears to have been a general tendency toward population increase and more numerous and larger settlements. At some sites, particularly those of the Menchian and Sebilian cultures on the Kom Ombo Plain, we find many grinding stones: artifacts that suggest the processing of plant foods, perhaps even wild seed-bearing grasses. None of these grasses has yet been identified with certainty, although millets, sorghum and even barley have been postulated. At similar sites elsewhere in Egypt flint blades with a gloss or polish resembling that found on much used stone sickle blades have been reported. It has also been suggested that there may have been some tentative efforts at controlling or taming wild cattle, gazelles and other animals at about this time.

If there was such a trend toward the manipulation and domestication of plants and animals in Egypt at the end of the Ice Age, it would seem to have been a false dawn. We do not know much about human activities at Kom Ombo during the interval after 10,000 B.C. that is sometimes called the Epipaleolithic or Mesolithic. We do know, however, that a complex series of small-scale climatic and environmental changes took place. Contrary to earlier hypotheses, although there was a warming trend in Egypt at the end of the Pleistocene, it was not accompanied by either a sudden

or a continuous period of desiccation. From about 10,000 B.C. until 3000 B.C. conditions fluctuated between the semiarid and the hyperarid. But no catastrophic drought, as some earlier archaeologists had believed, forced the hunter-gatherers out of the hills and plains into the narrow confines of the Nile Valley, where all at once, in propinquity with the appropriate plants and animals, they "invented" agriculture. Indeed, local rainfall seems actually to have increased for a time after 9000 B.C. and again about 5000 B.C.

Nevertheless, even though the tributaries continued their seasonal flow, the hydrological budget of the Nile itself now tended to be reduced as a result of climatic changes in East Africa. The river's floods were more restricted, the water table was lowered and the wetlands shrank in extent. Although there were still periodic fluctuations in the size of the Nile, conditions were never quite the same again at Kom Ombo. The plain seems to have become a marginal zone, unable to support a population as large as that of the late Paleolithic. Over the next few thousand years most of Kom Ombo slowly reverted to near-desert conditions; the ephemeral wadi waters gradually faded away, and sometime late in the third millennium B.C. the present hyperarid climate of Egypt became established.

We know that in other parts of Upper Egypt after 10,000 B.C., and in Lower Nubia as well, a hunting and fishing way of life continued for at least 4,000 years more, although its practitioners appear to have been reduced in numbers. At Kom Ombo too some hunting-gathering-fishing groups probably still lived on the western edge of the plain near the river. The general reaction of the inhabitants of the Nile Valley

HIPPOPOTAMUS JAW in a late Pleistocene deposit is cleared by author and a local worker. Presence of the animal four kilometers from today's Nile is evidence of swampy conditions.

IMPRESSION OF THE PALM OF A HUMAN HAND appears on a lump of hardened mud found in a Sebekian deposit. It is a rare example of a skin impression from the Paleolithic.

to the changing environmental conditions seems to have been to place a greater emphasis on fishing and the procurement of other riverine foods in order to supplement the increasingly scarce supply of game animals and land plants. Possibly some of the brief hyperarid periods after 10,000 B.C. led to a rapid reduction in the populations of these plants and animals. Unlike certain groups in southwestern Asia, however, the early Egyptians had not developed a sedentary way of life based on villages and on the collection of wild plants, which under conditions of demographic or ecological stress would have promoted the plants' domestication. If an indigenous trend toward plant and animal domestication developed in the Nile Valley at all, it apparently never passed the incipient level. Such a trend may, however, have helped to preadapt the Egyptians to a ready acceptance of food production later.

When diversified food production finally arose in Egypt, perhaps around 5000 or 4000 B.C., or at least 2,000 years after its development in western Asia, it was evidently introduced from outside and utilized the familiar animals (goats, sheep and pigs) and cereals (wheat and barley) domesticated long before in Asia. The imported plants quickly took the place of those indigenous to Egypt because they were more productive, particularly after the advent of irrigation. They and the imported animals provided the economic base for Pharaonic civilization, which emerged about 3000 B.C. Nevertheless, it is interesting to note that in the earliest Pharaonic era, that of the Old Kingdom, the Egyptians showed a lively interest in domesticating local animals—wild cattle, gazelles, antelopes and even hyenas—and continued to make use of cranes, geese and ducks in sacrifices and for food. The roots of this practice may lie in the preagricultural traditions of the Nile Valley.

In recent years prehistorians working in many areas of both the Old World and the New have uncovered a great diversity of human specializations and adaptations that developed in the closing phases of the Pleistocene. Our knowledge of the riparian hunters, fishermen and gatherers of the Nile Valley provides a valuable addition to the data on these processes of local adaptation. Although we should not exaggerate the role of environmental change in our attempts to explain cultural change, no one denies that there are close, if still poorly understood, articulations between the two, particularly at the hunting-gathering level of cultural evolution. What is being learned from the work on the Kom Ombo Plain and at other localities along the Nile should be of value to all prehistorians in search of the principles underlying the development of human behavior in the distant past.

6

A Paleolithic Camp at Nice

by Henry de Lumley
May 1969

Construction work on the French Riviera has uncovered the remains of man's earliest-known construction work: huts put up by hunters who visited the shore of the Mediterranean some 300,000 years ago

A Paleolithic site uncovered recently in the south of France contains traces of the earliest-known architecture: huts that were built some 300,000 years ago. The structures were evidently made by nomadic hunters who visited the Mediterranean shore briefly each year. They left behind artifacts and animal bones that, together with the plant pollen found at the site, yield a remarkably detailed picture of the occupants' activities during their annual sojourn by the sea. Because the discovery of the site and its excavation were unusual, I shall give a brief account of both before describing the new evidence the site provides concerning human life during this very early period of prehistory.

The city of Nice, in southeastern France, stands on a basement formation of limestone and marl. The bedrock is covered by layers of sand, clay and soil that mark the glacial oscillations of the ice age. During the construction of a shipyard some years ago certain glacial strata were exposed to view and attracted the attention of several scholars. In one sandy layer in 1959 Georges Iaworsky of the Monaco Museum of Prehistoric Anthropology found a few stone tools of typical Paleolithic workmanship. Two years later in another sandy section he found a tool of the early Paleolithic type known as Acheulean. Acheulean tools take their name from St. Acheul, a site in France where examples were first discovered, but since then Acheulean implements have been found at many other sites in Europe and in Asia and Africa. It had originally seemed that the sands had been deposited in the warm period between the glaciations called the Riss and the Würm, but Iaworsky pointed out that the age of the Acheulean tool indicated that these deposits were much older.

Then, in the course of foundation work during October, 1965, bulldozers cut a series of terraces into the sloping grounds of the Château de Rosemont, on the shoulder of Mont Boron in the eastern part of the city. The area of excavation, near the corner of Boulevard Carnot and an alley romantically named Terra Amata (beloved land), was scarcely 300 yards from Nice's commercial harbor and not far from the shipyard where Iaworsky and others, myself included, had studied the glacial strata. As the excavation proceeded the bulldozers exposed an extensive sandy deposit containing more Paleolithic implements. The significance of the discovery was quickly realized, and the builders agreed to halt operations temporarily. With the help of the French Ministry of Culture, a major archaeological salvage effort was mounted.

Starting on January 28, 1966, and continuing without interruption until July 5 more than 300 workers, including young students of archaeology from the universities and a number of enthusiastic amateurs, devoted a total of nearly 40,000 man-hours to the excavation of the Terra Amata site. The excavated area covered 144 square yards; in the course of investigating the 21 separate living floors found within the area the workers gradually removed a total of 270 cubic yards of fill, using no tools except trowels and brushes. The digging brought to light nearly 35,000 objects, and the location of each object was recorded on one or another of 1,200 charts. In addition, casts were made of 108 square yards of living floor and the progress of the work was documented in some 9,000 photographs.

In stratigraphic terms the deposits at Terra Amata begin at the surface with a layer of reddish clay that is nine feet thick in places and contains potsherds of the Roman period. Below the clay is a series of strata indicative of glacial advances during the Würm, Riss and Mindel periods and the warmer periods that intervened. The site embraces three fossil beaches, all belonging to the latter part of the Mindel glaciation. The youngest beach, marked by a dune and a sandbar, proved to be the site of human habitation.

When the youngest beach was deposited, the level of the Mediterranean was 85 feet higher than it is today. Soon after the beach was formed the sea level dropped somewhat, exposing the sandbar and allowing the wind to build a small dune inland. The hunters must have visited the area during or soon after a major period of erosion that occurred next. The evidence of their presence is found on or in the sands but not in the reddish-brown soil that later covered the eroded sand surface. Numerous shells of land snails, found at the base of the reddish soil, indicate a period of temperate climate.

The landscape of Terra Amata at the time of the hunters' visits differed in a number of respects from today's. The backdrop of the Alps, dominated by Mont Chauve, was much the same, but the sea covered most of the plain of Nice and even penetrated a short distance into what is now the valley of the Paillon River. The climate, though temperate, was somewhat brisker and more humid than the one we know. Pollen studies, undertaken by Jacques-Louis de Beaulieu of the pollen-analysis laboratory at the University of Aix-Marseilles, indicate that fir and Norway pine on the alpine heights grew farther down the slopes than is now the case, and that heather, sea pine, Aleppo pine and holm oak covered Mont Boron and its coastal neighbors.

In the limestone of Mont Boron's western slope the sea had cut a small cove opening to the south. Within the cove a sandy, pebble-strewn beach extended down to the sea, sheltered from the north and east winds. A small spring to one side provided a source of fresh water. A few seashore plants—grasses, horsetails, short-stemmed plantain and various shrubs—grew in the cove. The stream from the spring held water lilies of the genus *Euryale,* which, as De Beaulieu notes, can be found only in Asia today. All things considered, it appears that nothing was lacking even 300 millenniums ago to make Terra Amata a beloved land.

The superimposed living floors at Terra Amata are located in three separate areas. Four are on the section of beach that had formed the sandbar until the sea level dropped; six are on the beach seaward of the bar, and 11 are on the dune inland. The huts that were built on the living floors all had the same shape: an elongated oval. They ranged from 26 to 49 feet in length and from 13 to nearly 20 feet in width. Their outline can be traced with two kinds of evidence. The first is the imprint of a series of stakes, averaging some three inches in diameter, that were driven into the sand to form the walls of the hut. The second is a line of stones, paralleling the stake imprints, that apparently served to brace the walls. One of the earliest of the huts is perfectly outlined by an oval of stones, some as much as a foot in diameter and some even stacked one on the other. The living floor within the oval consisted of a thick bed of organic matter and ash.

The palisade of stakes that formed the walls was not the huts' only structural element. There are also visible the imprints left by a number of stout posts, each about a foot in diameter. These supports were set in place down the long axis of the hut. Evidence of how the palisade and the center posts were integrated to form the roof of the hut has not survived.

A basic feature of each hut is a hearth placed at the center. These fireplaces are either pebble-paved surface areas or shallow pits, a foot or two in diameter, scooped out of the sand. A little wall, made by piling up cobbles or pebbles, stands at the northwest side of each hearth. These walls were evidently windscreens to protect the fire against drafts, particularly from the northwest wind that is the prevailing one at Nice to this day.

The fact that the hunters built windscreens for their hearths makes it clear that their huts were not draft-free. This suggests that many of the palisade stakes may have been no more than leafy branches. Certainly nothing more permanent was required. As we shall see, the huts were occupied very briefly. As we shall also see, the time of the annual visit can be narrowed down to the end of spring and the beginning of summer, a season when such a building material would have been readily available.

In the huts on the dune the hearths were apparently designed for small fires. If one can judge from the larger amounts of charcoal and ash, the hearths in the huts closer to the sea must have accommodated much bigger fires. It is worth noting that the hearths at Terra Amata, together with those at one other site in Europe, are the oldest yet discovered anywhere in the world. The hearths that

OVAL HUTS, ranging from 26 to 49 feet in length and from 13 to 20 feet in width, were built at Terra Amata by visiting hunters. A reconstruction shows that the hut walls were made of stakes, about three inches in diameter, set as a palisade in the sand and braced on the outside by a ring of stones. Some larger posts were set up along the huts' long axes, but how these and the walls were joined to make roofs is unknown; the form shown is conjectural. The huts' hearths were protected from drafts by a small pebble windscreen.

equal them in age were found by László Vértes in strata of Mindel age at Vértesszölös in Hungary. Like some of the hearths at Terra Amata, those at the Hungarian site are shallow pits a foot or two in diameter.

Also from Vértesszölös comes a significant early human fossil: the occipital bone of a skull that has been assigned to modern man. No such human remains were found in our excavation at Terra Amata, but we came on two indirect sources of information about the site's inhabitants. One is the imprint of a right foot, 9½ inches long, preserved in the sand of the dune. Calculating a human being's height from the length of the foot is an uncertain procedure. If, however, one uses the formula applied to Neanderthal footprints found in the grotto of Toirano in Italy, the individual whose footprint was found at Terra Amata may have been five feet one inch tall.

Our other indirect source of information consists of fossilized human feces found in the vicinity of the huts. De Beaulieu's analysis of their pollen content shows that all of it comes from plants, such as *Genista*, that shed their pollen at the end of spring or the beginning of summer. This is the finding that enables us to state the precise time of year when the hunters came to Terra Amata.

How did the visitors occupy themselves during their stay? The evidence shows that they gathered a little seafood, manufactured stone tools and hunted in the nearby countryside. The animal bones unearthed at Terra Amata include the remains of birds, turtles and at least eight species of mammals. Although the visitors did not ignore small game such as rabbits and rodents, the majority of the bones represent larger animals. They are, in order of their abundance, the stag *Cervus elaphus*, the extinct elephant *Elephas meridionalis*, the wild boar (*Sus scrofa*), the ibex (*Capra ibex*), Merk's rhinoceros (*Dicerothinus merki*) and finally the wild ox *Bos primigenius*. Although the hunters showed a preference for big game, they generally selected as prey not the adults but the young of each species, doubtless because they were easier to bring down.

The visitors did not systematically exploit the food resources available in the Mediterranean. Nevertheless, they were not entirely ignorant of seafood. A few shells of oysters, mussels and limpets at the site show that they gathered shellfish; fishbones and fish vertebrae indicate that on occasion the hunters also fished.

The large majority of all the artifacts found at Terra Amata are stone tools. They represent two different but closely related stone industries. Both appear to be contemporary with the earliest "biface" industries of the Paleolithic period (so named because many of the tools are made out of stone "cores" that are shaped by chipping flakes from both faces rather than from one face only). They bear certain resemblances to the tools of an early Paleolithic biface industry named the Abbevillian (after the site in France where they were first discovered) and to the Acheulean biface industry, which is somewhat more advanced. On balance, both Terra Amata industries should probably be characterized as early Acheulean.

The more primitive of the two Terra Amata industries is represented by the tools found in the huts closest to the sea. Mainly pebble tools, they include many pieces of the type designated choppers, a few of the type called chopping tools and some crude bifaces made by detaching flakes from one end of an oval cobble but leaving a smooth, unflaked "heel" at the other end. Among the other tools found in the seaside huts are cleavers, scrapers, projectile points of a kind known in France as *pointes de Tayac*

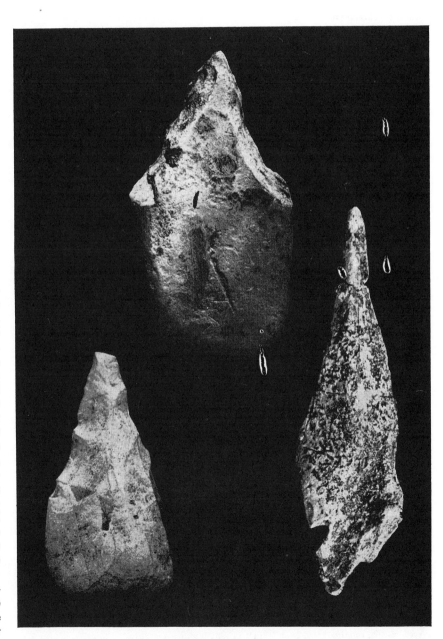

REPRESENTATIVE TOOLS unearthed at Terra Amata include a pebble (*middle*) that has been flaked on one of its faces to form a pick, another stone tool (*left*), flaked on both faces but with one end left smooth, and a bone fragment (*right*) pointed to make an awl.

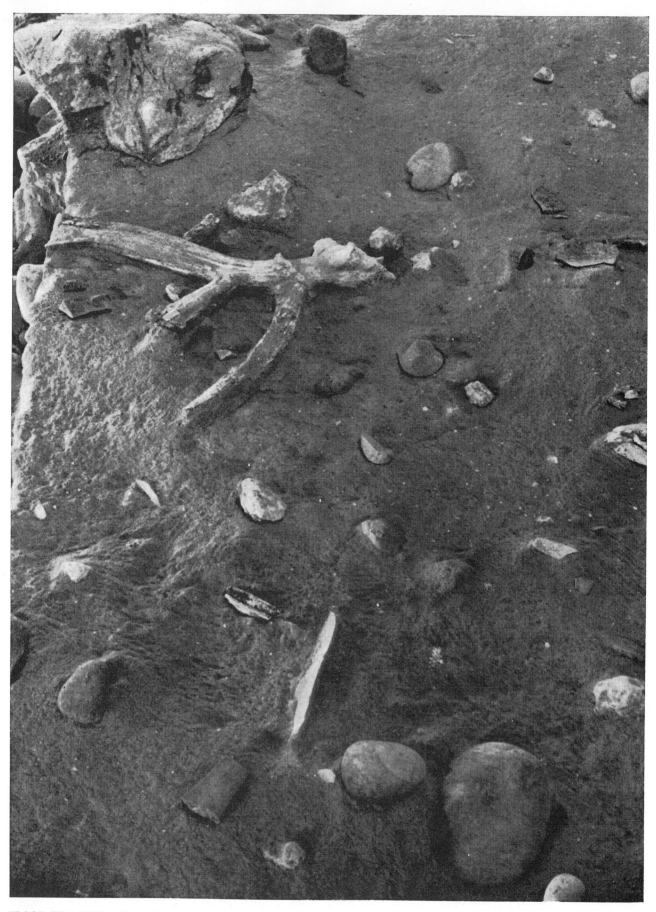

FLOOR OF A HUT at Terra Amata is one of several brought to light by the excavators, revealing the ancient debris left behind by the occupants. The whole pebbles are raw material for tools; the chips and flakes, toolmakers' waste. The antler is from a stag.

and pebble tools flaked on one face only.

The stone industry represented by the tools found in the huts on the dune is more advanced, although it too includes choppers, chopping tools and cobble bifaces with a smooth heel. There are no single-faced pebble tools or cleavers on the dune, however, and tools made from flakes rather than from cores are relatively numerous. The tools made from flakes include those designated scrapers with abrupt retouch, end scrapers with toothed edges and flakes of the kind named Clactonian (after the English site Clacton-on-Sea). Some of the Clactonian flakes have been notched on one edge; others have been made into perforators by chipping out two notches side by side so that a point of stone protrudes. Projectile points from the dunes include, in addition to *pointes de Tayac,* some that are triangular in cross section and others of a kind known in France as *pointes de Quinson.*

Some of the tools found at Terra Amata were probably made on the spot. The hut floors show evidence of tool manufacturing, and the toolmaker needed only to walk along the beach to find workable pebbles and cobbles of flint, quartzite, limestone and other rock. The toolmaker's place inside the huts is easily recognized: a patch of living floor is surrounded by the litter of tool manufacture. The bare patches are where the toolmakers sat, sometimes on animal skins that have left a recognizable impression.

Not all the stone debris represents the waste from finished work. In one instance the excavators found a cobble from which a single chip had been struck. Nearby was a chip that fitted the scar perfectly. In another toolmaker's atelier several flakes had been removed from a cobble by a series of successive blows. Both the core and the flakes were found, and it was possible for us to reassemble the cobble. Scarcely a flake was missing; evidently the toolmaker did not put either the core or the flakes to use.

At least one of the projectile points unearthed at Terra Amata could not have been produced locally. The stone from which it is made is a volcanic rock of a kind found only in the area of Estérel, southwest of Cannes and some 30 miles from Nice. This discovery allows us to conclude that these summer visitors' travels covered at least that much territory in the south of France, although we cannot be sure how much more widely they may have roamed.

A few tools made of bone have been

FIRE PIT (*right*) was protected from drafts and from the prevailing northwest wind in particular by a windscreen built of cobbles and pebbles, seen partially preserved at left.

TOOLMAKER'S ATELIER occupies one section of a hut. It is easily identified by the debris of tool manufacture that surrounds the bare patch of floor where the toolmaker sat.

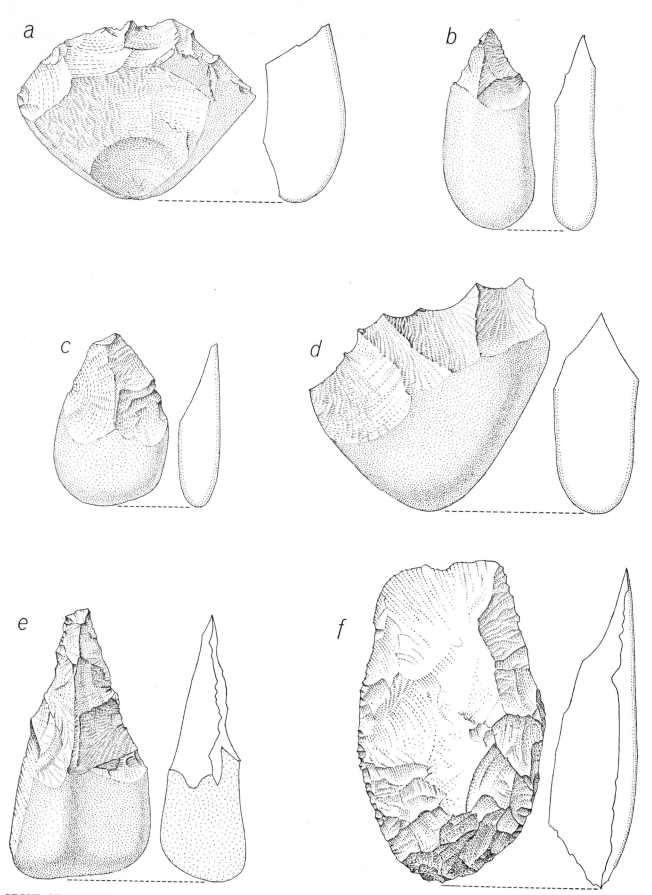

GROUP OF PRIMITIVE TOOLS was found in association with the huts closest to the sea at Terra Amata. They include choppers (*a*) and picks (*b,c*), made from pebbles that are flaked on one face only; chopping tools (*d*) that are flaked on both faces; crude bifaces (*e*), made by detaching flakes from one end of a cobble but leaving an unflaked "heel" at the opposite end; cleavers (*f*), and two other kinds of stone artifacts (*illustrated on opposite page*): scrapers and projectile points of a kind known as *pointes de Tayac*.

found at Terra Amata. One leg bone of an elephant has a hammered point at one end. Another bone has a point that was probably hardened in a fire (a technique used today by some primitive peoples to harden the tips of wooden spears). A third bone fragment has one end smoothed by wear; still another may have served as an awl, and some fragments of bone may have been used as scrapers.

As for other kinds of artifacts, there are traces of only two. On the dune a spherical imprint in the sand, filled with a whitish substance, may be the impression left by a wooden bowl. Some pieces of red ocher found at the site obviously belonged to the visitors: the ends are worn smooth by wear. They recall the red ocher found at sites belonging to the much later Mousterian period, which François Bordes of the University of Bordeaux suggests were used for body-painting.

Let us see if the pattern of the hunters' annual visits to Terra Amata can be reconstructed. We know from the pollen evidence that they arrived in the late spring or early summer, and we can assume that they chose the sheltered cove as their camping ground as much because of its supply of fresh water as for any other reason. On arrival they set up their huts, built their hearths and windscreens, hunted for a day or two, gathered some seafood, rested by their fires, made a few tools and then departed. How do we know that their stay was so short? First, the living floors show no sign of the compaction that would characterize a longer occupation. Second, we have independent evidence that the huts collapsed soon after they were built. A freshly chipped stone tool that is left in the sun will quickly become bleached on the exposed side whereas the bottom side retains its original coloring. Many of the tools on the living floors at Terra Amata are bleached in this way. For the implements to be exposed to the full force of the Mediterranean summer sun the huts must have fallen apart soon after they were abandoned.

In the fall the winds covered the living floors, the leveled palisades and the rest of the camp debris with a layer of sand perhaps two inches deep. The rains then spread out the sand and packed it down, so that when the hunters returned to the cove the following year the evidence of their earlier stay had been almost obliterated. Only a few objects, such as the windscreens for the hearths, still protruded from the sand. The visi-

tors then built new huts, often digging the hearth pit exactly where the preceding year's had been and rekindling their fires on the ashes of the previous season. After a day or two of hunting, gathering seafood and making tools the annual visit was ended. The 11 living floors on the dune at Terra Amata are so precisely superimposed that they almost certainly represent 11 consecutive yearly visits, probably involving many of the same individuals.

There is no older evidence of man-

made structures than that at Terra Amata. Until this site was excavated the record for antiquity was held by the traces of construction discovered at Latamne, an open-air site in Syria, by J. Desmond Clark of the University of California at Berkeley. An early Acheulean site, Latamne is believed to be as old as the Mindel-Riss interglacial period. Terra Amata, which evidently was inhabited at the end of the Mindel glacial period, is therefore even earlier.

The evidence indicating that the hunt-

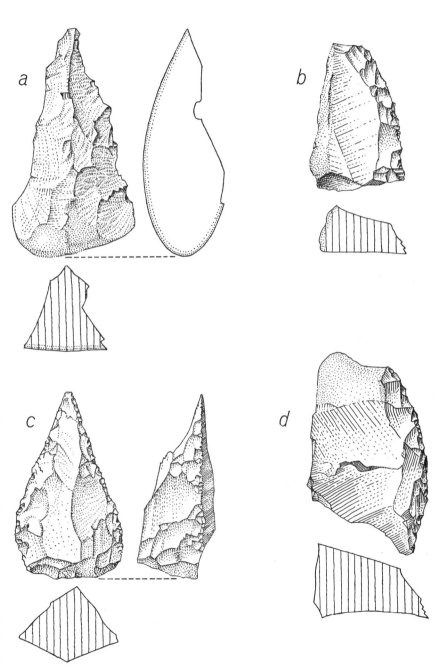

LESS PRIMITIVE TOOLS were found in the huts on the dune at Terra Amata. There were no cleavers or single-faced pebble tools and many more of the tools were made from flakes rather than from cores. Tools common to both areas are *pointes de Tayac* (*a*) and flakes made into simple scrapers (*b*), choppers, chopping tools and bifaces like those on the opposite page. Flakes were also made into projectile points (*c*) and more elaborate scrapers (*d*).

YEARS BEFORE PRESENT	GLACIAL STAGES	STONE INDUSTRY	SITES IN SOUTHEAST FRANCE	CULTURAL ADVANCES
				FIRST AGRICULTURE
10,000		UPPER PALEOLITHIC		
	WÜRM			
		MOUSTERIAN	GRIMALDI CAVES	OLDEST BURIALS
100,000				
	RISS	ACHEULEAN	LAZARET CAVE	
200,000				
			TERRA AMATA	OLDEST MAN-MADE DWELLINGS
	MINDEL			
		ABBEVILLIAN		
500,000				OLDEST EVIDENCE OF FIRE
				OLDEST BIFACE TOOLS
1,000,000	GÜNZ	PEBBLE CULTURE	VALLONNET CAVE	
			UPPER TERRACES ROUSSILLON VALLEY	
				OLDEST STONE TOOLS
2,000,000	DONAU			

CHRONOLOGICAL POSITION of Terra Amata in prehistory is indicated on this chart, which shows (*left to right*) the time, given in thousands of years before the present, of the major glacial advances and retreats in Europe, the successive stone industries of the Paleolithic period, sites in southeastern France where the industries have been found and early man's progress in technology.

ers came to Terra Amata at about the same time year after year, together with the likelihood that the dune huts sheltered some of the same individuals for more than a decade, suggests that the visitors possessed stable and even complex social institutions. It is thus appropriate to conclude with the words of the French historian Camille Jullian, written soon after the Terra Amata living floors had been exposed. "The hearth," Jullian wrote, "is a place for gathering together around a fire that warms, that sheds light and gives comfort. The toolmaker's seat is where one man carefully pursues a work that is useful to many. The men here may well be nomadic hunters, but before the chase begins they need periods of preparation and afterward long moments of repose beside the hearth. The family, the tribe will arise from these customs, and I ask myself if they have not already been born."

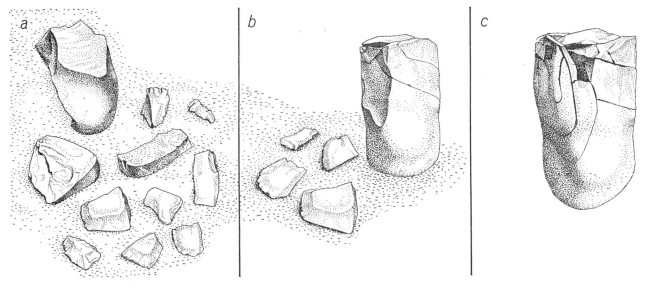

UNUTILIZED RAW MATERIAL was found in one Terra Amata toolmaker's atelier. Near the shattered half of a large cobble lay most of the fragments that had been struck from it (a). They could be reassembled (b) so that the cobble was almost whole again (c).

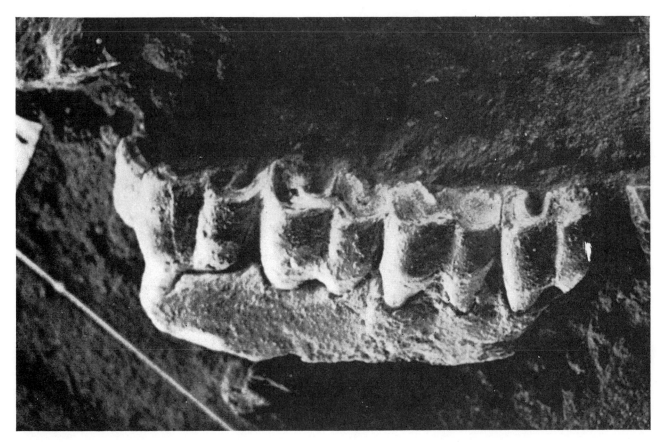

ANIMAL BONE, photographed *in situ* near one corner of an excavation unit, is a fragment of rhinoceros mandible, complete with teeth. The visitors preferred large mammals to other game. Along with rhinoceros they hunted stag, elephant, boar, ibex and wild ox.

MOUTH OF SHANIDAR CAVE is an opening in the flank of Baradost Mountain, some 250 miles from Baghdad. The cave is 130 feet deep; its mouth is 26 feet high and 82 feet wide. From November to April it is inhabited by Kurdish goatherds (*see photograph below*).

FLOOR OF SHANIDAR CAVE is covered with simple shelters for its Kurdish inhabitants and corrals for their animals. In this photograph Kurdish workmen have just begun the excavation of the earthen floor of the cave. Bedrock was reached at a depth of 45 feet.

Shanidar Cave

by Ralph S. Solecki
November 1957

*This rocky shelter in Iraq has been inhabited by man
for 100,000 years. Digging down through the earth of
its floor, archaeologists have even uncovered
the remains of the predecessors of Homo sapiens*

In a mountainside in the Zagros Mountains of northern Iraq is a human dwelling place known as "The Big Cave of Shanidar." It is a high-vaulted natural cave about the size of four tennis courts—capacious enough to house a considerable band of people. The cave has a warm southern exposure and is well protected from winter winds. Nearby are springs and a stream to supply water. Remnants of wild game and the few stands of still-undisturbed virgin forest on the hillsides testify that the place has long had a fertile and livable climate. Today the Cave of Shanidar is inhabited by a clan of Kurdish goatherds and their animals. It is not hard to imagine that men have lived in this commodious, sun-warmed shelter for generation after generation. Out of scientific curiosity we have dug into the floor of the cave, and found to our delight that this conjecture is a feeble understatement. The inhabitation of the Shanidar Cave apparently goes back at least 100,000 years! Remains unearthed from deep beneath its trampled floor give evidence that Neanderthal man once lived here, and that the cave has been a home of man more or less continuously for something like 3,000 generations.

Needless to say, the Shanidar Cave has become one of our most important and fruitful sites for tracing the early history of mankind. Rarely do archaeologists have a chance to see so clear a succession of man's development over so long a period as we have in the layers that make the pages of the story of Shanidar. The story is not lessened in interest by the fact that Shanidar Cave is close to the birthplace of the first great civilizations in Mesopotamia [see "The Sumerians," by Samuel Noah Kramer, beginning on page 178].

Mesopotamia itself is a poor place to look for the Stone Age cultures that preceded its ancient civilizations. A hunting and foraging people would have found little food in its marshes and deserts; moreover, it would be difficult to discover or to date any of their camp sites in this sea-flooded and river-washed plain. Archaeologists have long realized that the best chance of finding Stone Age human remains lay in the foothills and mountains north of the Tigris and Euphrates. In 1928 a small party led by Dorothy Garrod of the University of Cambridge found such remains in two caves near a town called Suleimaniyah in the Zagros foothills [*see map on next page*]. There were no other serious excavations until Robert Braidwood of the University of Chicago began his explorations of Stone Age sites in the same vicinity in 1950 [see "From Cave to Village," by Robert J. Braidwood, SCIENTIFIC AMERICAN October 1952]. Braidwood discovered evidences of the beginnings of human agriculture and village settlements. But the dream of archaeologists looking into man's distant past is to find a site where the stages of his development are piled layer upon layer so that we can get a consecutive, slow-motion picture, so to speak.

In 1951, while working in Iraq with a University of Michigan expedition, I heard about Shanidar Cave and decided to stay on, after the expedition went home, to do some exploratory digging in the cave. These first soundings were so promising that I returned in 1953, and again in 1956, for two more full seasons of excavation. The investigations have been conducted on behalf of the Iraq Directorate-General of Antiquities and the Smithsonian Institution, with support from several other organizations.

The Zagros Mountains resemble the highlands of Scotland; their foothills look like the hills of the U. S. Southwest. Shanidar Cave is in a mountain called Baradost, overlooking Shanidar Valley. From the cave mouth one can see the Greater Zab River, a tributary of the Tigris. The cave, now some 2,500 feet above sea level, was dissolved out of the mountain's limestone rock, originally laid down by an ancient sea. It has a flat earthen floor, about 11,700 square feet in area, and a high ceiling (45 feet at the highest point) blackened with a centuries-old deposit of soot. The Kurdish goatherds and their families, who live in the cave all winter from November to April, have built individual brush huts inside it, each with a small fireplace, and corrals for goats, chickens, cows and horses [*see drawing on page 69*]. The Kurds are a proud, self-sufficient, but backward people. They make fire with flint and steel and grind wheat by hand with circular stones. The women cut hay in the mountain meadows with short iron sickles and toil barefooted up a mountain trail with goatskins to fetch water from the springs. Compared with modern Baghdad, only 250 miles away, the present dwellers in Shanidar Cave could just as well be living in the days of the Assyrian herdsmen 2,500 years ago.

It was from this level of culture, then, that we began our digging journey into man's early history. We marked off a small area in the center of the cave and started our slow, careful excavation down through the floor. In three seasons of work we have cut through the full depth of the cave's earthen accumulations, down to bedrock at 45 feet, and have sifted about a tenth of the total bulk of its deposits. The excavations have yielded a rich record of human

CAVE IS LOCATED on this map of the region north of the Persian Gulf. Suleimaniyah is the site of earlier cave excavations by Dorothy Garrod of the University of Cambridge.

occupation—ancient hearths, tools, animal bones, even Neanderthal skeletons—going back some 100,000 years.

We found four main layers, distinguishable by soil color and the types of artifacts they contained. Each corresponded to a recognizable stage of man's development. I shall first review briefly the general contents of these layers, which are identified, according to an archaeological convention, by the letters A to D from the top down [see drawing on page 70].

Layer A, averaging about five feet thick, is a black, greasy soil, compacted by many generations of feet. It dates from the present back to some time in the Neolithic (New Stone) Age, perhaps 7,000 years ago. This layer covers the revolutionary period in man's way of life when he emerged from mere hunting to food gathering, agriculture and animal herding. Throughout Layer A we found ash beds of communal fires, bones of domesticated animals and domestic tools such as stone mortars (which the Kurds still use for cracking nuts). The circular millstones with which they still grind wheat showed up only in the upper part of Layer A; apparently these are a comparatively recent development. About a foot below the surface we found some primitive clay tobacco bowls—mute evidence that the tobacco habit came to this part of Asia about 300 years ago. A little farther down was a bit of burnished pottery similar to the kind known as "Uruk" ware, named for the city of Erech in ancient Mesopotamia. This pottery dates from the time of the invention of cuneiform writing in Sumer.

Layer B, just below A, is a fairly thin, brown-stained deposit which, according to carbon-14 measurements, dates back to the Middle Stone Age, about 12,000 years ago. It contains the primitive artifacts of a people who knew neither agriculture nor animal domestication nor pottery making. There is no sign that they even collected edible nuts. Apparently snails made up a considerable part of their diet, for there are heaps of snail shells strewn about. Animal bones are relatively scarce in this layer: there are no domestic animals and few wild ones. Possibly it was a period of game scarcity in Shanidar Valley.

Nonetheless the prehistoric people of Layer B seem to have thrived and even to have had some leisure. They made exquisitely chipped projectile points, and bone awls which must have been used for sewing or lacing. What is more, there are engraved pieces of slate, and also fragments of well-rubbed coloring stones which suggest that these people may have made paintings or decorations.

Below Layer B we come to a gap of some 17,000 years during which the cave apparently was not occupied. The next layer, C, dates from about 29,000 to more than 34,000 years ago, according to radiocarbon measurements of charcoal in its firebeds. Near the top of the layer are many boulders, which probably fell from the ceiling during an

earthquake and may well have discouraged residence in the cave. The soil layer itself, a yellowish deposit about eight feet thick with the remains of many fires, bespeaks a long occupation by the late Paleolithic (Old Stone Age) people who had lived in the cave in this period.

Now these people are an anomaly in the Iraq region. Their flint tools—so-called "blade tools"—were like the implements of a late Paleolithic culture in Europe known as the Aurignacian (which used to be identified with Cro-

Magnon man). But no such culture has been found anywhere in Iraq except at Shanidar, although other sites in the area have yielded earlier and later cultures. To the distinctive culture of Layer C we therefore gave the name "Baradostian," after the name of the mountain on which Shanidar Cave is located.

The people of Layer C, like their counterparts in Europe and elsewhere, must have been good woodworkers, for their deposits contain many flint woodworking tools, including scrapers and

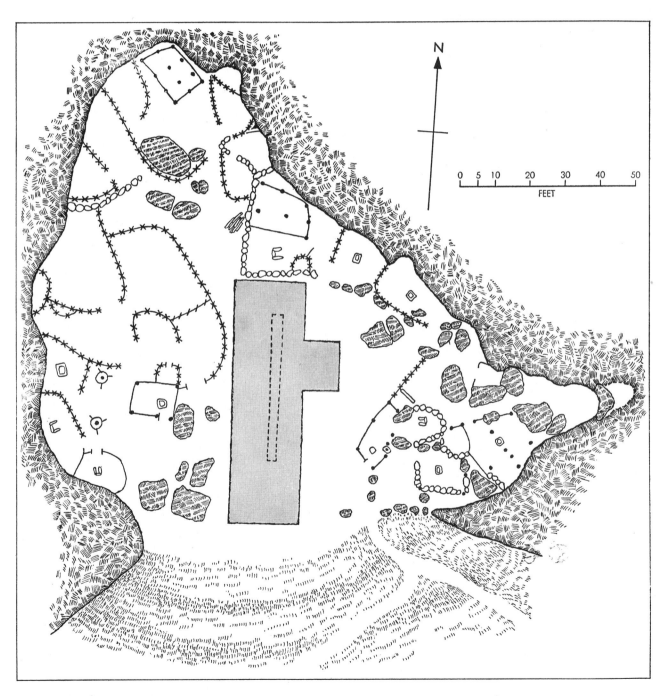

EXCAVATION IS LOCATED by the gray area on this map of the cave. The broken line in the gray area, and its extension toward the mouth of the cave, is the outline of a test trench dug in 1951. The floor of the cave is littered with rocks from the ceiling.

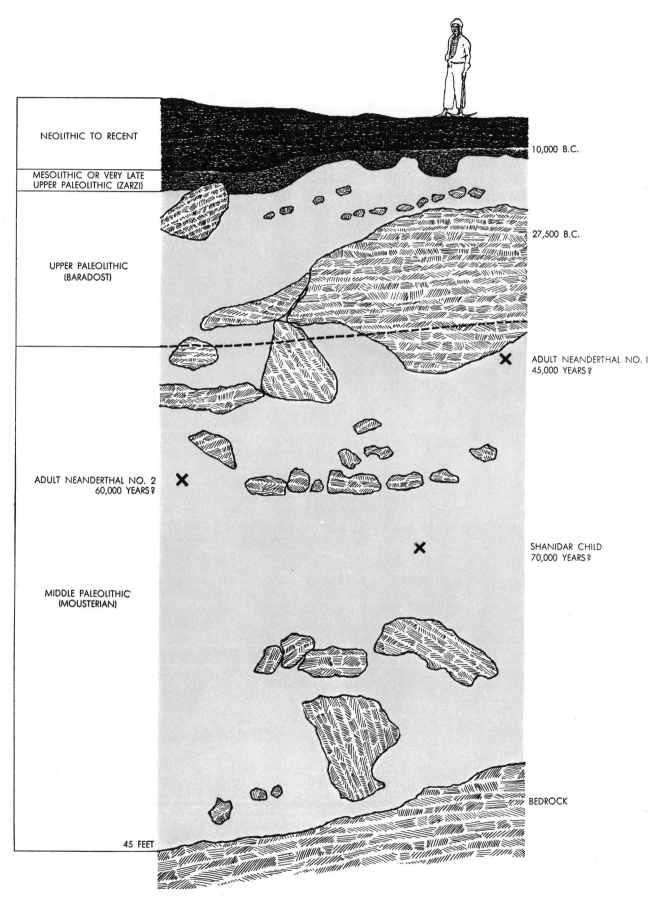

NEOLITHIC TO RECENT

MESOLITHIC OR VERY LATE
UPPER PALEOLITHIC (ZARZI)

UPPER PALEOLITHIC
(BARADOST)

ADULT NEANDERTHAL NO. 2
60,000 YEARS?

MIDDLE PALEOLITHIC
(MOUSTERIAN)

45 FEET

10,000 B.C.

27,500 B.C.

ADULT NEANDERTHAL NO. 1
45,000 YEARS?

SHANIDAR CHILD
70,000 YEARS?

BEDROCK

LAYERS IN THE FLOOR of the cave are indicated on this cross section. At the top (Neolithic to Recent) is Layer A; second from the top (Mesolithic or Very Late Upper Paleolithic), Layer B; third from the top (Upper Paleolithic), Layer C; fourth from the top (Middle Paleolithic), Layer D. The location of the Neanderthal finds are marked by crosses. The rocks fell from roof of the cave.

gravers. Of course none of their wood products has survived in the soil of the cave, but we know from the reports of ancient explorers that Stone Age peoples were capable of a wonderful wood technology.

In Layer D of the cave, a 29-foot-thick series of deposits extending from about 16 feet below the surface to bedrock at 45 feet, we arrived at a distinct break in the human line. The peoples above were presumably all *Homo sapiens:* here, some 45,000 years ago and earlier, we discover the extinct *Homo neanderthalensis*. Not only do we recognize his crude tools, but by incredibly good luck the Shanidar Cave yields up no fewer than three skeletons of Neanderthal man, including the first Neanderthal infant!

First, a brief word about his artifacts, of which, naturally, there are not many. The flint implements of Neanderthal man are called Mousterian, after a site in France where typical ones were found. Like those unearthed elsewhere, the Neanderthal tools in Shanidar Cave are simple flakes of flint with one worked face, struck to form a cutting edge or a point. Apparently Neanderthal man was smart enough to make the most of his material, because every flint core we found had been hacked down to the last flake that could be extracted from it.

We have no clue to what clothing he wore, but he must have wrapped himself in some sort of covering, for this was a cold period in the history of Shanidar Cave—the height of the last Ice Age. In Layer D there is a dark, eight-foot stratum with an especially heavy concentration of fire remains, probably representing a period when the cave was continually occupied because of the cold outside. Apparently the occupants kept a constant fire going, for warmth and to repel wild animals. The period was not only cold but also very wet: there is a layer of stalagmitic lime—drippings from the ceiling—which marks the only era of appreciable dampness in the history of this cave.

Although the cave afforded protection from the miserable climate, it was not without its hazards to the Neanderthal occupants. From time to time there were terrific rockfalls from the ceiling, probably caused by earthquakes. We found firebeds and an animal buried under such falls, and the skeletons of both of the Neanderthal adults lay crushed under boulders which may have crashed down and killed them.

Neanderthal man has been found in a number of places in Europe, but he is a rarity in Asia. Shanidar Cave is only the fifth site in Asia where his bones have turned up. (The nearest to Shanidar is Mount Carmel in Palestine.) This alone gives the skeletons in our cave extraordinary interest, for we may learn something about man's evolution by comparing these skeletons with Neanderthals elsewhere. And added to this is the fact that one of the Shanidar finds is a year-old baby, the only infant Neanderthal yet unearthed.

The three skeletons lay at three different levels, separated by thousands of years [*drawing on opposite page*]. The most recent, and best preserved because its bones were least crushed by rocks and the overburden, is that of an adult estimated to have lived in the cave about 45,000 years ago. A rockfall shattered some of its bones badly, but the skeleton is fairly complete, and much of the skull is intact. The second adult skeleton was found about 23 feet below the surface and is believed to be about 60,000 to 65,000 years old. It was considerably more damaged than the first: a rockfall crushed not only its bones but also its skull. The child lay at a still lower level, perhaps 70,000 years old. Its skeleton was found doubled up, with the legs tucked under the chin and the arms folded close to the body. Most of the fragile skeleton, including the head, was crushed under the earth overburden, and only its teeth and the hand and foot bones are in good condition.

Every frequenter of museums is familiar with the classic picture of Neanderthal man of Europe: the low, sloping forehead, the bulging brow ridges, the massive, prognathous jaw, the receding chin, the worn teeth. Our best-preserved specimen, the Shanidar 45,000-year-old, is generally faithful to this picture. He was what anthropologists call a "conservative" type—almost fully Neanderthaloid, with few suggestions of progress toward the features of *Homo sapiens*. But he does show one feature which is more human than Neanderthaloid: his brow bulge is not one continuous ridge running across the forehead but has a depression in the middle between the eyes, and it flares at the sides. This skeleton is about five feet three inches long—the typical height of Neanderthal man. Two of the front teeth are missing, and he evidently lost them while he was alive, because there is some replacement of tissue in the jawbone where they were rooted. The teeth of both of our Neanderthal adults show heavy wear: they were worn quite flat.

It will take time to analyze the skeletons, to relate them to the Neanderthals of Europe and of other sites in Asia, to discover whether the three Neanderthals of different eras at Shanidar differ from one another, to reconstruct their posture and other attributes and to read any clues they may offer to the evolution of early man in the Middle East. It is possible that the still unexcavated part of Shanidar Cave will yield more skeletons; indeed, we have found two human skeletons from the Neolithic Period and one from the time of Mohammed.

Meanwhile the priceless hoard of remains in Shanidar Cave is being studied by archaeologists, physical anthropologists, zoologists, geologists, climatologists and other specialists. With the combined insights of all these investigators we can hope to translate the scraps of evidence into a comprehensive account of the peoples who lived in the cave and of how they wrested a living from nature in various times and conditions. The Kurdish families who still live at Shanidar are, of course, a vivid and illuminating part of the picture. Stone Age archaeology would be a vague and frustrated science were it not for the assistance that anthropologists and their living subjects are able to give in enriching the meaning of artifacts. As a prehistorian once put it, in anthropology "one catches one's archaeology alive." We see an excellent illustration of what this may mean when we look at the remarkable products made by "primitive" tribes with seemingly crude and limited tools. An archaeologist unearthing a prehistoric wood-scraper made of stone or a shell has no idea of what its users manufactured with it, for the wood objects have long since decayed. But when we discover what living aborigines have done with similar tools, we begin to realize that prehistoric man may well have been far more resourceful, and capable of more exquisite workmanship, than his tools suggest.

We still know comparatively little about the history of the Big Cave of Shanidar. But standing before the deep cut that we have sliced into its floor, we can see the general outlines of that history. We see Neanderthal man crouching over a fire nearly 100,000 years ago, and looking out from the cave mouth at a valley landscape not too different from the one today. He goes forth to hunt tortoises, wild goats and wild pigs (which still roam the valley but are now untouched by the Kurds because of a religious taboo). Apparently he does not try to catch the swift deer or tackle the dangerous bear, wolf or leopard (at least their bones are practically absent in the deposits of Shanidar Cave). The splintered bones of his game show that he cracked open the bones to suck out every bit of marrow.

For tens of thousands of years Neanderthal man hangs on at the cave, surviving the Ice Age, rockfalls and unremitting rains. Although he is a backward type, he lingers on in this mountain fastness for thousands of years after physically more "progressive" Neanderthals have died out in Palestine, only 600 miles away. Century after century his life continues with a monotonous sameness; even his flint tools do not change. Eventually he is succeeded by *Homo sapiens*. Now the curve of culture begins to rise gradually: the new men improve their hunting weapons, fashion tools for woodworking and sit around a communal fire. Thousands of years later the inhabitants of the cave have advanced to finely chipped tools, sewing and painting. But the curve of progress still clings low on the horizon. Then, some 7,000 years ago (only yesterday in the long history of the cave), the curve suddenly begins to shoot up with a burst of power. The people of Shanidar Cave learn to domesticate animals, till the soil, grind wheat, make pottery, spin thread. They remain, however, an isolated, pastoral people, in spite of the successive Sumerian, Babylonian, Assyrian and Persian civilizations that rise and fall in nearby Mesopotamia.

So the story of Shanidar Cave ends just a little beyond the Stone Age. Soon, it seems, its story will come to a final end, because the Iraq Government plans to build a dam on the Greater Zab which will flood Shanidar Valley and cut off access to the cave. Fortunately it was discovered in time to tell us its history.

NEANDERTHAL SKELETONS were exposed by an extension of earlier soundings made in the spring of 1957. The first adult Neanderthal to be discovered is at lower right. The arrow on the rear wall points to the location of the second adult Neanderthal.

8

Isimila: A Paleolithic Site in Africa

by F. Clark Howell
October 1961

The stone tools of early man have seldom been found exactly where he left them. Now excavations in Tanganyika have exposed campsites littered with tools that provide clues to their users' way of life

The prehistorian who studies the earlier part of the Old Stone Age is attempting to reconstruct the habits and behavior of peoples dead for more than 75,000 years. In going about the task he is not encumbered by an oversupply of evidence: the total inventory comprises a few fragments of human skeletons; some bones of the animals that the early hunters killed (and vice versa); pieces of wooden implements, preserved through rare accidents; and large numbers of the chipped stones with which man then carved, scraped and battered out his living.

If one is to extract much valid information about the way of life these artifacts represent, one must examine them in the settings in which they were used—in "archaeological context." For a long time, when Europe was the main theater of archaeological exploration, stone tools dating from the early Paleolithic period were not seen this way. Abandoned at the exposed sites where their makers had lived (men did not become cave dwellers until rather late in the Old Stone Age), the tools were subsequently disturbed and even transported over considerable distances during the glaciations of the Pleistocene epoch. During the past 30 years or so much research on early man has been conducted in the unglaciated landscape of central Africa. A number of undisturbed, open living sites have been turned up. One of these, at Isimila in southern Tanganyika, has provided an assortment of Paleolithic tools in archaeological context. Together with my colleagues Maxine R. Kleindienst and Glen H. Cole, I have spent a considerable part of the past several years excavating and analyzing the material. It has provided valuable new insights into the activities of early man.

A number of the undisturbed sites are situated in or are adjacent to the Great Rift Valley of eastern central Africa. These include Kariandusi and Olorgesailie in Kenya and Olduvai Gorge in northern Tanganyika. Olduvai Gorge presents the longest known sequence of Pleistocene living sites. There L. S. B. Leakey of the Coryndon Museum in Nairobi has recently discovered remains of the oldest known toolmakers, dating back some 1,750,000 years. The Isimila site is situated not in the Rift Valley but in the Iringa highlands of southern Tanganyika, and the tools there are not nearly so old. They belong to the style of manufacture known as Acheulean, after the place in northern France where an abundance of such tools has been found. Current estimates place the be-

ginning of the Acheulean industry about 300,000 years ago, in the middle of the Pleistocene, and the end about 75,000 years ago, toward the end of the last interglacial period. Judging by the geological formations represented there, Isimila seems to have been inhabited for only a few thousand years near the end of the long span of the Acheulean period.

The geological history of the site was traced for us by Edward G. Haldemann and Ray Pickering of the Department of Geological Survey of Tanganyika. Millions of years ago the place was a major river valley. Then a series of upward and downward geological movements transformed the landscape, leaving the old valley as a small trough at an

EXCAVATION SITE was dotted with tools and rubble, exposed by erosion of Isimila beds. Nine living sites were excavated in three upper levels. One was excavated in fourth.

AERIAL VIEW of Isimila, looking northeast, shows main areas of sheet erosion. Trenches at middle right are excavation H20 in Level 4, the only bed containing fossil animal bones.

elevation of 5,400 feet, drained only by a small stream. During a period of increased rainfall in the middle of the Pleistocene the surrounding hills were covered with trees. Later the climate became drier and scrub vegetation replaced the woodland. Soil slipped and washed down from the deforested hills, choking the outlet of the basin and damming up an elongated body of water. This was alternately a marsh and a shallow pond, sometimes with an overflow. A steady deposition of silt in this basin eventually filled it to a depth of more than 60 feet with alternating beds of fine clay and coarser sandy sediment. The whole silting process seems to have required a few thousand years at most, and during this time early Stone Age hunters camped around the water hole.

There are five distinct beds of coarse sediment. Recent erosion has bared a good part of the upper three, and we have excavated them extensively. They contain an extraordinary number of living areas, all of them littered with tools. Indeed, it is hardly possible to walk over the site in any direction without stepping over quantities of finished and partly finished tools and waste chips. Since these upper layers are quite acid, no bone (except for a single hippopotamus tooth) has been found in them. In the fourth layer, however, we found bones of a number of animals, representing both extinct and still existing species. The skeleton of a hippopotamus, with the head and legs missing, looks very much as though it had been slaughtered or scavenged by human beings. The lower layers also yielded tools, but very few living areas to provide context.

With artifacts scattered so liberally through the three upper layers, the delimitation of a living area is somewhat arbitrary. In certain places, however, the pieces lie at the bottom of the sandy bed, on the surface of the underlying clay or within an inch or two of it. Horizontally they are densely distributed in a central region, becoming sparser with distance from the center. Although the boundaries may be uncertain, it seems quite clear that these assemblages mark out a site occupied for some time.

Nine living areas have been extensively excavated in the upper three levels, and one in the fourth bed has been partially exposed. The existence of several occupation areas on each level provides the first opportunity to compare different assemblages of tools known to be roughly contemporaneous. At other sites it has been possible only to compare them with those from different strata. Con-

HIPPOPOTAMUS BONES found in Level 4 form skeleton lacking head and extremities. The animal may have been slaughtered or scavenged by early man. This level contained fossil animal bones, of both extinct and extant species. No human bones were found.

HAND AXES found on Level 1 were resting on edge, as their users left them. Only one other Paleolithic site in Africa yielded tools resting in this position. It has been suggested that implements left lying thus were used for a specialized purpose, as yet unknown.

sequently the work at Isimila is forcing a revision of some widely held notions about the earlier Old Stone Age.

Our method of studying the occupation site was simple enough in principle but tedious and exacting in practice. After carefully excavating an area, we examined, classified and tabulated each one of the hundreds of tools that were exposed, as well as the numerous bits of rubble and waste chips. From these counts we were able to prepare charts showing the relative frequency of each type of object at each place [see illustration on pages 78 and 79].

Of what use is all this detail? In part the answer is still uncertain. When the same sort of analysis has been carried out at other sites, a comparison of the data may bring out new facts and relations. At Isimila alone, however, there was enough diversity to provide an entirely new idea of the full range of the Acheulean tool complex and to reveal an unsuspected degree of specialization.

Before proceeding to a description of what we found, a word about the different kinds of tool is in order. Unlike earlier toolmakers, the Acheulean craftsmen did not merely trim up likely looking stones that were ready to hand. They knew how to strike flakes from boulders or large stones and then fashion the blanks into a wide variety of standardized shapes. The kinds of rock with which they worked—mylonite (a strongly coherent rock containing fine mineral grains), granite, quartz and quartzite—show that they had mastered the most intractable raw materials.

The stone artifacts at Isimila fall into several classes. These include large and small shaped tools, pieces that were modified or slightly trimmed, pieces that were used but not trimmed and waste products. Within these classes various types of tool can be recognized and differentiated on the basis of the kind and the treatment of edges, the nature of the secondary trimming and so on. The tool types also exhibit different shapes or forms, and these vary between assemblages from the same site as well as between those from different sites. The large shaped tools with sharp cutting edges are usually made of mylonite and occasionally of quartz or quartzite. According to their shape and type of edge they are designated as hand axes, cleavers, knives, flake scrapers and "discoids" [see illustration on page 81]. The list of the blunter large pieces—generally of granite, quartz or quartzite—includes picks, core scrapers, choppers and "spheroids." Small tools are most often quartz, and their worked edges are frequently notched or otherwise shaped for scraping or perhaps for piercing.

Although many of the names suggest that the purposes for which the different tools were used are known, this is not at all true. In some cases, however, the most common guesses seem fairly plausible. It appears likely that the large blunt tools, which were always made of particularly durable varieties of stone, were meant for heavy duty. The small tools may have been used for working wood.

The hand ax was formerly thought to be an all-purpose tool, used for cutting, skinning, digging and so on, but the evidence from the undisturbed living sites at Isimila and elsewhere contradicts this notion. The sharp edges of the hand axes and some of the other large tools suggest beyond doubt that they were used only on soft substances. Recently some authorities have suggested that certain of the large sharp pieces were used for skinning and dismembering thick-skinned animals.

There is no proof for any of these hypotheses. Some of the evidence is distinctly mysterious. For example, both at Isimila and at another East African site several hand axes were found resting on one edge. Were they merely stuck in the ground after their users had finished their work or does their position indicate some specialized application? With further research such questions may be answered. Meanwhile the list of names serves to describe an assortment of well-defined tool types, whatever their purpose. The conventional labels furnish the prehistorian with an essential system of classification.

Among the various living areas at Isimila we could distinguish three distinct types of tool assemblage. The first type, represented in six places, has been traditionally regarded as the typical Acheulean tool kit. It consists mostly (up to 70 per cent and in one case even more) of large, sharp-edged tools—notably hand axes, cleavers and knives. The rest of the collection is divided about equally into large blunt tools and small flake tools. There are few waste products. The second type, of which there are two examples, is just the reverse:

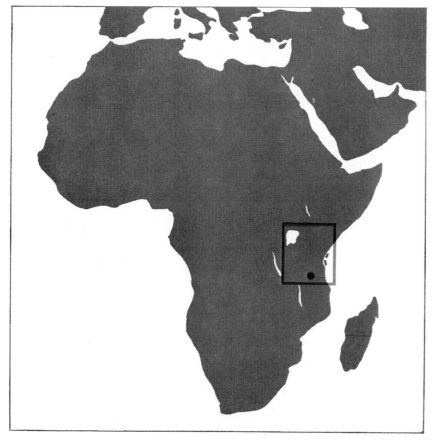

LOCATION OF ISIMILA is shown by the blue dot at right of center on this map of Africa. Most of the continent escaped glaciation during the ice age and still preserves some of the open-air sites at which early man camped in the period before he began to inhabit caves.

small tools predominate (40 to 60 per cent). Here there are few large cutting-edged tools and a fairly large quantity of waste products.

Both of these general categories have been observed in other Paleolithic sites in East Africa. The third type is new. Found at one place in the third level,

it contains a few small tools and a few large cutting-edged ones, the latter of an unusual shape. About half of the total is made up of large, heavy-duty tools—principally picks, core scrapers and choppers.

Before the excavations at Isimila were undertaken, different styles of individual

tools and different tool kits had always been found at separate sites, or in separate levels of the same site. Therefore they were usually held to reflect the passage of time and changes in culture or technology. Some authorities have attributed the first two types of tool kit we found at Isimila to distinct "cultures"

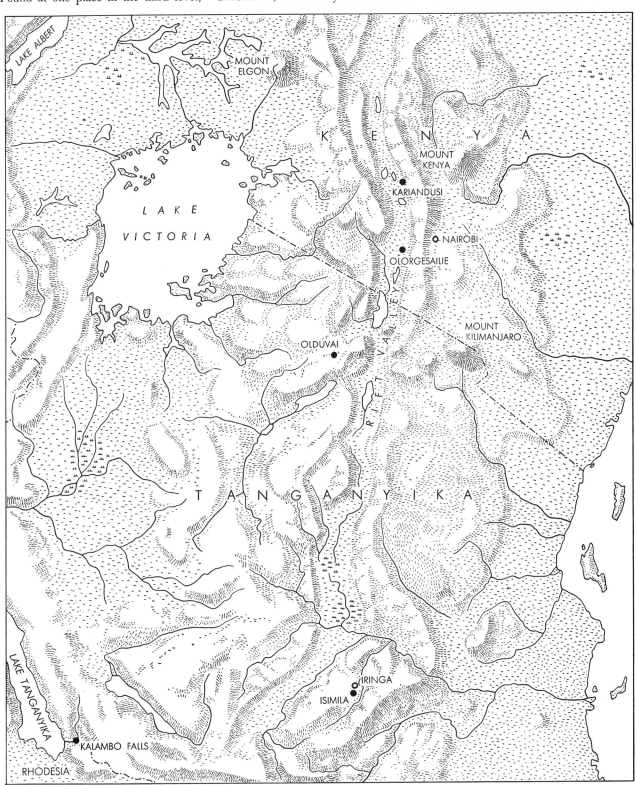

RIFT VALLEY AREA holds most of the human occupation sites recently excavated in eastern Central Africa. Shown here as black dots, from Kenya in the north to Rhodesia in the south, are Kariandusi, Olorgesailie, Olduvai Gorge, Isimila and Kalambo Falls.

with different ecological adjustments and subsistence patterns. There has even been talk of two different species of man.

The results at Isimila make such interpretations highly questionable. The place was occupied for a relatively short time. Yet a wide variety of tools and tool kits appears at different places within a single level. It seems most likely that in this case differences in tool kits reflect different activities. Members of the same group may well have been simultaneously performing different tasks requiring different tools.

On the other hand, variations in in-dividual styles in similar assemblages also found at Isimila may mean that more than one band of early men occupied the site at about the same time. For example, in one living area most of the hand axes are shaped like spearheads, in another most are egg-shaped. In one tool kit the sides of many of the cleavers converge; in a similar one they are largely parallel. Miss Kleindienst has discovered regional differences in the workmanship of certain tools at a number of East African Acheulean sites. Perhaps groups from different localities may have concentrated at the same campsite together. Stylistic variations had been known in the tools of hunters and gatherers of the present day and of Neolithic times, but it was interesting to find them so much earlier.

Similarly, there are differences in materials from one occupation site to another even in the same level. In some locations the full range of raw materials is represented; in others, only one or two varieties. The mylonite used for large cutting-edged tools also varies from site to site in color, hardness and flaking qualities. To some extent the variation may simply reflect the sources that were available at a given time. But it could also mean that the toolmakers selected

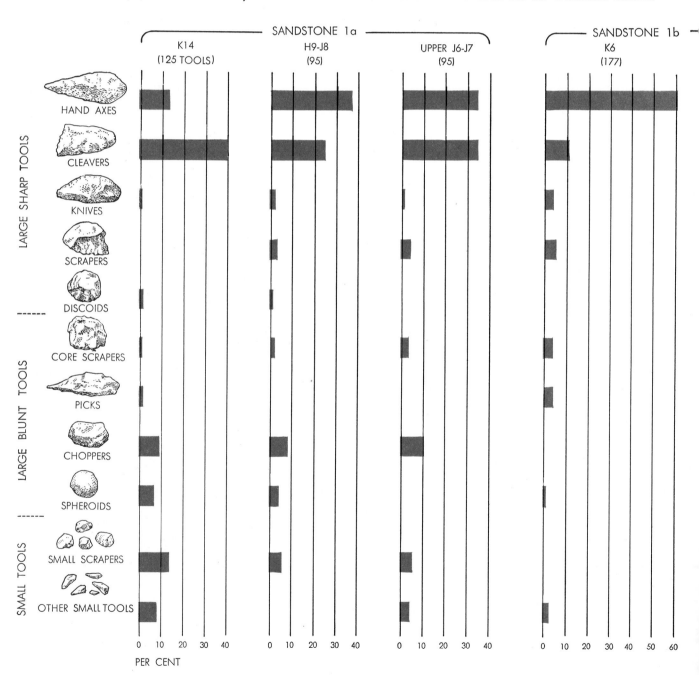

TOOL ASSEMBLAGES at nine sites in the three upper levels of the Isimila beds are shown in this chart based on an analysis by Maxine R. Kleindienst. At six sites (K14, H9-J8, Upper J6-J7, K6, J12, K19) large sharp tools predominate. At two (Lower K18, Lower J6-J7) small tools are numerous. At one (Lower H15) large blunt tools form the majority. This assemblage is unique for this

their materials from a number of exposed deposits, choosing the kinds best suited to the pieces they were working on. Conceivably different bands may even have enjoyed exclusive rights of exploitation to sources they had discovered. This would account for differences between the varieties of stone used at different sites in the same level.

The pattern of stone rubble found at different locations varies with the type of tool kit and tells its own story. Where there are small tools there is usually a good deal of rubble, most of it chips of the tool material. Evidently

these pieces were fashioned at the living sites where they were used. In the case of large tools, on the other hand, the living areas contain relatively few waste products of the same materials. Such waste as is there looks as though it was the product of minimal reworking or sharpening. Most of the tools were evidently made elsewhere.

One factory site has been uncovered at Isimila. The frequencies of both tools and waste products there are quite unlike those at any living place. The workshop contains few finished, or even semifinished, large tools. There are some roughed-out specimens and some fresh

blanks. Most of the inventory consists of large flakes of mylonite struck off in shaping the blocks of raw material from which the blanks were subsequently produced.

Certain of the living areas contain a puzzling distribution of stone pieces: a good many large tools and, as usual, little or no factory waste products but a large amount of extraneous rubble. In these places the inhabitants must have deliberately amassed stone rubble. What they wanted it for we have no idea, but there is little doubt that they went out and collected it. Other open sites in East Africa as well as some caves in Europe

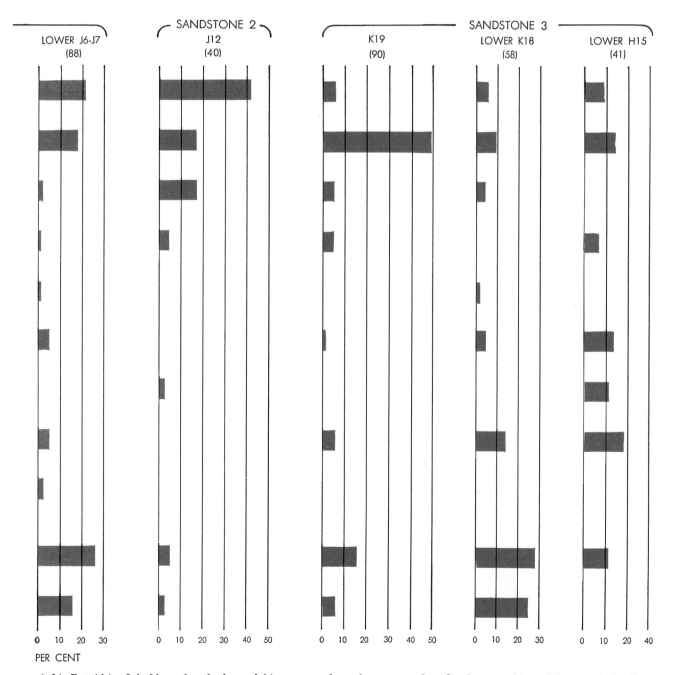

period in East Africa. It had been thought that each kit represented a different time or culture. But all kits are present on Level 3, at roughly contemporaneous sites. It may be that they were made by

the same people and each was used for a different task. At all sites except one (Lower J6-J7) a few tools are omitted from the count. These were broken and too damaged to be identified by name.

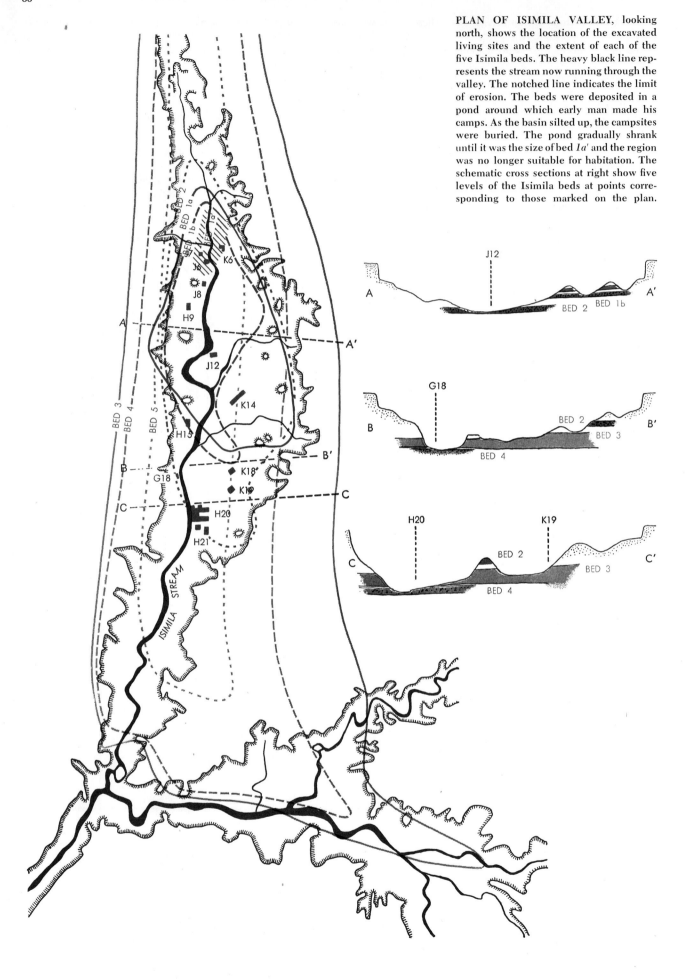

PLAN OF ISIMILA VALLEY, looking north, shows the location of the excavated living sites and the extent of each of the five Isimila beds. The heavy black line represents the stream now running through the valley. The notched line indicates the limit of erosion. The beds were deposited in a pond around which early man made his camps. As the basin silted up, the campsites were buried. The pond gradually shrank until it was the size of bed *1a'* and the region was no longer suitable for habitation. The schematic cross sections at right show five levels of the Isimila beds at points corresponding to those marked on the plan.

STONE TOOLS at Isimila were made some 75,000 years ago. Their diversity in size, shape and material suggests each type had its own use. Shown here, from top left to bottom right, are: two hand axes, two cleavers, knife, scraper, "discoid," pick, core scraper, chopper and "spheroid." The hand axes are 11 inches long. Chopper and spheroid are made of quartz; all others, of the mineral mylonite.

reveal evidence of the same activity.

At Isimila we found no wood or any evidence of fire. Both have been uncovered at other Acheulean sites, however. Pieces of wood preserved at Kalambo Falls in Rhodesia and at three European deposits—in Germany, Spain and England—indicate that men in the earlier Old Stone Age made wooden implements and weapons, including hardwood spears and what are probably clubs and throwing sticks. Charred wood, charcoal and ash at Kalambo Falls and in two African caves testify to the use of fire during the latter part of the Acheulean period.

From the recent work at Isimila, as well as at other undisturbed open-air sites, a much fuller picture of the life of Paleolithic man has begun to emerge. It shows a more varied and specialized technology and perhaps a higher degree of social organization than had been envisaged before. As always, the new information suggests still further questions: How large were the groups that camped at the open-air sites? Were there several different families in the same band? Were there different bands? How long did the people stay? Days? Weeks? Did they come back several times a year?

The very profusion of the remains at Isimila constitutes a puzzle in itself. What did the people want with all those tools? To be sure, the objects are not hard to make; a skilled prehistorian can turn one out in a few minutes. It is likely that the cutting-edged tools were discarded and replaced as soon as they lost their edge. Even so, the quantity seems out of proportion to any conceivable need.

Not all the problems may be solvable. But further studies of evidence in the archaeological context of the earlier Old Stone Age cannot fail to enlarge our understanding of man's place in nature.

II

NEOLITHIC VILLAGERS
AND FARMERS

NEOLITHIC VILLAGERS AND FARMERS   II

INTRODUCTION

The transition from hunter-gatherer to food producer is one of the most important areas in which archaeology can contribute to an understanding of human society. Indeed, probably the only subject of equal significance is the emergence of tool-making hominids several million years ago. These two changes, perhaps more than any other, have transformed cultural conditions and altered our environment, human biology, and, to a degree, our planet.

The definition of food production is in part dependent upon the ambiguous concept of domestication itself. Domestication is best seen as a continuum of relationships among human beings, plants, and animals. It is often difficult, if not impossible, to distinguish morphologically domesticated from wild plants. For some plants the essential factor in domestication is a shift in adaptation to new habitats that are modified or destroyed by people; the emphasis is on ecological rather than morphological change. Some domesticated plants—maize, dates, bananas, breadfruit—are forever tied to people, having lost their independent power of seed dispersal and germination; others, even if controlled or manipulated by humans, revert to the original wild state if not constantly tended.

If it is difficult to determine the extent of domestication in past cultural systems on morphological or ecological bases, it follows that the agricultural status of a community is often ambiguous. There are degrees of food production, and the assignment must be an arbitrary one. Anthropologists and archaeologists can, however, agree on a working definition of domestication that posits, at a minimum, (1) a reasonably efficient level of food production entailing situations in which food acquired through direct production amounts to over half of the community's dietary needs for part of the year; and (2) both plant and animal domesticates are no longer bound to their natural habitat.

After hundreds of millennia of predatory food gathering, hunting, and collecting, how did people move to controlling their own food supply? What were the sociocultural consequences of this new development in human history?

The economic foundation for civilization in the Old and New Worlds differed. The parallel and independent processes for development of civilization in both hemispheres are distinctive in their subsistence pattern. Old World and New World civilizations developed essentially independently of each other and thus they provide opportunity for the comparative study of the rise of civilizations.

The economic foundations on which Near Eastern civilizations were built depended upon wheat, barley, certain legumes (especially peas and lentils), sheep, goats, pigs, cattle, and dogs, with horses and camels arriving as later domesticates./These subsistence resources are remarkably different in kind from those that established the economic foundation for the New World, and in their difference may be found a partial explanation for the distinctive paths that both hemispheres followed toward civilization. In the New World the vegetable domesticates were principally maize, beans, and squash; the animal domesticates, the llama of Peru and guinea pig of Mesoamerica, were far more limited geographically than those of the Old World./

Most writers have emphasized the similarities in the evolution of urban societies in the Old and New Worlds. One point, however, appears to have attracted little attention: The differences in the subsistence patterns established fundamentally distinctive cultural patterns in both areas. The Near Eastern subsistence economy from earliest times supported two distinctive cultural patterns—the sedentary farmer and the nomadic herder. The relationship between these two provides one of the leitmotifs of Near Eastern civilization—at times it was built upon animosity and suspicion, as over grazing rights and property ownership; at other times it provided important services and information between settled areas through which the nomads moved./Without an understanding of the tensions and interrelations between these two cultural systems, we can only partially comprehend the civilization process in the Near East. By contrast, New World foundations for civilization lack this sedentary agriculturalist–nomad herder relationship.

Until around 1925, when V. Gordon Childe began to stress the food-producing or "neolithic" revolution, the matter of domestication received little attention. Throughout the eighteenth and nineteenth centuries, cultural-evolutionary schemes of universal history were posited and accepted as idealized explanations of cultural evolution. Human beings progressed from "savagery"—hunting and gathering—to "barbarism"—agriculture or pastoralism—to civilization. The stages were nicely outlined, each with its consequent impact on the social order. If it all seemed very neat and logical, it was because it was based on no empirical evidence. All was mere speculation: Hypotheses were formulated, even arguments of detail discussed, but no one chose to test these ideas by actual archaeological fieldwork. These untested cultural-evolutionary models received their most concise formulation in the writings of Childe./He was interested in the impact a newly introduced food-producing way of life had upon the savage hunters and food collectors of Europe following the end of the last Ice Age. He turned his attention to the Near East as the probable center of origin from which food-production was diffused to Europe, thousands of years before conventional ancient history began.

According to Childe, the time during which the food-producing revolution took place was one of major climatic changes./He postulated that, with the retreat of the ice sheets from continental Europe around 10,000 B.C., the summer rains that watered North Africa and Arabia shifted northward to Europe, resulting in the desiccation of much of the Near East. Such desiccation, Childe argued, provided the stimulus for adopting a food-producing economy. An enforced concentration of people and animals along banks of streams and in oases entailed an intensive readaptation; the enforced juxtaposition of animals, plants, and humans in restricted areas promoted a new symbiosis leading to domestication.

Today the geographical expanse for the early neolithic has been greatly expanded./In "An Earlier Agricultural Revolution," W. G. Solheim argues that a wholly independent Neolithic Revolution occurred in Southeast Asia and was dependent upon different plants than those exploited in the Near East. Of equal significance is Jacobsen's article, which suggests that in southeastern Europe domestication of plants and animals was brought about by diffusion from western Asia within an indigenous cultural setting far earlier than previously thought.

In the Near East the presence of animals that could be domesticated—sheep, goats, cattle, and pigs—and the wide progenitors of wheat, barley, peas, lentils, and bitter vetch provide the crucible in which the Neolithic Revolution took place. The manipulation of these plants and animals within their native habitat or their removal to a different one brought about selective processes that resulted in genetic changes. These genetic changes, in turn, altered morphology, which enables paleobotanists and paleozoologists to differentiate between wild and domesticated varieties of plants and animals.

The geographical area in which this process took place extends from the Anatolian plateau to the deserts of Central Asia and from the uplands of Palestine to the Caucasian range. In this large area several primary centers can be isolated where domestication of plants and animals was first accomplished. This occurred in the millennia following the stablization of our modern climate (after the last Ice Age); by 9000–8000 B.C. in the Syro-Palestinian Levant, the hilly flanks of the Zagros in Iraq and Iran, the south Anatolian plateau and eastern Elburz; in short, in the highland zones of the Near East. The presence at Nahal Oren, Israel, around 18,000 B.C., of seeds of precisely those plants later domesticated indicates that already at such an early date particular plants were selected for exploitation.

The high percentage of gazelle bones, three times more than any other species, in early neolithic sites of the Near East may indicate their domestication, or, at the very least, their selective exploitation. Studies on the herding behavior of animals suggest that certain species may be preadapted for domestication; thus in recent times the red deer, eland, and musk-ox have, for all practical purposes, been "domesticated," perhaps in the same manner that the gazelle was in the early neolithic. The transition from extensive dependence on gazelle to sheep and goats may have resulted from the fact that sheep and goats utilize a wider range of foods and are better integrated into a sedentary economy than are gazelle.

Archaeologists feel increasingly uneasy in using the traditional Grecized sequence of Paleolithic, Mesolithic, and Neolithic. Recent research has expanded, modified, and confounded this system by introducing such "stages" as protoneolithic, Aceramic, Prepottery neolithic, and pre- or proto-Urban, all with various subdivisions. This proliferation of stages has resulted in baffling terminology. Archaeologists believe it most helpful, and theoretically most illuminating, to approach the data through an understanding of the successive economic patterns that led to food production. In this manner the development of food production is seen as a successive and increasingly dependent adaptive manipulation of environmental resources.

Theories on the origins of domestication tend to be of two types: those that involved purposeful direction, the conscious manipulation of animals and plants by human beings and those that stress environmental pressures, such as desiccation or glacial advances and retreats, which brought about ideal conditions for domestication. F. E. Zeuner, a pioneer in paleozoological studies, believed that "social relationships" between humans and certain exploited wild animals led inevitably to a symbiotic relationship developing into domestication. This focus differs from that of ecologically oriented archaeologists in the Near East, whose approach deals not with social relationships but with environmental pressures and adaptations of specific ecosystems as the primary causes leading to domestication.

In examining the Neolithic Revolution Robert Braidwood has discerned two levels in the evolution of food production: an era of incipient cultivation and animal domestication and a later era of primary village farming. It is important to realize that these "levels" of socioeconomic evolution did not develop contemporaneously, nor did they inevitably succeed each other. Though it is difficult to support from archaeological evidence, we may assume that the mosaic of interdependence between village agriculturalists and nomadic herders was an early development, with the principal actors often changing their roles. It is also important to recognize that cultural developments are never uniform over large geographical expanses, nor are innovators restricted to a single area. The archaeological record suggests a slow, often faltering adaption toward food production, a process that in retrospect we erroneously perceive as directed toward a final goal—food production. Cultural evolution, like biological evolution, is entirely random, not directed toward final goals but only establishing boundaries for what is possible. So fundamental a change as food production has obvious social consequences. When people sow crops, food supplies and populations remain in one place. The practice of agriculture tends toward the establishment of permanent settlements, which in turn lead to the establishment of storage activities, enabling food produced at any time of the year to be consumed at other times. Animal husbandry has a similar effect in "banking" food supplies: Meat can be kept on the hoof until needed.

It is not true, however, that permanent settlements occur only with the appearance of food production. There are a number of archaeological sites without evidence of domestication that indicate permanence of settlement. In fact, increasing sedentism among forager-fisher populations exploiting reliable food supplies may have resulted in population pressures, leading to more effective manipulation of food resources and the "budding-off" of excess population migration in search of new food sources. This, in turn, may have provided a selective advantage to groups developing practices of husbandry and sowing.

Over the years there have been many explanations purporting to understand the causes that led to the Neolithic Revolution. Among the earliest and most persistent are ones dealing with environmental determinism, in which severity of environmental factors is seen to cause populations to cluster in oases, where they formed symbiotic relationships. This theory is no longer favored for a number of reasons, not least of which is the absence of evidence for large-scale environmental desiccation at the end of the Pleistocene.

Robert J. Braidwood was first to test the theories dealing with the Neolithic Revolution through archaeological excavation. His excavations at Jarmo (see "The Agricultural Revolution") led him to reject notions of catastrophic climatic change. Braidwood, in confronting the absence of evidence for radical environmental change, felt that the shift to a food-producing economy resulted from an "ever increasing cultural differentiation and specialization of human communities." Though this may be so, it still fails to provide an understanding of *why* food production was adopted.

Beginning with Carl Sauer's essay in 1952, "Seeds, Spades, Hearths, and Herds," an ecological approach to the origins of food production has been of paramount importance. Sauer confronts the origins of food production as a change in adaptation, a change in the manner of interaction between culture and environment. More than fifteen years later Lewis Binford (1968) added an important dimension to this ecological approach when he suggested that, at the end of the Pleistocene, population increases forced settlements from coastal to inland areas. These population movements, in turn, led to demographic pressures in areas where potentially domestic plants and animals could be found. The development of agricultural techniques are seen by Binford as adaptively advantageous to the populations of these regions. This hypothesis, entailing a series of causes, has a number of weaknesses; for example, we still await evidence to support the contention that populations moved inland and that demographic pressures existed. We may also wonder why such a process was not set in motion in earlier interglacials, leading to similar demographic stress and culture change.

Kent Flannery has proposed, in a series of papers, what is today the most widely accepted theory. Flannery advances a hypothesis based on systems models to explain not the cause but the mechanisms for the transition to food production. Flannery's hypothesis contains three important assumptions: (1) Hunter-gatherer populations increased prior to food production; (2) food production began in marginal areas of the mountain zones of Iran-Iraq-Turkey and the woodland zones of Palestine; and (3) there were many centers of food production at the start.

Flannery suggests that preagricultural peoples adapted not to specific environments but to the exploitation of certain plants and animals that inhabited several environments. In order to successfully exploit these resources, populations had to be in specific areas at specific times; the procuring of foods required a *scheduling* of seasonal movement. The seasonal use of different environments is typical of both the Near East and Mesoamerica, enabling populations to schedule their exploitation of differing plants or animals in different seasons. Increasing populations would lead to new groups splitting off to exploit more marginal areas, where they would be forced to cultivate the plants they brought with them.

In recent years a number of research programs have indicated that hunting and gathering populations, well adapted to particular environments, remain stable and below the point of resource exhaustion. In such conditions a disequilibrium is brought about either through environmental change or through demographic stress. The absence of clear evidence for the first pressure has resulted in models that concentrate on demography as the "prime mover" in the domestication of plants and animals. Flannery took Binford's model of demographic stress and applied it to the Near East. His systems model begins with population growth, or movement to marginal areas, where producers tried to grow plants artificially around the margins of optimum zones, and concludes with that population's gradual adaptation to a food-producing economy. Populations in areas of unpredictable resources could bank surplus animals in times of poor crop harvest, or vice versa to further insure their existence in such marginal areas.

The essays in this section all address themselves to varying aspects of the Neolithic Revolution. The extraordinary complexity of such a community is fully elucidated in the articles by Mellaart and by Kenyon. The existence of craft specialization, corporate labor, and even a metal technology would have stunned V. G. Childe as wholly unanticipated aspects of a neolithic community. The presence of copper implements as reported by Çambel and Braidwood points to the beginnings of a metal technology as early as 7000 B.C.

Two additional aspects emerge in our understanding of these neolithic communities that were unanticipated prior to their archaeological recovery. The article by Dixon, Cann, and Renfrew points out the extraordinary range in the geographical distribution of a single resource: obsidian. Obsidian is geologically restricted in the Near East, and through chemical analyses archaeologists can determine the source area. Through the recovery and analyses of obsidian from excavations it has been shown that obsidian was utilized in most neolithic communities and that this obsidian came from restricted geological deposits. The exploitation of this single resource points to an exchange system that brought seemingly isolated neolithic communities into contact.

Equally significant in transforming our understanding of the neolithic communities is the hypothesis presented in the article by Schmandt-Besserat. The systematic recovery of geometrically shaped clay objects from neolithic sites— cones, discs, pyramids, and so on—has been long known. Schmandt-Besserat presents an entirely plausible argument that these geometric forms represent "counters," allowing individuals to send quantities of produce at a distance by encapsulating the geometric forms in clay containers. The correctness of the quantity sent could then be checked at the destination by breaking the sealed clay envelope. Schmandt-Besserat suggests that this early form of symbolic communication can be traced back to 6000 B.C. and earlier, thus providing a foundation for the development of writing.

Certainly, as the following pages indicate, we have added immeasurably to our understanding of the neolithic transition from hunting and gathering to agriculture.

REFERENCES

Binford, L. 1968. "Post Pleistocene Adaptations." In *New Perspectives in Archeology*, ed. S. R. and L. R. Binford. Aldine, Chicago.

Childe, V. G. 1951. *Man Makes Himself*. Mentor Books, New York.

Flannery, K. 1972. "The Cultural Evolution of Civilizations." In *Annual Review of Ecology and Systematics*, vol. 3, pp. 399–426.

Sauer, C. O. 1952. *Seeds, Spades, Hearths, and Herds*. American Geographical Society, Washington, D.C.

Zeuner, F. E. 1963. *A History of Domesticated Animals*. Hutchinson, London.

9

The Agricultural Revolution

by Robert J. Braidwood
September 1960

*Until some 10,000 years ago all men lived by hunting,
gathering and scavenging. Then the inhabitants of hills
in the Middle East domesticated plants and animals
and founded the first villages*

Tool-making was initiated by pre-*sapiens* man. The first comparable achievement of our species was the agricultural revolution. No doubt a small human population could have persisted on the sustenance secured by the hunting and food-gathering technology that had been handed down and slowly improved upon over the 500 to 1,000 millennia of pre-human and pre-*sapiens* experience. With the domestication of plants and animals, however, vast new dimensions for cultural evolution suddenly became possible. The achievement of an effective food-producing technology did not, perhaps, predetermine subsequent developments, but they followed swiftly: the first urban societies in a few thousand years and contemporary industrial civilization in less than 10,000 years.

The first successful experiment in food production took place in southwestern Asia, on the hilly flanks of the "fertile crescent." Later experiments in agriculture occurred (possibly independently) in China and (certainly independently) in the New World. The multiple occurrence of the agricultural revolution suggests that it was a highly probable outcome of the prior cultural evolution of mankind and a peculiar combination of environmental circumstances. It is in the record of culture, therefore, that the origin of agriculture must be sought.

About 250,000 years ago wide-wandering bands of ancient men began to make remarkably standardized stone hand-axes and flake tools which archeologists have found throughout a vast area of the African and western Eurasian continents, from London to Capetown to Madras. Cultures producing somewhat different tools spread over all of eastern Asia. Apparently the creators of these artifacts employed general, non-specialized techniques in gathering and preparing food. As time went on, the record shows, specialization set in within these major traditions, or "genera," of tools, giving rise to roughly regional "species" of tool types. By about 75,000 years ago the tools became sufficiently specialized to suggest that they corresponded to the conditions of food-getting in broad regional environments. As technological competence increased, it became possible to extract more food from a given environment; or, to put the matter the other way around, increased "living into" a given environment stimulated technological adaptation to it.

Perhaps 50,000 years ago the mod-

AIR VIEW OF JARMO shows 3.2-acre site and surroundings. About one third of original area has eroded away. Archeologists dug the square holes in effort to trace village plan.

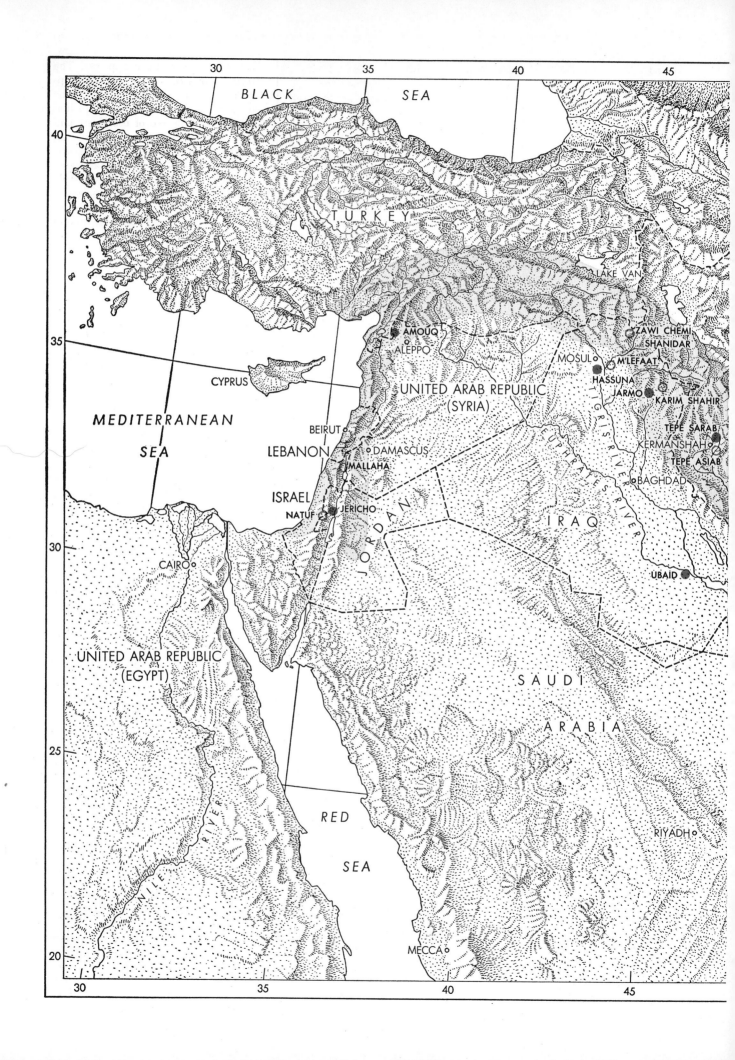

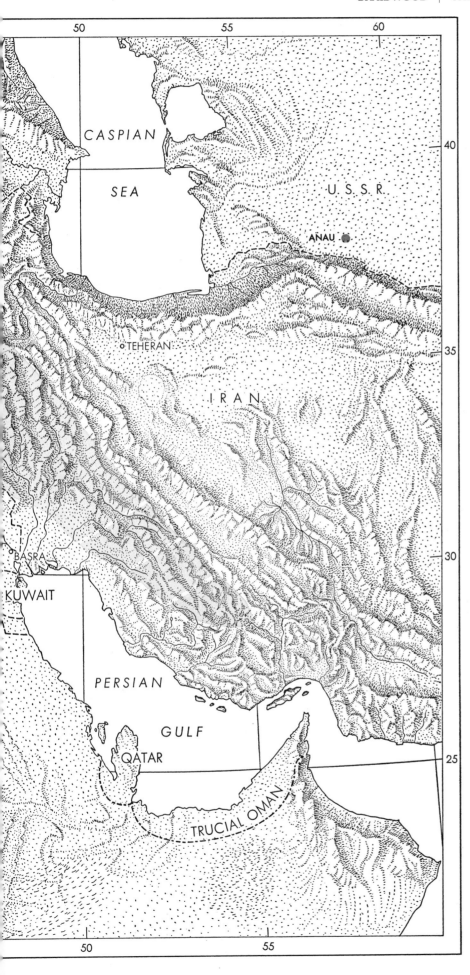

ern physical type of man appeared. The record shows concurrently the first appearance of a new genera of tools: the blade tools which incorporate a qualitatively higher degree of usefulness and skill in fabrication. The new type of man using the new tools substituted more systematic food-collection and organized hunting of large beasts for the simple gathering and scavenging of his predecessors. As time passed, the human population increased and men were able to adjust themselves to environmental niches as diverse as the tropical jungle and the arctic tundra. By perhaps 30,000 years ago they spread to the New World. The successful adaptation of human communities to their different environments brought on still greater cultural complexity and differentiation. Finally, between 11,000 and 9,000 years ago some of these communities arrived at the threshold of food production.

In certain regions scattered throughout the world this period (the Mesolithic in northwestern Europe and the Archaic in North America) was characterized by intensified food-collection: the archeological record of the era is the first that abounds in the remains of small, fleet animals, of water birds and fish, of snails and mussels. In a few places signs of plant foods have been preserved, or at least we archeologists have learned to pay attention to them. All of these remains show that human groups had learned to live into their environment to a high degree, achieving an intimate familiarity with every element in it. Most of the peoples of this era of intensified food-collecting changed just enough so that they did not need to change. There are today still a few relict groups of intensified food-collectors—the Eskimos, for example—and there were many more only a century or two ago. But on the grassy and forested uplands bordering the fertile crescent a real change was under way. Here in a climate that provided generous winter and spring rainfall, the intensified food-collectors had been accumulating a rich lore of experience with wild wheat, barley and other food plants, as well as with wild dogs,

HILLS FLANKING fertile crescent, where agricultural revolution occurred, are indicated in color. Hatched areas are probably parts of this "nuclear" zone of food-producing revolution. Sites discussed in this article are indicated by large circles. Open circles are prefarming sites; solid circles indicate that food production was known there.

goats, sheep, pigs, cattle and horses. It was here that man first began to control the production of his food.

Not long ago the proponents of environmental determinism argued that the agricultural revolution was a response to the great changes in climate which accompanied the retreat of the last glaciation about 10,000 years ago. However, the climate had altered in equally dramatic fashion on other occasions in the past 75,000 years, and the potentially domesticable plants and animals were surely available to the bands of food-gatherers who lived in southwestern Asia and similar habitats in various parts of the globe. Moreover, recent studies have revealed that the climate did not change radically where farming began in the hills that flank the fertile crescent. Environmental determinists have also argued from the "theory of propinquity" that the isolation of men along with appropriate plants and animals in desert oases started the process of domestication. Kathleen M. Kenyon of the University of London, for example, advances the lowland oasis of Jericho as a primary site of the agricultural revolution [see the article "Ancient Jericho," by Kathleen M. Kenyon, beginning on page 117].

In my opinion there is no need to complicate the story with extraneous "causes." The food-producing revolution seems to have occurred as the culmination of the ever increasing cultural differentiation and specialization of human

communities. Around 8000 B.C. the inhabitants of the hills around the fertile crescent had come to know their habitat so well that they were beginning to domesticate the plants and animals they had been collecting and hunting. At slightly later times human cultures reached the corresponding level in Central America and perhaps in the Andes, in southeastern Asia and in China. From these "nuclear" zones cultural diffusion spread the new way of life to the rest of the world.

In order to study the agricultural revolution in southwestern Asia I have since 1948 led several expeditions, sponsored by the Oriental Institute of the University of Chicago, to the hills of Kurdistan north of the fertile crescent in Iraq and Iran. The work of these expeditions has been enriched by the collaboration of botanists, zoologists and geologists, who have alerted the archeologists among us to entirely new kinds of evidence. So much remains to be done, however, that we can describe in only a tentative and quite incomplete fashion how food production began. In part, I must freely admit, my reconstruction depends upon extrapolation backward from what I know had been achieved soon after 9,000 years ago in southwestern Asia.

The earliest clues come from sites of the so-called Natufian culture in Palestine, from the Kurdistan site of Zawi Chemi Shanidar, recently excavated by

Ralph S. Solecki of the Smithsonian Institution, from our older excavations at Karim Shahir and M'lefaat in Iraq, and from our current excavations at Tepe Asiab in Iran [see map on preceding two pages]. In these places men appear to have moved out of caves, although perhaps not for the first time, to live in at least semipermanent communities. Flint sickle-blades occur in such Natufian locations as Mallaha, and both the Palestine and Kurdistan sites have yielded milling and pounding stones—strong indications that the people reaped and ground wild cereals and other plant foods. The artifacts do not necessarily establish the existence of anything more than intensified or specialized food-collecting. But these people were at home in a landscape in which the grains grew wild, and they may have begun to cultivate them in open meadows. Excavations of later village-farming communities, which have definitely been identified as such, reveal versions of the same artifacts that are only slightly more developed than those from Karim Shahir and other earlier sites. We are constantly finding additional evidence that will eventually make the picture clearer. For example, just this spring at Tepe Asiab we found many coprolites (fossilized excrement) that appear to be of human origin. They contain abundant impressions of plant and animal foods, and when analyzed in the laboratory they promise to be a gold mine of clues to the diet of the Tepe

SICKLE BLADES FROM JARMO are made of chipped flint. They are shown here approximately actual size. When used for harvest-ing grain, several were mounted in a haft of wood or bone. Other Jarmo flint tools show little advance over those found at earlier sites.

Asiab people. The nature of these "antiquities" suggests how the study of the agricultural revolution differs from the archeology of ancient cities and tombs.

The two earliest indisputable village-farming communities we have so far excavated were apparently inhabited between 7000 and 6500 B.C. They are on the inward slopes of the Zagros mountain crescent in Kurdistan. We have been digging at Jarmo in Iraq since 1948 [see "From Cave to Village," by Robert J. Braidwood, SCIENTIFIC AMERICAN October 1952], and we started our investigations at Tepe Sarab in Iran only last spring. We think there are many sites of the same age in the hilly-flanks zone, but these two are the only ones we have so far been able to excavate. Work should also be done in this zone in southern Turkey, but the present interpretation of the Turkish antiquities law discourages our type of "problem-oriented" research, in which the investigator must take most of the ancient materials back to his laboratory. I believe that these northern parts of the basins of the Tigris and Euphrates rivers and the Cilician area of Turkey will one day yield valuable information.

Although Jarmo and Tepe Sarab are 120 miles apart and in different drainage systems, they contain artifacts that are remarkably alike. Tepe Sarab may have been occupied only seasonally, but Jarmo was a permanent, year-round settlement with about two dozen mud-walled houses that were repaired and rebuilt frequently, creating about a dozen distinct levels of occupancy. We have identified there the remains of two-row barley (cultivated barley today has six rows of grains on a spike) and two forms of domesticated wheat. Goats and dogs, and possibly sheep, were domesticated. The bones of wild animals, quantities of snail shells and acorns and pistachio nuts indicate that the people still hunted and collected a substantial amount of food. They enjoyed a varied, adequate and well-balanced diet which was possibly superior to that of the people living in the same area today. The teeth of the Jarmo people show even milling and no marginal enamel fractures. Thanks apparently to the use of querns and rubbing stones and stone mortars and pestles, there were no coarse particles in the diet that would cause excessive dental erosion. We have calculated that approximately 150 people lived in Jarmo. The archeological evidence from the area indicates a population density of 27 people per square mile, about the same as today. Deforestation, soil deteriora-

JARMO WHEAT made imprint upon clay. Cast of imprint (*left*) resembles spikelet of present-day wild wheat *Triticum dicoccoides* (*right*). Specimens are enlarged seven times.

tion and erosion, the results of 10,000 years of human habitation, tend to offset whatever advantages of modern tools and techniques are available to the present population.

Stone vessels of fine craftsmanship appear throughout all levels at Jarmo, but portable, locally made pottery vessels occur only in the uppermost levels. A few impressions on dried mud indicate that the people possessed woven baskets or rugs. The chipped flint tools of Jarmo and Tepe Sarab, in both normal and microlithic sizes, are direct and not very distant descendants of those at Karim Shahir and the earlier communities. But the two farming villages exhibit a geo-

metric increase in the variety of materials of other types in the archeological catalogue. Great numbers of little clay figurines of animals and pregnant women (the "fertility goddesses") hint at the growing nonutilitarian dimensions of life. In both communities the people for the first time had tools of obsidian, a volcanic glass with a cutting edge much sharper and harder than stone. The obsidian suggests commerce, because the nearest source is at Lake Van in Turkey, some 200 miles from Jarmo. The sites have also yielded decorative shells that could have come only from the Persian Gulf.

For an explanation of how plants and animals might have been domesticated

KERNELS OF JARMO WHEAT were carbonized in fires of ancient village. They resemble kernels of wild wheat growing in area today. They are enlarged approximately four times.

between the time of Karim Shahir and of Jarmo, we have turned to our colleagues in the biological sciences. As the first botanist on our archeological team, Hans Helbaek of the Danish National Museum has studied the carbonized remains of plants and the imprints of grains, seeds and other plant parts on baked clay and adobe at Jarmo and other sites. He believes that the first farmers, who grew both wheat and barley, could

only have lived in the highlands around the fertile crescent, because that is the only place where both plants grew wild. The region is the endemic home of wild wheat. Wild barley, on the other hand, is widely scattered from central Asia to the Atlantic, but no early agriculture was based upon barley alone.

Helbaek surmises that from the beginning man was unintentionally breeding the kind of crop plants he needed.

CARBONIZED BARLEY KERNELS from Jarmo, enlarged four times, are from two-row grain. The internodes attached to kernels at right indicate tough spikes of cultivated barley.

Wild grasses have to scatter their seeds over a large area, and consequently the seed-holding spike of wild wheat and barley becomes brittle when the plant ripens. The grains thus drop off easily. A few wild plants, however, exhibit a recessive gene that produces tough spikes that do not become brittle. The grains hang on, and these plants do not reproduce well in nature. A man harvesting wild wheat and barley would necessarily reap plants with tough spikes and intact heads. When he finally did sow seeds, he would naturally have on hand a large proportion of grains from tough-spike plants—exactly the kind he needed for farming. Helbaek points out that early farmers must soon have found it advantageous to move the wheat down from the mountain slopes, from 2,000 to 4,300 feet above sea level (where it occurs in nature), to more level ground near a reliable water supply and other accommodations for human habitation. Still, the plant had to be kept in an area with adequate winter and spring rainfall. The piedmont of the fertile crescent provides even today precisely these conditions. Since the environment there differs from the native one, wheat plants with mutations and recessive characteristics, as well as hybrids and other freaks, that were ill adapted to the uplands would have had a chance to survive. Those that increased the adaptation of wheat to the new environment would have made valuable contributions to the gene pool. Domesticated wheat, having lost the ability to disperse its seeds, became totally dependent upon man. In turn, as Helbaek emphasizes, man became the servant of his plants, since much of his routine of life now depended upon the steady and ample supply of vegetable food from his fields.

The traces and impressions of the grains at Jarmo indicate that the process of domestication was already advanced at that place and time, even though human selection of the best seed had not yet been carried far. Carbonized field peas, lentils and vetchling have also been found at Jarmo, but it is not certain that these plants were under cultivation. Apparently farming and a settled community life were cultural prerequisites for the domestication of animals. Charles A. Reed, zoologist from the University of Illinois, has participated in the Oriental Institute expeditions to Iraq and Iran and has studied animal skeletons we have excavated. He believes that animal domestication first occurred in this area, because wild goats, sheep, cattle, pigs, horses, asses and dogs were all present there, and settled agricultural communities had already been established/The wild goat (*Capra hircus aegagrus*, or pasang) and sheep (*Ovis orientalis*), as well as the wild ass (onager) still persist in the highlands of southwestern Asia. Whether the dog was the offspring of a hypothetical wild dog, of the pariah dog or of the wolf is still uncertain, but it was undoubtedly the first animal to be domesticated. Reed has not been able to identify any dog remains at Jarmo, but doglike figurines, with tails upcurled, show almost certainly that dogs were established in the domestic scene. The first food animal to be domesticated was the goat; the shape of goat horns found at Jarmo departs sufficiently from that of the wild animal to certify generations of domestic breeding. On the other hand, the scarcity of remains of cattle at Jarmo indicates that these animals had not yet been domesticated; the wild cattle in the vicinity were probably too fierce to submit to captivity.

No one who has seriously considered the question believes that food needs motivated the first steps in the domestication of animals. The human proclivity for keeping pets suggests itself as a much simpler and more plausible explanation/ Very young animals living in the environment may have attached themselves to people as a result of "imprinting," which is the tendency of the animal to follow the first living thing it sees and hears during a critically impressionable period in its infancy [see "'Imprinting' in Animals," by Eckhard H. Hess; SCIENTIFIC AMERICAN Offprint 416].

Young animals were undoubtedly also captured for use as decoys on the hunt. Some young animals may have had human wet nurses—a practice in some primitive tribes even today. After goats were domesticated, their milk would have been available for orphaned wild calves, colts and other creatures. Adult wild animals, particularly goats and sheep, which sometimes approach human beings in search of food, might also have been tamed.

Reed defines the domesticated animal as one whose reproduction is controlled by man. In his view the animals that were domesticated were already physiologically and psychologically preadapted to being tamed without loss of their ability to reproduce/The individual animals that bred well in captivity would have contributed heavily to the gene pool of each succeeding generation. When the nucleus of a herd was established, man would have automatically selected against the aggressive and un-

CLAY FIGURES from Sarab, shown half size, include boar's head (*top*), what seems to be lion (*upper left*), two-headed beast (*upper right*), sheep (*bottom left*) and boar.

"FERTILITY GODDESS" or "Venus" from Tepe Sarab is clay figure shown actual size. Artist emphasized parts of body suggesting fertility. Grooves in leg indicate musculature.

STONE PALETTES from Jarmo show that the men who lived there were highly skilled in working stone. The site has also yielded many beautifully shaped stone bowls and mortars.

JARMO IN IRAQI KURDISTAN is the site of the earliest village-farming community yet discovered. This photograph of an upper level of excavation shows foundation and paving stones. Site was occupied for perhaps 300 years somewhere around 6750 B.C.

EXCAVATION AT KARIM SHAHIR contained confused scatter of rocks brought there by ancient men and disturbed by modern plowing. This prefarming site had no clear evidence of permanent houses, but did have skillfully chipped flints and other artifacts.

manageable individuals, eventually producing a race of submissive creatures. This type of unplanned breeding no doubt long preceded the purposeful artificial selection that created different breeds within domesticated species. It is apparent that goats, sheep and cattle were first husbanded as producers of meat and hides; wild cattle give little milk, and wild sheep are not woolly but hairy. Only much later did the milk- and wool-producing strains emerge.

As the agricultural revolution began to spread, the trend toward ever increasing specialization of the intensified food-collecting way of life began to reverse itself. The new techniques were capable of wide application, given suitable adaptation, in diverse environments. Archeological remains at Hassuna, a site near the Tigris River somewhat later than Jarmo, show that the people were exchanging ideas on the manufacture of pottery and of flint and obsidian projectile points with people in the region of the Amouq in Syro-Cilicia. The basic elements of the food-producing complex —wheat, barley, sheep, goats and probably cattle—in this period moved west beyond the bounds of their native habitat to occupy the whole eastern end of the Mediterranean. They also traveled as far east as Anau, east of the Caspian Sea. Localized cultural differences still existed, but people were adopting and adapting more and more cultural traits from other areas. Eventually the new way of life traveled to the Aegean and beyond into Europe, moving slowly up such great river valley systems as the Dnieper, the Danube and the Rhone, as well as along the coasts. The intensified food-gatherers of Europe accepted the new way of life, but, as V. Gordon Childe has pointed out, they "were not slavish imitators: they adapted the gifts from the East . . . into a new and organic whole capable of developing on its own original lines." Among other things, the Europeans appear to have domesticated rye and oats that were first imported to the European continent as weed plants contaminating the seed of wheat and barley. In the comparable diffusion of agriculture from Central America, some of the peoples to the north appear to have rejected the new ways, at least temporarily.

By about 5000 B.C. the village-farming way of life seems to have been fingering down the valleys toward the alluvial bottom lands of the Tigris and Euphrates. Robert M. Adams believes that there may have been people living in the lowlands who were expert in collecting food from the rivers. They would have

POTTERY MADE AT JARMO, in contrast to the stonework, is simple. It is handmade, vegetable-tempered, buff or orange-buff in color. It shows considerable technical competence.

taken up the idea of farming from people who came down from the higher areas. In the bottom lands a very different climate, seasonal flooding of the land and small-scale irrigation led agriculture through a significant new technological transformation. By about 4000 B.C. the people of southern Mesopotamia had achieved such increases in productivity that their farms were beginning to support an urban civilization. The ancient site at Ubaid is typical of this period [see the article "The Origin of Cities," by Robert M. Adams, beginning on page 170].

Thus in 3,000 or 4,000 years the life of man had changed more radically than in all of the preceding 250,000 years. Before the agricultural revolution most men must have spent their waking moments seeking their next meal, except when they could gorge following a great kill. As man learned to produce food, instead of gathering, hunting or collecting it, and to store it in the grain bin and on the hoof, he was compelled as well as enabled to settle in larger communities. With human energy released for a whole spectrum of new activities, there came the development of specialized nonagricultural crafts. It is no accident that such innovations as the discovery of the basic mechanical principles, weaving, the plow, the wheel and metallurgy soon appeared.

No prehistorian worth his salt may end or begin such a discussion without acknowledging the present incompleteness of the archeological record. There is the disintegration of the perishable materials that were primary substances of technology at every stage. There is the factor of chance in archeological discovery, of vast areas of the world still incompletely explored archeologically, and of inadequate field techniques and interpretations by excavators. There are the vagaries of establishing a reliable chronology, of the whimsical degree to which "geobiochemical" contamination seems to have affected our radioactive-carbon age determinations. There is the fact that studies of human paleo-environments by qualified natural historians are only now becoming available. Writing in the field, in the midst of an exciting season of excavation, I would not be surprised if the picture I have presented here needs to be altered somewhat by the time that this article has appeared in print.

10

An Earlier Agricultural Revolution

by Wilhelm G. Solheim II
April 1972

*It has generally been assumed that man first
domesticated plants and animals in the Middle East.
Excavations in Southwest Asia now suggest that
there the revolution began some 5,000 years earlier*

Agriculture is known to have been invented at least twice. Plants and animals were domesticated in the Old World and the process was repeated quite independently some millenniums later in the New World. Evidence of a third domestication has now been uncovered. The agricultural revolution, which was thought to have first occurred some 10,000 years ago among the emerging Neolithic societies of the Middle East, seems to have been achieved independently thousands of miles away in Southeast Asia. This separate agricultural revolution involved plants and animals for the most part unknown in the Middle East, and it may have begun as much as 5,000 years earlier.

The fact that some of the most technologically advanced cultures in the world in the period from about 13,000 B.C. to 4000 B.C. flourished not in the Middle East or the adjacent Mediterranean but in the northern reaches of mainland Southeast Asia is not easy to accept. Nonetheless, recent excavations in Thailand have convinced my colleagues and me that somewhere among the forest-clad mountains of the region man's first tentative efforts to exploit wild plants and animals opened the way first to horticulture and then to full-scale agriculture and animal husbandry.

In terms of prehistory mainland and island Southeast Asia are together the largest unknown region in the world. It is only in the past decade that they have been recognized as rewarding areas for archaeological investigation. My own work in the region began in the Philippines in 1949 and has since included investigations both in other island areas and on the mainland. The need for salvage archaeology in advance of construction work in the lower basin of the Mekong River resulted in the excavation of two sites in northern Thailand

by my colleagues and me in 1965–1966. The first of these sites, a prehistoric mound called Non Nok Tha, is close to the area that was flooded by the waters of the Nam Phong Reservoir. Our work there, sponsored jointly by the Thai Government Department of Fine Arts, the University of Otago in New Zealand and my department at the University of Hawaii, began during the 1965–1966 dry season with the support of the National Science Foundation. Simultaneously my department sponsored a second excavation at a promising site in the northwest corner of Thailand. This was Spirit Cave; its discoverer and excavator, Chester F. Gorman, was a student of mine at the University of Hawaii.

The mound called Non Nok Tha was tilled jointly by a few of the farmers of a nearby hamlet. They had almost covered it with plantings of bananas, chili peppers and mulberry bushes, but there were two cleared areas on the mound where the rice from the surrounding paddy fields was threshed at harvesttime. Digging at the edge of a mulberry planting, we found that the uppermost strata of the mound contained a few iron implements and numerous remains of individuals who had been cremated before burial. Below these levels were earlier graves whose occupants had not been cremated; the burials included various grave furnishings. Among them were stone molds for casting bronze axe blades, some of the axes themselves, other bronze objects and a number of polished stone tools. The graves also held pottery that was well made but generally lacked decoration. In the lowest levels of the site we found still more polished stone tools and a few specimens of decorated pottery but no bronze at all.

These were significant discoveries. First, never before had a site been

found in Southeast Asia that contained evidence of a substantial interval when bronze was known but iron was not. Second, the pottery from the lowest strata included two vessels decorated with a pattern that I had first seen in the Philippines and had later observed on pottery from excavations elsewhere in Southeast Asia.

The Non Nok Tha site proved to be so rich in burials that our work went more slowly than we had expected. Eventually we pieced together more than 100 pottery vessels for the Thai National Museum, sent samples off for carbon-14 analysis and packed up a number of other finds for laboratory study back in Hawaii. Several of the site's deepest burials we left untouched but mentally reserved for later excavation. We were convinced that the lowest levels of the mound were quite old, going back perhaps as far as 1000 B.C., but we could not be certain until the carbon-14 results were known.

As we unpacked, cleaned and examined the specimens in Hawaii we continued to find the unexpected. For example, we found among the potsherds from the lowest levels some that bore the imprint of cereal grains and husks. It appeared that the cereal might be rice, and we sent a number of samples to an authority on cereal grains, Hitoshi Kihara of the Kihara Institute for Biological Research in Japan. Kihara concluded that the cereal had been *Oryza sativa,* the common species of rice that is grown throughout Asia today.

We had also found animal bones in many of the burials at Non Nok Tha. They gave the impression that portions had been cut from large animals and placed in the graves. Charles Higham of the University of Otago offered to identify the bones. He found them indistinguishable from the bones of *Bos indicus,* the common species of humped cattle from India.

At last we received the carbon-14 results. They showed that the mound was much older than we had anticipated. The lowest levels we had excavated at the site had been deposited before 3000 B.C., some of them possibly before 4000 B.C. None of the uppermost strata, however, was more than 1,000 years old.

Early in 1968 Donn T. Bayard of the University of Otago was able to excavate in a new area at Non Nok Tha. He opened several deep graves; one contained a remarkably well-preserved human skeleton and, resting on the skeleton's chest, a socketed tool made of copper. This body must have been buried sometime during the fourth millennium B.C., which makes the copper im-

HUMAN BURIAL of the fourth millennium B.C. was unearthed in 1968 at Non Nok Tha, a rich archaeological site in northern Thailand, by Donn T. Bayard of the University of Otago in New Zealand. In addition to a skeleton the burial contained a socketed implement made of copper (*arrow*). The copper contains traces of arsenic and phosphorus, suggesting that, if the tool was not actually a casting, the metal had at least been heat-treated by roasting the ore to prepare it for cold hammering. No older socketed tool is known.

ANIMAL LIMB BONES (*right foreground*) are typical of the many aggregates of animal bone, some of them more than 5,000 years old, found in burials at Non Nok Tha. They are probably the bones of the familiar species of Indian humped cattle, *Bos indicus.*

plement the oldest-known socketed metal tool in the world.

In summary, the findings at Non Nok Tha included several surprises. They showed that rice was an established cereal and that humped cattle were commonplace in mainland Southeast Asia perhaps as early as the fifth millennium B.C. Bronze metallurgy had flourished in the region for a considerable interval before the appearance of iron, and a unique form of copper tool had appeared on the scene even earlier. None of these developments had taken place in a vacuum: some of the earliest pottery in this corner of the mainland bore designs that are found elsewhere in mainland and island Southeast Asia. Even bigger surprises, however, were in store at Spirit Cave.

Gorman's site lies high up on the face of a limestone cliff that overlooks a small stream not far from the border between Thailand and Burma. The cave was last occupied, Gorman found, about 5600 B.C. The levels that underlie the top level span more than 4,000 years, and the earliest strata were formed about 10,000 B.C. The artifacts from all these occupation levels (except for those in the levels of the last 1,200 years or so) proved to be very much the same: simple stone tools representative of a Southeast Asian hunters' and gatherers' culture. The culture is called Hoabinhian because the cave sites where its simple artifacts were first unearthed during the 1920's are in the mountains near the town of Hoa Binh in North Vietnam. Since the initial discovery, many other sites containing Hoabinhian artifacts have been found in the mountainous terrain of northern Southeast Asia, almost always in small caves not far from streams. At first sight Gorman's cave looked like one more Hoabinhian find, remarkable only for being farther west than any previously discovered.

Two findings soon demonstrated the importance of Spirit Cave. The first was the result of Gorman's careful search for plant material. By sifting all the soil as it was removed from his test trench-es, Gorman recovered the fragmentary remains of 10 separate plant genera, among them pepper, butternut, almond, candlenut and betel nut. Of even greater significance was evidence of a species of cucumber, a bottle gourd, the Chinese water chestnut and certain legumes: the pea (*Pisum*), either the bean or the broad bean (*Phaseolus* or *Vicia*) and possibly also the soybean (*Glycine*). Some of these plant remains were present in all levels at the site.

It seems probable that several of the plants were cultivated by the inhabitants of Spirit Cave. The relatively small number of specimens that Gorman recovered in 1966, however, does not make it possible to draw a clear-cut conclusion on this crucial point. Last year Gorman did further work at Spirit Cave and recovered additional specimens. They are now being analyzed by Douglas Yen of the Bernice P. Bishop Museum in Honolulu, so that the question may soon be settled.

Let us assume for the sake of argument that Yen's finding will be negative

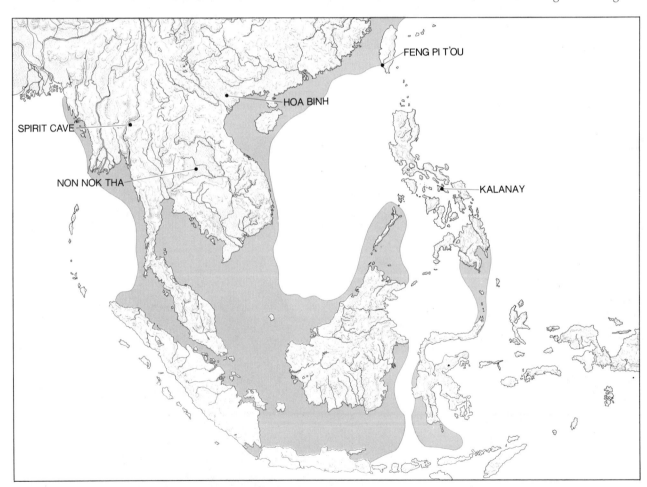

MAJOR EARLY SITES in Southeast Asia include Hoa Binh, in North Vietnam, where remains of a hunters' and gatherers' culture were found during the 1930's, and another Hoabinhian site, Spirit Cave in Thailand, where the earliest-known evidence of farming may have been found. Pottery at Spirit Cave, among the oldest in the world, resembles later wares found on Formosa. A second site in Thailand, Non Nok Tha, not only yielded a uniquely early kind of metal tool but also contained pots with designs like those found on Malayan and Philippine pottery. Lower seas in the past greatly enlarged the land area; color shows one estimate of the increase.

and that the plants unearthed at Spirit Cave are merely wild species that had been gathered from the surrounding countryside to supplement the hunters' diet. What should we then conclude? Such a finding would be evidence of an advanced stage in the utilization of wild plants in Southeast Asia, a stage that in my opinion is at least as early as any equivalent stage known in the Middle East. On the other hand, what if Yen's finding is positive? This would be evidence that the inhabitants of Spirit Cave were engaging in horticulture at least 2,000 years before the date that has been suggested for the first domestication of plants in the Middle East.

Gorman's next major finding was evidence that a clearly non-Hoabinhian influence had reached Spirit Cave about 6800 B.C. This was indicated by the presence of new and distinctive artifacts among the simple Hoabinhian tools, including rectangular stone adzes with partially polished surfaces and knives made by grinding both sides of a flat piece of slate to form a wedge-shaped cutting edge. Tools such as these are unknown anywhere else in mainland Southeast Asia at such an early date.

Even more important was the presence in the upper strata of pottery fragments that showed a variety of finishes. Most of the potsherds bore imprints that were probably produced by striking the soft clay with a cord-wrapped paddle before the pot was fired. Other potsherds show evidence of polishing, still others had been incised by cutting into the soft clay with a comblike tool, and a few are coated with what appears to be a resin glaze. Except for certain extremely early examples of pottery that have been unearthed in Japan, these fragments from Spirit Cave are the oldest pottery in the world. Moreover, the variety of decoration and finish they display testifies to the existence of a sophisticated potter's tradition with a considerable past.

In addition to collecting more plant material last year, Gorman found examples of a new class of artifacts to add to the inventory from Spirit Cave. These are small pellets of baked clay. In excavating Non Nok Tha we had found similar pellets that were more recent. Our workmen had suggested that they were projectiles for use with a "pellet bow," a weapon that children in northern Thailand still use to hunt birds. The device is like a conventional bow except that a slingshot-like pouch for the pellet is attached to the bowstring.

It is a peculiarity of Southeast Asian

SPIRIT CAVE, located near the Burma border in northwestern Thailand, is being excavated by Chester F. Gorman of the University of Hawaii. From the start, during 1965–1966, Gorman has found the remains of many kinds of edible plants, including nuts, water chestnuts, a species of cucumber and two or three legumes. Some of the material is 12,000 years old. If cultivated and not picked wild, the plants represent man's earliest farming endeavor.

archaeology that stone projectile points, which are among the most abundant artifacts elsewhere in the world, are rarely found in the region. The reason is presumably that the early hunters in the area made their projectiles of wood, as the Southeast Asians who hunt with the bow and arrow still do; objects made of wood, of course, quickly rot and leave no trace in the archaeological record. If the clay pellets at Spirit Cave were indeed made for pellet bows, then such weapons and possibly conventional bows and arrows could have been in use there 9,000 or more years ago.

Taking into account both the range

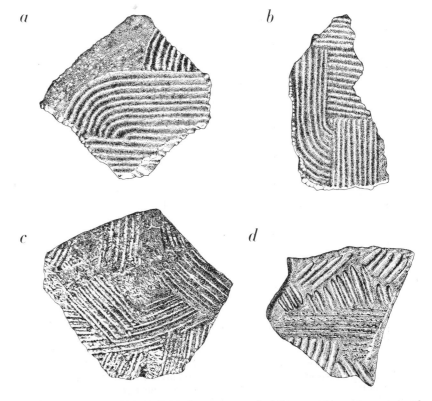

POTTERY FRAGMENTS from Spirit Cave, some nearly 9,000 years old, are decorated with sophisticated incised designs (a, b), suggesting that the potter's art had evolved at a still earlier date elsewhere in Southeast Asia. The designs resemble some on pottery more than 4,000 years old (c, d), found on Formosa in 1964 by Kwang-chih Chang of Yale University.

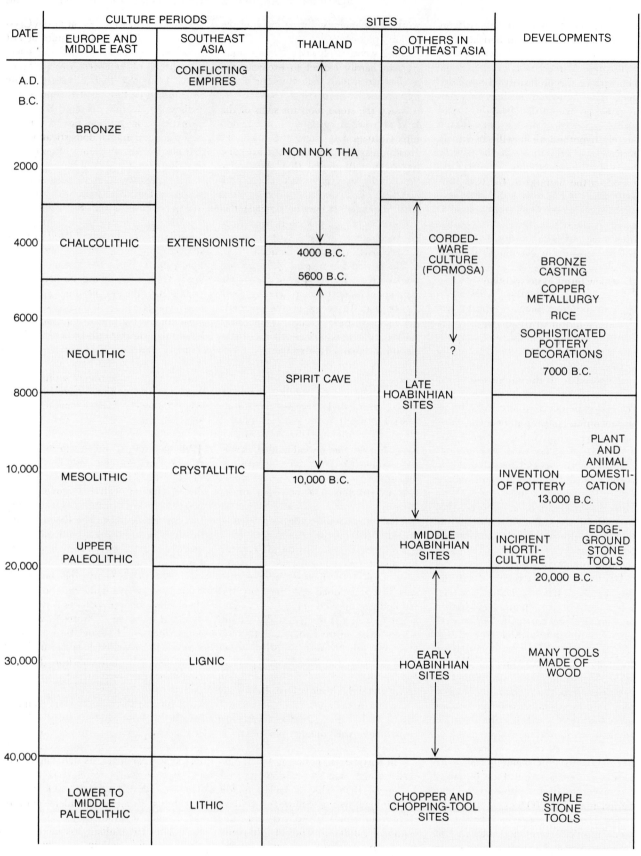

| DATE | CULTURE PERIODS | | SITES | | DEVELOPMENTS |
	EUROPE AND MIDDLE EAST	SOUTHEAST ASIA	THAILAND	OTHERS IN SOUTHEAST ASIA	
A.D.		CONFLICTING EMPIRES			
B.C.					
	BRONZE		NON NOK THA		
2000		EXTENSIONISTIC			
4000	CHALCOLITHIC		4000 B.C.	CORDED-WARE CULTURE (FORMOSA)	BRONZE CASTING
			5600 B.C.		COPPER METALLURGY
6000					RICE
	NEOLITHIC		SPIRIT CAVE		SOPHISTICATED POTTERY DECORATIONS
				LATE HOABINHIAN SITES	7000 B.C.
8000					
	MESOLITHIC	CRYSTALLITIC			INVENTION OF POTTERY
10,000			10,000 B.C.		PLANT AND ANIMAL DOMESTI-CATION
					13,000 B.C.
	UPPER PALEOLITHIC			MIDDLE HOABINHIAN SITES	INCIPIENT HORTI-CULTURE	EDGE-GROUND STONE TOOLS
20,000					20,000 B.C.
		LIGNIC		EARLY HOABINHIAN SITES	
30,000					MANY TOOLS MADE OF WOOD
40,000					
	LOWER TO MIDDLE PALEOLITHIC	LITHIC		CHOPPER AND CHOPPING-TOOL SITES	SIMPLE STONE TOOLS

NEW FRAMEWORK for the prehistory of Southeast Asia has been developed on the basis of recent excavations. The traditional subdivisions of the stone and metal ages of Europe, which cannot be applied in Southeast Asia, are shown at left. Beside them are the five new divisions of the past in Southeast Asia, ranging from prehistoric up to historic times. The names of the earliest periods indicate the kind of material most used for tools: Lithic suggests stone tools; Lignic, wooden ones. The later period names indicate the principal trends during each period. The local cultures of the region took shape during the Crystallitic period. Major population shifts away from mountain habitats occurred in the Extensionistic period. The Period of Conflicting Empires witnessed the rise of states after the start of the Christian Era. Elsewhere the chart shows the relation of five periods to specific sites and basic developments.

of the carbon-14 dates and the rich inventory of remains unearthed at Spirit Cave and Non Nok Tha, it is apparent that a radical revision is needed in our concepts of the prehistory of Southeast Asia. The theoretical outline of a new regional prehistory that follows is based on such a revision. My reconstruction is largely hypothetical; it will need to be tested by further excavation both in mainland and island areas. Much of it is based on the findings at the two Thailand sites, but I have included additional data from my own work and the work of others in the region. Because the outline uses some unfamiliar terms, I shall first briefly review the conventional terminology of prehistory in order to place these new terms in perspective.

For more than a century archaeologists have referred to three stages of the Stone Age: the Paleolithic ("old stone"), the Mesolithic ("middle stone") and the Neolithic ("new stone"). The terms were first defined to fit the prehistory of Europe, but they have since been applied so widely that it is often unthinkingly assumed that cultures all over the world have passed through these three stages. It is quite clear, however, that in many regions the European terms do not correctly describe the sequence of events; this is particularly true of Southeast Asia. The evolution of cultures there has been distinctly different from that in Europe and the Middle East. I am therefore suggesting the substitution of new terms for Southeast Asia.

For the earliest period in Southeast Asia I propose the term Lithic. The term refers to the early human use of chipped and flaked stone for tools. This period, roughly equivalent to the early and middle Paleolithic of Europe, is, I suggest, the only one of the three Stone Age stages that all mankind has shared. In Southeast Asia the technology of chipping and flaking stone developed slowly and never did reach the level of extremely fine workmanship found in many other parts of the world. A possible reason for this seeming backwardness is proposed below. In any event I have arbitrarily set the end of the Lithic period around 40,000 B.C.

For the next period I propose the name Lignic, a term derived from the Latin word for wood. It is part of my hypothesis that during this period tools made of wood—particularly those made of bamboo—became more important to the peoples of Southeast Asia than tools made of stone. Such a change in the preferred material for tools would help to account for the slow progress in stone-

working technology during much of the region's prehistory.

Since wood rarely lasts in the ground, we can hardly expect to excavate the ancient wood tools that would prove my hypothesis. It is possible, however, to examine the stone tools for signs of the kind of wear suggestive of woodworking. Gorman has done this with the Hoabinhian tools from Spirit Cave, and he has found several that show edge wear indicating their use to shape both large pieces of wood and wood shafts of small diameter. It may be significant in this connection that a high percentage of the charcoal in the hearths at Spirit Cave consists of charred bamboo.

The period when wood tools proliferated I have arbitrarily defined as beginning about 40,000 B.C. and ending about 20,000 B.C. In terms of the currently known prehistoric cultures of Southeast Asia this dating would equate the Lignic period with early Hoabinhian.

For the third period in the region I propose the name Crystallitic. The term has nothing to do with raw materials but is intended to suggest that during this interval distinct local cultures began to take shape, or crystallize, in Southeast Asia. Before the period ended, sometime around 8000 B.C., I believe there had developed many elements of culture that are still found in the region today. In terms of known prehistoric sites the Crystallitic period equates with middle and late Hoabinhian.

I suggest that it was during Crystallitic times that the technique of shaping stone tools by grinding and polishing was first developed. At the start this method was applied only to a tool's cutting edge; later it was gradually extended over the entire surface. Stone tools that are ground and polished rather than chipped and flaked are typical of the Neolithic stage of the Stone Age in Europe and the Middle East; they make their first appearance about 8000 B.C. in the Middle East. I believe the same technology was being pioneered in Southeast Asia much earlier.

The Crystallitic period is also the interval when plants were domesticated. I suggest that what is called middle Hoabinhian was a culture or cultures whose adherents were experimenting with many different kinds of wild plants for many different reasons. At some point, probably about 13,000 B.C. somewhere in the northern reaches of Southeast Asia, such experiments culminated in the domestication of some of these plants and the consequent appearance of horticulture as a new means of food procurement.

Having advanced this far in the Crystallitic period, we make contact at last with some of our newfound evidence: the contents of the lowest levels at Spirit Cave. I suggest that it was the late Hoabinhian culture, as it is represented in these levels, that achieved the transformation from horticulture to generalized plant and animal domestication and that also achieved the invention of pottery. In different parts of the region different plants would have been selected for cultivation. The same was probably true of the animals involved: the pig, the chicken and possibly even the dog. All these different elements of late Hoabinhian culture spread and accumulated as time passed. When the lowest levels at Spirit Cave were being formed, about 10,000 B.C., the people there appear to have possessed such elements of late Hoabinhian culture as an advanced knowledge of horticulture and perhaps domesticated pigs. They had no pottery, however, nor would they acquire any until an entire spectrum of sophisticated wares arrived at Spirit Cave from elsewhere in Southeast Asia some three millenniums later.

For the fourth period in Southeast Asia I propose the name Extensionistic. The term refers to the major trend during the interval: the movement of peoples out of the mountains where they had previously lived. The Extensionistic trend, which began around 8000 B.C. and ended at about the beginning of the Christian Era, led the mountain peoples not only into the many other hospitable habitats of the mainland but also beyond them; the mountain peoples traveled by overland routes or by water in virtually every direction. I believe future investigation will show that local cultures that were distinctly different from the late Hoabinhian evolved at the start of this period.

At present the only known candidate for one of these newly evolved cultures is the complex of traits that appeared in the upper levels at Spirit Cave, with its rectangular adzes, its slate knives and its sophisticated cord-marked pottery. That complex, however, is not eligible for status as an independent culture; one cannot separate its elements from their late Hoabinhian associations. Is there a similar complex elsewhere, free of a Hoabinhian matrix?

There is on the island of Formosa (Taiwan). Its artifacts include rectangular adzes, polished slate points and cord-marked pottery, some of it decorated with comb incisions like the ware at Spirit Cave. This Formosan complex

SIMPLE COPPER TOOL, perhaps used as an adze or an axe, is the one found in 1968 in a deep burial at Non Nok Tha. The socket at one end (*see section*) makes the tool unique.

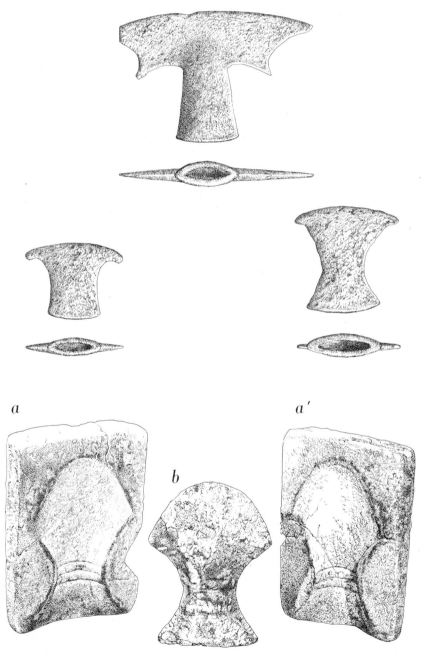

a   *a'*

b

WORK IN BRONZE at Non Nok Tha included casting axe heads in stone molds. Illustrated are two halves of a mold and a matching axe head (*a, a', b*), and profile and top views of three typical axe heads, showing the sockets for inserting the wooden axe handles.

has been named the Corded-Ware Culture by its discoverer, Kwang-chih Chang of Yale University. Little is known about its age except that, at the two open-air sites where it has been unearthed, the culture ceased to exist sometime before 2500 B.C. Considering the winds of change that marked the Extensionistic period, it is worth emphasizing two points here. First, Formosa is a long way from Spirit Cave. Second, the remains of the Corded-Ware Culture on Formosa are found not in a conventional Hoabinhian cave setting but out in the open.

What were the consequences of the population movements during this period? I suggest that the earliest movements brought the people no farther from the mountains than into the adjacent piedmont. Even this movement led to enough of an environmental change, however, to make the hunting of wild animals and the gathering of wild plants activities of diminishing significance and to make farming much more important. The transition from dependence on wild food resources to dependence on domesticated ones would of course have been gradual. Indeed, the transition is not complete in Southeast Asia even today. People in towns and even in cities still collect wild produce, and many such items are found in the markets. Wild animals are hunted and trapped wherever possible and make an important addition to the limited human intake of protein.

The beginning of the Extensionistic period coincided with the end of the Pleistocene epoch. The lower level of the sea during the Pleistocene ice ages gave Southeast Asia about twice the land area it has today. The seacoast ran along the edge of what is now the Sunda Shelf, and the islands of western Indonesia and the Philippines were connected to the mainland. Few Hoabinhian sites have been found adjacent to the present coastline; it seems logical to expect that many of the Extensionistic settlements were located in river valleys and on shores that are now submerged. The slowly rising sea that accompanied the last retreat of the continental glaciers must have forced some peoples to retreat to the mainland and have left others marooned on the islands. The inhabitants of the Sunda Shelf who retreated to the coast of South China and North Vietnam were probably the ancestors of the people who took readily to the sea starting about 4000 B.C. and ultimately pushed as far as Madagascar off the coast of Africa and Easter Island off the coast of South America.

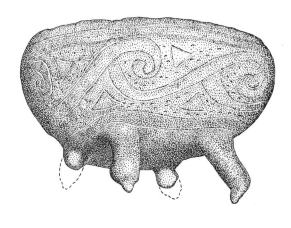

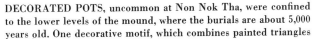

DECORATED POTS, uncommon at Non Nok Tha, were confined to the lower levels of the mound, where the burials are about 5,000 years old. One decorative motif, which combines painted triangles with a curvilinear scroll (*left*), is repeated in the incised decorations on pottery found at offshore sites in the region such as the cave site near Kalanay on the Philippine island of Masbate (*right*).

What material changes would have been evident as various local cultures evolved during this period? Again the material from Spirit Cave and Non Nok Tha is suggestive. The slate knives from the upper levels at Spirit Cave closely resemble the kind used today to harvest rice in parts of Indonesia. Is it possible that rice was one of the plants the final residents of Spirit Cave collected and perhaps cultivated? The cereal was certainly known at Non Nok Tha perhaps no more than 1,500 years later, as the pottery impressions of rice grains and rice husks have demonstrated.

Metallurgical analysis of the copper tool that Bayard unearthed at Non Nok Tha shows that it contains traces of phosphorus and arsenic. This fact suggests that the tool was not merely pounded into shape from a large nugget but that the copper was smelted or otherwise heat-treated, and it implies some degree of metallurgical sophistication among the fourth-millennium inhabitants of the site. Not long afterward the people of Non Nok Tha were casting bronze in the form of socketed tools much like the earlier copper one. No trace of copper, tin or lead ores—the three metals used in this region to make bronze—has been found in association with the bronze-casting equipment at Non Nok Tha. Either the ores were smelted at some other part of the site or the refined metals, or the alloyed bronze itself, reached Non Nok Tha through trade channels.

We are led to the conclusion that the relatively advanced metallurgy practiced at Non Nok Tha during the fourth and third millenniums B.C. had its roots in earlier metallurgical developments elsewhere in the region. If one gives due weight to the evidence that socketed metal tools were unknown outside the region until about 2000 B.C., a further conclusion seems inescapable: The development of metallurgy in Southeast Asia was probably independent of and unrelated to the development of metallurgy in the Middle East.

A major puzzle remains. Given the spread of plant and animal domestication, the advances in metallurgy and the development of trade, it is surprising that the entire Extensionistic period was unmarked by the kind of social evolution that accompanied the same events in the Middle East. We find neither the rise of cities nor the growth of centralized political power. Even as late as the second and first millenniums B.C. fortifications are unknown anywhere in Southeast Asia, which strongly suggests that organized warfare was also unknown. With one possible exception the various cultures of the region seem to have shared much the same kind of economic base and to have enjoyed contact with one another but to have remained politically independent. The exception is the culture of the region of what is now North Vietnam and the adjacent parts of China; during the second millennium B.C. a centralized authority that was quite independent of the imperialistic dynasties in northern China may have arisen in this area. More archaeological investigation is needed, however, before the actual extent of the development can be determined.

The first years of the Christian Era coincided with the start of the most recent period in Southeast Asia, which I call the Period of Conflicting Empires. It was then that, as a result of Indian political and religious influences, the first centralized states finally made their appearance in the region, just as they had in India itself. Once established, a number of petty states flourished in succession for some 1,500 years; they were largely parasitic on the population of the region. Beginning in the 16th century and continuing into the 20th, European imperialism gradually supplanted the native variety; the change in rulers made no appreciable difference to the inhabitants. The occupation of Spirit Cave had of course ended long before the Period of Conflicting Empires began; except for the appearance of iron and the water buffalo the archaeological record at Non Nok Tha was scarcely affected by the events of the period.

Following the withdrawal of the European colonialists after World War II, the Period of Conflicting Empires also came to an end. Southeast Asia today is in an interval of readjustment that has been complicated equally by the collapse of empires and of philosophies. The least one may hope for a region where early man took so many remarkable strides along the road to civilization is a return to the live-and-let-live pattern of cultural independence that characterized much of its prehistory.

11 Obsidian and the Origins of Trade

by J. E. Dixon, J. R. Cann, and Colin Renfrew
March 1968

*Objects made of this volcanic glass are found at
many Neolithic sites around the Mediterranean.
Spectroscopic analysis indicates that the raw material
often came from hundreds of miles away*

The transition from hunting to farming, which started mankind on the road to civilization, presents a number of interesting questions for investigators, not the least of which is the extent of communication among early human settlements. Archaeological explorations in recent years have unearthed the sites of prehistoric villages that were widely scattered in southwestern Asia and around the Mediterranean. The earliest communities—for example Jarmo in what is now Iraq and Jericho in Jordan—apparently were settled some 10,-000 years ago [see the article "The Agricultural Revolution," by Robert J. Braidwood, beginning on page 91]. One might suppose the primeval villages, separated by hundreds of miles and often by mountains or water, were isolated developments, not even aware of one another's existence. There have been reasons to suspect, however, that this was not the case, and we have now found definitive evidence that the prehistoric communities throughout the Near East and the Mediterranean region were in active communication.

What kinds of evidence of communication between geographically separated peoples might one look for? Obviously in the case of prehistoric peoples the only materials available for study are the remains of the objects they made or used. In the search for signs of possible contact between two cultures archaeologists have generally depended on a comparative examination of the artifacts. If the two cultures show strong similarities in knowledge or technique—say in the method of working flint or the style of pottery—this is taken to signify mutual contact and perhaps actual trade in objects. At best, however, such evidence is only suggestive and is always subject to doubt; it leaves open the possibility that the similarities, no matter how close they are, may be mere coincidence, the two peoples' having hit independently on a natural and obvious way of doing things.

The raw materials of which the objects were made, on the other hand, may offer an opportunity for a more decisive inquiry. If a material used by a community does not occur locally in the raw state, one must conclude it was imported, and the possibility exists that it was obtained in trade with another population. One can then start on the task

OBSIDIAN BOWL made during the fourth millennium B.C. is seen from above, its spout jutting out at the right. The translucent bowl, which is nearly eight inches in diameter, comes from the Mesopotamian site of Tepe Gawra [*see illustration on page 116*]. Trace-element analysis shows that the obsidian comes from Acigöl, 400 miles to the west in Turkey.

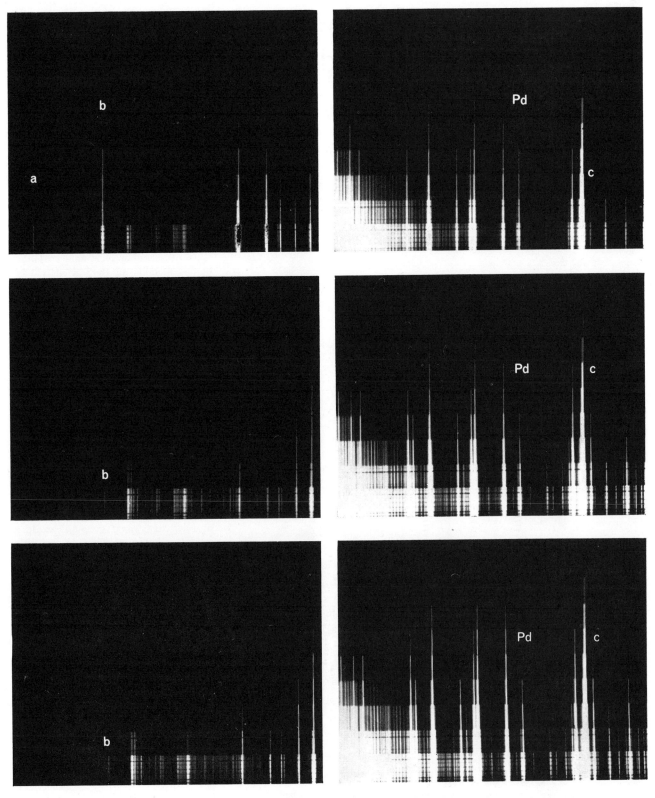

SPECTROGRAMS of three obsidian samples, reproduced here in part, show that differing proportions of trace elements make possible the identification of obsidian from different volcanic deposits. At top are two parts of the spectrogram of raw volcanic glass from Melos in the Aegean Sea. Matching parts of a spectrogram of a piece from an obsidian blade unearthed at Ali Kosh in Iran are at center. Matching parts of a spectrogram of volcanic glass from Nemrut Dağ, near Lake Van in Armenia, are at bottom. In the top specimen the spectral lines of strontium ("a" *at left, 4,607.4 angstrom units*) and barium ("b" *at left, 4,554 angstroms*) are relatively long, indicating proportions of some 200 parts per million and 700 parts per million respectively. The same lines are almost invisible in the center and bottom specimens. The spectral line of zirconium ("c" *at right, 3,438 angstroms*) is relatively short in the top specimen, indicating a concentration of about 50 parts per million. In the other two specimens the long zirconium lines indicate a concentration of about 700 parts per million. Palladium (*spectral lines labeled "Pd" to the left of "c"*) is not a normal trace element in obsidian; the element is added to provide a standard for calibration. The trace-element differences show that the Ali Kosh artifact (*center*) could not have been made of obsidian from Melos but instead is chemically similar to the obsidian found at Nemrut Dağ.

OBSIDIAN FROM MELOS, in the form of a core from which blades have been flaked, shows the characteristic glistening surface of this volcanic glass. Obsidian was probably traded in the form of glass lumps or cores that the final purchaser turned into tools himself.

SCULPTURED SEASHELL, carved from a variety of obsidian with distinctive white spots, was found in a Minoan site on Crete. Sir Arthur Evans, the pioneer student of Cretan prehistory, thought the obsidian had come from Lipari, off Sicily, where similarly spotted volcanic glass is common. Analysis now proves that it came from nearby Giali in the Aegean.

of tracing the material to its source.

It occurred to us that obsidian might be an ideal material for a tracer investigation of this kind. Obsidian is a hard, brittle volcanic glass that can be chipped like flint and fashioned into a sharp tool. It is known to have been used for knives and scrapers by prehistoric men as early as 30,000 years ago. Obsidian tools have been found in nearly every early village site in the Near East and the Mediterranean region. Yet for most of these sites it was an indubitably foreign material; it can be obtained only in certain areas of recent volcanic activity, which in that part of the world means the region around Italy, some islands in the Aegean Sea and certain areas in modern Turkey and Iran. Some of the ancient villages where obsidian tools were used were many hundreds of miles from the nearest natural source of the material.

How could one identify the particular source from which the obsidian was obtained in each case? Clearly our first task was to determine whether or not obsidian samples showed distinguishable differences that could be connected with their source. We considered several possible criteria. Physical appearance obviously would not be a reliable guide, because obsidian samples from a single volcanic deposit may vary greatly in visible characteristics such as color. Microscopic examination was not helpful: the obsidian tools were generally made of material that is uniform in structure, without crystalline inclusions. Chemical analysis of the main components was also of no avail, because all samples of obsidian are substantially alike from this point of view. We decided finally on a chemical test based on the presence of trace elements. Perhaps the obsidian samples would show distinct differences in their trace-element content that could be identified with the deposits from which they came.

In order to explore this possibility we began by analyzing samples of obsidian collected from various well-known volcanic sources in the Mediterranean area: Lipari, a volcanic island north of Sicily, two areas in Sardinia, the islands of Pantelleria and Palmarola and the island of Melos in the Aegean Sea.

For chemical analysis of the samples we used a convenient spectrographic method that archaeologists have long employed on metal objects. Every element emits characteristic wavelengths of light when it is heated to incandescence; a familiar example is the yellow light of burning sodium. By passing the light

SOURCES OF OBSIDIAN in the Mediterranean and the Near East during Neolithic times included volcanic areas in Sardinia and on Palmarola, Lipari and Pantelleria in the central Mediterranean, the islands of Melos and Giali in the Aegean Sea, two central Anatolian sites, Acigöl and Çiftlik, and several places in ancient Armenia, including Bingöl in eastern Turkey and Nemrut Dağ near Lake Van.

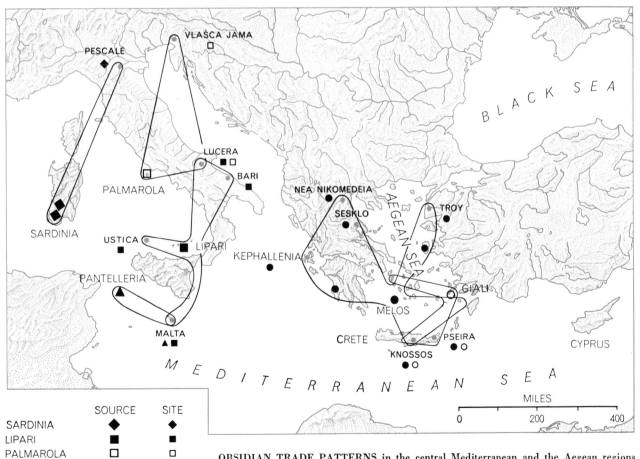

	SOURCE	SITE
SARDINIA	◆	◆
LIPARI	■	■
PALMAROLA	□	□
PANTELLERIA	▲	▲
MELOS	●	●
GIALI	○	○

OBSIDIAN TRADE PATTERNS in the central Mediterranean and the Aegean regions show that, although the volcanic glass was often shipped long distances from its sources, trade apparently did not take place between the two regions. Within each region, however, obsidian from two sources is often found at one site. Not all the sites indicated are named.

from a mixture of elements through a prism or diffraction grating that spreads out the wavelengths in a spectrum, one can separate the emissions of the various elements and detect trace elements that are present even in the amount of only a few parts per million. The beauty of the method for studying archaeological specimens is that accurate measurements can be obtained from very small amounts of material. Sixty milligrams taken from a sample is sufficient. Ground to a fine powder, mixed with an equal amount of carbon and ignited in a carbon arc, this material yields a spectrographic picture that gives a measure of the quantity of each trace element in the sample; the quantity is indicated by the intensity (photographically the height) of the element's spectral lines.

We obtained readings for 16 elements in our samples of obsidian. Among the trace elements found to be present, the two that showed the greatest quantitative variation over the range of samples were barium and zirconium. We there-fore tried using the relative concentra-tions of these two elements as a test for identification of the source [see illustra-tion on this page]. To our immense satis-faction these quantities were found to indicate the geographical source quite well. Samples from various flows and outcrops at Lipari, for instance, all showed much the same proportion of barium to zirconium; those from Melos had characteristic contents of these ele-ments different from those at Lipari. The Pantelleria and Sardinia samples like-wise could be distinguished on the same basis. The Palmarola samples turned out to be similar to the Lipari ones on the barium-zirconium graph, but we found we could distinguish them from the Lipari type by their content of another trace element, cesium.

Having established these markers for identifying the obsidian sources, we were in a position to determine the raw-material origins of obsidian tools found at the sites of ancient settlements. The little island of Malta, south of Sicily, of-fered objects for a clear-cut test. The re-mains of a remarkable prehistoric society of 5,000 years ago, marked by colossal stone temples, have been unearthed on this island. The finds include small obsid-ian tools. There are, however, no natu-ral obsidian deposits on the island. Where, then, did the material come from? Some archaeologists had suggest-ed that it might have been brought there by Minoan traders from the island of Melos, 600 miles to the east. Our trace-element analysis of the Malta tools dis-closed that this conjecture was incorrect: the obsidian was of the types found on Lipari and on Pantelleria, a tiny island 150 miles northwest of Malta.

The findings revealed two important facts about the ancient Maltese settle-ment. They showed that the island peo-ple in that early Neolithic period were already accomplished seafarers, travel-ing frequently to Sicily, Lipari and Pantelleria. On the other hand, the ob-sidian evidence also indicated that the Maltese people had little or no contact with the contemporary Minoan settle-ments of the Aegean area. Their stone temples may well have been their own invention.

Our tests resolved another question involving the Minoan culture. Sir Arthur Evans, the illustrious archaeologist who excavated the palace at Knossos on Crete more than half a century ago, found a number of finely carved objects there that were made of a variety of obsidian marked by prominent white spots. He concluded that this material came from

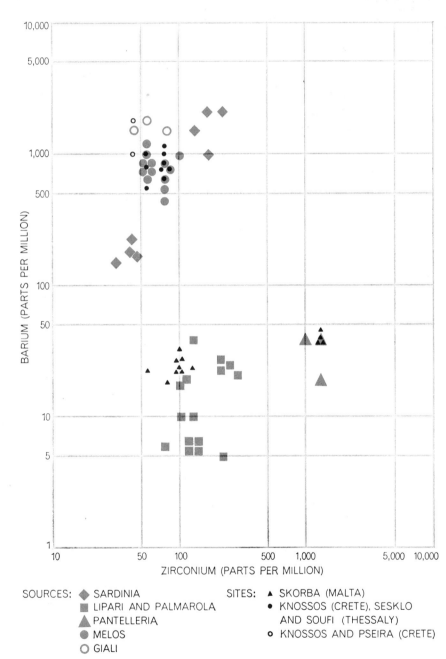

SOURCES: ◆ SARDINIA
◼ LIPARI AND PALMAROLA
▲ PANTELLERIA
● MELOS
○ GIALI

SITES: ▲ SKORBA (MALTA)
● KNOSSOS (CRETE), SESKLO AND SOUFI (THESSALY)
○ KNOSSOS AND PSEIRA (CRETE)

TWO TRACE ELEMENTS, barium and zirconium, provide the principal means of identify-ing the sources of obsidian artifacts from central Mediterranean and Aegean sites. Obsidian from both Sardinian sources is richer in barium than obsidian from Pantelleria, Lipari and Palmarola, whereas Pantellerian obsidian is the richest of all in zirconium. Other trace ele-ments, not plotted here, allow additional distinctions to be drawn. Although their barium and zirconium contents are similar, the high calcium content of Gialian obsidian distin-guishes it from Melian, whereas Palmarolan obsidian is much richer in cesium than Liparian.

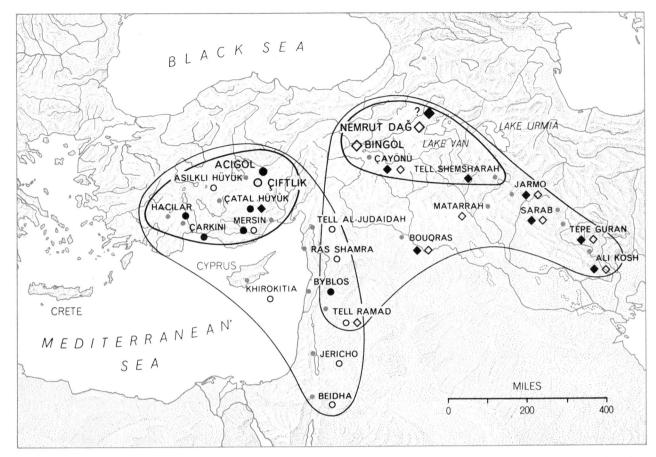

	SOURCE	SITE
ARMENIAN OBSIDIAN 1G	◆	◆
4C	◇	◇
ANATOLIAN OBSIDIAN 1E-F	●	●
2B	○	○

NEOLITHIC NEAR EAST was another scene of active obsidian trade. Cypriot, Anatolian and Levant villages obtained obsidian mainly from two sources in Anatolia: Acigöl and Çiftlik. Mesopotamian villages, in turn, depended on sources in Armenia. The locations of two, Nemrut Dağ and Bingöl, are known. A third variety of obsidian, found at many Mesopotamian sites, is also probably Armenian but its source is not yet known. A heavy line surrounds a nuclear zone within each trade area. These are designated "supply zones" by the authors: more than 80 percent of the chipped-stone tools at supply-zone sites are obsidian.

Lipari, some of whose obsidian also has white spots. On trace-element examination, however, it now turns out that the white-spotted obsidian at Knossos came not from Lipari but from the small island of Giali some distance north of Rhodes. The Knossos remains also include tools made of unspotted obsidian. Analysis shows that this material came from Melos, which is to be expected, since Melos is the nearest obsidian source to Crete. In general, the obsidian evidence establishes the early Aegean islanders as skilled sailors and traders, disseminating the material not only among the islands but also to settlements in Greece and Turkey.

The obsidian tracer work, begun only six years ago, has given rise to investigations at various institutions in Britain, the U.S. and elsewhere, and studies are going forward on material from early settlements in Europe, in the Middle East, in Mexico, California and the Great Lakes region of the New World, in New Zealand and in Africa, where early man

made hand axes of obsidian as long as 100,000 years ago. Our own group at the University of Cambridge, having verified the validity of the method by the Mediterranean tests, has proceeded to apply it to an investigation of the origins of trade among the earliest settlements of man in the Near East, that is to say, in Mesopotamia and in Turkey, Palestine and Egypt.

The first problem in the study of this region was to locate the natural sources of obsidian. A number of sources (all volcanic, of course) have now been identified in mountainous areas of Turkey and northern Iran [*see top illustration on page 111*] and in Ethiopia to the south. All the available geological evidence indicates that the entire region between these places, including Egypt, is devoid of natural deposits of obsidian. This means that every prehistoric village in the "fertile crescent," where farming began, had to import its obsidian.

Samples from all the natural deposits and from the obsidian artifacts found

in the village sites were analyzed. They were found to be definable in eight different groups, or types, according to their barium-zirconium content, and in some groups the presence of another trace element (like that of cesium in the Palmarola obsidian) served additionally to distinguish the particular source of the material. Some of the obsidian artifacts could not be matched to any known natural source. This necessarily called for searches for the missing sources. The composition of the natural obsidian samples suggested a certain geographical pattern of distribution, and this clue led to the discovery of at least one missing source. A few sources have not yet been located precisely, but the basic pattern of sources and destinations is now clear enough to provide a good picture of the movement and trade routes of obsidian in the period when the first steps toward civilization (variously called the "agricultural revolution" or the "neolithic revolution") were taking place.

By about 9000 B.C. groups of people

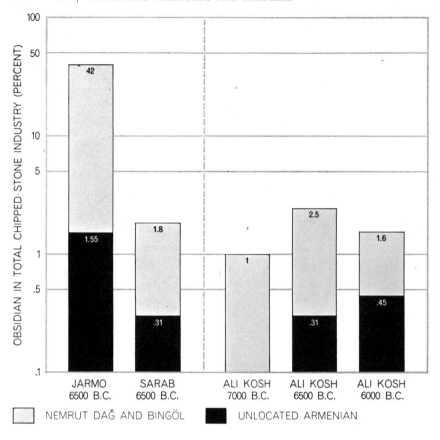

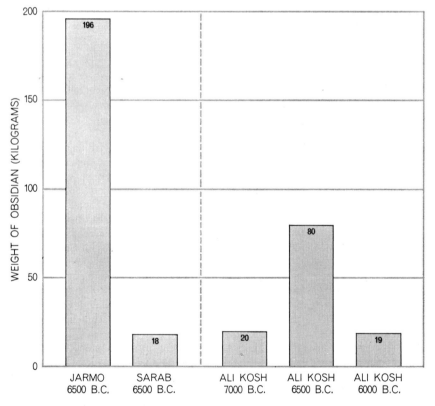

INFLUENCE OF GEOGRAPHY on trade in tool materials is apparent from the total obsidian and its proportion to other stone tools at three Zagros villages that imported Armenian obsidian during the seventh to sixth millenniums B.C. Jarmo, although outside the Armenian supply zone (*see illustration on preceding page*), was nonetheless well supplied with obsidian in terms both of percentage (*top graph*) and of estimated total weight of the material (*bottom graph*). The reduction in both percentage and weight at two more distant towns, Sarab and Ali Kosh (*plotted for three periods*), is drastic. Both distance and the difficult terrain apparently contributed to the scantiness of trade in the case of Sarab, a hill town.

in the Near East had begun to practice an incipient agriculture: selectively hunting and perhaps herding sheep and goats and harvesting wild prototypes of wheat and barley. They were not yet using obsidian to any appreciable extent. By the time the first farming villages were founded, probably a little after 8000 B.C., obsidian had come into rather general use. Naturally the extent of adoption of the material varied with distance from the sources of supply, and this is clearly traceable in the obsidian objects found at the sites of the ancient villages.

Within 150 to 200 miles of the obsidian deposits in Turkey and Armenia most of the chipped-stone tools found in the early prehistoric village sites are of obsidian: 80 percent, as against only 20 percent of flint. From that zone the proportion of obsidian falls off nearly exponentially with distance. This is clearly illustrated by the distribution of obsidian from a natural source in the volcanic area around Çiftlik, near the present town of Niğde in Turkey. At Mersin, the site of an early village on the Mediterranean coast not far from Çiftlik, obsidian was the most common chipped-tool material. From there its use diminished rapidly down the Levant coast, until at Jericho, 500 miles from the source, it is found only in very small quantities, most of the chipped tools there being made of flint. A few pieces of Çiftlik obsidian have been found, however, even at a Neolithic settlement on Cyprus, which indicates at least a trading contact across the water. Some of the obsidian from Turkish sources was distributed over distances of more than 600 miles in the early Neolithic period.

The early villages near the sources in Turkey developed a rich art and craftsmanship in obsidian. Particularly impressive are the objects found at Çatal Hüyük, a 6000 B.C. village that was so large it can be called a town. Among its obsidian products were beautifully made daggers and arrowheads and carefully polished mirrors, as sophisticated as any of those made 7,000 years later in Aztec Mexico.

Jarmo, one of the earliest-known villages in the fertile crescent, was favored by proximity to several obsidian sources. At least two of these sources furnished considerable amounts of the material, estimated to total 450 pounds or more, to Jarmo in very early times. From this it appears that well before 6000 B.C. Jarmo must have been conducting a thriving trade across the mountains that brought it into contact with the communities to the north in Armenia. There were then no wheeled vehicles (they were not invented until 3,000 years later) and not even pack animals. Hence all the traded goods, including obsidian, must have been transported on foot, or perhaps part of the way in boats down the Tigris River.

Tracing the varieties of obsidian from their sources to the villages where they turn up in manufactured objects, we can reconstruct the trade routes of

that early time in man's economic and social history. The routes, crossing mountains, deserts and water, connect the early settlements with a network of communications that must have influenced their development profoundly. No doubt goods besides obsidian were traded over these routes; indeed, it seems likely that there was a trade in perishable commodities that was much greater in size and economic significance than that in obsidian. Clearly, however, the most impor-

tant traffic must have been in ideas. The network of contacts arising from the trade in goods must have been a major factor in the rapid development of the economic and cultural revolution that within a few thousand years transformed mankind from a hunting animal to a builder of civilization.

Obsidian now furnishes us with a tool for retracing the communications at the beginning of the revolution, more than 3,000 years before the invention of writ-

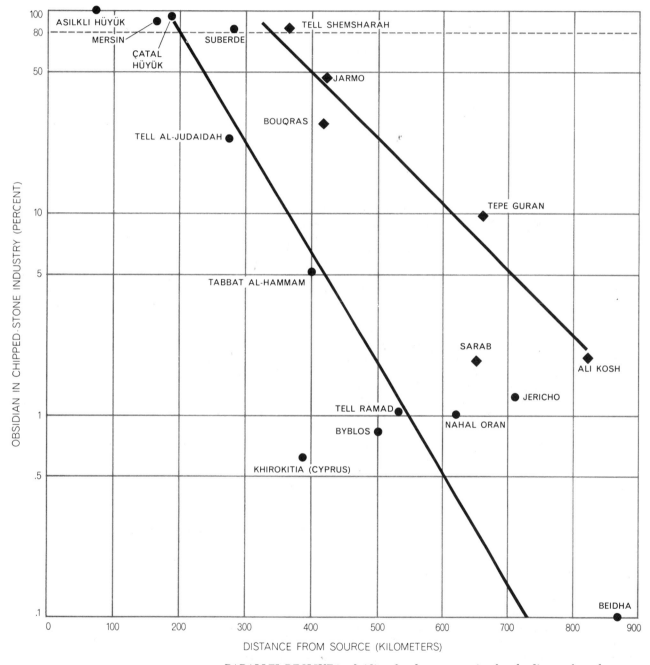

PARALLEL DECLINE in obsidian abundance proportional to the distance from the source is evident in both Near East trade areas during the period from 6500 to 5500 B.C. Not all the sites named here are included in the map on the next page. The boundary between a supply zone and the wider hinterland that the authors call a "contact zone" appears to lie about 300 kilometers from each area's obsidian sources. Poor supply of obsidian at the Cyprus site in spite of its nearness to sources in Turkey is a second example of the influence of geographical factors other than distance. The necessary ocean voyage apparently inhibited trade.

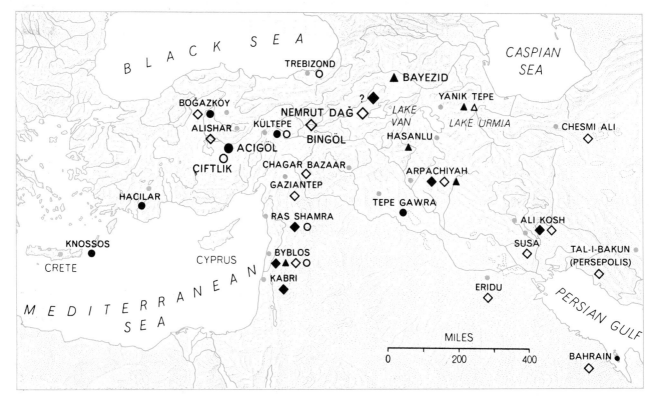

		SOURCE	SITE
ARMENIAN OBSIDIAN	1G	◆	◆
	3A	▲	▲
	4C	◇	◇
ANATOLIAN OBSIDIAN	1E-F	●	●
	2B	○	○

POST-NEOLITHIC TRADE, its directions often traceable by means of luxury items made from obsidian, was cosmopolitan in its extent. Two new sources of supply in the Lake Urmia area of Armenia were developed and Armenian obsidian was traded as far west as the Levant and as far south as Bahrain on the Persian Gulf. Obsidian from Turkey was carried westward to Crete and was transported for the first time across the desert to Mesopotamia. Ethiopian obsidian holds the Near East travel record; a slab of this material, bearing a 16th-century B.C. Egyptian inscription, has been discovered at Boğazköy, a Hittite site in Turkey.

ing. In addition to revealing the pattern and range of contacts among the prehistoric settlements, it gives us a rough picture of trade statistics (through the amounts of material involved) that indicates the strength of the communication links between particular communities. Furthermore, the development of communications over the millenniums after the villages were first established can be traced in the record of the obsidian trade.

As time went on and transportation, aided by the domestication of the ass, improved, the trade in obsidian expanded, both in the number of sources mined and in the distances of distribution. Trade routes developed across the Syrian desert in both directions, and more obsidian began to appear on the Levant coast. Obsidian from Armenia was exported to villages as far distant as Bahrain on the Persian Gulf and the Teheran area near the Caspian Sea. The use of obsidian for tools declined with the coming of the metal ages after 4000 B.C., but it continued to be prized for ornamental objects such as bowls, statuettes and even small articles of household furniture, such as tables. By that time the

Egyptians, apparently obtaining the material from Ethiopia, also had begun to use obsidian for this purpose. A remnant of a little toilette table of obsidian made in Egypt and bearing a hieroglyphic inscription of Pharaoh Chian, of the 16th century B.C., has been found at Bogazköy, the capital of the ancient Hittite kingdom in Turkey. It may have been a gift sent by the Pharaoh to the Hittite king.

By then obsidian itself was no longer an important material of commerce. Nonetheless, the great trade routes that had developed between the cities of the Near East may well have followed the same paths that had first been blazed by the obsidian trade thousands of years earlier.

The analysis of the early obsidian objects now throws new light on the revolution, some 10,000 years ago, that led to man's emergence from the hunter's way of life. There has been a tendency to think of this beginning as an isolated, small-scale phenomenon—of a little tribal group of people settling down somewhere and developing an agricultural system all by itself. In recent years an intensive search has been pursued for

the "birthplace" of this event: Did the first village spring up in the Levant or in the Zagros Mountains on the rim of the fertile crescent or in Turkey? That question now becomes less interesting or significant than it was thought to be. The farming way of life, it appears, originated not at some single location but over whole regions where the peoples of various settlements exchanged ideas and the material means of sustenance.

Throughout the 2,000 years or more during which agriculture was first developing in the Near East the communities dispersed through the region were in more or less continual communication with one another, primarily trading goods but also inevitably sharing their discoveries of agricultural techniques and skills. There is every reason to believe the region functioned essentially as a unit in moving along the road of technological advance. The early villages show considerable diversity in the customs and beliefs that make up what is called a society's "culture," but there can be little doubt that their mutual contact greatly influenced not only their material progress but also their social development and world view.

Ancient Jericho

by Kathleen M. Kenyon
April 1954

*By digging through its layered remains
archaeologists have found that it flourished 4,000 years
before it fell to the Israelites. Indeed, it may be
the oldest town in the world*

And it came to pass at the seventh time, when the priests blew with the trumpets, Joshua said unto the people, Shout; for the Lord hath given you the city . . . and the people shouted with a great shout [and] the wall fell down flat. . . . And they utterly destroyed all that was in the city . . . with the edge of the sword. . . . And they burnt the city with fire, and all that was therein.

Jericho fell to Joshua and the Israelites sometime between 1400 and 1250 B.C. It had had a long, long history before that. Modern archaeologists are greatly interested in the site of this ancient city, for in addition to the romantic attraction of the Biblical story,

the site has other claims to importance. There is reason to believe that Jericho may be the oldest town in the world, and we are finding there a wealth of material evidences of man's first steps toward civilization some 7,000 years ago.

The site of ancient Jericho today is a great mound—a heap entombing dead towns. It contains a series of cities, each built on the ruins of those that went before. The Arabian name for a mound formed of the accumulated remains of human occupation is *tell*. The Jericho tell has a great deal to say indeed; its lowest levels go back to Neolithic times —the late stone-age period when man first took the revolutionary step from a nomadic life of hunting to the settled life of agriculture and community build-

ing. From that step has sprung all human progress: the beginning of architecture, arts, crafts and manufacture, community organization, religion, laws, the invention of writing and ultimately civilization.

Although archaeologists have long been convinced that the Near East is the region where man first made the transition from a wandering to a settled life, the early stages of this transition have been shrouded in the mists of time. There are plenty of human artifacts from the Early Bronze Age in the Near East, but very few from the Neolithic period that preceded it. When, during the latter part of the 19th century and the early years of the 20th, archaeological expeditions began to explore the site of

EARLY NEOLITHIC houses of Jericho had curved walls such as those at left center in this excavation. Running from upper left to lower right are the stones of a Neolithic city wall, probably the oldest in the world. At the left is the base of a later structure.

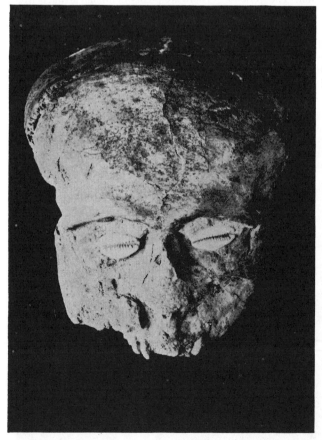

NEOLITHIC PORTRAIT HEADS were made by covering skulls with plaster. The head at the top is shown as it was found. The one at lower left has eyes of cowrie shells. The one at lower right has bands of paint across the top and eyes with vertical slits.

ancient Jericho, there was no suspicion that a prehistoric period lay beneath their spades. Their object was primarily to investigate the story of the capture of Jericho by Joshua's people, to date that event and thereby to throw light on the date of the first Israelite settlement in Palestine.

Between 1930 and 1936 the archaeologist John Garstang, of Liverpool University, carried out a series of deeper and more thorough excavations at Jericho. Far down in the mound, beneath the debris of Early Bronze Age cities, he found some flints and building remains which showed that men had occupied the site in the Neolithic age. His discoveries aroused in some archaeologists a keen desire to investigate the deep Jericho levels further.

The Second World War delayed this investigation. During the 20-year period between the two world wars Palestine in general had been the scene of much archaeological activity, principally by British and U. S. expeditions. Palestine is an area with a remarkably small written history, apart from the Bible. Very few ancient written records of the country have survived, and its history has had to be built up piece by piece from the results of excavations. These have yielded a consecutive history of Palestine from very early times, which has been set down in books such as *The Archaeology of Palestine and the Bible*, by William F. Albright of The Johns Hopkins University.

After the long interruption of World War II and the postwar political troubles in Palestine, archaeologists were keen to resume digging as soon as it became feasible. The British School of Archaeology in Jerusalem sent me to Jordan in 1951 to investigate the possibilities. I found that the Jordan Department of Antiquities was ready to welcome archaeologists and that the American School of Oriental Research in Jerusalem, with which our school had collaborated closely in the past, also wished to undertake excavations again. We had no difficulty in choosing a site: Jericho offered an ideal opportunity. So in January, 1952, a joint Anglo-American expedition of some 20 workers, with myself as director and A. Douglas Tushingham of the American School as assistant director, camped at the Jericho tell and went to work.

The ancient mound is a mile from the modern town of Jericho on the left bank of the River Jordan. It lies in a flat plain 840 feet below sea level. What

LATER NEOLITHIC houses had straight walls. Both walls and floors were covered with polished plaster. However, the people who lived in the houses had not invented pottery.

MIDDLE BRONZE AGE defenses are marked by the two farther men. The nearest man stands atop a later Bronze Age wall. In the foreground is a still later Iron Age structure.

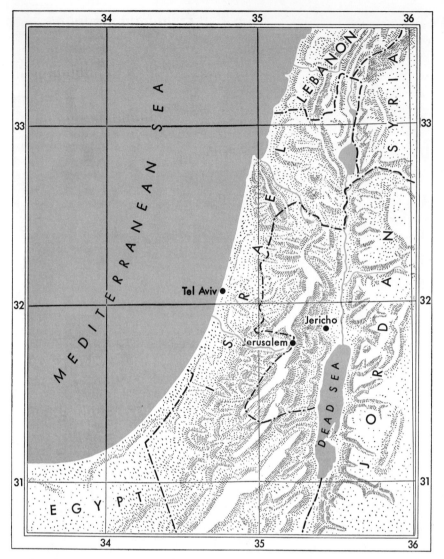

JERICHO IS LOCATED in Jordan near the Dead Sea. It is in the midst of a desert, but has been made habitable for 7,000 years by the copious waters of Elisha's Fountain.

notebook and labels the finds. Drawings are made, so that we have a permanent record of the structures excavated.

The process of excavation is a process of dissection. The archaeologist breaks down the history of the site by peeling off the layers one by one; he traces the history backward from the top down. At Jericho we have found that the surviving deposits go down in some places to depths of about 70 feet. Excavations are still in progress, and only in a very few places have we reached the earliest layers, but we have enough to tell something of a consecutive story of the site.

Garstang had discovered the Neolithic levels at the northwest end of the tell. The depth of deposit is so great there that he sounded the lowest levels only with a relatively narrow shaft. The present expedition is continuing the clearance of the levels he sounded. One of our first surprises was the discovery of Neolithic artifacts at a place on the west side of the tell some distance from where Garstang had found his. The Stone Age remains here were only about four feet below the surface, presumably because later levels in this place have been eroded or quarried away. What was remarkable about this discovery was that it showed that even in Neolithic times the settlement already covered a considerable area and had grown beyond the dimensions of a mere village.

In this area on the west side of the tell excavation has reached bedrock in some places. Just above the rock we have found rude huts which may be the Jericho settlers' earliest experiments in architecture. They are mud-brick structures with curved walls, and they look like a translation of the round tents and temporary structures of nomadic hunters into a more permanent material. This phase appears to have been short. The next stage (represented by a type of house discovered by Garstang at the north end) was a very big advance. These houses were rectangular, with solidly built walls, wide doorways and rooms grouped around courtyards. Most striking of all is the fact that the walls and floors were finished with highly burnished coats of fine plaster, giving a most sophisticated appearance. These houses belonged to a firmly established community, and moreover a well-organized one, for at this stage the settlement apparently was surrounded by a massive town wall.

These Stone Age people still had no pottery—a fact which underlines how close we are here to the beginnings of

has made it habitable through all these thousands of years is a never-failing supply of fresh water gushing from Elisha's Fountain. We began systematically to uncover the ancient Jerichos, layer by layer. Modern archaeological research is built upon foundations laid by the great 19th-century archaeologist Sir Flinders Petrie, a pioneer far ahead of his time. The dating of ancient cultures must depend, when inscriptions are lacking, upon the evolution of artifacts, especially pottery. Petrie showed that each stage of human history in the East had a distinctive pottery, and that one could establish a pottery sequence, some stages of which could be linked with inscriptions of known date in Egypt or Mesopotamia. On the foundations created by Petrie this sequence has now been built up, period by period, so that it is now possible for an archaeologist to date finds with considerable accuracy

as far back as the beginning of the Early Bronze Age, about 3000 B.C.

The basic method of stratigraphy, as Petrie enunciated it in 1890, is to establish a fixed reference point and record the level of each find (in number of feet) above that point. This technique has its limitations, because an archaeological layer may slope instead of being horizontal or may have been cut into by later occupants. Since Petrie's time the method has been considerably refined. Each layer of soil is now traced through and treated as an entity; the finds discovered in that structure (*e.g.*, a floor level) are then dated by it.

Obviously such work requires close supervision by experts, for the workmen doing the digging cannot be expected to identify or understand the significance of the layers. Each small gang works under the direct supervision of a field assistant, who records the layers in a

settled life, for pots and pans, a primary necessity, are one of the first technical inventions of settled man. No doubt the reason men settled here lies in the natural advantages of the site. The copious stream that emerges from the rock beside the settlement made the soil of the Jordan Valley, with its tropical climate, exceedingly fertile; the modern Jericho is still a brilliant green oasis in this arid land. The inhabitants of Jericho could be assured of success in their first experiments in agriculture, and the settlement could become truly permanent.

The progress of those early settlers was not in material things alone. In the Neolithic levels we unearthed a room which in all probability was a small shrine. At one end of the room we found a niche with a rough stone pedestal, and nearby lay a carefully worked bit of volcanic stone which must have been a cult object and probably stood on the pedestal. Figurines of animals modeled in clay suggest that the religion of these early agriculturists was a fertility cult..

Our expedition's most remarkable find so far is a group of seven portrait heads. On actual human skulls the artist had modeled features in plaster. The heads have an astonishingly lifelike appearance. There can be little doubt that they are portraits, probably of venerated ancestors. Thus we are looking at the faces of individuals who died 7,000 years or more ago. These portraits are among the earliest examples of human art.

We do not yet know the exact date of this early settlement, but we guess it to be about 5000 B.C., and hope soon to have our guess tested by radiocarbon analysis of the charcoal from its layers. Its life was certainly a long one, for its successive layers of houses make a mound many feet high. Above this pre-pottery Neolithic stage we find the ruins of a second Neolithic stage in which pottery appears. This stage again lasted a considerable time, and added further height to the mound. By the time Jericho approaches the dawn of the historic period, after 3000 B.C., its walls crown a mound already some 60 feet high.

In the Early Bronze Age, a period of great urban development in Palestine, Jericho became an important walled city. It guarded a gateway through which nomads from the desert to the east were continually trying to force their way into the more fertile lands of Palestine. The Jericho city walls were breached and rebuilt no fewer than 17 times; time and again they were damaged or destroyed by enemies or by natural agencies such as earthquakes. About 2100 B.C. they

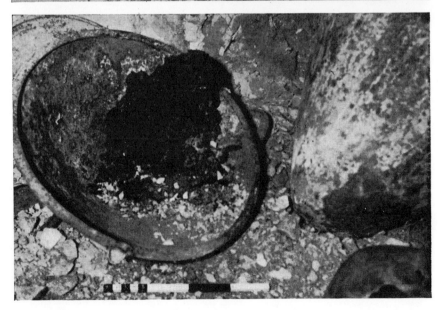

MIDDLE BRONZE AGE TOMB was occupied by a skeleton and remarkably well-preserved grave goods. The skeleton is shown at the top. In the middle is a basket containing toilet articles. At the bottom is a dish containing the remains of a large slab of meat.

were totally destroyed by the nomadic Amorites who overran much of Palestine. The city was burned to the ground.

There followed some 200 years of cultural sterility. The newcomers were not town dwellers. Their houses and equipment were simple and primitive. But about 1900 B.C. well-built houses and city walls again begin to appear at Jericho. They were built by a new people, probably from the north, who brought with them the advanced culture of the Middle Bronze Age. Under them Jericho grew to the greatest size it has ever attained. Its walls were rebuilt on a new system with the base defended by a sloping ramp, presumably against the approach of chariots.

Our best evidence for the culture of these people comes from a number of tombs which we have been fortunate enough to find intact. The hot climate of the Jordan Valley has preserved their contents—wood, textiles, basketwork, even food. Everywhere else in Palestine such objects have perished; hence the Jericho remains are the first material evidences of the culture of Palestine in the period around the 17th century B.C.

Each tomb is rich in provisions of food, drink and household equipment that were left with the dead for the afterlife. The furniture was simple: wooden tables, stools and beds, all made with considerable skill. Wooden or pottery bowls held the food, and great four-handled jars, each provided with a small dipper, contained the drink. There were rush mats, toilet accessories in wooden boxes or in alabaster flasks, many wooden combs and other small objects in baskets. We have even recovered fragments of clothing, which when they are analyzed should tell us how they were woven and of what materials.

The Middle Bronze Age came to an end with another sack of the city, probably at the hands of the Egyptians about 1560 B.C. There, unfortunately, most of the archaeological history of Jericho comes to an end. Garstang found a few remnants of structures going down to about 1350 B.C. But over most of the rest of the mound erosion and human depredations have removed all traces of the Jericho after the 16th century B.C. No sign of the walls attacked by Joshua has been found. Nevertheless, though we have been disappointed in our search for the city of the Biblical story, this disappointment has been more than compensated by the uncovering of its remarkable earlier history. It is hoped that our further excavations will continue to be as richly rewarded.

A Neolithic City in Turkey

by James Mellaart
April 1964

*An ancient mound now known as Çatal Hüyük has
yielded evidence that communities with highly
developed economic structure, religion and art existed
as long ago as 7000 B.C. and perhaps even earlier*

Excavations on the Anatolian plateau of Turkey a few years ago
provided an answer to an archaeological question of long standing about
Neolithic culture. The Neolithic is the
stage of civilization at which men began
to cultivate crops and to domesticate
animals and as a result of these activities
to dwell in permanent settlements; in
the Near East this stage occurred roughly between 7000 B.C. and 5000 B.C. The
question was how Neolithic culture had
moved from the Near East into Europe.
The answer was that the movement was
overland, by way of the Anatolian plateau. Such a route had long seemed to
archaeologists a logical supposition, but
until Neolithic communities were excavated on the plateau there had been
no direct evidence to support the supposition [see "Hacilar: A Neolithic Village Site," by James Mellaart, SCIEN-
TIFIC AMERICAN, August, 1961].

In answering one question, however,
these excavations raised another: What
were the origins of the culture of which
Hacilar was representative? The Late
Neolithic culture found at Hacilar had
arrived there fully developed. The long
gap between its arrival, probably about
6000 B.C., and the desertion of a pre-
pottery village on the same site some
500 years earlier needed investigation.
The gap appeared to correspond to the
Early Neolithic period. If an Early Neolithic site could be excavated on the
plateau, it might indicate the origin of
the Hacilar culture and provide a longer
culture sequence.

We had such a site in mind. I had
found it about 30 miles southeast of the
modern city of Konya in 1958: an ancient mound (*hüyük* in Turkish) bearing
the name Çatal. The mound, covered
with weeds and thistles, stood in the
middle of a great plain. Lying on what

was once the bank of a river (now ca-
nalized into other channels to prevent
flooding) that flows from the Taurus
Mountains onto the plain, it rose gently
from the fields to a height of 50 feet.

Çatal Hüyük seemed to be the most
promising of some 200 sites we had visited on the Konya plain. A preliminary
investigation indicated, to our delight,
that the site belonged substantially, if
not wholly, to the Early Neolithic period. Small fragments of pottery and
broken obsidian arrowheads showed
an unmistakable resemblance to those
found in the deepest Neolithic levels at
Mersin on the southern coast of Turkey,
and at Çatal Hüyük they were on top
of the mound. Moreover, the pottery
looked more primitive than anything we
had found at Hacilar.

So it was that Çatal Hüyük's 8,000
years of slumber came to an end on May
17, 1961, when our party began excavations. Ten days later the first Neolithic
paintings ever found on man-made walls
were exposed, and it was clear that
Çatal Hüyük was no ordinary site. Succeeding excavations in 1962 and 1963
have confirmed this impression. With its
story only partly revealed by the excavations to date, Çatal Hüyük has already
added to the archaeological evidence
that the development of towns and
cities (as distinct from villages) goes
farther back in antiquity than had been
thought. Çatal Hüyük deserves the
name of city: it was a community with
an extensive economic development,
specialized crafts, a rich religious life,
a surprising attainment in art and an
impressive social organization.

For the opportunity to explore this
story we are indebted to several organizations. Our excavations have been supported by the Wenner-Gren Foundation
for Anthropological Research, the Bol-

lingen Foundation, the British Academy,
the University of London, the University of Edinburgh, the Royal Ontario
Museum, the Australian Institute of
Archaeology, the University of Canter-
bury in New Zealand and the late
Francis Neilson. The Shell Oil Company
and British Petroleum Aegean Limited
provided technical help. Numerous
other institutions have contributed in
such ways as sending experts to the site
or making analyses of material found at
the site.

Çatal Hüyük covers 32 acres and so
is easily the largest known Neolithic site, although how much of the
site was occupied at any given period
cannot be said with certainty. Apparently the settlement grew up from the
riverbank, and the substantial part of
the mound that spreads back from the
river therefore dates from later phases
of settlement. Our excavations, covering
about one acre, have so far been concentrated on the southwest side of the
mound, in a quarter that appears to have
been sacred and residential. Because
we have found nothing but finished
goods in this area, we assume that the
bazaar quarter with the workshops lies
elsewhere in the mound.

With different quarters for different
activities, a clear specialization in crafts
and a social stratification that is obvious
in both the size of the houses and the
quality of burial gifts, this settlement
was not a village of farmers, however
rich. It was far more than that. In fact,
its remains are as urban as those of any
site from the succeeding Bronze Age yet
excavated in Turkey.

We have found at Çatal Hüyük 12
superimposed building levels, which we
have numbered from 0 to VI-A and
VI-B to X according to their apparent

chronology from latest to earliest [*see illustration on page 129*]. All these levels belong to a single culture that was uninterrupted in development and shows no signs of destruction attributable to outside forces. The entire sequence so far discovered appears to cover the seventh millennium B.C., although radiocarbon dating of Çatal Hüyük materials now in progress at the University of Pennsylvania may provide a more precise time scale. The core of the mound, however, remains to be sounded, and a full 10 meters of deposit there may take the origins of Çatal Hüyük back to the end of the last continental glaciation.

Houses at Çatal Hüyük were built of shaped mud brick of standard sizes. Because the nearest stone was several

miles away and would have been difficult to bring to the site, the foundations of the houses also consist of mud brick, laid in several courses. By these foundations it is possible to recognize buildings even if their floors are gone, as is the case in Level 0. The houses were rectangular, usually with a small storeroom attached [*see the illustration on page 126*]. Apparently these dwellings were one-story structures, perhaps with a wooden veranda.

The houses show a remarkable consistency of plan inside. Along the east wall there were two raised platforms with a higher bench at the southern end. This arrangement constituted a "divan," used for sitting, working and sleeping. The smaller corner platform evidently belonged to the male owner and the

larger central platform to the women and children. This hierarchic convention appears from Level X to Level II and probably existed in Levels I and 0, of which little remains. There are numerous variations on this arrangement of built-in furniture, including situations in which platforms appear along the north or west wall. The hearth was invariably at the south end of the room, sometimes accompanied by an oven and less often by a kiln. There was a reason for this location of the fires: it had to do with the manner in which the houses were entered.

The entrance was, as in some American Indian villages, a hole in the roof, over which there was surely some sort of canopy-like shelter. The roof opening was always on the south side of the

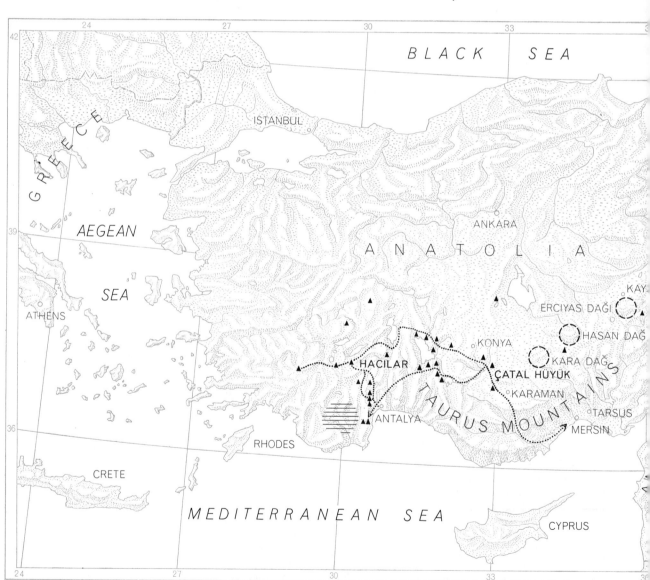

AREA OF NEAR EAST in which the culture represented by Çatal Hüyük was located is shown. Triangular symbols show Neolithic sites; circled areas indicate sources of obsidian; hatched areas, sources of flint. Çatal Hüyük was chosen for extensive archaeological work after excavations at Hacilar revealed a Late Neolithic culture that had arrived fully developed from some other place. Çatal

dwelling; thus it served both as a smoke hole and as an entrance. All access from the outside to the roof was by a movable ladder. From the roof into the dwelling the usual access was by a fixed ladder, although some buildings had another entrance through a well-plastered ventilation shaft that apparently had a movable ladder. Communication between dwellings was accomplished over the rooftops. There is little evidence of lanes and passages, and the courtyards that exist (often merely a ruined house) appear to have been used only for rubbish disposal and excreta.

The system of roof entrances meant that the outside of the settlement presented a solid blank wall. This was a check against enemies and also against

Hüyük apparently represents a culture that was a forerunner of Hacilar's and eventually may be traced back farther than 7000 B.C.

floods. It was evidently a successful defense system, as is indicated by the absence of any signs of massacre. About all any attackers could do—armed as they were with nothing more than bow and arrow, slings and stone tools—was to raid the cattle kept in corrals on the edge of the settlement or to set fire to the roofs. The defenders, in contrast, had the advantage of height and probably of superior numbers. In any case, because of the successful defense the only form of destruction suffered by Çatal Hüyük was fire. Most of the buildings in levels from VI to II were destroyed by fire; but with numerous hearths and ovens and the high winds of the region a disastrous fire about once a century is no more than could be expected.

As a result of these fires the carbonized remains of cereal grains and other foods are plentiful at Çatal Hüyük. There are also many animal bones. The food remains and the bones tell a great deal about the domestic economy of the settlement; the studies being made of them by the paleoethnobiologist Hans Helbaek of the National Museum of Denmark and the zoologist Dexter Perkins, Jr., of Harvard University will probably yield important additional information.

On the basis of what is now known Helbaek has described the grain finds as "the largest, richest and best preserved of all early cereal deposits so far recovered," providing "some of the most significant genetical and cultural" data yet obtained about early civilization. The grains, unlike the finds in other early Near Eastern settlements of cultivated plants little removed from their wild ancestors, include such hybrids and mutants as naked six-row barley and hexaploid free-threshing wheat, which were introduced into Europe from Anatolia in the sixth millennium B.C. The use made of the grains is indicated by the grain bins found in every house and the many mortars for dehusking and querns for grinding. In addition to cereals, peas and lentils the community grew bitter vetch and some other crops; the residents also collected nuts, fruits and berries.

The zoological remains are no less interesting: they show the presence of domesticated sheep even below Level X and cows as early as Level VII. Goats and dogs also appear to have been domesticated, but there is no indication that pigs were. Their absence may be due to religious considerations. Although the domesticated animals provided the community with wool, milk, meat and

skins, the people had by no means abandoned hunting. Wild cattle and red deer were extensively hunted, as were wild asses, wild sheep, boars and leopards.

With such an abundant diet it is not surprising to find from the skeletons that the inhabitants were generally healthy. Bone disease was rare, teeth were good and this dolichocephalic (long-headed) people were fairly tall: the males ranged from about five feet six inches to five feet 10 and the females from five feet to five feet eight. Still, as is to be expected of such an ancient era, few individuals reached middle age.

The burials were inside the houses, beneath the platforms. Most of the skeletons we have found are those of women and children; presumably many of the males died away from home on hunting or fighting forays. The dead were buried in a contracted position, usually lying on their left side with feet toward the wall. Isolated burials were rare; some buildings contain several generations of a family, with 30 or more burials. It appears to have been the practice before final burial to strip the bodies of flesh by a preliminary interment, or by exposure to vultures, insects or microorganisms on an outdoor platform, sheltered by gabled structures built of reeds and mats. Thereafter the bones, still more or less held in position by the ligaments, were wrapped in cloth and given final burial, often being laid out on mats of cloth, skin or fur.

The burials provide information about the dress, weapons and jewelry of the Çatal Hüyük people. Male dress consisted of a loincloth or a leopard skin, fastened by a belt with a bone hook and eye; the men appear also to have worn cloaks fastened with antler toggles in the winter. The women wore sleeveless bodices and jerkins of leopard skin, with fringed skirts or string skirts—the ends of the string being encased in copper tubes for weighting. The women used bone pins for fastening garments.

Weapons buried with the men included polished stone maceheads, obsidian arrowheads and javelin heads and sometimes an obsidian spearhead. Frequently there was a fine flint dagger with a chalk or bone handle and a leather sheath.

Jewelry was mainly for the women and children. They wore the necklaces, armlets, bracelets and anklets we found made of beads and pendants in a great variety of stone, shell, chalk, clay, mother-of-pearl and (as early as Level IX) copper and lead. Cosmetics were

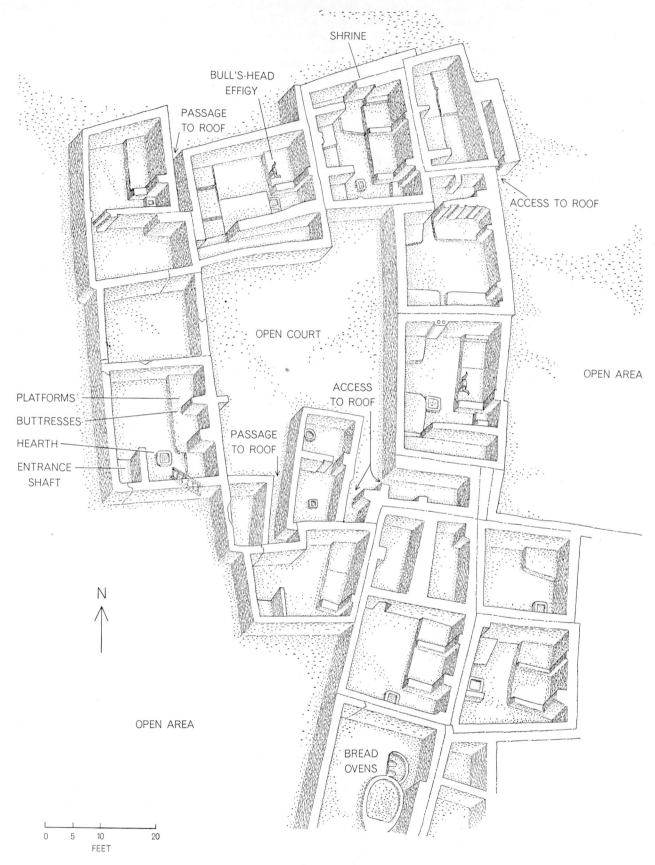

SHRINE

BULL'S-HEAD
EFFIGY

PASSAGE
TO ROOF

ACCESS TO ROOF

OPEN COURT

OPEN AREA

PLATFORMS

BUTTRESSES

HEARTH

ENTRANCE
SHAFT

ACCESS
TO ROOF

PASSAGE
TO ROOF

ACCESS
TO ROOF

N

OPEN AREA

BREAD
OVENS

0   5   10   20
FEET

COMMUNITY ARRANGEMENTS of 8,000 years ago in a Neolithic city are depicted on the basis of recent excavations. This is a reconstruction of an area in the fifth of 12 building layers so far found at the Çatal Hüyük site on the Anatolian plateau of Turkey.

Access to the buildings was solely from the roof, so that the exterior walls presented a solid blank face, which served effectively as a defense against both attackers and floods. Çatal Hüyük showed a surprising evolution of civilization for so early a community.

SITE OF NEOLITHIC CITY is this mound on the Anatolian plateau of Turkey. The Turkish word for mound is *hüyük*, and this one, which rises 50 feet above the plain, has the modern name of Çatal. After the inhabitants left about 6000 B.C. it lay deserted for 8,000 years; when excavations were started in 1961, it was heavily overgrown. In this photograph the view is from west of the site.

GENERAL VIEW OF EXCAVATIONS at Çatal Hüyük shows work in progress in Level VI, which is near the middle of the 12 levels of construction explored to date. The author chose Çatal Hüyük as the most promising of more than 200 sites he visited on the Anatolian plateau in a search for a representative Early Neolithic community. The site proved to have been a major settlement.

EXCAVATED SHRINE is in Level VI. Three plaster heads of bulls appear atop one another on the west wall, with a half-meter scale below them; on the north wall is a ram's head made of plaster. At bottom right is the remaining part of a small pillar.

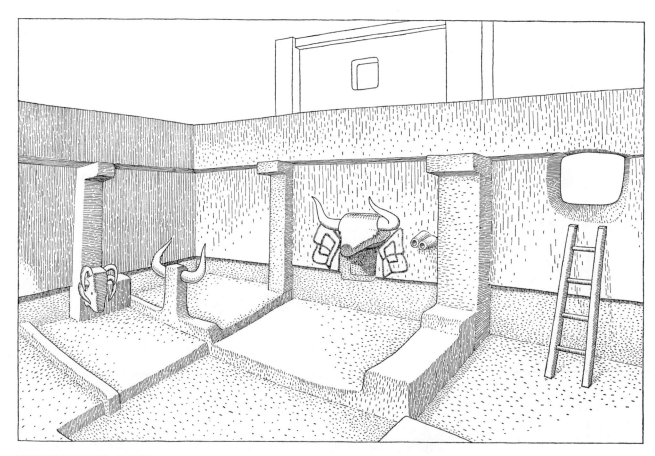

RECONSTRUCTED SHRINE is the same as that shown above. The drawing represents the author's conception, based on excavations of several shrines at Çatal Hüyük, of how the room might have looked in Neolithic times. The stylized heads of animals and women's breasts probably were fertility symbols. Many of the city's shrines also had wall paintings of remarkable sophistication.

widely used, judging from the number of related articles we found, such as palettes and grinders for their preparation, baskets or the shells of fresh-water mussels for their containers and delicate bone pins for their application. The cosmetics probably consisted of red ocher, blue azurite, green malachite and perhaps galena. The women, once arrayed, used mirrors of highly polished obsidian to see the effect.

Several times we found food remains with the dead: berries, peas, lentils, eggs or a joint of meat put next to the deceased in baskets or in wooden bowls and boxes, which are carved with great delicacy. These wooden vessels are a characteristic of the Çatal Hüyük culture, and even when pottery began to appear in quantity around 6500 B.C., baskets and wooden bowls continued in use and had a strong influence on the pottery. The ovals and boat shapes, the lozenges and rectangles that appear in the pottery, not only from Level VI-A upward at Çatal Hüyük but also in the following Late Neolithic of Hacilar, have their origins in the wood-carving tradition of early Çatal Hüyük. In the same way numerous pottery vessels have features such as handles that derive from the earlier basketry.

The first production of pottery at Çatal Hüyük is found in Levels X and IX, but evidently this soft ware could not compete with traditional wood and woven products. It was not until the end of Level VI-A, when technical improvements had led to the production of an excellent hard baked ware, that pottery came into general use. The pottery was handmade and highly burnished. At first it was all dark brown or black; cooking pots were left that way but other objects were soon turned out in red, buff or mottled tones. In the upper levels of the mound animal heads start to appear on oval cups, and an over-all red slip, or coating, is in use, but painting on pottery was apparently never achieved. This pottery develops without a break into that of Late Neolithic Hacilar.

Another area in which Çatal Hüyük shows a people of remarkable technical competence and sophistication is textiles. We found some carbonized textiles in burials as far down as Level VI. They appear to have been wool, and at least three different types of weaving can be distinguished. These are the earliest textiles yet known; Helbaek has written of them that "we shall be hard put to it to find evidence of more perfect work anywhere within the following thousand years."

It is singular that with all these products of human workmanship we have found so few traces of the workmen. None of the 200 houses and shrines excavated so far has shown any evidence that any art or craft other than food preparation was carried on within. We have much fine woolen cloth but only one or two spindle whorls or loom weights, and these are from fill rather than from floor deposits. We have thousands of finely worked obsidian tools but only two small boxes of chips, thousands of bone tools but no piles of waste or splinters. Somewhere in the mound there must be the workshops of the weavers and basketmakers; the matmakers; the carpenters and joiners; the men who made the polished stone tools (axes and adzes, polishers and grinders, chisels, maceheads and palettes); the bead makers who drilled in stone beads holes that no modern steel needle can penetrate and who carved pendants and used stone inlays; the makers of shell beads from dentalium, cowrie and fossil oyster; the flint and obsidian knappers who produced the pressure-flaked daggers, spearheads, lance heads, arrowheads, knives, sickle blades, scrapers and

borers; the merchants of skin, leather and fur; the workers in bone who made the awls, punches, knives, scrapers, ladles, spoons, bowls, scoops, spatulas, bodkins, belt hooks, antler toggles, pins and cosmetic sticks; the carvers of wooden bowls and boxes; the mirror makers; the bowmakers; the men who hammered native copper into sheets and worked it into beads, pendants, rings and other trinkets; the builders; the merchants and traders who obtained all the raw material; and finally the artists—the carvers of statuettes, the modelers and the painters.

The unusual wealth of the city of Çatal Hüyük, as manifested by this great variety of sophisticated workmanship, is a phenomenon as yet without parallel in the Neolithic period. At the base of course lay the new efficiency of food production, transplanted from its probable origin in the hills to the fertile alluvial plain. Although that may account for the unprecedented size of the city, something else is needed to explain the community's almost explosive development in arts and crafts.

The key undoubtedly lies in the community's dependence on the import of

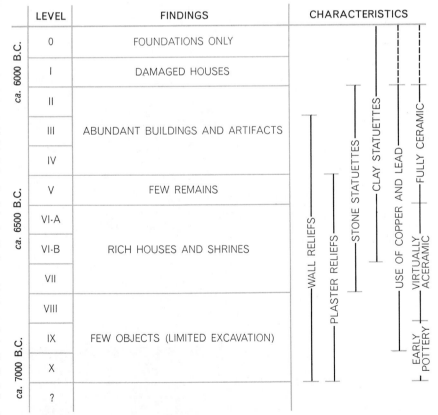

CHRONOLOGY OF HABITATION at Çatal Hüyük is indicated in this chart. Each level above VI-B apparently was built because of fire damage to the preceding level; the site appears to have been deserted after a fire in Level 0. Levels may yet be found below X.

NEOLITHIC ARTIFACTS found at Level VI of Çatal Hüyük and dating from about 6500 B.C. include bone necklace, bone pin, stone beads, limestone bracelet and obsidian mirror.

WALL PAINTING found in Level VI shows children's hands. Çatal Hüyük yielded the earliest known paintings on man-made walls. Most of the painting had a religious purpose.

raw materials (other than clay, timber and food) from near and far. One cannot possibly be wrong in suggesting that it was a well-organized trade that produced the city's wealth. Moreover, it appears likely that the trade in obsidian was at the heart of this extensive commerce. This black volcanic glass, which first appeared in the preceding Mesolithic period, became the most widespread trading commodity during the Neolithic period in the Near East. It has been found in the "proto-Neolithic" and prepottery Neolithic periods at Jericho; it occurs as far south as Beidha near Petra; it reached Cyprus in the sixth millennium. The origin of this obsidian, which was the best material of the time for cutting tools, was almost certainly central Anatolia, and it is extremely likely that the city of Çatal Hüyük controlled this source and organized the trade. The then active volcanoes of Hasan Dağ, Karaca Dağ, Mekke Dağ and others lie on the edge of the Konya plain. The nearest is some 50 miles east of Çatal Hüyük, and all are visible on a clear day. These sources of obsidian were well within the limits of the culture area of which Çatal Hüyük was the undisputed center.

This hegemony was not only economic but also religious and therefore political; in the ancient world no authority could exist without religious sanction. About the political system of Çatal Hüyük one can do little more than guess because there are no writings from the community. It seems likely, however, that at such an early stage of civilization only the priests could have been the bearers of authority.

Of the religious system one can say more because of the shrines and religious art we have found at Çatal Hüyük. In my view they constitute the community's most important archaeological contribution. I would maintain, perhaps wrongly, that the Neolithic religion of Çatal Hüyük (and of Hacilar) was created by women. In contrast to nearly all other earlier and later "fertility cults" of the Near East, it significantly lacks the element of sexual vulgarity and eroticism that is almost automatically associated with fertility and probably is the male's contribution. If the Çatal Hüyük religion is a creation of women, one has the rare opportunity of exploring Neolithic woman's mind by studying the symbolism she used in her effort to comprehend and influence the mysteries of life and death.

Of these symbols there is an abundance. In addition to schematic clay figurines of people and more naturalistic animal figures, there is a unique collection of fine statuettes. Those from the upper layers are modeled in clay; those in the lower layers are carved from stone. Beyond these, which together with burial rites are usually the archaeologist's only sources of information about religion, Çatal Hüyük has produced no fewer than 40 shrines and sanctuaries. They are at every level, but the nine in Level VI-A, the 12 in Level VI-B and the eight in Level VII are particularly rich in information. Wall decorations occur in most: painted scenes with numerous human figures in Levels III and IV; modeled and sometimes painted reliefs in Levels VI-A through X.

The shrines, although frequently large and well appointed, do not differ in plan from the houses, but they are much more lavishly decorated [*see illustration on page 128*]. Even if they were not continuously lived in, they served as burial places, presumably for their priestesses and the priestesses' families. It is only in the shrines that we have found reliefs and symbolism connected with life and death. From these it is possible to reconstruct in some degree the Neolithic pantheon.

The supreme deity was the Great Goddess. Often represented beside her are a daughter and a young son. A bearded god, who is always shown on a bull, was perhaps the Great Goddess' husband. No other deities appear. This group, therefore, probably constitutes the "holy family." Statues and reliefs represent the female deities either as two goddesses or as twins. The idea behind the duplication is evidently that of age and fertility, the whole aim of the religion being to ensure the continuity of life in every aspect: wildlife for the hunter, domesticated life for the civilized communities and finally the life of Neolithic man himself.

It is doubtful that Neolithic thought regarded these as four distinct deities. More likely the representations show aspects of the goddess as mother or as daughter and virgin, with the god as consort or son. The role of the male deity is more pronounced at Çatal Hüyük than it is at Hacilar, perhaps because in Çatal Hüyük hunting and the domestication of wild animals still held major importance, but in general the male plays a subsidiary role.

Scenes dealing with life are generally found on the west wall of the shrines. A typical scene shows the goddess giving birth to a bull or ram. Scenes dealing with death are found on the east

CLAY SEALS, most about the size of a postage stamp, apparently were used for identification. No house had more than one, and all the designs differed. These were in Levels II–IV.

STATUE OF GODDESS, done in clay and about eight inches high, shows her giving birth. Many representations of the goddess were found at Çatal Hüyük; this was in Level II.

wall: in three shrines the east-wall paintings show vultures attacking headless human corpses. Usually, however, the subject of death is expressed in more subtle ways. Representations of women's breasts, for example, which are of course symbolic of life, contained such items as the skulls of vultures, the lower jaws of wild boars and the heads of foxes and weasels—all scavengers and devourers of corpses.

The symbolism of west and east walls, or right and left, is matched by black and red: the red associated with life, the black with death. Panels of red hands are common, and several burial sites show remains of a coating of red ocher, which was evidently intended to be a substitute for blood and so a means of restoring life, at least symbolically. A great black bull covered the vulture paintings; both were symbolic of death. Contrasted with these was another painting of an enormous red bull surrounded by minute jubilant people.

There are some strange figures in the shrines. A stern-looking representation of the goddess was found with a headless bird, probably a vulture. Numerous figures roughly carved out of stalactites suggest a link with the dark world of caves, man's first refuge and sanctuary. An odd painting seems to represent a honeycomb with eggs or chrysalises on boughs and with bees or butterflies, which perhaps symbolize the souls of the dead. It is framed by alternate red and black hands along the top and gray and pink hands along the base. An earlier painting shows alternate red and black lines, resembling a net, similarly framed by hands. Net patterns decorate several other religious scenes, together

with symbols of horns, crosses and hands. Crosses, perhaps a simplified form of a four-petaled flower, were painted on a statuette of the goddess as well as on numerous walls; probably they are to be interpreted as fertility symbols. Rosettes and the double ax (or butterfly) are in the same category.

In several shrines and houses schematized heads of bulls in the form of a pillar serve as a cult symbol for protection. We have found curious benches with one, two, three or seven pairs of the bone cores of horns stuck in the sides. These defy explanation. Perhaps they figured in the burial rites, conceivably serving as a bier while the grave was dug.

Of the rites performed in the shrines little can be said. It is apparent, however, from the absence of blood pits and animal bones that there was no sacrificing of animals in the shrines. There were offerings of other kinds. In a shrine in Level II we found grain that had been burned on the plastered ceremonial altar and then covered by a new coat of plaster; this suggests the first offering after the harvest. In the earlier buildings, particularly in Level VI, there are offerings of all sorts: pots that doubtless contained food and drink; groups of hunting weapons, maces, axes and ceremonial flint daggers; tools; bags of obsidian; beads and many other objects, all unused or in pristine condition.

The wall paintings were mostly created for religious occasions and were covered with white plaster after they had outlived their usefulness. The paint was made of minerals mixed with fat; the painter worked with a brush on a white, cream or pale pink surface. The

range of colors is extensive. Red in all shades, including pink, mauve and orange, is predominant. The other colors are white, lemon yellow, purple, black and (very infrequently) blue. We have yet to find green. In a class apart from the religious paintings are several paintings of textile patterns, which attest the importance attached to weaving. Many of them show kilims, or woven carpets, making carpet weaving an art that can now be traced back to Neolithic times.

Many seasons of work remain at Çatal Hüyük. It is therefore premature to speak definitively about the origins of this remarkable civilization. It can be said, however, that the discovery of the art of Çatal Hüyük has demonstrated that the Upper Paleolithic tradition of naturalistic painting, which died in western Europe with the end of the ice age, not only survived but flourished in Anatolia. The implication is that at least part of the population of Çatal Hüyük was of Upper Paleolithic stock.

These people may not have been the first to learn the arts of cereal cultivation and animal husbandry, but they improved on the techniques to such an extent that they were able to produce the surplus of food that permits the beginning of leisure and specialization. By the seventh millennium they had created the first Mediterranean civilization, of which Çatal Hüyük is such an impressive representative. In time the offshoots of that civilization reached the Aegean shore, and by the sixth millennium Anatolian colonists were laying the foundations for the ultimate development of civilization in Europe.

17,000 Years of Greek Prehistory

by Thomas W. Jacobsen
June 1976

Excavations at a site in the Peloponnesus show evidence of human habitation from the Ice Age through Neolithic times. They reveal the basic economic foundation of the Classical Greek civilization

The contribution of Classical Greece to modern civilization is so well known that Athens is virtually a synonym for high culture. The earlier Bronze Age cultures of the Mycenaean Greeks and the Minoans of Crete are also familiar to many. Until recently, however, little was known about still earlier stages in the human history of Greece: the Old Stone Age and the New. Now archaeological fieldwork at a site in southern Greece has uncovered a remarkable record of those earlier stages. Stratified deposits formed in late Paleolithic times, more than 20,000 years ago, are overlain by a virtually uninterrupted sequence of remains that extends to the end of Neolithic times, only 5,000 years ago. The site, a cave and its immediate surroundings on a rocky headland named Franchthi on the coast of the Argive Peninsula, is unique in Greece for the span of cultural development it preserves. Its archaeological record documents some of man's earliest efforts to come to terms with an environment that was often hostile and testifies to his increasingly complex interactions with the plant and animal life and the land and sea of Greece. It was these interactions that provided the foundations of Greek civilization.

The rich stratigraphic record of Franchthi Cave enables us to ask seminal questions about conditions in Greece during and immediately after the last major glaciation in Europe. For example, how· was the area affected by the retreat of the European ice sheet some 10,000 years ago? What can we learn, beyond a mere descriptive inventory of material remains, about the daily life of the people who lived in the area? How did the environment that confronted a Neolithic Greek farmer differ from that encountered by a Paleolithic hunter-gatherer in the same area thousands of years earlier? For that matter, how did man's activities over the millenniums affect the environment?

Environmental studies suggest that the earliest human activity known at Franchthi approximately coincided with the coldest phase of the Würm glaciation, the last of the European ice ages. In other parts of southeastern Europe, in certain areas of the Middle East and apparently in much of Greece

the climate was cold and dry. Vegetation was sparse; the landscape was open and resembled a steppe. Shorelines were some kilometers seaward of today's coast because much of the earth's water was stored in the great ice sheets.

This cold and dry period, when the annual range of temperatures in southern Greece may have been much like that in mountainous areas of northern Greece today, was followed by a time of gradually increasing warmth and moisture. As the Würm ice sheet shrank, the sea level slowly rose and the coastline moved inland. Trees invaded the sparsely vegetated landscape until the steppe became a region of woodland and open glades. As we shall see, this climatic change seems to have had a marked effect on the lives of the hunter-gatherers in the Argive.

In the Franchthi area the surface rocks are heavily eroded limestones that rest on a substrate of igneous rocks. Here and there, where the erosion has removed the limestone cover and exposed the harder substrate, the soils that have developed are particularly fertile. On the fringes of these exposures, where the limestones and the impermeable igneous rock meet, springs are fairly common. Elsewhere the terrain is marked by features such as caves and sinkholes that are characteristic of what geologists call a karst landscape. Franchthi Cave, which shelters much of the archaeological deposit at the site, is one such feature. In this semiarid environment, notable for its long, dry summers, the perennial springs in the vicinity of the cave must have been a major attraction to man.

The cave lies at the western tip of the Franchthi headland. Today its mouth is no more than 15 meters above sea level and only about 75 meters from the shore. The cave is now about 150 meters deep, but originally it was much larger. Rockfalls in the interior have blocked off most of the sheltered area, and one of them left a window in the roof of the cave. This catastrophic event, possibly caused by an earthquake, seems to have taken place about 3000 B.C. It may have been the main reason the cave

was abandoned as a living site late in the Neolithic period.

The archaeological excavations at Franchthi were begun in 1967. Since then there have been five additional seasons of fieldwork, the most recent in 1974. Our group from Indiana University has conducted the investigation in collaboration with workers from the University of Pennsylvania and other American and European institutions; the work has been done under the auspices of the Greek Archaeological Service and the American School of Classical Studies at Athens. In the opening seasons our interests were focused on the cave, where we made several trial soundings. Two of them, designated H/H-1 and F/A on our site plan, were ultimately excavated to a depth of nine and 11 meters respectively. They provide the stratigraphic framework for the site as a whole.

The two soundings revealed well-stratified and mutually complementary sequences of archaeological remains that document successive human occupations of the cave. The earlier of the cultures represented are reminiscent of the Upper Paleolithic and the Mesolithic elsewhere in Europe. (The Mesolithic is the transitional period between the Paleolithic and the Neolithic in the Old World.) Thanks largely to the efforts of the radiocarbon laboratory at the University of Pennsylvania we now have more than 50 carbon-14 age determinations from different human occupation levels in Franchthi Cave. The two earliest determinations, based on samples found near the bottom of the Paleolithic deposit, yield dates around 20,000 B.C.

It is these age determinations that place the earliest indications of human activity at Franchthi in the time of the final Würm glaciation. The first occupants of the cave, probably a small band of seasonal visitors, seem to have been engaged principally in hunting. The animal remains at this level are dominated by the bones of a species of horse, probably a wild ass. The seasonal occupants of the site seem also to have gathered wild plants, but studies of plant remains from these levels are incomplete. The occupants' tools, made from flint or chert,

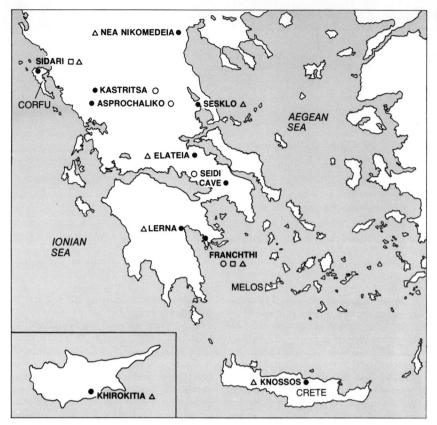

PRE-BRONZE-AGE SITES in and near European Greece include six where only Neolithic or later remains were found: four on the mainland and one each on Crete and Cyprus (*triangles*). Three mainland sites contain Paleolithic remains (*circles*). A site on Corfu contains late Mesolithic (*rectangle*) and early Neolithic levels. Franchthi contains remains of all three periods, including Mesolithic and Neolithic tools made of obsidian from Melos, an Aegean island.

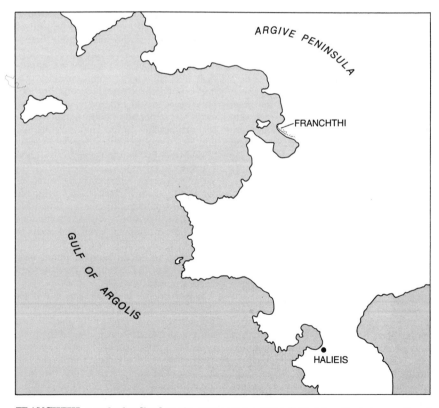

FRANCHTHI, a rocky headland on the eastern shore of the Gulf of Argolis, is in a region of limestone where erosion has produced many caves and sinkholes. The archaeological remains of the Paleolithic, Mesolithic and Neolithic periods accumulated in one such cave at Franchthi.

include "backed" (that is, blunted on one edge) bladelets of a type well known from Upper Paleolithic contexts elsewhere in the Old World.

As the Würm ice sheet retreated and warm and moist conditions came to prevail, the successive inhabitants of the site appear to have adapted successfully to the changing environment. Among the remains of the larger animals the bones of the red deer and the bison begin to outnumber those of the horse. The bones of a fourth animal, probably a wild goat, also appear. Plants too were being collected in a wider variety; we find the remains of wild pulses such as vetch and lentil. Other food resources were exploited, as is indicated by the shells of land snails and marine mollusks. The first fishbones appear, revealing that small-scale fishing has begun.

Tools of flint and chert have become abundant. Their shape and their small size are typical of many stone-tool industries in the eastern Mediterranean during the Final Paleolithic, some 12,000 to 10,000 years ago. Backed bladelets are still present; we also find small disk-shaped scrapers and microliths, some with "geometric" shapes such as triangles and trapezoids. Denticulated (notched) pieces, whose function is uncertain, are particularly common in the latest Paleolithic strata.

Our analysis of the material from the lowermost strata at the cave is not yet sufficiently advanced to enable us to reconstruct how these seasonal hunter-gatherers exploited the Franchthi area in terms either of how much ground they covered or of when during the year they were present. It may be significant, however, that we have found two open-air Paleolithic sites within six kilometers of the cave. One is near the mouth of a magnificent gorge to the east of Franchthi where water is available the year round. This would have been an ideal place for the hunters to ambush game. Their prey may have been animals that funneled into the narrow passage during annual migrations or resident animals that came to drink.

As for how long the visitors stayed at Franchthi, preliminary paleotemperature analyses of marine-mollusk shells suggest that during the Final Paleolithic the site was occupied at least throughout the summer. There is no clear-cut indication of winter activity at the cave. This negative finding may be due at least in part to the inhospitable dampness of the cave during the winter rainy season.

The Paleolithic strata in Franchthi Cave are overlain by a long record of the activities of two successive Mesolithic occupations. The earlier Mesolithic strata in the cave, deposited during the late ninth and early eighth millenniums B.C., yield some evidence of continuity with the Final Paleolithic strata just below them. The Mesolithic occupation can nonetheless be distinguished from the preceding occupation in several ways. Perhaps the most striking is that the inventory of animal bones no longer includes those of the wild horse and the wild goat. Now it is the bones of the red deer, which had become the favored prey in Final Paleolithic times, that make up the majority of the remains of larger animals.

The prominence of the red deer in the early Mesolithic levels at Franchthi could of course represent a change in the hunting preference or practices of the inhabitants. It is also possible, however, that a gradual change in the environment was accompanied by a greater abundance of deer. It is at this time that the landscape seems to have been transformed into open forest. Part of the evidence for the transition is the remains of plant foods at the site. Small quantities of wild pulses (now including the pea) continue to be found in the early Mesolithic strata. At the same time the shells of pistachios and almonds suddenly become abundant. However forested or unforested

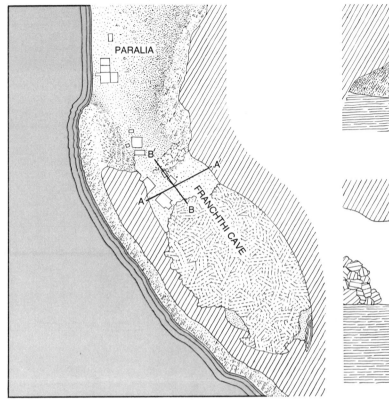

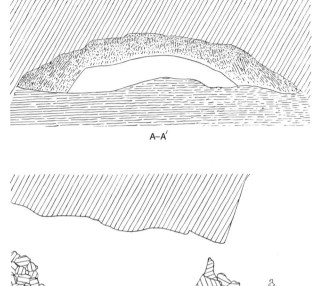

A–A'

B–B'

HILLSIDE CAVE AND SHORELINE at Franchthi (*left*) are where the author and his colleagues unearthed a consecutive series of occupation strata deposited between 20,000 and 3000 B.C. The shoreline deposit, exclusively Neolithic in age, was some two meters in depth; the two main excavations within the cave, yielding artifacts from Paleolithic to Neolithic in age, were nine and 11 meters deep. Solid lines inside the cave (*left*) indicate the orientation of the two profiles of the cave (*right*). Most of the cave is filled with fallen rock.

| | WILD ANIMALS | | | | | | | | | WILD PLANTS | | | DOMESTIC ANIMALS | | | DOMESTIC PLANTS | |
	ASS	GOAT	RED DEER	CATTLE/BISON	PIG	LAND SNAILS	MARINE MOLLUSKS	SMALL FISHES	LARGE FISHES	PULSES	PISTACHIO	ALMOND	SHEEP/GOAT	PIG	CATTLE	PULSES	CEREALS
FINAL NEOLITHIC			H	?	?	G	G	F	?		G	G	h	h	h	f	f
LATE NEOLITHIC			?	?	?	G	G	F	F		G	G	h	h	?	f	f
MIDDLE NEOLITHIC			?	?	?	G	G	F	F		G	G	h	h	h	f	f
EARLY NEOLITHIC			H	?	?	G	G	F	F		G	G	h	h	?	f	f
UPPER MESOLITHIC			H	H	H	G	G	F	F	G	G	G					
LOWER MESOLITHIC			H	H	H	G	G	F		G	G	G					
UPPER PALEOLITHIC	H	H	H	H	H	G	G	F		G							

PROCUREMENT METHOD

HUNTING   H
GATHERING G
FISHING   F
HERDING   h
FARMING   f

FOOD RESOURCES in the vicinity of Franchthi were exploited in differing degrees by seasonal visitors to the site. Both Paleolithic and Mesolithic visitors hunted game, gathered wild plant foods and fished, but their hunting and gathering choices were often limited by environmental conditions. For example, the Paleolithic climate evidently did not favor pistachio and almond trees but suited wild ass, wild goat and bison. Mesolithic conditions seem to have favored animals more at home in a woodland setting, such as red deer and wild boar. Visitors during both periods caught fish and gathered shellfish and land snails. Before upper Mesolithic times, however, only small fishes were caught. Hunting and fishing continued during Neolithic but generally fell off as domesticated plants and animals appeared.

the landscape may have been, the trees that bore these fruits were certainly present.

The occupants of the site continued to do some fishing and to supplement their diet with land snails and marine mollusks. For that matter, the early Mesolithic hunting and gathering activities were in the main still comparable to the economic strategies that had been pursued by the occupants' Paleolithic predecessors; the differences in the archaeological evidence are more reflective of an environmental adjustment than of a major change in the manner of subsistence. We expect, however, that with further study it will be possible to estimate more accurately the relative importance of each component of the overall subsistence pattern at any given time in the history of the site. Once that is accomplished we should be better able to understand the changing relations between man and his environment

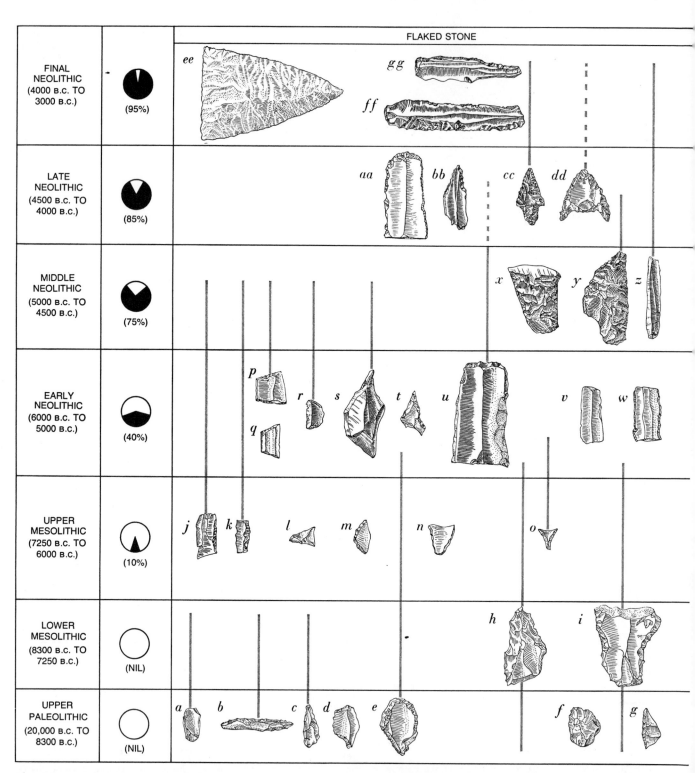

SELECTED ARTIFACTS from successive levels at Franchthi are made from flint and obsidian (*above and right*) and from bone (*far right*). The gray lines indicate when similar objects are found in more than one of seven temporal intervals (*far left*); pie charts show the increasing preference for obsidian as a raw material. Upper Paleolithic and Mesolithic tools include "backed" bladelets (*a–c, j, k*), microburins (*d*), small scrapers (*e, f*), microliths (*g, l–o*) and denticulated pieces (*h, i*). Similar forms (*p–r*) were still produced in the earlier phases of the Neolithic but are often slightly larger. Perhaps the most typical Neolithic tool is the simple blade (*z*), sometimes worked further to produce a variety of specialized forms (*v, w, aa, bb, ff, gg*). Projectile points—transverse (*x*), shouldered (*y*), tanged (*cc*) or

during the long period of human occupation at Franchthi.

The later Mesolithic levels at the site, the earliest of which may be dated at about 7250 B.C., are marked by two notable innovations. One is the appearance among the animal bones of fish vertebrae that are much larger than any found in the earlier levels. The vertebrae are comparable in size to those of the modern tunny, a fish that typically weighs several hundred pounds. The bones clearly point toward an increased exploitation of marine resources in the vicinity of the site. The second innovation provides strong confirming evidence for the first. It is the sudden appearance of a new tool material: obsidian, a handsome and distinctive volcanic glass. The oldest obsidian at Franchthi antedates by at least 1,000 years the earliest-known occurrence of the material anywhere else in the Aegean basin.

Obsidian is superior to flint in some respects; for example, although it is not as strong, it lends itself to a sharper cutting edge. As a result the material was intensively sought in later prehistory, not only in Neolithic times but also during the Bronze Age. Colin Renfrew of the University of Southampton and his colleagues have located many of the main sources of raw obsidian in the eastern Mediterranean. Thanks to their cooperation we now know that the Mesolithic obsidian found at Franchthi probably came from a deposit of the volcanic glass at Adhamas, on the northern side of the island of Melos, which is separated from Franchthi by some 150 kilometers of open sea.

The sudden and simultaneous appearance of large fishbones and obsidian in the later Mesolithic strata at Franchthi, taken together with the close quantitative correlation between these two kinds of material in subsequent Mesolithic strata, strongly suggests that the acquisition of obsidian from Melos was intimately connected with the new fishing practices on the Argive Peninsula. It remains for us to identify those practices. For example, we can only guess at the nature of the craft used by these pioneer voyagers. Until quite recently, however, the lobstermen of Corfu put out to sea in simple boats made of reeds. Vessels of this kind should have been within the technological competence of Mesolithic fishermen; they might also have been adequate for the Melos voyage.

Apart from a comparative abundance of microlithic implements—now made out of both flint and obsidian—and a smaller number of bone tools, little has survived to give a picture of the material culture of the Mesolithic residents of Franchthi. The microliths, many of them geometric, would have been equally useful to hunters as projectile points, to fishermen as harpoon barbs and possibly even to the collectors of plants as a cutting edge for primitive sickles. Studies of the microliths' working edges for evidence of different kinds of wear may eventually enable us to choose among such possibilities, but the required analyses remain to be carried out. The bone tools are largely in the form of points and could have served a variety of purposes, but again detailed study lies in the future. Simple items of personal adornment such as pebble pendants and pierced shells, which are quite rare in the Paleolithic strata, are somewhat commoner in the Mesolithic ones.

We have found one complete burial belonging to the Mesolithic period. It contained the oldest entire skeleton yet uncovered in Greece. The burial provides at least indirect information about the ideology of the people then living at the site. A man

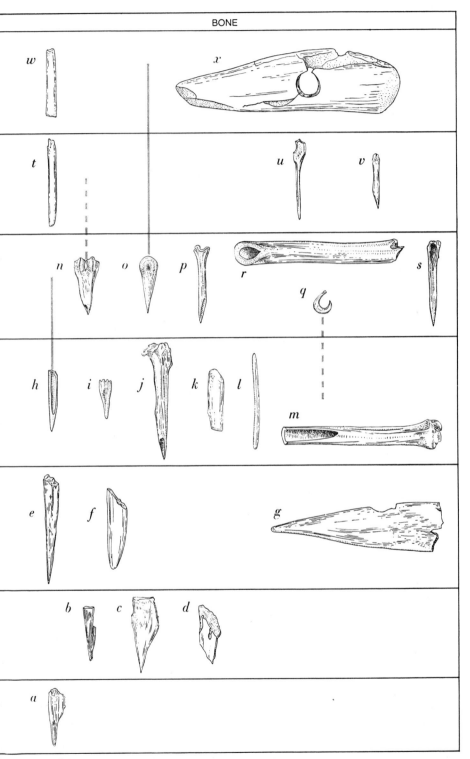

BONE

tanged and barbed (dd)—may have been used in both fishing and hunting; large "lance heads" (ee) appear in final Neolithic strata. Bone tools, particularly common in the Neolithic, include many points that vary in form and workmanship (a, b, e, h, n and u are typical). Bone points could have been applied to many kinds of task. Other forms typical of the Neolithic are scoops or gouges (m, r) and fishhooks (q). Perforated hoes or mattocks made from antler (x) are uncommon in the deposits, and they are confined to the later phases of the Neolithic period.

aged about 25 had been interred in a shallow depression just inside the present mouth of the cave. The body had been put into the grave with its knees drawn up and had been covered with a pile of fist-sized stones. The young man seems to have died from severe blows on the forehead, but it is possible that he had already been near death from malaria. That is the diagnosis of J. Lawrence Angel of the Smithsonian Institution, based on his analysis of certain bone abnormalities. We take the lack of any recognizable grave offerings as reflecting the absence among the Mesolithic occupants of Franchthi of any significant concern about life after death, or at any rate the absence of any clearly developed sense of personal property. As for the possibility that the young man had been suffering from malaria, it may be relevant that the postglacial rise in sea level could well have created marshy coastal areas suitable as breeding grounds for malarial mosquitoes.

About 6000 B.C. or shortly thereafter something new began to happen at Franchthi. There is no marked discontinuity in the occupational sequence, but the materials excavated from these levels differ in many respects from anything found in earlier ones. For example, the animal bones tentatively identified in Paleolithic strata as being those of some kind of wild goat were entirely absent from Franchthi during the 2,000-year Mesolithic occupation of the site. About 6000 B.C., however, the bones of goats (and sheep) reappear in substantial numbers. Moreover, they seem to be the bones not of wild forms but of domesticated ones. Sheep and goats are the domesticated animals most commonly associated with Neolithic cultures in this part of the Old World, particularly in southwestern Asia and southeastern Europe.

At about the same time two new plants—wheat and barley, both probably domesticated—make their first appearance at Franchthi. This combination of zoological and botanical evidence, strongly suggesting that the inhabitants of Franchthi had begun to engage in animal husbandry and agriculture early in the sixth millennium B.C., is supported by the appearance of new kinds of stone tools in the same levels of the cave.

The new tools include celts: ax heads made of hard stone that are given their final shape by grinding and polishing instead of flaking. Mounted on a handle of wood or antler, an implement of this kind can be used to clear the land of small trees and brush or to loosen the soil for planting. Coarse millstones also appear for the first time, along with flint blades that show evidence of having served as the cutting edge of sickles.

Our present correlation of these strata within the existing framework of carbon-14 dates at Franchthi is not precise enough to settle the question of whether or not the first evidence for pottery making at the site is exactly contemporaneous with the evidence for animal husbandry and agriculture. It is

reasonably certain, however, that if there was any delay between these first indications of the transition from a Mesolithic to a Neolithic way of life and the start of pottery making, it was not a long one. We should perhaps have expected this; among early agricultural societies elsewhere the need for

durable nonporous containers for the storage of food seems to have led to experimentation in the shaping and firing of clay vessels. The earliest pots at Franchthi, which are among the earliest found anywhere in Greece, were made without benefit of a potter's wheel; their forms are simple and

	GROUND AND POLISHED STONE		
FINAL NEOLITHIC (4000 B.C. TO 3000 B.C.)			
LATE NEOLITHIC (4500 B.C. TO 4000 B.C.)			
MIDDLE NEOLITHIC (5000 B.C. TO 4500 B.C.)			
EARLY NEOLITHIC (6000 B.C. TO 5000 B.C.)			
LOWER AND UPPER MESOLITHIC (8300 B.C. TO 6000 B.C.)			
UPPER PALEOLITHIC (20,000 B.C. TO 8300 B.C.)			

OTHER FRANCHTHI ARTIFACTS include stone objects (*above*) finished by means other than flaking, such as grinding and polishing. Most are Neolithic but one (*a*), a deeply grooved stone, is from a Mesolithic level. It may have been used for making bone points. The Neolithic pieces include a quern (*b*) for milling grain, a rubbing stone (*c*) to be used with the quern, a polished stone celt (*d*) and a tiny marble bowl (*e*) found in the grave illustrated on page 140. It is the

they are generally undecorated. In these respects they resemble the pottery found in a number of comparably early sites elsewhere in the eastern Mediterranean.

This innovative period at Franchthi coincides with the first extension of the area of occupation beyond the shelter of the cave.

The new area was to the northwest of the cave, running along the present shoreline. Here in 1973 and 1974 we uncovered a stratified Neolithic deposit that turned out to be some two meters deep; its bottom level rests on virgin soil. The Paralia deposit, as we call it, contains some remnants of structural stonework. Sea erosion and the breakdown of the craggy slopes above the deposit, together with the limited extent of our excavations in the area, leave the exact nature of the structures obscure. We have considered the possibility that they are the remains of agricultural terraces, but the most

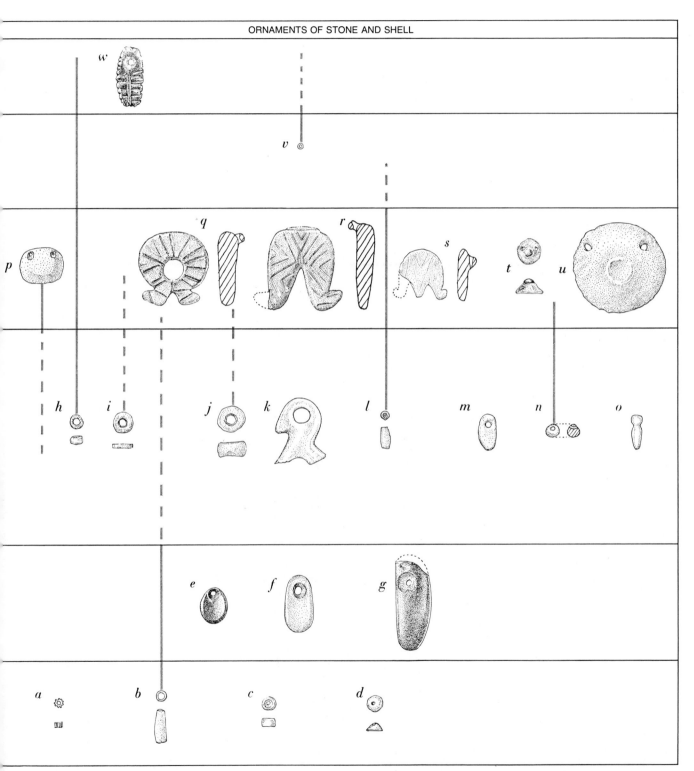

ORNAMENTS OF STONE AND SHELL

most complete of a number of stone vessels, usually found in fragments, from the earlier Neolithic levels. Ornaments (*above*) range from simple Paleolithic and Mesolithic articles to more complex Neolithic ones. Beads (*a, b*) were made from naturally fluted and smooth seashells; others (*c, d*) were made from stone, as were the Mesolithic pendants (*e-g*). Among the Neolithic ornaments stone studs (*o*) and bossed pendants (*t, u*) are noteworthy, as are zoomorphic (*k*) and anthropomorphic (*q-s*) amulets. The last, representing half-trunks and legs, may be fertility charms; they have not been found elsewhere in Greece. One pendant (*w*) had ocher in its grooves.

probable explanation is that they were retaining walls on the uphill side of a small settlement. There may be vestiges of dwellings here, but much of the seaside Neolithic settlement could now be submerged in Franchthi bay.

The lowest Neolithic strata in the Paralia deposit contain the earliest evidence for pottery making at Franchthi. Until the age of these strata can be more precisely determined we are placing it a little later than 6000 B.C. With the possible exception of a hiatus around 4000 B.C. the deposit is thereafter made up of a succession of strata that continue to the end of the Neolithic period in Greece, about 3000 B.C. This coincides generally with the Neolithic sequence in the cave itself, and so we can add some three millenniums of Neolithic settlement to the long record of the Paleolithic and Mesolithic occupation of Franchthi.

These must have been millenniums of considerable growth of population throughout Greece, as the establishment of the Paralia settlement itself suggests. Nevertheless, a slight puzzle remains. In spite of the implication of permanence normally associated with an agricultural way of life and in spite of the presence of stone structures, we still lack evidence of definite overwinter occupation at Franchthi. Such evidence may become available as our study of animal remains continues, but we must accept the possibility that a seasonal regime governed the social and economic life of these farming people much as we think it governed the life of the people of earlier times. One point to be considered in this connection has been suggested by our preliminary study of the botanical remains: the cultivation of olive trees, fig trees and grapevines, a major winter activity of the Greek farmer today, was unknown to the Neolithic farmers of Franchthi. Indeed, evidence from elsewhere in Greece indicates that the cultivation of these important Mediterranean staples was not fully established in the Aegean basin until the Bronze Age.

Many of the differences between the Mesolithic and Neolithic ways of life at Franchthi are apparent in the contrasting elements of material culture. For example, to the extent that Mesolithic ideology was reflected in personal ornament its expression was limited to a few simple pendants and beads made from pebbles and shells. The Neolithic deposits are far richer in such artifacts. Among other objects, they have yielded a number of clay figurines of both animals and human beings. Most of the figurines are represented only by fragments, but the anthropomorphic figures are mostly female, and many of them emphasize sexual characteristics.

The Paralia excavations have yielded a good deal of evidence concerning an important component of the social and economic life of these early farmers: their craft activities. We may not be justified in speaking of craft specialization at that early time, but the presence of an industry for the production of shell beads is certainly noteworthy. We first recognized the possibility that such an industry existed when during the 1973 season at Paralia we unearthed a large number of small drill-like implements, from two to three centimeters long, flaked out of a reddish flint of poor quality.

The most popular raw material for the production of flaked stone tools at Franchthi during the Neolithic was obsidian; indeed, by the end of the Neolithic obsidian was virtually the only material so used. Nevertheless, the special flaking qualities of the reddish flint seems to have made it more suitable than obsidian for drills, even though it is good for little else. We were at first surprised when we found the poor-quality flint was a far commoner raw material in certain Paralia deposits than obsidian. The reason became apparent when we found finished beads by the score together with bead "blanks" in various stages of completion. Evidently the flint drills are associated with the production of shell beads.

Our excavations at Paralia indicate that the bead industry was active at the site for a short time in the latter part of the sixth millennium B.C. This marks one of the rare occasions in Aegean prehistory when an early craft has been identified by the discovery not only of the finished product but also of the tools that were used to make it. Whether or not these objects were made by an individual or a group whose special occupation it was, the absence of either beads or drills in other Neolithic contexts at Franchthi suggests that the bead industry was localized in the settlement along the shore.

Although stone beads and pendants had been made at Franchthi as early as Mesolithic times, their number and quality increase markedly in the Neolithic levels. Several of the pendants are of particular interest because they represent only the lower half of a human body. They could have been intended as fertility charms; at least this would have been in keeping with the ideology of a society that placed a social and economic emphasis on the fecundity of man and nature alike.

INFANT BURIAL, the only one of eight such child burials of the Neolithic period at Franchthi to contain grave offerings, was inside the cave. To the right of the forearm, partly concealed by one of the stones that covered the burial, is half of a broken clay pot; it is suggestive of the widely followed practice of "killing" pottery that was used as a grave offering. Also under the rock, above the infant's skull, is a small marble vessel that was nearly intact when it was found; the vessel is among the artifacts that are depicted in the illustration on preceding two pages.

FRANCHTHI CAVE appears as a low, shadowed arch halfway up the steep hillside that rises from the water's edge. When the first bands of Paleolithic hunters used the cave as a campsite, the sea level was lower, fresh water was nearby and the coast was kilometers away.

MOUTH OF CAVE (*right*) and one of two deep excavations, *H/H*-1, are visible in this photograph looking across the interior of the cave. Most of the cave floor is now buried under substantial falls of ceiling rock (*left*); the falls may have led to the abandonment of the cave.

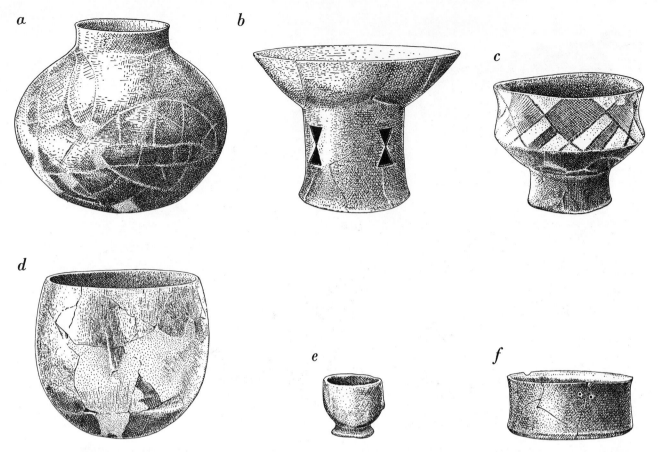

NEOLITHIC POTTERY from the earlier levels at Franchthi (*d, e*) is undecorated but skillfully made. The deep hemispherical pot has a burnished surface, as does the footed piece, a cup or small bowl of sophisticated design. The potter's skill reached its height in the middle Neolithic. The collared jar (*a*) is simple in form, but its lustrous finish results from the chemical composition of the paint that was applied before firing. Other middle Neolithic decorative devices include cutouts (*b*) and painted geometric designs (*c*). The holes in the rim of the shallow basin (*f*) were made after the piece had been cracked during use; the break was probably repaired with a tightly tied thong.

It should not be supposed, however, that such an emphasis implies any neglect of the collateral economic activities of the society: hunting, gathering and fishing. It is not unlikely that women continued to collect wild plants in season. Moreover, entirely new kinds of artifacts—bone fishhooks and tanged projectile points made of both flint and obsidian—show that fishing and hunting were still important activities.

Burial customs are almost always a reflection of ideological attitudes, and the Neolithic burials we uncovered at Franchthi are significant in this respect. Generally the Neolithic practices follow what little we know of the Mesolithic tradition; the burials are distributed seemingly at random within the confines of the settlement (inside the cave or along the shore), the graves are shallow pits and the bodies were buried with their knees drawn up. At the same time certain innovations are evident. For example, the custom of secondary burial seems to have arisen in the later phases of the Neolithic. This practice called for letting the soft parts of the body decay by either leaving the body exposed or burying it temporarily. Thereafter the bones were bundled together and deposited in their final resting place.

Grave offerings are rare in the Neolithic burials at Franchthi. The two exceptions are worth mentioning. The first is an infant burial of the early Neolithic that we found inside the cave during the 1973 season. It was one of a total of eight Neolithic burials of infants or children unearthed at Franchthi, four inside the cave and four outside. It was also the only one of the eight to include grave goods. Although the infant was only a few weeks old when he died, an unusually fine vessel made of marble and almost exactly half of a broken clay pot were buried with him. One wonders why, in a time when grave goods were so rare, such a young person should have been honored with any. One also wonders whether the pot had been broken symbolically ("killed," as some ethnologists say) during a funeral ceremony, as was still customary in the vicinity of Franchthi until just a few years ago. These questions must remain unanswered, but it seems safe to guess that the infant or his parents had some kind of special status in the community.

The other noteworthy Neolithic burial is that of a 40-year-old woman whose skeleton was wedged so tightly into a small pit in the Paralia settlement that it almost certainly represents a secondary burial. A complete but well-worn pot that shows signs of having been mended was buried with her; its style suggests that the woman died sometime before 4500 B.C. Among the other grave goods is a group of bone tools that includes several well-made points and a number of obsidian blades. Such a set of tools would be appropriate for a person engaged in any one of several crafts. Whether the objects were gifts indicative of the woman's status in the community or were merely personal possessions is hard to ascertain. It seems likely, however, that among the later Neolithic inhabitants of Greece a sense of personal property was growing.

The Neolithic settlement at Franchthi is in most respects typical of early village-farming communities throughout the eastern Mediterranean. Once established it flourished for some 3,000 years. Over that span the inhabitants of the cave and the shoreline settlement seem to have had increasing contact with other parts of the Aegean basin and even with areas well beyond the Aegean. That, however, is another story, and perhaps I should conclude this account by discussing a key question: To what extent does the Neolithic settlement at Franchthi represent a natural or inevitable development of the local Paleolithic and Mesolithic occupations? A clear answer to the question would contribute greatly to our understanding of early Greek prehistory and would help to clarify the relations between this area and the prehistoric cultures of neighboring regions to the north and the east.

To review the record briefly, the most dramatic innovations over some 17,000 years at Franchthi came at the end of the Mesolithic, about 8,000 years ago. The physical limits of the settlement were enlarged, the size of the local population may have increased accordingly and a host of new elements can be perceived in the archaeological record. The most striking of these elements is the sudden appearance of species of plants and animals previously unknown in the area. The new plants and animals appear to be domesticated, and so it is unlikely that they represent the culmination of a long period of local experimentation in plant and animal husbandry. The evidence thus leads us to conclude that a basically agricultural economy, with all the term implies from the technological, social and ideological points of view, was introduced from elsewhere and imposed on a native Greek Mesolithic substratum. Whether or not this cultural revolution was accompanied by an influx of new people cannot now be established. All things considered, however, at least a modest infusion of new blood seems likely.

It might be noted that the situation at Franchthi bears a striking resemblance to that which is thought to have prevailed in much of Europe when agriculture first arose. It would be incautious, however, to suggest that the circumstances at Franchthi were necessarily typical even of Greece. To be sure, there is no evidence from elsewhere in Greece to contradict such a suggestion, but for the present it would be prudent to insist that something approaching a true picture will emerge only after considerably more excavation and research have been conducted throughout the region.

One conclusion that does seem to be justified at this point is that the establishment of the village-farming stage at Franchthi (and apparently at most other sites in Neolithic Europe) fits the generally accepted reconstruction that perceives agriculture as beginning in the "nuclear" Middle East. A growing body of evidence indicates that experimentation with potentially domesticable plants and animals was in progress at several locations in the Middle East during the millenniums represented at Franchthi by the late Paleolithic and Mesolithic occupations. This early experimentation was greatly facilitated by the availability in that part of the Old World of those same plant and animal species (indeed, many of the same species that eventually appeared at Franchthi). It is this fact more than any other that distinguishes conditions in the Middle East from those that seem to have prevailed in Greece and elsewhere in con-

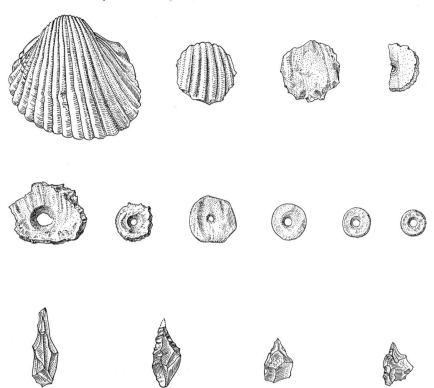

BEAD INDUSTRY, utilizing cockleshells as the raw material, was practiced only at Paralia during a few score years of the Neolithic occupation of Franchthi. Drill-like tools, made from a poor grade of flint (*bottom*), heavily outnumber obsidian tools in strata at Paralia representing a short span of time in the late sixth millennium. Their function as bead-making artifacts became apparent when they were found together with unfinished beads, blanks and complete beads.

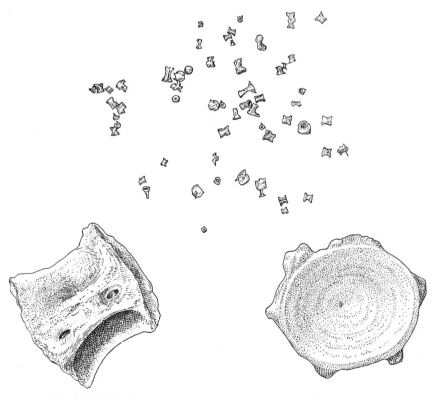

IMPROVED FISHING is dramatically demonstrated by the sudden appearance in upper Mesolithic strata of fish vertebrae (*bottom*) much larger than the vertebrae (*top*) found in Paleolithic and lower Mesolithic strata. The appearance of the larger fishbones coincides with the appearance of obsidian at Franchthi. Obsidian came from Melos, a 150-kilometer voyage away.

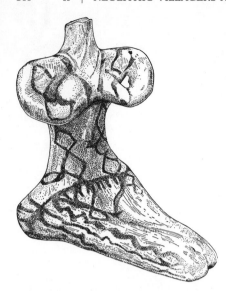

FEMALE FIGURINE, made late in the fifth millennium B.C., is remarkable both for its seated posture and for the painted suggestions of clothing. Figurines representing human beings and, less frequently, animals first appear in the Neolithic levels. Most are in fragments, which may indicate deliberate destruction. All the figures of identifiable sex are female.

tinental Europe before the advent of agriculture.

Given this chronological priority, it has usually been assumed as a corollary that the village-farming way of life spread from the Middle East to Greece by some process of diffusion, probably at the same time bringing the first farmers (and even possibly the first human inhabitants) to Cyprus and Crete before ultimately reaching the southern shore of Europe. Such may well have been the case; at least we finally have some evidence that generally supports the hypothesis. Before dismissing our question with a simplistic "Noah's ark" answer, however, we must recognize that not all the problems have been solved and that many related questions are still unanswered.

For example, much more needs to be learned about the complex of factors that must bear on the origins of agriculture in the Middle East itself. To mention one unanswered question, archaeologists have only now begun to deal with the problem of why it all happened there when it did. As for Greece, the picture is even cloudier. Our preliminary findings at Franchthi constitute an important beginning, but they are only a beginning. Did the Neolithic of southern Greece really come into being as abruptly as it now appears it did? What factors led the Mesolithic hunter-gatherers to modify their long established way of life so markedly? What was happening elsewhere in the Greek peninsula at that time? These and other questions will occupy us as we press on with our study of this significant site.

An Early Farming Village in Turkey

by Halet Çambel and Robert J. Braidwood
March 1970

*Çayönü Tepesi, a site in a little-studied part of Asia
Minor, adds to the growing record of man's agricultural
origins. Also revealed there is the earliest evidence of
man's use of metal*

When and where did men first turn to farming and animal husbandry as a way of life? This question has increasingly come to occupy the attention of archaeologists in recent years. The first direct attempt to discover just when in human prehistory farming villages appeared was made in the Near East a little more than 20 years ago when a party from the Oriental Institute of the University of Chicago began digging at Jarmo in the foothills of the Zagros Mountains in northeastern Iraq. Today scores of such investigations are in progress in several parts of the Old World and the New World. In the Near East alone the area of interest has grown until it stretches from Turkestan and the Indus valley on the east to the Aegean and the Balkans on the west. This article concerns one Near Eastern investigation that has opened up a new area and has by chance brought to light the earliest evidence of man's use of metal.

Field results in the years since Jarmo allow a few broad generalizations about the dawn of cultivation and animal husbandry. We now know that somewhat earlier than 7500 B.C. people in some parts of the Near East had reached a level of cultural development marked by the production, as opposed to the mere collection, of plant and animal foodstuffs and by a pattern of residence in farming villages. It is not clear, however, when this level of development became characteristic of the region as a whole. Nor do we yet have a good understanding of conditions in the period immediately preceding. The reason is largely that few sites of this earlier period have yet been excavated, and that during the earliest phases of their manipulation the wild plants and animals would not yet possess features indicat-

ing that they were on the way to domestication. Moreover, even the most painstaking excavation may fail to turn up materials that constitute *primary* evidence for domestication, that is, the physical remains of the plants and animals in question. Fragments of plant material and bone—the objects that could tell us exactly which of a number of possible organisms were then in the process of domestication—are often completely missing from village sites.

What should be said of villages that yield plant and animal material that we cannot positively identify as being the remains of domesticated forms? Until recently we tended to believe that if

such sites had every appearance of being permanently settled, and if their inventory of artifacts included flint "sickle" blades, querns (milling stones), storage pits and similar features, then they probably represented the next-earliest level of cultural development; we called it the level of incipient cultivation and animal husbandry. Over the years, however, it has become increasingly probable that early village-like communities of a somewhat different kind may also have existed in the Near East. At these sites the food supply tends at first to include plant and animal forms that were not subsequently domesticated. In other words, even though such items as flint sickles,

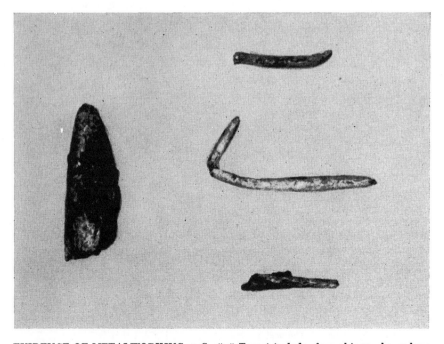

EVIDENCE OF METALWORKING at Çayönü Tepesi includes four objects, shown here twice actual size. At left is the point of a reamer, formed from a lump of native copper by hammering. Beside it are two copper pin fragments and a whole pin that has been bent. The pinpoints have been formed by abrasion. A source of native copper lies quite near the site.

querns and the like appear in their inventories, and the architectural traces of their settlement suggest some degree of permanence, it looks as if we are dealing here with villagers living on a level of intensive collection of wild foods alone. Our older notion that villages had to mean farmers has gone by the board.

A prime example of such a non-food-producing community is the village-like site of Mallaha, in northern Israel. The excavator of Mallaha, Jean Perrot of the French Archaeological Mission in Israel, was the first to suggest that when other sites of a similar nature were unearthed, they too might lack any evidence of food production. Mallaha was inhabited about 9000 B.C. The village site of Mureybet, on the middle reaches of the Euphrates in Syria, is somewhat later, say about 8250 B.C. Mureybet, which was excavated by Maurits N. van Loon for the Oriental Institute in 1964 and 1965, also shows no trace of food production. An even later example is the "hunters' village" of Suberde in Turkey, excavated by Jacques Bordaz of the University of Montreal in 1964 and 1965 [see "A Hunters' Village in Neolithic Turkey," by Dexter Perkins, Jr., and Patricia Daly; SCIENTIFIC AMERICAN, November 1968]. As late as 6500 B.C. the people of Suberde fed themselves mainly by killing large numbers of wild sheep and wild cattle.

In very rough outline the available evidence now suggests that both the level of incipient cultivation and animal domestication and the level of intensified food-collecting were reached in the Near East about 9000 B.C. In contrast to the moderately intensive food-collecting characteristic of the preceding level of development (the level of the late Upper Paleolithic period), what allowed this second kind of community to flourish was collecting of a most intensive kind. We believe such communities can be regarded as being incipiently food-producing, in the sense that their inhabitants were doubtless already manipulating both plants and animals to some extent. It seems to us that in much of the Near East this interval of incipient food production was just before or at the same time as what in Europe is called the Mesolithic period: a phase of cultural readaption, still on a food-collecting level, to the sequence of postglacial forested environments that formed in Europe about 11,000 years ago. (Food production proper did not reach most of Europe until sometime after 5000 B.C.)

The inventory of artifacts known as the Natufian assemblage, after the valley in Palestine where it was first discovered, provides examples, found both in caves and in village-like sites, of communities without food production. The artifacts uncovered at Mallaha, for instance, fit the Natufian classification. A different but contemporary inventory, found east of the Euphrates and Tigris rivers, is named the Karim Shahirian assemblage, after Karim Shahir, a site on the flanks of the Zagros Mountains. The artifacts from Zawi Chemi, another early site in Iraq, are of this second kind, and Zawi Chemi appears to have the earliest evidence for domesticated sheep (about 9000 B.C.). A somewhat later site in neighboring Iran—Ganj Dareh, near Kermanshah—contains an assemblage that, although it is similar, is somewhat more developed than the basic Karim Shahirian. It is not yet clear, however, either along the Mediterranean littoral or in the regions east of the Euphrates, through how many successive phases the incipient food producer—hunters' village level may have passed before the next developmental step took place.

The early phase of that next step—the level of effective village-farming communities—is now known from sites throughout the Near East. Representative early-phase villages have been unearthed in most of the region's grassy uplands, in some middle reaches of its major river valleys, along the Mediterranean and even beyond the Near East in Cyprus, Crete and Greece. Originally one of us (Braidwood) believed the most ancient evidence of this early phase

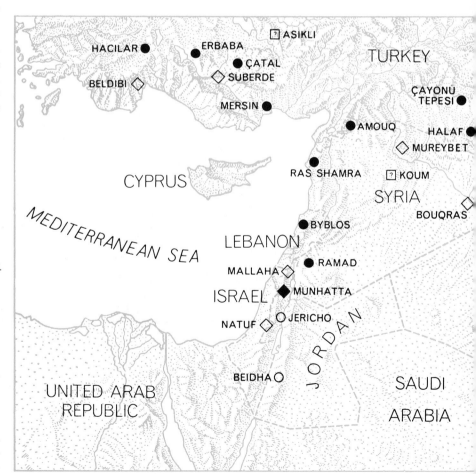

● SITES WITH ESTABLISHED FOOD PRODUCTION.

○ SITES WITH SEVERAL PERIODS OF OCCUPATION. SOME FOOD-PRODUCING.

◆ SITES WITH EVIDENCE OF "INCIPIENT" FOOD PRODUCTION.

◇ SITES WITH INSUFFICIENT EVIDENCE OR NO EVIDENCE OF FOOD PRODUCTION.

▣ SITES KNOWN FROM BRIEF TESTS OR SURFACE COLLECTIONS; NO EVIDENCE OF FOOD PRODUCTION.

SOUTHWESTERN ASIA, from beyond the Caspian (right) to the Mediterranean shore (left), contains many of mankind's earliest farming settlements, most of them in or near the hilly regions flanking the Fertile Crescent of Mesopotamia. The region also contains a number of village-like sites whose inhabitants were only incipient food producers or won a living by means of intensified hunting and gathering (see key above).

would be found only within a geographically restricted area, which was defined as the hilly flanks of the Fertile Crescent [*see illustration below*]. Moreover, even within this area the expectation was that the evidence would be confined to the zone naturally occupied today by certain wild but potentially domesticable plants and animals. One consequence of this view was that for a time the search for early sites was restricted to the "hilly flank" area, with the result that a large proportion of the early village sites now known are either in that area or immediately adjacent to it.

Recently it has become apparent that in past millenniums the natural range of the potentially domesticable forms of what may be called the "wheat-barley/sheep-goat-cattle-pig complex" extended well beyond the hilly flanks of the Fertile Crescent. For example, while extending earlier investigations by the Oriental Institute in Iran, Herbert E. Wright, Jr., of the University of Minnesota and Willem van Zeist of the University of Groningen have collected samples from the beds of lakes and ponds for analysis of their pollen content. Wright and van Zeist find that since about 17,000 years ago the vegetation and climate along the flanks of the Zagros Mountains have

changed much more than had been supposed. At the same time test excavations by an Oriental Institute group at Koum, in the dry steppe country west of the Euphrates in Syria, have added another site to the growing list of early non-food-producing settlements. Koum, like Mureybet, lies well south of the hilly-flanks zone, just as Suberde in Asia Minor lies well north of it. We have yet to learn precisely how wide the natural range of the domesticable plants and animals constituting this Near Eastern complex was in early times. The question will be answered only with the continued help of our colleagues in the natural sciences.

In the 1950's there was a substantial increase of archaeological activity in the Near East, but not until the 1960's did it become possible to investigate one untouched area that formed a virtual keystone in the arch. This was the southern slopes and the piedmont of the Taurus Mountains in southeastern Turkey, an area that includes the entire northern watershed in the upper reaches of the Tigris and the Euphrates. We reasoned that, however extensive the ancient range of domesticable plants and animals may have been, the upper basin of the Tigris and the Euphrates must have been

somewhere near the center of the zone.

Much of this unexplored territory lay within three Turkish border provinces (Urfa, Diyarbakir and Siirt), which for reasons of national security are normally out-of-bounds to foreign visitors. It seemed to us that if the area was to be reconnoitered, a joint Turkish-American venture was in order. In late 1962 the Oriental Institute joined forces with the department of prehistory of Istanbul University to establish a joint Prehistoric Project, and the authors of this article were made its codirectors. The project received the support of the National Science Foundation and the Wenner-Gren Foundation for Anthropological Research.

We proposed that a surface survey of the three provinces be made in the fall of 1963 and that exploratory digging be undertaken in the spring of 1964. We presently received the necessary approvals, which in this border region meant not only the cooperation of the Directorate of Antiquities of the Turkish Republic but also the active support of the Prime Minister, of many high civil and military authorities and of the governors of the three provinces and their staffs.

Thanks to the interest of all concerned, we were able to begin our sur-

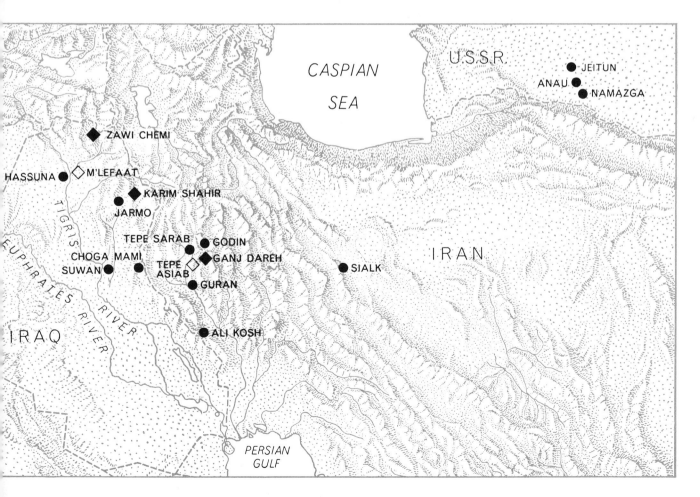

face survey in the province of Siirt early in October of 1963. We moved on to Diyarbakir in mid-November and ended the season with a five-day survey in Urfa in mid-December. Since the three provinces cover a total of more than 46,000 square kilometers, the reconnaissance could scarcely be an intensive one. The most detailed work was done in two valley regions: the plains of Kurtalan in Siirt and the Ergani plain in Diyarbakir. We found a total of 134 archaeological sites, plotted their location and roughly classified the materials we could collect on the surface at the main sites.

Our survey showed that this part of Turkey had been continuously occupied by men at least from the time (between 100,000 and 200,000 years ago) when stone tools of the Acheulean type were commonplace. So far as our particular interests were concerned, sites that looked as though they might be the remains of early farming villages were located in both the Kurtalan and the Ergani valleys. Still other sites in these val-

leys evidently represented more fully evolved village-farming communities. Some of the sites belonged to the developed village-farming phase termed Halafian (after Tell Halaf in northern Syria).

So far as settlements that might have belonged to the initial level of incipient food production are concerned, the most we can say at the moment is that our survey turned up no artifacts that, even in general terms, could be called representative of either the Natufian or the Karim Shahirian assemblages. Although it is probable that an unrelated third cultural tradition at the general level of incipient food production existed in this part of Turkey, we have yet to identify its traces.

In late April of 1964 we returned to the area of our survey prepared to undertake a number of test excavations. Bruce Howe of Harvard University, who had joined the project with the support of the American Schools of Oriental Re-

search, tackled two small open sites in the area northwest of the provincial capital of Urfa. Named Biris Mezarligi and Sögüt Tarlasi, the sites contained numerous specialized stone tools produced from blades of flint. The inventory seems to represent some end phase of the Paleolithic period in the region. The sites did not yield samples adequate for carbon-14 dating, so that the age of this blade industry is a matter of conjecture; our guess is that the tools were made around 10000 B.C. or perhaps a little later. At Sögüt Tarlasi, but not at Biris Mezarligi, the blade-tool horizon was overlain by material of a time somewhat before 3000 B.C., contemporary with the Uruk phase of Sumerian culture in neighboring Mesopotamia.

While Howe worked in Urfa, the majority of the workers on the project moved on to Diyarbakir in order to investigate a promising mound some five kilometers southwest of the town of Ergani. Known as Çayönü Tepesi, the mound is about 200 meters in diameter;

SUCCESSIVE LEVELS exposed during excavation on the crest of the mound are shown in a drawing based on composite photographs. At the rear of the dig, only a little below the mound surface, are the stone foundations of mud-brick structures that had been built at Level 2. In the middle distance (a, a'), still surrounded by unremoved earth, are the bases of the two stone monoliths found at Level 4. Sections of the cobble pavement found at Level 5 are in the foreground at left. In the foreground at right is the grill-like stone foundation of the elaborate structure exposed at Level 5. The two-by-two-meter pit, foreground, descends beyond Level 6.

it stands on the north bank of a minor tributary of the Tigris. At some time in the past part of the mound's south side was washed away. At the foot of the talus slope on the river side we found fragments of crude and easily crumbled pottery that had been made by hand, rather than with the potter's wheel. Some additional potsherds were present on the northeast slope of the mound and in the top 10 or 15 centimeters of soil in our test excavations (about the depth to which the soil had been disturbed by modern plowing). Below that our 1964 excavations revealed no pottery. The presence in these lower levels of figurines made of clay shows that clay was known and used in the early days of Çayönü Tepesi. Like the people of Jarmo and some other early village-farming communities, however, the inhabitants of Çayönü Tepesi evidently got along without the clay bowls, jars and other containers that are commonplace in the villages of later farmers.

We worked at Çayönü Tepesi for two seasons—in 1964 and again in 1968—and we expect to work there again this year. Our main evidence concerning the early occupation of the site comes from a 10-by-15-meter area we excavated on the crest of the mound and a five-by-eight-meter trench we cut into the mound on the river side; both excavations were undertaken during the 1964 season [see illustrations on page 150]. Those who explore village sites in southwestern Asia come to expect that each new excavation will exhibit an exuberant characteristic that is distinctively its own. Çayönü Tepesi was no exception: its special characteristic is its architecture. Among the buildings we uncovered, several must have been quite imposing. The trench we cut back from the river revealed part of what could have been a building interior or perhaps an open court. The area was floored with a broad pavement of smooth flagstones, around which the stone bases of thick walls rose to a height of a meter or more. Spaced along the main axis of the paved area were the broken bases of a pair of large stone slabs that had once stood upright. From one of the stone walls buttresses projected at the points nearest the broken slabs. Another partly intact slab marked the area's short axis. Unfortunately erosion had eaten away the southern portions of this elaborate structure, so that its full plan is beyond recovery.

At the crest of the mound we dug down to a depth of more than three meters, encountering traces of at least six

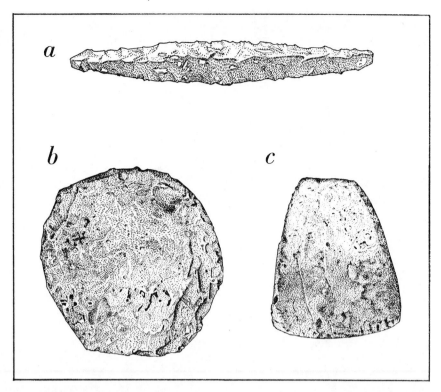

THREE STONE IMPLEMENTS from Çayönü Tepesi are a flint projectile point (a), found during the 1968 season, a scraper of flint (b) and a polished stone celt, the bit of a compound cutting tool (c), unearthed in 1964. The artifacts are shown at their actual size.

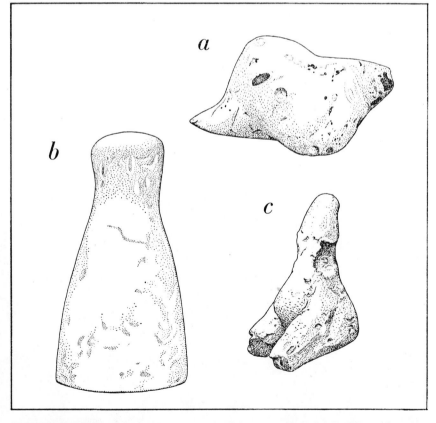

THREE ODDITIES from the site are a snail shell (a), a polished stone object (b) and a crude clay figurine (c). The shell, imported from the Mediterranean, has been smoothed and drilled with holes, presumably for decorative inserts. The stone, about three inches high, is one of 22 found in a cache during the 1968 season; their function is unknown. The figure seems to represent a pregnant woman; it may be a portrayal of the familiar "fertility deity."

AIR VIEW of Çayönü Tepesi, on the bank of a tributary of the Tigris River in southwestern Turkey, shows the work done by the authors in 1964. Near the river (*right*) digging uncovered stone walls and a floor of flagstones. On the crest of the village mound (*left*) six successive levels of occupation have been exposed; the next-to-lowest level contained objects made from copper.

GROUND VIEW of Çayönü Tepesi, from a rise on the south side of the river, shows a stretch of the broad Ergani plain beyond the site. On the northern horizon are the first ranges of the Taurus Mountains, here distinctively marked by light-colored bands of rock.

successive levels of occupation. At the fourth level the bases of two more upright slabs rose from a broad pavement of fist-sized limestone cobbles; the broken upper portion of one slab lay beside its base. The fifth level, also paved with cobbles, contained the stone foundations of still another substantial structure. What we could perceive of the foundation plan showed a curious grill-like pattern [see illustration on page 148]. Our work in 1968 exposed another of these grill-like foundations. A similar foundation, although it is smaller and built of sun-dried mud walling rather than stone, was unearthed at Jarmo. We are still puzzled as to the function of such foundations.

The purpose of the upright slabs at Çayönü Tepesi is equally puzzling. We are of two minds about whether they could have been supports for roof beams. Our first notion was that the slabs might have been ceremonial stones set up within unroofed courts, but the actual function of the structures containing them is not yet clear. We are much impressed by the substantial proportions of the buildings and by the relative sophistication of their construction, but we are still loath to press any suggestion that they served a public or a sacred purpose.

In addition to its impressive architecture, Çayönü Tepesi yielded tools chipped from flint and obsidian or fashioned from stone by grinding, ornaments made of polished stone, the clay figurines mentioned above and one shell ornament. The last object indicates contact, direct or indirect, with the Mediterranean coast. If one adds to this inventory evidence what seems to be a primitive form of wheat and the remains of domesticated dogs, pigs, sheep and probably goats, one gains some sense of the quality of life here and in similar communities across southwestern Asia as the arts of farming and animal husbandry became established during the eighth millennium B.C. If that were all Çayönü Tepesi had to tell us, it would be enough. A combination of geological propinquity and archaeological good fortune, however, has made the site even more significant. We have found here what is so far the earliest evidence of man's intentional use of metal.

Turkey is rich in minerals; one of its major mining centers today—a deposit of native copper, copper ores and related minerals such as malachite—is less than 20 kilometers from Çayönü Tepesi. In our excavation at the crest of the mound we noticed, from just below the surface downward, dozens of fragments of a bright green substance that we took to be malachite. Below the fourth occupation level we began to find actual artifacts made of malachite: drilled beads, a carefully smoothed but undrilled ellipsoid and a small tablet. Next we found part of a tool—one end of a reamer with a square cross section—that had been hammered into shape out of a lump of native copper. Finally we uncovered three tiny objects of copper that are perhaps analogous to the ordinary modern straight pin. In two of these pins, which do not appear to be complete, the metal had been abraded to form a point at one end; the third pin was pointed at both ends and was sharply bent [see illustration on page 145].

Metallurgy, of course, involves the hot-working of metals, including such arts as smelting, alloying, casting and forging. We are making no assertion that any kind of metallurgy, however primitive, existed at Çayönü Tepesi; there is not even any unanimity of opinion among the experts about whether the reamer, the only article that had certainly been hammered, was worked cold or hot. The fact remains that sometime just before 7000 B.C. the people of Çayönü Tepesi not only were acquainted with metal but also were shaping artifacts out of native copper by abrading and hammering.

What we suggest is that the Çayönü Tepesi copper reveals the moment in man's material progress when he may first have begun to sense the properties of metal as metal, rather than as some peculiar kind of stone. Looking back from the full daylight of our own age of metals, these first faint streaks of dawn are exciting to behold.

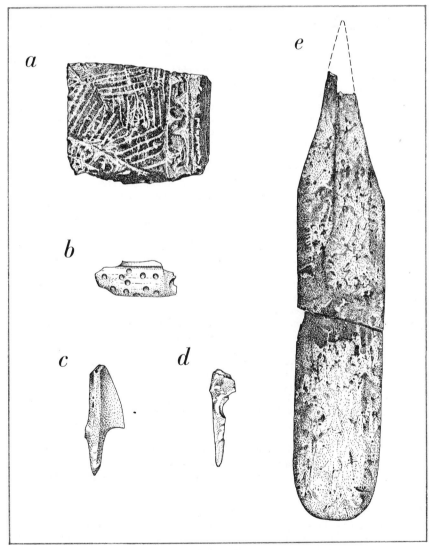

CRAFTSMANSHIP at Çayönü Tepesi included the decoration of stone bowls with incisions (a) and bone objects with drilled patterns (b). Drills flaked from flint (c, d) were used to work the bone. Bone awls (e) were probably used to produce wooden and leather items.

16

The Earliest Precursor of Writing

by Denise Schmandt-Besserat
June 1978

Long before the Sumerians invented writing, accounts in western Asia were kept with clay tokens of various distinctive shapes. It appears that the tokens gave rise to the Sumerian ideographs

What led to writing? The art itself is a good example of what students of the past call independent invention, since systems of writing have evolved in isolation at different times in different parts of the world. For example, one system—the Chinese ideogram—can be traced to its origin in archaic signs engraved on the scapular bones of sheep or the shells of turtles in the second millennium B.C. as a means of asking questions of heaven. Roughly 1,000 years later an entirely independent system of writing arose halfway around the world in Mesoamerica. It combined a simple system of numerical notation with complex hieroglyphs and was principally used to indicate the dates of various events according to an elaborate calendrical system.

Both Chinese and Maya writing were relatively late inventions. Some one system of writing must have been the earliest, and it is from such an initial point that we may begin the search for the antecedents of the art. The credit for being the first to write texts is usually given to the Sumerians of Mesopotamia. By the last century of the fourth millennium B.C. the officials of such Sumerian city-states as Uruk had developed a system of recording numerals, pictographs and ideographs on specially prepared clay surfaces. (A pictograph is a more or less realistic portrayal of the object it is supposed to represent; an ideograph is an abstract sign.)

At Uruk a team of German archaeologists directed by Julius Jordan turned up many examples of these archaic records in 1929 and 1930. The texts, about 1,000 of them, were first analyzed by Adam Falkenstein and his students. Today additional discoveries have increased the total number of Uruk and Uruk-style texts to about 4,000, and Falkenstein's pioneer efforts are being continued mainly by Hans J. Nissen of the Free University of Berlin and his associate Margaret W. Green.

Although the clay blanks used by the Uruk scribes are universally referred to as tablets, a word with the connotation of flatness, they are actually convex. Individual characters were inscribed in the clay by means of a stylus made of wood, bone or ivory, with one end blunt and the other pointed. The characters were basically of two kinds. Numerical signs were impressed into the clay; all other signs, pictographs and ideographs alike, were incised with the pointed end of the stylus. The repertory of characters used by the Uruk scribes was large; it is estimated at no fewer than 1,500 separate signs.

Hypotheses about the origin of writing generally postulate an evolution from the concrete to the abstract: an initial pictographic stage that in the course of time and perhaps because of the carelessness of scribes becomes increasingly schematic. The Uruk tablets contradict this line of thought. Most of the 1,500 signs (Falkenstein compiled 950 of them) are totally abstract ideographs; the few pictographs represent such wild animals as the wolf and the fox or items of advanced technology such as the chariot and the sledge. Indeed, the Uruk texts remain largely undeciphered and an enigma to epigraphers. The few ideographic signs that have been identified are those that can be traced back stage by stage from a known cuneiform character of later times to an archaic Sumerian prototype. From the fragmentary textual contents that such identities allow it appears that the scribes of Uruk mainly recorded such matters as business transactions and land sales. Some of the terms that appear most frequently are those for bread, beer, sheep, cattle and clothing.

After Jordan's discovery at Uruk other archaeologists found similar texts elsewhere in Mesopotamia. More were found in Iran: at Susa, at Chogha Mish and as far off as Godin Tepe, some 350 kilometers north of Uruk. In recent years tablets in the Uruk style have been unearthed in Syria at Habuba Kabira and Jebel Aruda, nearly 800 kilometers to the northwest. At Uruk the tablets had been found in a temple complex; most of the others came to light in the ruins of private houses, where the presence of seals and the seal-marked clay stoppers for jars indicate some kind of mercantile activity.

The fact that the Uruk texts contradict the hypothesis that the earliest form of writing would be pictographic has inclined many epigraphers to the view that the tablets, even though they bear the earliest-known writing, must represent a stage in the evolution of the art that is already advanced. The pictographic hypothesis has been revived anew. The fact that no writing of this kind has yet appeared at sites of the fourth millennium B.C. and even earlier is explained away by postulating that the writing of earlier millenniums was recorded exclusively on perishable mediums that vanished long ago, such as parchment, papyrus or wood.

I have an alternative proposal. Research into the first uses of clay in the Near East over the past several years suggests that several characteristics of the Uruk material provide important clues to what kinds of visible symbols actually preceded the archaic Sumerian texts. These clues include the choice of clay as a material for documents, the convex profile of the Uruk tablets and the appearance of the characters recorded on them.

Nuzi, a city site of the second mil-

CLAY TOKENS FROM SUSA, a city site in Iran, are seen in the composite photograph on the opposite page. The tokens, in the collection of the Musée du Louvre, are about 5,000 years old. The five tokens in the top row represent some of the commonest shapes; a sphere, a half-sphere, a disk, a cone and a tetrahedron. The more elaborate tokens in the next row have been marked with incisions or impressions. Unperforated and perforated versions of similar tokens appear in the third and fourth rows. Tokens in the bottom two rows vary in shape and marking; some can be equated with early Sumerian ideographs (*see illustration on pages 158 and 159*).

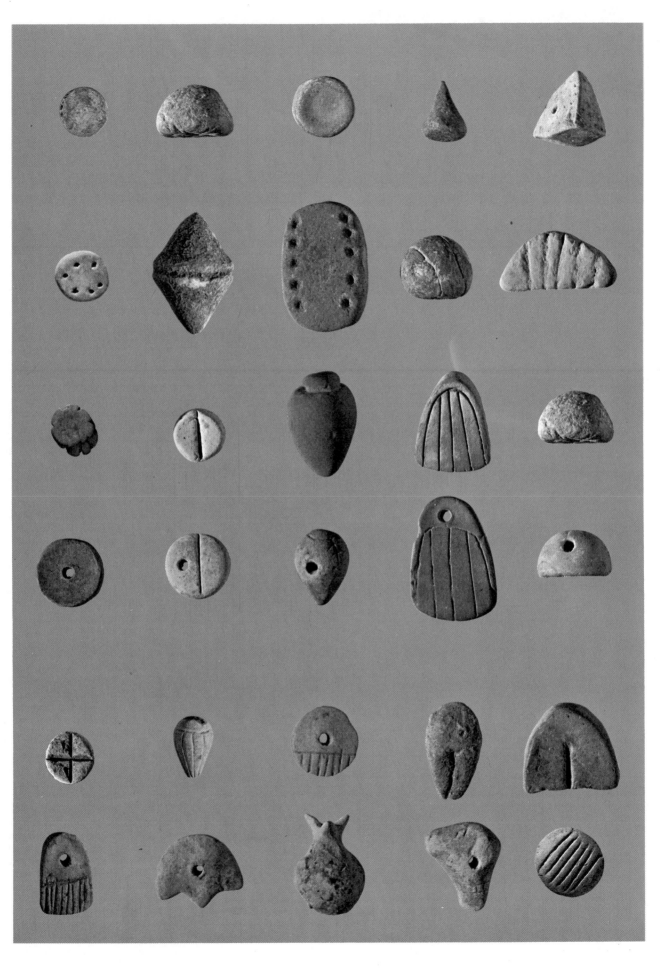

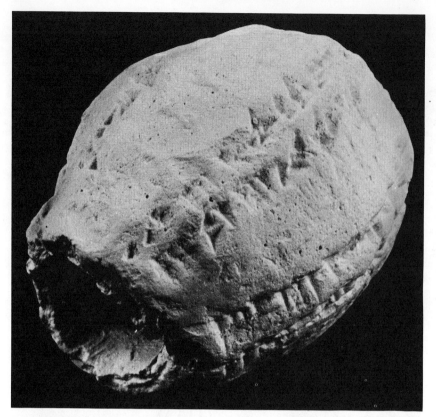

EGG-SHAPED HOLLOW TABLET was found in the palace ruins at Nuzi, a Mesopotamian city site of the second millennium B.C. The cuneiform inscription on its surface lists 48 animals. On being opened the tablet was found to contain 48 counters. The counters were lost before an accurate description had been prepared, but Nuzi texts suggest their use for reckoning.

SPHERICAL BULLA, an envelope of clay with tokens enclosed, was excavated from levels of the third millennium B.C. at Tepe Yahya, a site in south-central Iran halfway between the Indus Valley and lower Mesopotamia. Three tokens (*right*) were enclosed: a cone and two spheres.

lennium B.C. in Iraq, was excavated by the American School of Oriental Research in Baghdad between 1927 and 1931. Nearly 30 years later, reviewing an analysis of the Nuzi palace archives, A. Leo Oppenheim of the Oriental Institute of the University of Chicago reported the existence of a recording system that made use of "counters," or tokens. According to the Nuzi texts, such tokens were used for accounting purposes; they were spoken of as being "deposited," "transferred" and "removed."

Oppenheim visualized a kind of dual bookkeeping system in the Nuzi texts; in addition to the scribes' elaborate cuneiform records the palace administration had parallel tangible accounts. For example, one token of a particular kind might represent each of the animals in the palace herds. When new animals were born in the spring, the appropriate number of new tokens would be added; when animals were slaughtered, the appropriate number of tokens would be withdrawn. The tokens were probably also moved from one shelf to another when animals were moved from one herder or pasture to another, when sheep were shorn and so forth.

The discovery of a hollow egg-shaped tablet in the palace ruins supported Oppenheim's hypothesis. The inscription on the face of the tablet turned out to be a list of 48 animals. The hollow tablet rattled, and when one end of it was carefully opened, 48 tokens were found inside. Presumably the combination of a written list and countable tokens represented a transfer of animals from one palace service to another. Unfortunately we have no accurate description of the tokens; they were subsequently lost.

The Nuzi archives are dated to about 1500 B.C. The great Elamite site, Susa, has levels that are more than 1,500 years older. The digging at Susa, undertaken by French investigators, began in the 1880's and continues to this day. Six years after Oppenheim's 1958 report Pierre Amiet of the Musée du Louvre was able to confirm the existence of a similar accounting system at Susa. The token containers at Susa, unlike the container from Nuzi, were hollow clay spheres. Amiet called them "bullae"; so far about 70 of them have been found. The tokens they contain are clay modeled in a variety of geometric forms, including spheres, disks, cylinders, cones and tetrahedrons.

Amiet's finding was one of great significance; not only did it demonstrate that bullae and tokens were in existence at least a millennium and a half before they appeared at Nuzi but also it showed that they were as old or older than the earliest written records at Uruk. Indeed, it later became clear that the tokens, at least, were very much older.

In 1969 I began a research project

BULLA FROM SUSA shows two rows of surface impressions that match in number and shape the tokens it contained (*foreground*): one large cone, three small cones (*bottom row*) and three disks (*top row*). Tablets with incised representations of tokens probably evolved next.

with the objective of discovering when and in what ways clay first came to be used in the Near East. The making of pottery is of course the most familiar use of clay, but before the appearance of pottery man was making clay beads, modeling clay figurines, molding bricks out of clay and using clay for mortar. As a start on my project I visited museums in the U.S., in Europe and in various Near Eastern cities that had collections of clay artifacts dating back to the seventh, eighth and ninth millenniums B.C. This interval of time, beginning around 11,000 years ago and ending a little more than 8,000 years ago, saw the firm establishment of the first farming settlements in western Asia.

In the museum collections, along with the beads, bricks and figurines I had expected to find, I encountered what was to me an unforeseen category of objects: small clay artifacts of various forms. As I later came to realize, the forms were like those Amiet had found inside his Susa bullae: spheres, disks, cones, tetrahedrons, ovoids, triangles (or crescents), biconoids (double cones joined at the base), rectangles and other odd shapes difficult to describe. Could these artifacts, some of them 5,000 years older than the tokens from Susa, also have served as tokens?

I began to compile my own master catalogue of these oddities, listing each

token that was known to have come from a specific site. In summary, I found that whereas all of them were small, measuring on the average from one centimeter to two centimeters in their greatest dimension, many were of two distinct sizes. For example, there were small cones about a centimeter high and large cones three to four centimeters high. There were also thin disks, only three millimeters thick, and thick ones, as much as two centimeters thick. Other variations were evident. For example, in addition to whole spheres I found quarter-, half- and three-quarter spheres. Some of the tokens had additional features. Many were incised with deep lines; some had small clay pellets or coils on them and others bore shallow circular punch marks.

The tokens had all been modeled by hand. Either a small lump of clay had been rolled between the palms of the hands or the lump had been pinched between the fingertips. The clay was of a fine texture but showed no sign of special preparation (such as the addition of tempering substances, a practice in pottery making that enhances hardness after firing). All the tokens had, however, been fired to ensure their durability. Most of them varied in color from buff to red, but some had become gray and even blackish.

I found that the tokens were present

in virtually all museum collections of artifacts from the Neolithic period in western Asia. An extreme example of abundance is provided by the early village site of Jarmo in Iraq, first occupied some 8,500 years ago. Jarmo has yielded a total of 1,153 spheres, 206 disks and 106 cones. Reports generally indicate that the excavators found the tokens scattered over the floors of houses located in various parts of a site. If the tokens had once been kept in containers, such as baskets or pouches, these had disintegrated long ago. Nevertheless, there is evidence suggesting that the tokens were segregated from other artifacts and even implying what their function was. The reports indicate that many were found in clusters numbering 15 or more and that the clusters were located in storage areas within the houses.

As I reviewed the museum collections and the related site reports I became increasingly puzzled by the apparent omnipresence of the tokens. They had been found in sites from as far west as Beldibi in what is now southwestern Turkey to as far east as Chanhu Daro in what is now Pakistan. Tokens had even been unearthed at an eighth-millennium-B.C. site on the Nile near Khartoum.

At the same time I found that some site reports failed to take note of the tokens that had been collected, or men-

BULLAE	CYLINDERS	DISKS	SPHERES	CONES	SITE	MILLENNIUMS B.C. (II–IX)
		■			NUZI	
		■			MEGIDDO	
	■	■			KISH	
	■				FARA	
■	■	■	■	■	TELLO	
■	■	■			NIPPUR	
■	■	■	■		UR	
■	■	■	■	■	JEMDET NASR	
■	■	■			TEPE YAHYA	
■		■			SHAHDAD	
■	■				TALL-I MALYAN	
■	■	■			CHOGHA MISH	
■	■	■	■	■	SUSA	
■	■				TEPE HISSAR	
■	■	■	■	■	URUK	
	■	■			TALL-I-BAKUN	
■	■	■			TEPE GAWRA	
	■	■			TELL BILLA	
	■	■			CHAGAR BAZAR	
	■	■			HABUBA KABIRA	
	■		■		JAFFARABAD	
	■	■			CAN HASAN	
	■	■			MUNHATTA	
	■				ANAU	
	■	■			JEITUN	
	■	■			TAL-I-IBLIS	
	■				CHAGA SEFID	
	■	■			TELL ARPACHIYAH	
	■	■			TELL AS-SAWWAN	
	■	■			HAJJI FIRUZ	
	■	■			SEH GABI	
	■				JERICHO	
	■	■			TELL RAMAD	
	■				GHORAIFE	
	■	■			GIRD ALI AGHA	
	■	■			SUBERDE	
		■			DEH LURAN	
	■				BELT CAVE	
	■	■			TEPE SARAB	
	■	■			JARMO	
	■				TELL ASWAD	
	■				TEPE GURAN	
	■				CAYÖNÜ TEPESI	
		■			KHARTOUM	
					GANJ-I-DAREH TEPE	
		■			TEPE ASIAB	
					BELDIBI	

SITES WHERE TOKENS APPEAR represent a span of time from the ninth millennium B.C. to the second. As many as 20 variations on four basic token shapes are present at the earliest sites. Clay envelopes as containers for tokens do not appear before the fourth millennium B.C.

tioned them only casually. When the tokens were noted, the heading might read "objects of uncertain purpose," "children's playthings," "game pieces" or "amulets." As an example, the tokens from Tello in Iraq were interpreted by their discoverer, Henri de Genouillac, as amulets that expressed the residents' desire for "personal identification." Another example appears in Carleton S. Coon's report on Belt Cave in Iran. "From levels 11 and 12 come five mysterious...clay objects, looking like nothing in the world but suppositories. What they were used for is anyone's guess."

The realization that the tokens were all artifacts of the same kind was also hampered because, when they were listed at all in the site reports, they usually appeared under not one heading but several headings depending on their shape. For example, cones have been described as schematic female figurines, as phallic symbols, as gaming pieces and as nails, and spheres were mostly interpreted as marbles or as sling missiles.

Having studied at the École du Louvre, I was familiar with the work of Amiet. Nevertheless, I had compiled a catalogue of hundreds of tokens before I at last realized how much like Amiet's tokens from Susa these far earlier clay artifacts were. At first it seemed impossible that the two groups could be related; a minimum of 5,000 years separated the tokens of Neolithic times from those of Bronze Age Susa. As I extended my investigations to include later clay artifacts, dating from the seventh millennium B.C. to the fourth millennium and later, I found to my surprise that similar clay tokens had been found in substantial numbers at sites representative of the entire time span. Evidently a system of accounting that made use of tokens was widely used not only at Nuzi and Susa but throughout western Asia from as long ago as the ninth millennium B.C. to as recently as the second millennium.

The system appears to have been much the same as many other early, and even not so early, methods of account keeping. Classical scholars are familiar with the Roman system of making "calculations" with pebbles (*calculi* in Latin). Up to the end of the 18th century the British treasury still worked with counters to calculate taxes. For that matter, the shepherds of Iraq to this day use pebbles to account for the animals in their flocks, and the abacus is still the standard calculator in the markets of Asia. The archaic token system of western Asia was if anything only somewhat more complex than its later counterparts.

Considered overall, the system had some 15 major classes of tokens, further divided into some 200 subclasses on the basis of size, marking or fractional vari-

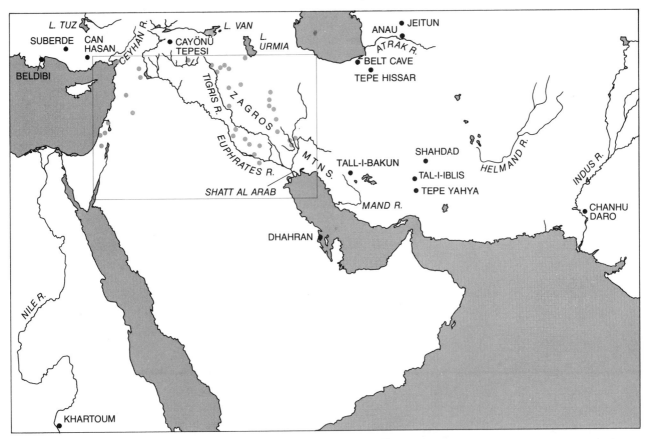

GEOGRAPHICAL DISTRIBUTION of tokens extends from as far north as the Caspian border of Iran to as far south as Khartoum and from Asia Minor eastward to the Indus Valley. Sites identified only by dots (*color*) within a rectangle here are named in the map below.

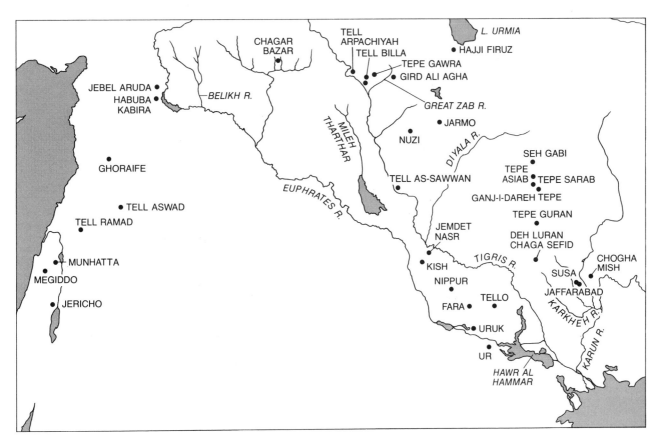

CLUSTERING OF SITES in the drainage of the upper and lower Tigris and the lower Euphrates and in the Zagros region of Iran is more a reflection of the availability of study collections than a measure of the actual extent and frequency of token use in the area.

ation, as in the case of the quarter-, half- and three-quarter spheres. Evidently each particular shape had a meaning of its own; a few appear to represent numerical values and others specific objects, commodities in particular.

It is not necessary to theorize about some of these meanings; a number of ideographs on the Uruk tablets almost exactly reproduce in two dimensions many of the tokens. For example, Uruk arbitrary signs for numerals, such as a small cone-shaped impression for the number one, a circular impression for the number 10 and a larger cone-shaped impression for the number 60 are matched by tokens: small cones, spheres and large cones. Further examples of ideographs that match tokens include, under the general heading of commodities, the Uruk symbol for sheep (a circle enclosing a cross), matched by disk-shaped tokens incised with a cross, and the Uruk symbol for a garment (a circle enclosing four parallel lines), matched by disk-shaped tokens incised with four parallel lines. Still other examples are ideographs for metal and oil and more clearly pictographic symbols for cattle, dogs and what are evidently vessels; each tablet sign can be matched with a similarly shaped and marked token. In addition, the forms of many still unread Sumerian ideographs appear to match other tokens.

Why did such a repertory of three-dimensional symbols come into existence? It cannot simply be a coincidence that the first tokens appear early in the Neolithic period, a time of profound change in human society. It was then that an earlier subsistence pattern, based on hunting and gathering, was transformed by the impact of plant and animal domestication and the development of a farming way of life. The new agricultural economy, although it un-

TOKEN TYPE I		II		III		IV		V		VI	
SPHERE		DISK		CONE		TETRAHEDRON		BICONOID		OVOID	
TOKENS	SUMERIAN PICTOGRAPHS	TOKENS	SUMERIAN PICTOGRAPHS	TOKENS	SUMERIAN PICTOGRAPHS	TOKENS	SUMERIAN PICTOGRAPHS	TOKENS	SUMERIAN PICTOGRAPHS	TOKENS	SUMERIAN PICTOGRAPHS
	NUMERAL 10		SEAT		NUMERAL 1				GOOD, SWEET		NAIL
	NUMERAL 10		GARMENT, CLOTH		NUMERAL 60				LEGAL DECISION, TRIAL, PEACE		OIL
	NUMERAL 10		GARMENT, CLOTH		NUMERAL 600				HEART, WOMB		ANIMAL (UNIDENTIFIED
	NUMERAL 100 OR 3,600		WOOL		BREAD		GARMENT, CLOTH		BRACELET, RING		
	NUMERAL 36,000		SHEEP		PERFUME				PLACE, COUNTRY		
			EWE								

FIFTY-TWO TOKENS, representative of 12 major categories of token types, have been matched here with incised characters that appear in the earliest Sumerian inscriptions. Most of the inscriptions cannot be read. Here, if the meaning of the symbol is known, the

doubtedly increased the production of food, would have been accompanied by new problems.

Perhaps the most crucial would have been food storage. Some portion of each annual yield had to be allocated for the farm family's own subsistence and some portion had to be set aside as seed for the next year's crop. Still another portion could have been reserved for barter with those who were ready to provide exotic products and raw materials in exchange for foodstuffs. It seems possible that the need to keep track of such allocations and transactions was enough to stimulate development of a recording system.

The earliest tokens now known are those from two sites in the Zagros region of Iran: Tepe Asiab and Ganj-i-Dareh Tepe. The people of both communities seem to have tended flocks and were possibly experimenting with crops around 8500 B.C., although at the same time they continued to hunt game and gather wild plants. The clay tokens they made were quite sophisticated in form. There were four basic types of token: spheres, disks, cones and cylinders. In addition there were tetrahedrons, ovoids, triangles, rectangles, bent coils and schematic animal forms. Subtypes included half-spheres and cones, spheres and disks with incisions and with punch marks. The set totaled 20 individual symbols.

The Neolithic period and the succeeding Chalcolithic period, or Copper Age, in western Asia lasted about 5,000 years. Over this substantial span one finds surprisingly few changes in the tokens, a fact that may indicate how well suited to the needs of an early agricultural economy this recording system was. In about 6500 B.C., 2,000 years after the rise of the first Zagros farming communities, another Iranian village, Tepe Sarab, began to flourish. The token inventory from excavations at Tepe

VII		IX		XI		XIII		XIV		XV	
CYLINDER		TRIANGLE		RECTANGLE		VESSEL		ANIMAL		MISCELLANEOUS	
TOKENS	SUMERIAN PICTOGRAPHS	TOKENS	SUMERIAN PICTOGRAPHS	TOKENS	SUMERIAN PICTOGRAPHS	TOKENS	SUMERIAN PICTOGRAPHS	TOKENS	SUMERIAN PICTOGRAPHS	TOKENS	SUMERIAN PICTOGRAPHS
	WOOD						TYPE OF VESSEL		DOG		BED
			STONE VESSEL		GRANARY		SHEEP'S MILK VESSEL		COW		
			METAL				TYPE OF VESSEL		LION		
			HILL				TYPE OF VESSEL				
					MAT, RUG						

equivalent word in English appears. The Sumerian numerical symbols equated with the various spherical and conical tokens are actual impressions in the surface of the tablet. In two instances (*sphere*) incised lines are added; in a third (*cone*) a circular punch mark is added.

Sarab shows no increase in the number of main types and an increase in subtypes from 20 only to 28, among them a four-sided pyramid and a stylized ox skull that is probably representative of cattle.

Perhaps it was during the Chalcolithic period that the agricultural surpluses of individual community members came to be pooled by means of taxes in kind, with the supervision of the surplus put into the hands of public officials such as temple attendants. If that is the case, the need to keep track of individual contributions evidently failed to bring any significant modification in the recording system. The tokens unearthed at four sites that flourished between 5500 and 4500 B.C.—Tell Arpachiyah and Tell as-Sawwan in Iraq and Chaga Sefid and Jaffarabad in Iran—reflect no more than minor developments. A new type of token, the biconoid, appears, and among some of the subtypes painted black lines and dots have taken the place of incisions and punch marks.

Early in the Bronze Age, between 3500 and 3100 B.C., there were significant changes in the recording system. This period saw an economic advance quite as remarkable in its own way as the rise of the farming economy that laid the foundation for it. The new development was the emergence of cities. Surveys of ancient sites in western Asia indicate a drastic increase in the population of Iraq and Iran; urban centers with many inhabitants begin to appear close to the earlier village settlements.

Craft specialization and the beginnings of mass production appear at this time. The bronze smithies and their products gave the age its name, but craftsmen other than smiths also arose, concentrated in various areas. The invention of the potter's wheel allowed the development of a pottery industry, and the output of various mass-production kilns came to be distributed over great distances. A similar trend is apparent in the manufacture of stone vessels, and the development of an expanded trade network is indicated by the appearance in Iraq of such exotic materials as lapis lazuli.

The development of an urban economy, rooted in trade, must have multiplied the demands on the traditional recording system. Not only production but also inventories, shipments and wage payments had to be noted, and merchants needed to preserve records of their transactions. By the last century of the fourth millennium B.C. the pressure of complex business accountancy on the token system becomes apparent both in the symbols and in how the tokens were used.

To consider the symbols first, six sites of the late fourth millennium B.C. in Iraq (Uruk, Tello and Fara), in Iran (Susa and Chogha Mish) and in Syria (Habuba Kabira) have yielded tokens representative of the full range of early shapes. In addition, some new shapes appear, among them parabolas, rhomboids and replicas of vessels. Even more significant than the appearance of new shapes, however, is the great proliferation of subtypes indicated by a variety of incised markings on the tokens. It is also now that a few of the tokens begin to have appliqué markings: added pellets or coils of clay.

The six sites have yielded a total of 660 tokens dating to about 3100 B.C. Of this number 363, or 55 percent, are marked with incisions. Most of the incisions are deep grooves made with the pointed end of a stylus; the grooves are placed conspicuously and with a clear concern for symmetry. On rounded tokens such as spheres, cones, ovoids and cylinders the incisions usually run around the equator and are thus visible from any aspect. On flat tokens such as disks, triangles and rectangles the incisions appear only on one face.

Most of the incisions present a pattern of parallel lines, although incised crosses and crisscross patterns are also found. The number of parallel lines would not seem to be random: there can be as many as 10 incisions, and the frequency of one-stroke, two-stroke, three-stroke and five-stroke patterns is conspicuous. It is noteworthy that with the exception of two-stroke patterns odd-numbered patterns are the most frequent.

Although incised patterns are by far the most abundant, 26 of the tokens (some 4 percent of the total) show circular impressions apparently made by punching the clay with the blunt end of a stylus. Some of the punched tokens bear a single impression. Others show a cluster of six punches, arranged either in a single row or in two rows with three impressions each.

As for changes in how the tokens were used, it is significant that 198 of them, or 30 percent of the total, are perforated. The perforated tokens run the gamut of types and include subtypes of the unmarked, incised and punched variety. In effect this means that tokens of any type or subtype were available in both unperforated and perforated forms. The perforations are so small that only a thin string could have passed through them. Of the explanations that come to mind one is that all 15 types of tokens and their 250 subtypes are nothing more than individual amulets that the early Bronze Age urban folk of western Asia wore on strings around their neck or wrist. I reject this explanation on two grounds. First, none of the perforated tokens that I have examined shows any evidence of being used as an amulet, such as wear polish or erosion around

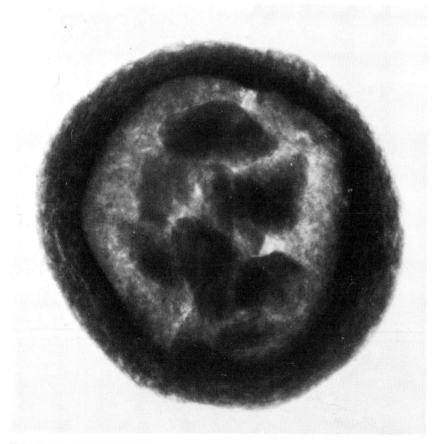

X RAY OF UNOPENED BULLA reveals tokens, some apparently cones and others ovoids. Age of the bulla is unknown; it was an isolated surface find near Dhahran in Saudi Arabia.

the string hole. Second, it seems preposterous that such a complex repertory of forms, so widespread in geographical distribution and manufactured with such remarkable uniformity, should have served as personal adornment in 30 percent of the cases and for some other purpose in the remaining 70 percent.

I prefer the hypothesis that some tokens representative of a specific transaction were strung together as a record. It seems at least plausible that the complexity of record keeping in an urban economy might have given rise to duplicate tokens suitable for stringing.

The stringing of tokens, if that is what the perforated tokens imply, would be only one change in how these symbolic bits of clay were used at the end of the fourth millennium B.C. A much more significant change is the first appearance at this time of clay bullae, or envelopes, such as those Amiet found as containers of tokens at Susa. The existence of a bulla is clear-cut direct evidence of the user's desire to segregate the tokens representing one or another transaction. The envelope could easily be made by pressing the fingers into a lump of clay about the size of a tennis ball, creating a cavity large enough to hold several tokens; the envelope could then be sealed with a patch of clay.

There is no doubt in my mind that such bullae were invented to provide the parties to a transaction with the kind of smooth clay surface that according to Sumerian custom could be marked by the personal seals of the individuals concerned as a validation of the event. The fact that most of the 350 bullae so far discovered bear the impressions of two different seals lends support to my conviction. Amiet has suggested that the Susa bullae may have served as bills of lading. In this view a rural producer of, say, textiles would consign a shipment of goods to an urban middleman, sending along with the shipment a bulla that contained a number of tokens descriptive of the kind and quantity of merchandise shipped. By breaking the bulla the recipient of the shipment could verify the makeup of the shipment; moreover, the need to deliver an intact bulla would inhibit the carrier from tampering with the merchandise in transit. This sealed transfer of tokens between trade partners represents an entirely new way of using the ancient recording system.

The innovation had one serious drawback. The seals impressed on the smooth exterior of the bulla served to validate each transmission, but if the seal impressions were to be preserved, the bulla had to remain intact. How, then, could one determine what tokens were enclosed and how many? A solution to the problem was soon found. The surface of the bulla was marked so that in addition to the validating seal impressions, it bore images of all the enclosed tokens.

TABLETS FROM URUK show the convex shape that may reflect their evolution from hollow bullae. Impressions represent numerals. Tablets are in the Pergamon Museum in Berlin.

The most striking example of this stratagem is a bulla that proved to contain six grooved ovoid tokens. Each of the six tokens had been pressed into the surface of the bulla before being stored inside it; they fit the surface imprints exactly. This means of recording the contents of a bulla on its exterior was not, however, universally practiced. On most bullae the impression was made with a thumb or a stylus; a circular impression stood for a sphere or a disk, a semicircular or triangular impression stood for a cone, and so forth.

The bulla markings were clearly not invented to take the place of the token system of record keeping. Nevertheless, that is what happened. One can visualize the process. At first the innovation flourished because of its convenience; anyone could "read" what tokens a bulla contained and how many without destroying the envelope and its seal impressions. What then happened was virtually inevitable, and the substitution of two-dimensional portrayals of the tokens for the tokens themselves would seem to have been the crucial link between the archaic recording system and writing. The hollow bullae with their enclosed tokens would have been replaced by inscribed solid clay objects: tablets. The strings, baskets and shelf loads of tokens in the archives would have given way to representative signs inscribed on tablets, that is, to written records.

The convex profile of the early Uruk tablets may well be a morphological feature inherited from the spherical bullae. Much the same may be true of the

selection as a writing surface of a material as unsuitable as clay, a soft and easily smeared medium that must be dried or baked if it is to be preserved. There can be little doubt about the relation between the shapes and markings of the tokens and the supposed arbitrary forms of many Uruk ideographs. No fewer than 33 clear-cut identities exist between the ideographs and two-dimensional representations of tokens and more than twice that many are possible.

To summarize, the earliest examples of writing in Mesopotamia may not, as many have assumed, be the result of pure invention. Instead they appear to be a novel application late in the fourth millennium B.C. of a recording system that was indigenous to western Asia from early Neolithic times onward. In this view the appearance of writing in Mesopotamia represents a logical step in the evolution of a system of record keeping that originated some 11,000 years ago.

On this hypothesis the fact that the system was used without significant modification until late in the fourth millennium B.C. seems attributable to the comparatively simple record-keeping requirements of the preceding 5,000 years. With the rise of cities and the development of large-scale trade the system was pushed onto a new track. Images of the tokens soon supplanted the tokens themselves, and the evolution of symbolic objects into ideographs led to the rapid adoption of writing all across western Asia.

BRONZE AGE CITIES AND CIVILIZATIONS

BRONZE AGE CITIES AND CIVILIZATIONS

III

INTRODUCTION

What is civilization? The word *civilization* is by no means an old word or concept. Boswell reported that in 1772 he urged Johnson to insert the word in his dictionary, but the doctor declined; he preferred the older word *civility*, which, in being derived from the Latin *civitas*, reflects the world of the city dweller. V. G. Childe (who defined the Neolithic Revolution, as we saw in Section II) listed the elements that he believed were involved in human transition from neolithic communities to urban centers. In his books *Man Makes Himself* and *What Happened in History*, he provided a list of material inventions that he believed were responsible for transforming people into urban dwellers: writing, use of animals for traction, wheeled carts, the plow, metallurgy, standard units of weight and volume, sailing boats, surplus production, specialization of craftsmen, irrigation technology, and mathematics. However, such a list is of very little help in defining a civilization, and it adds absolutely nothing to our understanding of how and why these inventions came about in the first place.

At neolithic Çayönü Tepesi about 7000 B.C. (see Çambel and Braidwood in Section II) there was metallurgy; sailing was already evident in Europe by 5000 B.C., as was irrigation at neolithic Beidha, Palestine; and specialized craftsmen may be posited as the artists of the Paleolithic. It is quite clear that neither a single criterion nor any list of criteria will succeed in defining civilization. Yet, if any single invention stands out as creating a dramatic change in social organization, I think it must be writing.

An attempt to define civilization made at a symposium held in 1958 at the Oriental Institute of the University of Chicago was perhaps more successful than others. (The proceedings of the symposium were published in 1960 in a book entitled *City Invincible*.) At that symposium the anthropologist Clyde Kluckhohn argued that there were three essential criteria for civilization: (1) towns containing 5000 or more people, (2) writing, and (3) monumental ceremonial centers. The Assyriologist I. Gelb stated, "I have reached the conclusion that writing is of such importance that civilization cannot exist without it, and, conversely, that writing cannot exist except in a civilization." I would agree with this, were it not for the Inca and Maya of the New World, peoples who lacked full writing and yet cannot be denied the status of civilization, however one chooses to define the concept. Robert M. Adams (see "The Origin of Cities"), an archaeologist and anthropologist, perhaps came closest to a working definition. He argued for a definition of civilization as a society with functionally interrelated sets of social institutions, which he listed as:

1. Class stratification, each stratum marked by a highly different degree of ownership or control of the main productive resources.

2. Political and religious hierarchies complementing each other in the administration of territorially organized states.

3. Complex division of labor, with full-time craftsmen, servants, soldiers, and officials existing alongside the great mass of primary, peasant producers.

Professor Adams' criteria thus concentrated on sociological phenomena that, when found working together, constitute a civilization.

If the earlier considerations presented by Childe failed to provide an understanding of how and why cities and civilizations evolved, it is worth considering how archaeologists today approach an answer to the question. The essays that follow discuss six of the earliest urban civilizations of the Old World: Sumerian, Indus, Persian Gulf ("Dilmun"), Proto-Elamite, Egyptian, and Mycenaean (see the articles by Kramer, Dales, Glob and Bibby, Lamberg-Karlovsky, Emery, and Chadwick, respectively). Each is wholly distinctive in architecture, ceramic and metallurgical technology, language, and political and economic organization. There are certain factors, however, that they all shared, particularly in their evolutionary development. It is these factors that archaeologists believe were fundamental to the evolution of cities and civilization.

Today scholars preoccupied with explaining the rise of civilization do not concentrate on single factors, such as the practice of irrigation leading to surplus agriculture and a bureaucratic state, but describe the rise of civilization as the result of the interaction of several different factors: environment and subsistence economy, population and demographic stress, trade, technology, and economic and social organization.

Environmental Conditions and Subsistence Economy

The environmental setting plays a fundamental role in the development of any civilization. It sets the conditions for the development of the subsistence economy. The environmental setting of Egypt, the Mycenaean world of the Aegean, and the world of the Maya civilization of the New World set constraints on the development of each civilization. The development of a viticulture—the production of grapes and wine—in the Aegean was essential to the Mycenaeans, and the floodplain agriculture of Egypt, based on cereals, was different from that of the Maya and the Mycenaeans. Each was determined by its own environmental setting. It is not mere coincidence that the four great civilizations of the Old World—Egypt, Mesopotamia, the Indus, and Shang China—were in alluvial plains. These riverine valleys, when irrigated, produced a surplus of agricultural crops, which differed in the various environments. Intensive food production through irrigation allows for a high population density and the production of a surplus agriculture. Intensive food production in each of the areas depended on irrigation agriculture, which, in turn, required a specific environmental setting.

It is one thing, however, to argue that civilization would not have emerged in these areas without irrigation and quite another to say that irrigation was the primary cause in the development of civilization. As noted, irrigation allowed for the settlement of previously unoccupied areas, whether in southern Mesopotamia or the Indus Valley. Irrigation produces higher yields than dry farming—an increase of up to 50 percent in modern times. This leads to differences in the quality and value of land, for irrigable land offers a far higher yield than land dependent on rainfall. Thus in the Near East or in the area of the Indus, where mountain valleys first saw the development of agriculture, smaller populations exploited a larger amount of land of equal value to that in the alluvial floodplains, where irrigation was possible and a smaller amount of available land could support a greater population. Differences in the value of the productivity of land led, in turn, to a competition for land ownership, a differential wealth from the surplus production, and a concomitant specialization of labor and social stratification.

It can hardly be doubted that a comprehensive understanding of environmental conditions sets the necessary conditions for the understanding of a civilization. However, though they are necessary conditions, they are not entirely sufficient, for such aspects as ideology, political systems, and social organization are also of great importance.

Population

The archaeological record confirms dramatically that the "food-producing revolution" resulted in a gradual increase in population. Earlier populations appear to have maintained an equilibrium between population and resources, whereas, following the development of agriculture, there was a clear and consistent increase in populations. This clearly documented fact has resulted in seeing population pressure as a prime cause in the development of prehistoric societies. As the permanent villages of the eighth through sixth millennia are larger in size than the earlier hunting and gathering sites, the towns of the fifth and fourth millennia in the Old World are larger than the earlier agricultural villages.

It appears certain that populations were increasing in Europe, Asia, and Africa, as well as in the New World, before the Urban Revolution. Population expansion may result in the growth of a specific community, or alternatively in the driving off of daughter communities. This driving off for the establishment of new communities is the typical mechanism for the geographical expansion of early farming communities and appears to have continued until Ubaid times in Mesopotamia, about 4000 B.C. After this time population increases are contained within restricted zones, and we see the gradual increase of settlement in Egypt and Mesopotamia such that by 3000 B.C. there are large towns and cities.

What brought about this change to the growth of towns and cities? Some scholars favor a direct demographic explanation: an increase in birth rate. Others prefer to consider a combination of factors: increasing population, increasing efficiency in the subsistence economy, sedentism of nomadic peoples, and a social organization directed toward the concentration of populations. The evidence from Egypt, Mesopotamia, and the Indus Valley seems to be clear that population increase—in all the above instances within a geographically circumscribed area that was agriculturally productive when exploited by irrigation—played a fundamental role in the development of civilization. And an expanding population was related to an increasing economic specialization and social stratification within the civilization of Mesopotamia, Egypt, and the Indus Valley.

Trade

In recent years trade has been seen as a primary factor in the development of complex societies. The excavation of such sites as Tepe Yahyā, in Iran (see article by Lamberg-Karlovsky and Lamberg-Karlovsky) and the recovery of the "Dilmun" civilization (see article by Glob and Bibby) have underscored the importance of economic interaction in the Near East. The alluvial plains of Mesopotamia and, to a lesser degree, those of Egypt and the Indus, lacked mineral materials—copper, gold, lapis lazuli, turquoise, carnelian—and even building timber. Essential as well as luxury materials had to be imported, often from very considerable distances, into the cities of these civilizations. Merchants involved in this trade operated not only as full-time traders but as foreign emissaries to distant city-states. Trade within the literate urban centers of Egypt, Sumer, and the Indus must have been organized differently from that which distributed obsidian throughout the neolithic communities, because neolithic communities could survive without obsidian but the Sumerian city-state depended on the uninterrupted supply of essential raw materials. The particular mechanism established by the Sumerians was to place the control of trade in the temples and the palaces, thus institutionalizing trade within the hands of the state and assuring its efficient continuity and the increased development and centralization of economic affairs.

The problem touched upon in the Özgüç article is particularly puzzling. The Assyrian trading colony at Kültepe was directly involved in the trade and exchange of tin. But where did the tin actually come from? There is not a *single* known source of tin in the Near East or in the eastern Mediterranean; the only tin known from Turkey to India and North Africa comes from the eastern deserts of Egypt. Yet throughout the third millennium copper-tin bronzes were produced not only by the Egyptians, Sumerians, and the Indus civilizations but by all communities throughout the Near East. Though the Assyrians were trading tin, we do not know where they obtained it. The known sources— Spain, Cornwall, Central Europe, and Burma—are either too distant or were not exploited in antiquity. The tin in the eastern deserts may have been exploited, but it seems unlikely that this simple resource supplied the entirety of Near Eastern demand. The resolution of this problem, like so many archaeological problems, awaits solution.

Social Organization

The social organization of each civilization was distinctive. In Egypt the entire country was unified under one political leader—the god king Pharaoh; in Mesopotamia each city-state was led by a king; the social organization of the Indus civilization is little understood, but it may have been, like that of Mesopotamia, organized into independent city-states. The social and economic factors necessary for the rise of cities are fundamentally dependent on the integration of a centralized economic and political power, social stratification, and economic specialization. These three factors contributed to the development of the Urban Revolution, and in each of the areas where they interacted, whether in Mesopotamia as discussed by Kramer in "The Sumerians" or the Mycenaean world as discussed by Chadwick, they led to the development of a complex society.

Economic specialization, a stratified society, and the centralization of power depend on the development of a *surplus* production of subsistence goods to support those engaged in trade, administration, and crafts. Social differentiation depends not only on surplus production but on the uneven distribution of this surplus—the development of a class-structured society. The individuals able to appropriate the greater surplus assumed greater power, not only economic but political as well. The development of a central authority became essential in the control of long-distance trade; warfare; the management of storage; and the redistribution of food, raw materials, and manufactured commodities. The situation resulting from an increasing economic specialization, social stratification, and centralization of authority initiated a process that, once set in motion, was irreversible.

Technology

That technology has an impact on the development of civilization would seem obvious. The discovery of new subsistence systems through domestication; increased population through surplus production by irrigation; the invention of metallurgy and the wheel; and the harnessing of animals are all major technological inventions that occurred prior to the Urban Revolution. Recognizing this fact, one may ask two questions: Could civilization have developed without the invention of these technologies? And what effect did these inventions have on the societies that developed them? In general, the answer involves three different, though related, considerations as recently outlined by Ruth Whitehouse in *The First Cities:*

1. Technological inventions encourage the rate of economic specialization.
2. Technological inventions increase the efficiency of production.
3. Technological inventions allow for the further elaboration of new activities: military, cermonial, recreational, and so on.

One example will suffice to illustrate the way these criteria function. (1) Processes involved in metallurgical production were far more complex than those for making stone tools. The production of metals involved smelting, casting, and ore extraction. The smiths that mastered these techniques were almost certainly full-time specialists removed from processing their own food supply. Such specialization resulted in the need to support specialist craftsmen from the surplus foods produced by those engaged exclusively in agricultural production. (2) The development of metallurgy not only increased specialization but increased the efficiency of production. Compared to stone, a metal tool holds its edge longer, is far easier to sharpen, and can be melted down and recast as a new tool. (3) It is all too obvious that the invention of metals led to the elaboration of new activities, still vital today, in practical, military, and recreational areas.

The above factors—environmental conditions and subsistence economy, population, trade, social organization, and technology—are not the only factors that led to the rise of complex societies. However, in recent years they have been thought to be the principal factors in the accomplishment of the Urban Revolution. Other factors, such as military activity and warfare, acted as a powerful force in the development of a central authority and the expansion of states. Further archaeological work will assign different emphases to the various factors.

REFERENCES

Childe, V. G. 1951. *Man Makes Himself.* Mentor Books, New York.
Childe, V. G. 1957. *What Happened in History.* Pelican Books, Baltimore.
Kraeling, E. and Adams, R. M. 1960. *City Invincible.* University of Chicago, Chicago.
Whitehouse, R. 1977. *The First Cities.* Phaidon, London.

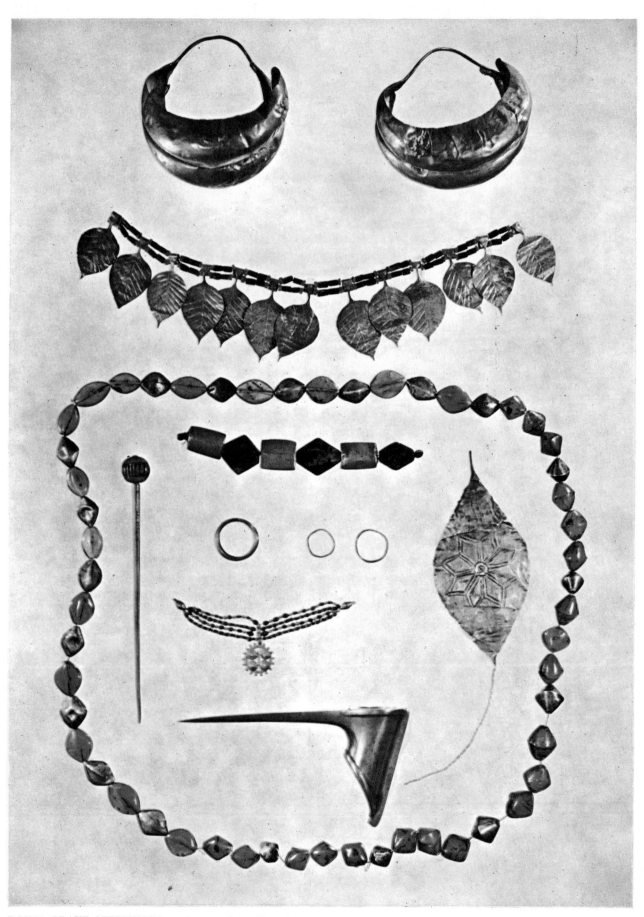

ROYAL GRAVE OFFERINGS from later tombs at Ur indicate the concentration of wealth that accompanied the emergence of a kingly class. Dated at about 2500 B.C., the objects include large gold earrings (*top*); a headdress with gold leaves; beads of gold, lapis and carnelian; gold rings; a gold leaf; a hairpin of gold and lapis; an ornament with a gold pendant; an adz head of electrum.

The Origin of Cities

17

by Robert M. Adams

September 1960

The agricultural revolution ultimately made it possible for men to congregate in large communities and to take up specialized tasks. The first cities almost certainly arose in Mesopotamia

The rise of cities, the second great "revolution" in human culture, was pre-eminently a social process, an expression more of changes in man's interaction with his fellows than in his interaction with his environment. For this reason it marks not only a turning but also a branching point in the history of the human species.

Earlier steps are closely identified with an increasing breadth or intensity in the exploitation of the environment. Their distinguishing features are new tools and techniques and the discovery of new and more dependable resources for subsistence. Even in so advanced an achievement as the invention of agriculture, much of the variation from region to region was simply a reflection of local differences in subsistence potential.

In contrast the urban revolution was

MAP OF NIPPUR on a clay tablet dates from about 1500 B.C. Two lines at far left trace the course of Euphrates River; adjacent lines show one wall of the city. Square structures at far right are temples; the two vertical lines at right center represent a canal.

EARLY GRAVE OFFERINGS from Mesopotamian tombs of about 3900 B.C. consist mainly of painted pottery such as two vessels at left. Vessels of diorite (*center and right center*) and alabaster (*far right*), found in tombs of about 3500 B.C. and later, reflect growth of trade with other regions and increasing specialization of crafts. These vessels and objects on opposite page are in the University Museum of the University of Pennsylvania.

a decisive cultural and social change that was less directly linked to changes in the exploitation of the environment. To be sure, it rested ultimately on food surpluses obtained by agricultural producers above their own requirements and somehow made available to city dwellers engaged in other activities. But its essential element was a whole series of new institutions and the vastly greater size and complexity of the social unit, rather than basic innovations in subsistence. In short, the different forms that early urban societies assumed are essentially the products of differently interacting political and economic—human —forces. And the interpretive skills required to understand them are correspondingly rooted more in the social sciences and humanities than in the natural sciences.

Even the term urban needs qualification. Many of the qualities we think of as civilized have been attained by societies that failed to organize cities. At least some Egyptologists believe that civilization advanced for almost 2,000 years under the Pharaohs before true cities appeared in Egypt. The period was marked by the development of monumental public works, a formal state superstructure, written records and the beginnings of exact science. In the New World, too, scholars are still searching the jungles around Maya temple centers in Guatemala and Yucatán for recognizably urban agglomerations of dwellings. For all its temple architecture and high art, and the intellectual achievement represented by its hieroglyphic writing and accurate long-count calendar, classic Maya civilization apparently was not based on the city.

These facts do not detract from the fundamental importance of the urban revolution, but underline its complex character. Every high civilization other than possibly the Mayan did ultimately

produce cities. And in most civilizations urbanization began early.

There is little doubt that this was the case for the oldest civilization and the earliest cities: those of ancient Mesopotamia. The story of their development, which we will sketch here, is still a very tentative one. In large part the uncertainties are due to the state of the archeological record, which is as yet both scanty and unrepresentative. The archeologist's preoccupation with early temple-furnishings and architecture, for example, has probably exaggerated their importance, and has certainly given us little information about contemporary secular life in neighboring precincts of the same towns.

Eventually written records help overcome these deficiencies. However, 500 or more years elapsed between the onset of the first trends toward urbanism and the earliest known examples of cuneiform script. And then for the succeeding 700 or 800 years the available texts are laconic, few in number and poorly understood. To a degree, they can be supplemented by cautious inferences drawn from later documents. But the earliest chapters rest primarily on archeological data.

Let us pick up the narrative where Robert J. Braidwood left it in *The Agricultural Revolution*, with the emergence of a fully agricultural people, many of them grouped together in villages of perhaps 200 to 500 individuals. Until almost the end of our own story, dating finds little corroboration in written records. Moreover, few dates based on the decay of radioactive carbon are yet available in Mesopotamia for this crucial period. But by 5500 B.C., or even earlier, it appears that the village-farming community had fully matured in southwestern Asia. As a way of life it then stabilized internally for 1,500 years or more, although it con-

tinued to spread downward from the hills and piedmont where it had first crystallized in the great river valleys.

Then came a sharp increase in tempo. In the next 1,000 years some of the small agricultural communities on the alluvial plain between the Tigris and Euphrates rivers not only increased greatly in size, but changed decisively in structure. They culminated in the Sumerian city-state with tens of thousands of inhabitants, elaborate religious, political and military establishments, stratified social classes, advanced technology and widely extended trading contacts [see the article "The Sumerians," by Samuel Noah Kramer, beginning on page 179]. The river-valley agriculture on which the early Mesopotamian cities were established differed considerably from that of the uplands where domestication had begun. Wheat and barley remained the staple crops, but they were supplemented by dates. The date palm yielded not only prodigious and dependable supplies of fruit but also wood. Marshes and estuaries teemed with fish, and their reeds provided another building material. There was almost no stone, however; before the establishment of trade with surrounding areas, hard-fired clay served for such necessary agricultural tools as sickles.

The domestic animals—sheep, goats, donkeys, cattle and pigs by the time of the first textual evidence—may have differed little from those known earlier in the foothills and northern plains. But they were harder to keep, particularly the cattle and the donkeys which were needed as draft animals for plowing. During the hot summers all vegetation withered except for narrow strips along the watercourses. Fodder had to be cultivated and distributed, and pastureland was at a premium. These problems of management may help explain why the herds rapidly became a responsibility of people associated with the temples. And control of the herds in turn may have provided the stimulus that led temple officials frequently to assume broader control over the economy and agriculture.

Most important, agriculture in the alluvium depended on irrigation, which had not been necessary in the uplands. For a long time the farmers made do with small-scale systems, involving breaches in the natural embankments of the streams and uncontrolled local flooding. The beginnings of large-scale canal networks seem clearly later than the advent of fully established cities.

In short, the immediately pre-urban society of southern Mesopotamia consisted of small communities scattered along natural watercourses. Flocks had to forage widely, but cultivation was confined to narrow enclaves of irrigated plots along swamp margins and stream banks. In general the swamps and rivers provided an important part of the raw materials and diet.

Where in this pattern were the inducements, perhaps even preconditions, for urbanization that explain the precocity of the Mesopotamian achievement? First, there was the productivity of irrigation agriculture. In spite of chronic water-shortage during the earlier part of the growing season and periodic floods around the time of the harvest, in spite of a debilitating summer climate and the ever present danger of salinity in flooded or over-irrigated fields, farming yielded a clear and dependable surplus of food.

Second, the very practice of irrigation must have helped induce the growth of cities. It is sometimes maintained that the inducement lay in a need for centralized control over the building and maintaining of elaborate irrigation systems, but this does not seem to have been the case. As we have seen, such systems came after the cities themselves. However, by engendering inequalities in access to productive land, irrigation contributed to the formation of a stratified society. And by furnishing a reason for border disputes between neighboring communities, it surely promoted a warlike atmosphere that drew people together in offensive and defensive concentrations.

Finally, the complexity of subsistence pursuits on the flood plains may have indirectly aided the movement toward cities. Institutions were needed to medi-

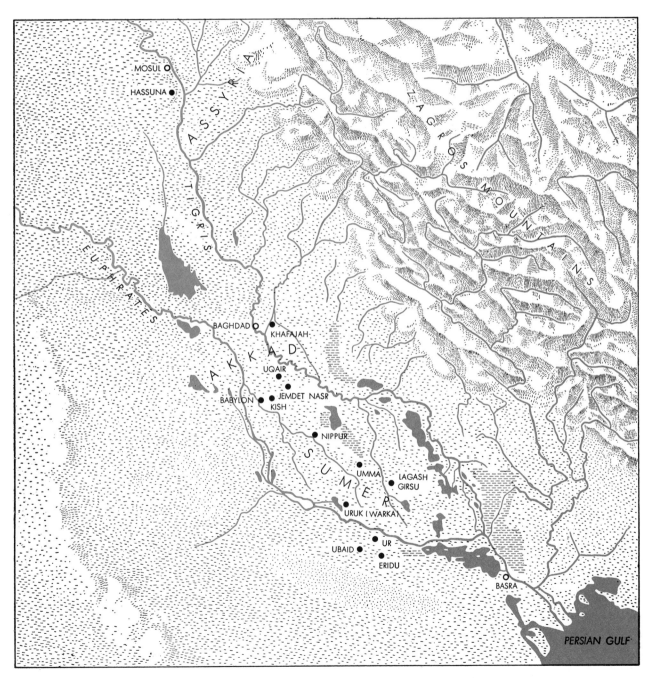

ANCIENT CITIES of Mesopotamia (*black dots*) were located mainly along Tigris and Euphrates rivers and their tributaries. In ancient times these rivers followed different courses from those shown on this modern map. Modern cities are shown as open dots.

CITY OF ERBIL in northern Iraq is built on the site of ancient city of Arbela. This aerial view suggests the character and ap-pearance of Mesopotamian cities of thousands of years ago, with streets and houses closely packed around central public buildings.

ate between herdsman and cultivator; between fisherman and sailor; between plowmaker and plowman. Whether through a system of rationing, palace largesse or a market that would be recognizable to us, the city provided a logical and necessary setting for storage, exchange and redistribution. Not surprisingly, one of the recurrent themes in early myths is a rather didactic demonstration that the welfare of the city goddess is founded upon the harmonious interdependence of the shepherd and the farmer.

In any case the gathering forces for urbanization first become evident around 4000 B.C. Which of them furnished the initial impetus is impossible to say, if indeed any single factor was responsible. We do not even know as yet whether the onset of the process was signaled by a growth in the size of settlements. And of course mere increase in size would not necessarily imply technological or economic advance beyond the level of the village-farming community. In our own time we have seen primitive agricultural peoples, such as the Yoruba of western Nigeria, who maintained sizable cities that were in fact little more than overgrown village-farming settlements. They were largely self-sustaining because most of the productive inhabitants were full-time farmers.

The evidence suggests that at the beginning the same was true of Mesopotamian urbanization: immediate economic change was not its central characteristic. As we shall see shortly, the first clear-cut trend to appear in the archeological record is the rise of temples. Conceivably new patterns of thought and social organization crystallizing within the temples served as the primary force in bringing people together and setting the process in motion.

Whatever the initial stimulus to growth and reorganization, the process itself clearly involved the interaction of many different factors. Certainly the institutions of the city evolved in different directions and at different rates, rather than as a smoothly emerging totality. Considering the present fragmentary state of knowledge, it is more reasonable here to follow some of these trends individually rather than to speculate from the shreds (or, rather, sherds!) and patches of data about how the complete organizational pattern developed.

Four archeological periods can be distinguished in the tentative chronology of the rise of the Mesopotamian city-state. The earliest is the Ubaid, named for the first site where remains of this period were uncovered [*see map on page 173*]. At little more than a guess, it may have lasted for a century or two past 4000 B.C., giving way to the relatively brief Warka period. Following this the first written records appeared during the Protoliterate period, which spanned the remainder of the fourth millennium. The final part of our story is the Early Dynastic period, which saw the full flowering of independent city-states between about 3000 and 2500 B.C.

Of all the currents that run through the whole interval, we know most about religious institutions. Small shrines existed in the early villages of the northern plains and were included in the cultural inventory of the earliest known agriculturalists in the alluvium. Before the end of the Ubaid period the free-standing shrine had lost its original fluidity of plan and adopted architectural features that afterward permanently characterized Mesopotamian temples. The development continued into the Early Dynastic period, when we see a complex of workshops and storehouses surrounding a greatly enlarged but rigidly traditional arrangement of cult chambers. No known contemporary structures were remotely comparable in size or complexity to these establishments until almost the end of the Protoliterate period.

At some point specialized priests appeared, probably the first persons released from direct subsistence labor. Their ritual activities are depicted in Protoliterate seals and stone carvings. If not immediately, then quite early, the priests also assumed the role of economic administrators, as attested by ration or wage lists found in temple premises among the earliest known examples of writing. The priestly hierarchies continued to supervise a multitude of economic as well as ritual activities into (and beyond) the Early Dynastic period, although by then more explicitly political forms of organization had perhaps become dominant. For a long time, however, temples seem to have been the

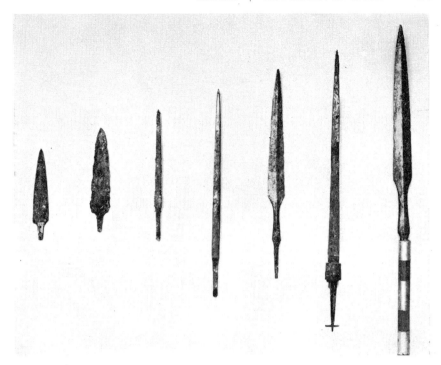

SPEARHEADS of copper and bronze from the royal cemetery at Ur date back to the third millennium B.C. The workmanship of these weapons matches that of the jewelry shown on page 170.

largest and most complex institutions that existed in the communities growing up around them.

The beginnings of dynastic political regimes are much harder to trace. Monumental palaces, rivaling the temples in size, appear in the Early Dynastic period, but not earlier. The term for "king" has not yet been found in Protoliterate texts. Even so-called royal tombs apparently began only in the Early Dynastic period.

Lacking contemporary historical or archeological evidence, we must seek the origins of dynastic institutions primarily in later written versions of traditional myths. Thorkild Jacobsen of the University of Chicago has argued persuasively that Sumerian myths describing the world of the gods reflect political institutions as they existed in human society just prior to the rise of dynastic authority. If so, they show that political authority in the Protoliterate period rested in an assembly of the adult male members of the community. Convoked only to meet sporadic external threat, the assembly's task was merely to select a short-term war leader.

Eventually, as the myths themselves suggest, successful war leaders were retained even in times of peace. Herein lies the apparent origin of kingship. At times springing up outside the priestly corporations, at times coming from them,

ROYAL WAR-CHARIOT carved on limestone plaque from city of Ur reflects increasing concern of Mesopotamian cities about methods of warfare in middle of third millennium B.C.

RELIGIONS of ancient Mesopotamia were dominated by the idea that man was fashioned to serve the gods. Here a worshipper followed by figure with pail brings a goat as an offering to goddess seated at right. A divine attendant kneels before her. This impression and the one below were made from stone cylinder-seals of Akkadian period (about 2400 B.C.).

new leaders emerged who were preoccupied with, and committed to, both defensive and offensive warfare against neighboring city-states.

The traditional concerns of the temples were not immediately affected by the new political leadership. Palace officials acquired great landed estates of their own, but the palace itself was occupied chiefly with such novel activities as raising and supplying its army, maintaining a large retinue of servants and entertainers and constructing a defensive wall around the city.

These undertakings took a heavy toll of the resources of the young city-states, perhaps too heavy to exact by the old "democratic" processes. Hence it is not surprising that as permanent, hereditary royal authority became established, the position of the assembly declined. In the famous epic of Gilgamesh, an Early Dynastic king of Uruk, the story opens with the protests of the citizenry over their forced labor on the city walls. Another episode shows Gilgamesh manipulating the assembly, obviously no longer

depending on its approval for his power. Rooted in war, the institution of kingship intensified a pattern of predatory expansionism and shifting military rivalries. The early Mesopotamian king could trace his origin to the need for military leadership. But the increasingly militaristic flavor of the Early Dynastic period also can be traced at least in part to the interests and activities of kings and their retinues as they proceeded to consolidate their power.

As society shifted its central focus from temple to palace it also separated into classes. Archeologically, the process can best be followed through the increasing differentiation in grave offerings in successively later cemeteries. Graves of the Ubaid period, at the time when monumental temples were first appearing, hold little more than a variable number of pottery vessels. Those in the cemetery at Ur, dating from the latter part of the Early Dynastic period, show a great disparity in the wealth they contain. A small proportion, the royal tombs

(not all of whose principal occupants may have belonged to royal families), are richly furnished with beautifully wrought weapons, ornaments and utensils of gold and lapis lazuli. A larger number contain a few copper vessels or an occasional bead of precious metal, but the majority have only pottery vessels or even nothing at all. Both texts and archeological evidence indicate that copper and bronze agricultural tools were beyond the reach of the ordinary peasant until after the Early Dynastic period, while graves of the well-to-do show "conspicuous consumption" of copper in the form of superfluous stands for pottery vessels even from the beginning of the period.

Early Dynastic texts likewise record social and economic stratification. Records from the main archive of the Baba Temple in Girsu, for example, show substantial differences in the allotments from that temple's lands to its parishioners. Other texts describe the sale of houseplots or fields, often to form great estates held by palace officials and worked by communities of dependent clients who may originally have owned the land. Still others record the sale of slaves, and the rations allotted to slaves producing textiles under the supervision of temple officials. As a group, however, slaves constituted only a small minority of the population until long after the Early Dynastic period.

Turning to the development of technology, we find a major creative burst in early Protoliterate times, involving very rapid stylistic and technical advance in the manufacture of seals, statuary and ornate vessels of carved stone, cast copper or precious metals. But the number of craft specialists apparently was very small, and the bulk of their products seems to have been intended only for cult purposes. In contrast the Early Dynastic period saw a great increase in production of nonagricultural commodities, and almost certainly a corresponding increase in the proportion of the population that was freed from the tasks of primary subsistence to pursue their craft on a full-time basis. Both stylistically and technologically, however, this expansion was rooted in the accomplishments of the previous period and produced few innovations of its own.

Production was largely stimulated by three new classes of demand. First, the burgeoning military establishment of the palace required armaments, including not only metal weapons and armor but also more elaborate equipment such as chariots. Second, a considerable vol-

GILGAMESH, early Mesopotamian king and hero of legend, may be figure attacking water buffalo (right center). Figure stabbing lion may be his companion, the bull-man Enkidu.

ume of luxury goods was commissioned for the palace retinue. And third, a moderate private demand for these goods seems to have developed also. The mass production of pottery, the prevalence of such articles as cylinder seals and metal utensils, the existence of a few vendors' stalls and the hoards of objects in some of the more substantial houses all imply at least a small middle class. Most of these commodities, it is clear, were fabricated in the major Mesopotamian towns from raw materials brought from considerable distance. Copper, for example, came from Oman and the Anatolian plateau, more than 1,000 miles from the Sumerian cities. The need for imports stimulated the manufacture of such articles as textiles, which could be offered in exchange, and also motivated the expansion of territorial control by conquest.

Some authorities have considered that technological advance, which they usually equate with the development of metallurgy, was a major stimulant or even a precondition of urban growth. Yet, in southern Mesopotamia at least, the major quantitative expansion of metallurgy, and of specialized crafts in general, came only after dynastic city-states were well advanced. While the spread of technology probably contributed further to the development of militarism and social stratification, it was less a cause than a consequence of city growth. The same situation is found in New World civilizations. Particularly in aboriginal Middle America the technological level remained very nearly static before and after the urban period.

Finally we come to the general forms of the developing cities, perhaps the most obscure aspect of the whole process of urbanization. Unhappily even Early Dynastic accounts do not oblige us with extensive descriptions of the towns where they were written, nor even with useful estimates of population. Contemporary maps also are unknown; if they were made, they still elude us. References to towns in the myths and epics are at best vague and allegorical. Ultimately archeological studies can supply most of these deficiencies, but at present we have little to go on.

The farming villages of the pre-urban era covered at most a few acres. Whether the villages scattered over the alluvial plain in Ubaid times were much different from the earlier ones in the north is unclear; certainly most were no larger, but the superficial appearance of one largely unexcavated site indicates that they may have been more densely built up and more formally laid out along a regular grid of streets or lanes. By the end of the Ubaid period the temples had begun to expand; a continuation of this trend is about all that the remains of Warka and early Protoliterate periods can tell us thus far. Substantial growth seems to have begun toward the end of the Protoliterate period and to have continued through several centuries of the Early Dynastic. During this time the first battlemented ring-walls were built around at least the larger towns.

A few Early Dynastic sites have been excavated sufficiently to give a fairly full picture of their general layout. Radiating out from the massive public buildings of these cities, toward the outer gates, were streets, unpaved and dusty, but straight and wide enough for the passage of solid-wheeled carts or chariots. Along the streets lay the residences of the well-to-do citizenry, usually arranged around spacious courts and sometimes provided with latrines draining into sewage conduits below the streets. The houses of the city's poorer inhabitants were located behind or between the large multiroomed dwellings. They were approached by tortuous, narrow alleys, were more haphazard in plan, were less well built and very much smaller. Mercantile activities were probably concentrated along the quays of the adjoining river or at the city gates. The marketplace or bazaar devoted to private commerce had not yet appeared.

Around every important urban center rose the massive fortifications that guarded the city against nomadic raids and the usually more formidable campaigns of neighboring rulers. Outside the walls clustered sheepfolds and irrigated tracts, interspersed with subsidiary villages and ultimately disappearing into the desert. And in the desert dwelt only the nomad, an object of mixed fear and scorn to the sophisticated court poet. By the latter part of the Early Dynastic period several of the important capitals of lower Mesopotamia included more than 250 acres within their fortifications. The city of Uruk extended over 1,100 acres and contained possibly 50,000 people.

For these later cities there are written records from which the make-up of the population can be estimated. The overwhelming majority of the able-bodied adults still were engaged in primary agricultural production on their own holdings, on allotments of land received from the temples or as dependent retainers on large estates. But many who were engaged in subsistence agriculture also had other roles. One temple archive, for example, records that 90 herdsmen, 80 soldier-laborers, 100 fishermen, 125 sailors, pilots and oarsmen, 25 scribes, 20 or 25 craftsmen (carpenters, smiths, potters, leather-workers, stonecutters, and mat- or basket-weavers) and probably 250 to 300 slaves were numbered among its parish of around 1,200 persons. In addition to providing for its own subsistence and engaging in a variety of specialized pursuits, most of this group was expected to serve in the army in time of crisis.

Earlier figures can only be guessed at from such data as the size of temple establishments and the quantity of craft-produced articles. Toward the end of the Protoliterate period probably less than a fifth of the labor force was substantially occupied with economic activities outside of subsistence pursuits; in Ubaid times a likely figure is 5 per cent.

It is not easy to say at what stage in the whole progression the word "city" becomes applicable. By any standard Uruk and its contemporaries were cities. Yet they still lacked some of the urban characteristics of later eras. In particular, the development of municipal politics, of a self-conscious corporate body with at least partially autonomous, secular institutions for its own administration, was not consummated until classical times.

Many of the currents we have traced must have flowed repeatedly in urban civilizations. But not necessarily all of them. The growth of the Mesopotamian city was closely related to the rising tempo of warfare. For their own protection people must have tended to congregate under powerful rulers and behind strong fortifications; moreover, they may have been consciously and forcibly drawn together by the elite in the towns in order to centralize political and economic controls. On the other hand, both in aboriginal Central America and in the Indus Valley (in what is now Pakistan) great population centers grew up without comprehensive systems of fortification, and with relatively little emphasis on weapons or on warlike motifs in art.

There is not one origin of cities, but as many as there are independent cultural traditions with an urban way of life. Southern Mesopotamia merely provides the earliest example of a process that, with refinements introduced by the industrial revolution and the rise of national states, is still going on today.

PARTLY EXCAVATED BURIAL of a lady-in-waiting to a Sumerian royal family of 2500 B.C. was moved intact from Ur to the University Museum of the University of Pennsylvania. Amid the rich ornaments of gold may be seen the teeth of their wearer.

The Sumerians

by Samuel Noah Kramer
October 1957

This gifted people lived at the head of the Persian Gulf roughly between 5,000 and 3,000 years ago. Their brilliant technological and social inventions laid the foundation of modern civilization

The Tigris-Euphrates plain is a hot, arid land. Six thousand years ago it was a wind-swept barren. It had no minerals, almost no stone, no trees, practically no building material of any kind. It has been described as a land with "the hand of God against it." Yet it was in this desolate region that man built what was probably the first high civilization. Here were born the inventions of writing, farming technology, architecture, the first codes of law, the first cities. Perhaps the very poverty of the land provided the stimulus that mothered these inventions. But the main credit must go to the people who created them—a most remarkable people called the Sumerians.

These Sumerians, as now revealed by long archaeological research, were a surprisingly modern folk. In many ways they were like the pioneers who built the U. S.—practical, ambitious, enterprising, jealous of their personal rights, technologically inventive. Having no stone or timber, they built with marsh reeds and river mud, invented the brick mold and erected cities of baked clay. They canalled the waters of the Tigris and Euphrates rivers into the arid fields and turned Sumer into a veritable Garden of Eden. To manage their irrigation systems they originated regional government, thus emerging from the petty social order of the family and village to the city-state. They created a written language and committed it to permanent clay tablets. They traded their grain surpluses to distant peoples for metals and other materials they lacked. By the third millennium B.C. the culture and civilization of Sumer, a country about the size of the state of Massachusetts, had spread its influence over the whole Middle East, from India to the Mediterranean. And there is hardly an area of our culture

today—in mathematics or philosophy, literature or architecture, finance or education, law or politics, religion or folklore—that does not owe some of its origins to the Sumerians.

One might suppose that the story of the Sumerians and their accomplishments would be one of the most celebrated in history. But the astonishing fact is that until about a century ago the modern world had no idea that Sumer or its people had ever existed. For more than 2,000 years they had simply vanished from the human record. Babylonia and ancient Egypt were known to every history student, but the earlier Sumerians were buried and forgotten. Now, thanks to a century of archaeological labor and to the Sumerians' own cuneiform tablets, we have come to know them intimately—as well as or better than any other people of the early history of mankind. The story of how the lost Sumerian civilization was discovered is itself a remarkable chapter. This article will review briefly how the history of the Sumerians was resurrected and what we have learned about them.

The Cuneiform Tablets

Modern archaeologists began to dig in Mesopotamia for its ancient civilizations around a century ago. They were looking for the cities of the Assyrians and Babylonians, who of course were well known from Biblical and Greek literature. As the world knows, the diggers soon came upon incredibly rich finds. At the sites of Nineveh and other ancient Assyrian cities they unearthed many clay tablets inscribed with the wedge-shaped writing called cuneiform. This script was taken to be the invention of the Assyrians. Since the Assyrians were apparently a Semitic people, the language was as-

sumed to be Semitic. But few clues were available for decipherment of the strange cuneiform script.

Then came a development which was to be as important a key to discovery in Mesopotamia as the famous Rosetta Stone in Egypt. In western Persia, notably on the Rock of Behistun, European scholars found some cuneiform inscriptions in three languages. They identified one of the languages as Old Persian, another as Elamite, and the third as the language of the Assyrian tablets. The way was now open to decipher the cuneiform writing—first the Old Persian, then the Assyrian, of which it was apparently a translation.

When scholars finally deciphered the "Assyrian" script, they discovered that the cuneiform writing could not have been originated by the Assyrian Semites. Its symbols, which were not alphabetic but syllabic and ideographic, apparently were derived from non-Semitic rather than Semitic words. And many of the cuneiform tablets turned out to be written in a language without any Semitic characteristics whatever. The archaeologists had to conclude, therefore, that the Assyrians had taken over the cuneiform script from a people who had lived in the region before them.

Who were this people? Jules Oppert, a leading 19th-century investigator of ancient Mesopotamia, found a clue to their name in certain inscriptions which referred to the "King of Sumer and Akkad." He concluded that Akkad was the northern part of the country (indeed, the Assyrians and Babylonians are now called Akkadians), and that Sumer was the southern part, inhabited by the people who spoke the non-Semitic language and had invented cuneiform writing.

So it was that the Sumerians were rediscovered after 2,000 years of oblivion. Oppert resurrected their name in 1869. In the following decades French, American, Anglo-American and German expeditions uncovered the buried Sumerian cities—Lagash, Nippur, Shuruppak, Kish, Ur (Ur of the Chaldees in the Bible), Erech, Asmar and so on. The excavation of ancient Sumer has proceeded almost continuously for three quarters of a century; even during World War II the Iraqi went on digging at a few sites. These historic explorations have recovered hundreds of thousands of Sumerian tablets, great temples, monuments, tombs, sculptures, paintings, tools, irrigation systems and remnants of almost every aspect of the Sumerian culture. As a result we have a fairly complete picture of what life in Sumer was like 5,000 years ago. We know something about how the Sumerians looked (from their statues); we know a good deal about their houses and palaces, their tools and weapons, their art and musical instruments, their jewels and ornaments, their skills and crafts, their industry and commerce, their *belles lettres* and government, their schools and temples, their loves and hates, their kings and history.

The Peoples of Sumer

Let us run quickly over the history. The area where the Sumerians lived is lower Mesopotamia, from Baghdad down to the Persian Gulf [*see the map at the right*]. It is reasonably certain that the Sumerians themselves were not the first settlers in this region. Just as the Indian names Mississippi, Massachusetts, etc., show that North America was inhabited before the English-speaking settlers came, so we know that the Sumerians were preceded in Mesopotamia by another people because the ancient names of the Tigris and Euphrates rivers (*Idigna* and *Buranun*), and even the names of the Sumerian cities (Nippur, Ur, Kish, etc.), are not Sumerian words. The city names must be derived from villages inhabited by the earlier people.

The same kind of clue—words that turn up in the Sumerian writing but are plainly not Sumerian in origin—tells us something about those first settlers in Sumer. As Benno Landsberger of the University of Chicago, one of the keenest minds in cuneiform research, has shown, among these pre-Sumerian words are those for farmer, herdsman, fisherman, plow, metal smith, carpenter, weaver, potter, mason and perhaps even

merchant. It follows that the predecessors of the Sumerians must already have developed a fairly advanced civilization. This is confirmed by excavations of their stone implements and pottery.

The dates of Sumer's early history have always been surrounded with uncertainty, and they have not been satisfactorily settled by tests with the new method of radiocarbon dating. According to the best present estimates, the first settlers occupied the area some time before 4000 B.C.; new geological evidence indicates that the lower Tigris-Euphrates Valley, once covered by the Persian Gulf, became an inhabitable land well before that date. Be that as it may, it seems that the people called Sumerians did not arrive in the region until nearly 3000 B.C. Just where they came from is in doubt, but there is some reason to believe that their original home had been in the neighborhood of a city called Aratta, which may have been near the Caspian Sea: Sumerian epic poets sang glowingly of Aratta, and its people were said to speak the Sumerian language.

Wherever the Sumerians came from, they brought a creative spirit and an extraordinary surge of progress to the land of Sumer. Uniting with the people who already inhabited it, they developed a rich and powerful civilization. Not long after they arrived, a king called Etana became the ruler of all Sumer: he is described in Sumerian literature as "the man who stabilized all the lands," and he may therefore be the first empire builder in human history. Sumer reached its fullest flowering around 2500 B.C., when its people had developed the cuneiform symbols and thereby originated their finest gift to civilization—the gift of written communication and history. Their own history came to an end some 800 years later: about 1720 B.C. In that year Hammurabi of Babylon won control of the country, and Sumer disappeared in a Babylonian kingdom.

Life in Sumer

The Sumerians' writings and disinterred cities, as I have said, make it possible to reconstruct their life in great detail. Their civilization rested on agriculture and fishing. Among their inventions were the wagon wheel, the plow and the sailboat, but their science and engineering went far beyond these elementary tools. For irrigation the Sumerians built intricate systems of canals, dikes, weirs and reservoirs. They developed measuring and surveying instru-

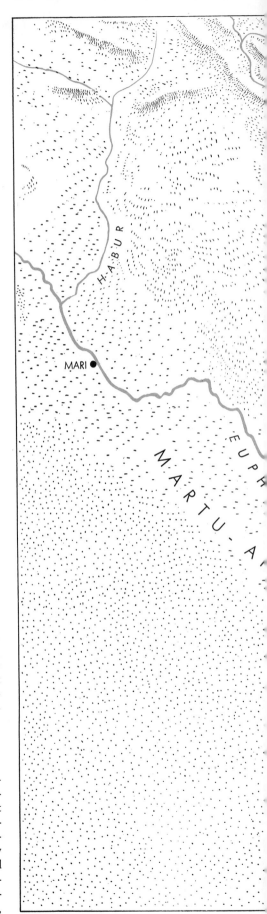

SUMER and its neighbors are located on this map of the area between modern

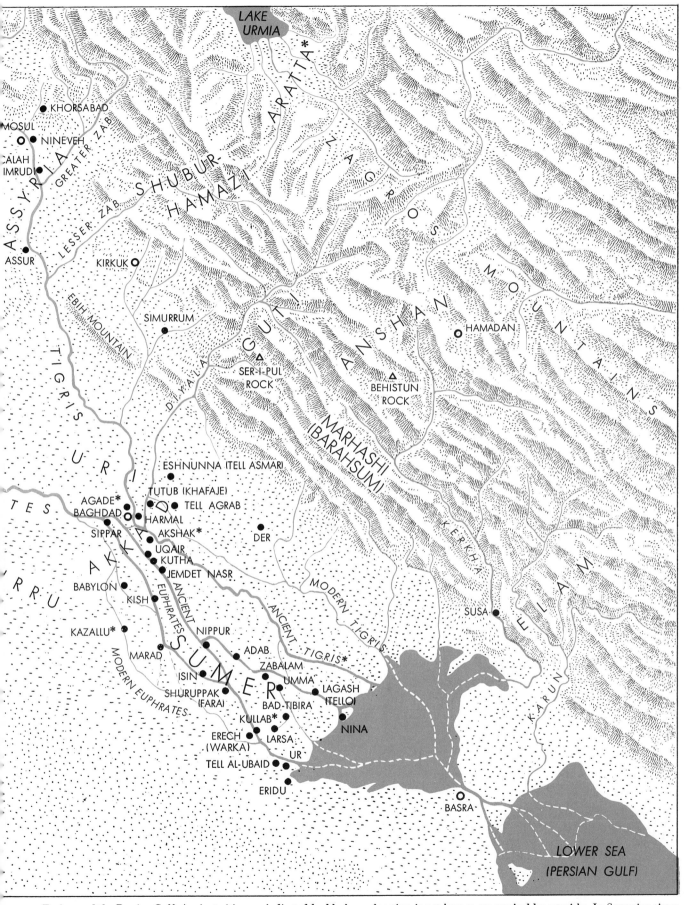

LAKE
URMIA

KHORSABAD

MOSUL
NINEVEH
CALAH
(IMRUD)

ASSYRIA

ASSUR

KIRKUK

GREATER ZAB

LESSER ZAB

SHUBUR-
HAMAZI

ARATTA*

ZAGROS

GUTIUM

ANSHAN

MOUNTAINS

EBIH MOUNTAIN

SIMURRUM

HAMADAN

DIYALA

SER-I-PUL
ROCK

BEHISTUN
ROCK

MARHASHI
(BARAHSUM)

TIGRIS

EUPHRATES

ESHNUNNA (TELL ASMAR)

TUTUB (KHAFAJE)

AGADE*
BAGHDAD
HARMAL
TELL AGRAB

SIPPAR
AKSHAK*

UQAIR
KUTHA

JEMDET NASR

BABYLON

KISH

DER

KERKHA

ELAM

AKKAD

ANCIENT EUPHRATES

MODERN TIGRIS

SUSA

KAZALLU*

NIPPUR

ANCIENT TIGRIS*

KARUN

MARAD

ADAB

MODERN EUPHRATES

ISIN

SHURUPPAK
(FARA)

SUMER

ZABALAM

UMMA

BAD-TIBIRA

LAGASH
(TELLO)

KULLAB*

NINA

ERECH
(WARKA)

LARSA

TELL AL-UBAID

UR

ERIDU

BASRA

LOWER SEA
(PERSIAN GULF)

Turkey and the Persian Gulf. Ancient cities are indicated by black dots; modern cities, by open dots. Cities and areas whose exact location is not known are marked by asterisks. In Sumerian times a large fresh-water lake lay beyond the head of the Persian Gulf.

SUMERIAN TABLETS are inscribed with cuneiform signs. At upper left is the medical tablet of which a section is shown on the cover (about 2000 B.C.). At upper right is a fragment of the epic poem "Enmerkar and the Lord of Aratta" (about 1800 B.C.). At lower left is part of the law code of Hammurabi (about 1700 B.C.). At lower right is a textile inventory (about 1950 B.C.).

ments, and a sexagesimal number system (*i.e.*, based on the number 60) with a place notation device not unlike our decimal system. Their farming was highly sophisticated: among their tablets is a veritable farmer's almanac of instructions in agriculture.

In the crafts, the Sumerians' inventions included the potter's wheel, metal casting (of copper and bronze), riveting, soldering, engraving, cloth fulling, bleaching and dyeing. They manufactured paints, leather, cosmetics, perfumes and drugs. Prescriptions recorded on some of their tablets show that the Sumerian physician had command of a large assortment of *materia medica*, prepared from plants, animals and inorganic sources.

Although the Sumerians' economy was primarily agricultural, their life was centered mainly in the cities. Here lived many of the farmers, herdsmen and fishermen, as well as merchants, craftsmen, architects, doctors, scribes, soldiers and priests. Artisans and traveling merchants sold their products in the central town market, and were paid in kind or in money—usually silver coin in the form of a disk or ring. The dozen or so cities in Sumer probably ranged from 10,000 to 50,000 in population. Each was enclosed by a wall and surrounded with suburban villages and hamlets.

The dominant feature of every Sumerian city was a massive temple mounted on a high terrace. It usually had the form of a ziggurat, Sumer's most distinctive contribution to religious architecture. This is a pyramidal tower with a series of ascending terraces winding around the outside. To break the unattractive blankness of the temple's mud-brick walls, the Sumerian architects introduced buttresses and recesses, and they also beautified the building with columns decorated in colored mosaics. Inside the temple were rooms for the priests and a central shrine with a niche for the statue of the god. Each city in Sumer had a different tutelary god, and the Sumerians considered the city the god's property. Thus the city of Nippur, for example, belonged to Enlil, the god of the air. Nippur became Sumer's chief religious and cultural center, and Enlil was elevated to the highest rank as father of all the gods.

Originally the cities were governed by the citizens themselves, presided over by a governor of their selection. On all important decisions the citizens met in an assembly divided into two chambers —the "elders" and the "men." But for military reasons they gradually relin-

TWO SUMERIAN CYLINDER SEALS are shown at left. Impressions were made with the seals by rolling them over wet clay. At right are two impressions made by this method.

quished this democratic system. Each city acquired a ruler—at first elected, later hereditary—who organized its defense against the other cities and against foreign invaders. In the course of time the king rivaled the city's religious leaders in wealth and influence. The rulers of Sumer's dozen or so city-states also contended with one another for control of the whole country, and the history of Sumer is largely a record of bitter conflicts among its cities, which eventually led to its downfall.

The life of the individual citizen in a Sumerian city was remarkably free and prosperous. The poorest citizen managed to own a farm and cattle or a house and garden. To be sure, slavery was permitted, and a man could sell his children or his entire family to pay off his debts. But even slaves had certain legal rights: they could engage in business, borrow money and buy their freedom. (The average price for an adult slave was 10 shekels— less than the price of an ass.) The great majority of Sumerians were free citizens, going about their business and the pursuit of happiness with a minimum of restrictions. This did not, however, apply to children, who were under the absolute authority of their parents, could be disinherited or sold into slavery, and had to marry mates chosen by the parents. But in the normal course of events Sumerian families cherished their children and were knit closely together by love

and mutual obligations. Women had many legal rights, including the right to hold property and engage in business. A man could divorce his wife on comparatively slender grounds, or, if they had no children, he was allowed to take a second wife.

Most Sumerian families lived in a one-story, mud-brick house consisting of several rooms grouped around an open court. The well-to-do had two-story houses of about a dozen rooms, plastered and whitewashed inside and out; these houses boasted servants' rooms and sometimes even a private chapel. Often the house had a mausoleum in the basement where the family buried its dead. The Sumerians believed that the souls of the dead traveled to a nether world where existence continued more or less as on earth. They therefore buried pots, tools, weapons and jewels with the dead. When a king died, the palace sometimes buried with him some of his courtiers and servants and even his chariot and animals.

Sumerian men were often clean-shaven, but many of them wore a long beard and had long hair parted in the middle. In early times their usual dress was a flounced skirt and felt cloak; later these were replaced by a long shirt and a big fringed shawl draped over the left shoulder, leaving the right arm bare. The common dress for women was a long shawl covering the body from head to foot, except for the right shoulder. Women usually braided their hair into a heavy pigtail and wound it around the head, but on important occasions they wore elaborate headdresses consisting of ribbons, beads and pendants.

Music apparently occupied a large place in the life of the Sumerians—at home, in school and in the temple. Beautifully constructed harps and lyres were found in the royal tombs at Ur. Research has also turned up references to drums, tambourines, reed and metal pipes, and hymns written on tablets. Some of the important personages in the palaces and temples of the Sumerian cities were musicians.

The Sumerians cannot be said to have produced any great art, but they did show considerable skill in carving and sculpture. Perhaps their most original contribution to the graphic arts was the cylinder seal—a stone cylinder with a carved design which was impressed in clay by rolling the cylinder over it. These designs, or seals, appear on clay tablets, jar covers and so on. They depict scenes such as a king on the battlefield, a shepherd defending his flock from wild beasts, heraldic arrangements of animals. Eventually the Sumerians settled on one favorite seal design which became almost their trademark—a scene showing a worshipper being presented to a god by his personal good angel.

Religion

The Sumerians lived by a simple, fatalistic theology. They believed that the universe and their personal lives were ruled by living gods, invisible to mortal

EARLIEST PICTOGRAPHS (3000 B.C.)	DENOTATION OF PICTOGRAPHS	PICTOGRAPHS IN ROTATED POSITION	CUNEIFORM SIGNS CA. 1900 B.C.	BASIC LOGOGRAPHIC VALUES		ADDITIONAL LOGOGRAPHIC VALUES		SYLLABARY (PHONETIC VALUES)
				READING	MEANING	READING	MEANING	
	HEAD AND BODY OF A MAN			LÚ	MAN			
	HEAD WITH MOUTH INDICATED			KA	MOUTH	KIRI₃ ZÚ GÙ DUG₄ INIM	NOSE TEETH VOICE TO SPEAK WORD	KA ZÚ
	BOWL OF FOOD			NINDA	FOOD, BREAD	NÍG GAR	THING TO PLACE	
	MOUTH + FOOD			KÚ	TO EAT	ŠAGAR	HUNGER	
	STREAM OF WATER			A	WATER	DURU₅	MOIST	A
	MOUTH + WATER			NAG	TO DRINK	EMMEN	THIRST	
	FISH			KUA	FISH			KU₆ HA
	BIRD			MUŠEN	BIRD			HU PAG
	HEAD OF AN ASS			ANŠE	ASS			
	EAR OF BARLEY			ŠE	BARLEY			ŠE

EVOLUTION OF SUMERIAN WRITING is outlined in the chart at left. The earliest pictographs were inscribed vertically on tablets. Around 2800 B.C. the direction of this writing was changed from vertical to horizontal, with a corresponding rotation of the pictographs. The pictographs were now reduced to collections of linear strokes made by a stylus which had a triangular point. Some of these cuneiform signs are logographic, i.e., each sign represents a spoken word. Some of the signs represent more than one word;

eyes. The chief gods were those of water, earth, air and heaven, named respectively Enki, Ki, Enlil and An. From a primeval sea were created the earth, the atmosphere, the gods and sky, the sun, moon, planets and stars, and finally life. There were gods in charge of the sun, moon and planets, of winds and storms, of rivers and mountains, of cities and states, of farms and irrigation ditches, of the pickax, brick mold and plow. The major gods established a set of unchangeable laws which must be obeyed willy-nilly by everything and everybody.

Thus the Sumerians were untroubled by any question of free will. Man existed to please and serve the gods, and his life followed their divine orders. Because the great gods were far away in the distant sky and had more important matters to attend to, each person appealed to a particular personal god, a "good angel," through whom he sought salvation. Not that the people neglected regular public devotions to the gods. In the Sumerian temples a court of professionals, including priests, priestesses, musicians and eunuchs, offered daily libations and sac-

rifices of animal and vegetable fats. There were also periodic feasts and celebrations, of which the most important was a royal ceremony ushering in each new year.

This ceremony is traceable to the cycle of nature in Mesopotamia. Every summer, in the hot, parched months, all vegetation died and animal life languished. In the autumn the land began to revive and bloom again. The Sumerian theology explained these events by supposing that the god of vegetation retired to the nether world in the summer and returned to the earth around the time of the new year; his sexual reunion with his wife Inanna, the goddess of love and procreation, then restored fertility to the land. To celebrate this revival and ensure fecundity, the Sumerians each year staged a marriage ceremony between their king, as the risen god, and a priestess representing the goddess Inanna. The marriage was made an occasion of prolonged festival, ritual, music and rejoicing.

The Sumerians considered themselves to be a chosen people, in more intimate contact with the gods than was the rest of mankind. Nevertheless they had a moving vision of all mankind living in peace and security, united by a universal faith and perhaps even by a universal language. Curiously, they projected this vision into the past, into a long-gone golden age, rather than into the future. As a Sumerian poet put it:

Once upon a time there was no snake,
   there was no scorpion,
There was no hyena, there was no lion,
There was no wild dog, no wolf
There was no fear, no terror,
Man had no rival.

Once upon a time . . .
The whole universe, the people in unison,
To Enlil in one tongue gave praise.

To students of the ancient religions of the Near East, much of the Sumerian cosmology and theology is easily recognizable. The order of the universe's creation, the Job-like resignation of sinful and mortal man to the will of the gods, the mystic tale of the dying god and his triumphant resurrection, the Aphrodite-like goddess Inanna, the ideals of "humaneness"—these and many other features of the Sumerian creed survive without much change in the later religions of the ancient world. Indeed, the very name of the Sumerian dying god, Dumuzi, endures as Biblical Tammuz, whose descent to the nether regions was still

CUNEIFORM SIGNS	TRANSLITERATION	TRANSLATION
	AMA-AR-GI₄	FREEDOM
	ARHUŠ	COMPASSION
	DINGIR	GOD, GODDESS
	DUB-SAR	SCRIBE
	É-DUB-BA	SCHOOL, ACADEMY
	HÉ-GÁL	PLENTY, PROSPERITY
	ME	DIVINE LAWS
	NAM-LÚ-LU₇	HUMANITY, HUMANENESS
	NAM-LUGAL	KINGSHIP
	NAM-TAR	FATE, DESTINY
	NÍG-GA	PROPERTY
	NÍG-GE-NA	TRUTH
	NÍG-SI-SÁ	JUSTICE
	SAG-GÍG	BLACK-HEADED ONES, THE SUMERIAN PEOPLE
	UKKIN	ASSEMBLY

some are syllabic, *i.e.*, they also represent syllables. The accents and subscript numbers on the modern transliteration of the cuneiform signs are used by modern scholars to distinguish between signs having the same pronunciation but different meanings. In the chart at right are 15 cuneiform words, their transliteration and their English translation.

STATUETTES show the appearance of the Sumerians. The four statuettes at left, made about 2500 B.C., were found at Tutub (modern Khafaje). The statuette at right, made about 1850 B.C., was found at Ur. It represents Princess Enannatumma, high priestess

mourned by the women of Jerusalem in the days of the prophet Ezekiel. It is not too much to say that, with the decipherment of the Sumerian tablets, we can now trace many of the roots of man's major religious creeds back to Sumer.

Cuneiform

But the Sumerians' chief contribution to civilization was their invention of writing. Their cuneiform script is the earliest known system of writing in man's history. The cuneiform system served as the main tool of written communication throughout western Asia for some 2,000 years—long after the Sumerians themselves had disappeared. Without it, mankind's cultural progress would certainly have been much delayed.

The Sumerian script began as a set of pictographic signs devised by temple administrators and priests to keep track of the temple's resources and activities. They inscribed the signs in clay with a reed stylus, and this accounts for the curious wedge-shaped characters. In the course of the centuries Sumerian scholars developed the signs into purely phonetic symbols representing words or syllables.

More than 90 per cent of the tablets that have been excavated in Sumer are economic, legal and administrative documents, not unlike the commercial and governmental records of our own day. But some 5,000 of the finds are literary works: myths and epic tales, hymns and lamentations, proverbs, fables, essays. They qualify as man's oldest known literature—nearly 1,000 years older than the *Iliad* and the Hebrew Bible. In addition the tablets include a number of Sumerian "textbooks," listing the names of trees, birds, insects, minerals, cities, countries and so forth. There are even commemorative narratives which constitute mankind's first writing of history.

From the Sumerians' invention of writing grew the first formal system of education—another milestone in human intellectual progress. They set up "professional" schools to train scribes, secretaries and administrators; in time these vocational schools became also centers of culture where scholars, scientists and poets devoted their lives to learning and teaching.

The head of the school was called "the school father"; the pupils, "school sons." Among the faculty members were "the man in charge of drawing," "the man in charge of Sumerian," "the man in charge of the whip." There was no sparing of the rod. The curriculum consisted in copying and memorizing the lists of

of the moon-god Nanna and sister of Lipit-Ishtar, king of Isin. Enannatumma presided at some of the most important reconstruction of Ur after it had been destroyed by the Elamites.

record was Lugalannemundu of the city of Adab; he is reported to have ruled 90 years and to have controlled an empire extending far beyond Sumer. But his empire also fell apart, and a king of Kish named Mesilim became the dominant figure in Sumer. Later rule over the country was won by the city of Lagash. The last ruler of the Lagash dynasty, a king named Urukagina, has the distinction of being the first recorded social reformer. He suppressed the city's harsh bureaucracy, reduced taxes, and brought relief to widows, orphans and the poor. One of King Urukagina's inscriptions contains the word "freedom"—the first appearance of this word in man's history. But within less than 10 years a king of the neighboring city of Umma overthrew Urukagina and put the city of Lagash to the torch.

The Fall of Sumer

The cities' incessant struggle for power exhausted Sumer. A Semitic people from the west, under the famous warrior Sargon the Great, marched into the country and established a new dynasty. Sargon founded a capital called Agade (from which came the name Akkadian) and made it the richest and most powerful city in the Middle Eastern world. He conquered almost all of western Asia and perhaps also parts of Egypt and Ethiopia. Sargon's sons held on to the empire, but his grandson, Naramsin, brought Sumer to disaster. For reasons unknown, he destroyed the holy city of Nippur, and soon afterward he was defeated by semibarbaric invaders from the mountains of Iran who overran Sumer and completely wiped out the city of Agade.

It took the Sumerians several generations to recover. But their civilization did come to life again, under a governor of Lagash named Gudea, whose face is the best known to us of all the Sumerians because a score of statues of him have been found in the ancient temples of Lagash. Gudea re-established contacts and trade with the rest of the known world and put Sumer on the path to prosperity. After Gudea, however, the rivalry among its cities broke out again and became Sumer's final undoing. The city of Ur, under a king named Ur-Nammu, defeated Lagash; Ur-Nammu founded a new rule called the Third Dynasty of Ur. It was to be Sumer's last dynasty.

Ur-Nammu was a strong and benevolent ruler. According to inscriptions that have recently come to light, he removed "chiselers" and grafters and established

words and names on the textbook tablets, in studying and composing poetic narratives, hymns and essays and in mastering mathematical tables and problems, including tables of square and cube roots.

Teachers in ancient Sumer seem to have been treated not unlike their counterparts in the U. S. today: their salaries were low and they were looked upon with a mixture of respect and contempt. The Sumerians were an aggressive people, prizing wealth, renown and social prestige. As their tablets suggest, they were far more concerned with accounts than with academic learning.

Their restless ambition and aggressive spirit are reflected in the bitter rivalry among their cities and kings. The history of Sumer is a story of wars in which one city after another rose to ascendancy over the country. Although there are many gaps in our information, we can

reconstruct the main outlines of that history from references in the tablets. The first recorded ruler of Sumer, as I have mentioned, was Etana, king of Kish. Probably not long afterward a king of Erech by the name of Meskiaggasher founded a dynasty which ruled the whole region from the Mediterranean to the Zagros Mountains northeast of Sumer. The city of Kish then rose to dominance again, only to be supplanted by the city of Ur, whose first king, Mesannepadda, is said to have ruled for 80 years and made Ur the capital of Sumer. After Mesannepadda's death, Sumer again came under the rule of the city of Erech, under a king named Gilgamesh who became the supreme hero of Sumerian history—a brave, adventurous figure whose deeds were celebrated throughout the ancient world of western Asia. The next great ruler who appears in the

AREA AROUND NIPPUR, one of the principal cities of Sumer (*see map on pages 180 and 181*), is covered with barren dunes today. Six thousand years ago much of the area was similarly barren. The Sumerians and their predecessors made it fertile by irrigation.

NIPPUR WAS EXCAVATED in 1951 and 1952 by a joint expedition of the University Museum of the University of Pennsylvania and the Oriental Institute of the University of Chicago. In this photograph the houses of Nippur's scribal quarter are uncovered.

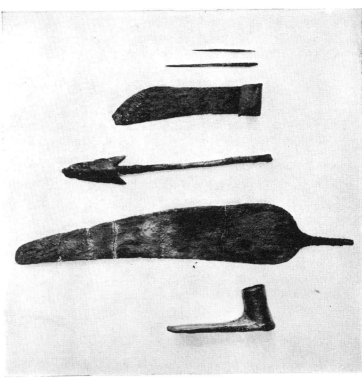

ARTIFACTS at left are Sumerian stone weights. The weight at top is one *mana* (505 grams); the weight at bottom, one *gin* (8.416 grams); the weight in middle, one *gin* 160 *shē* (15.896 grams).

At right is a group of copper and bronze tools and weapons. They are, from top to bottom, two bronze drills, a copper axhead, a copper spearhead, a copper saw blade and a bronze adzhead.

DIADEM of Queen Shub-Ad, who lived about 2500 B.C., was found in the royal cemetery of Ur. The horizontal band of the diadem is fashioned out of beads of lapis lazuli. Mounted on the band are tiny leaves, fruits, flowers and figures of rams, all made of gold.

a law code which insured honest weights and measures and took care that the poor should not "fall a prey to the wealthy." Ur-Nammu's code is especially significant for the fact that instead of the barbarous rule of "an eye for an eye and a tooth for a tooth" common among early societies it established a money fine as punishment for assaults.

In spite of Sumer's civilized kings and prosperity, time was running out for the Sumerians. Their internal rivalries and the growing pressure of surrounding peoples soon overwhelmed them. Semitic nomads from the Arabian desert to the west (the Amorites of the Bible) took over the Sumerian cities of Isin, Larsa and Babylon. Ur itself was conquered by the Elamites to the east, who carried off its last king, Ibbi-Sin. In the following two and a half centuries the Semitic rulers of Isin and Larsa, and then Larsa and Babylon, struggled for control of the country. Finally, in about the year 1720 B.C., Hammurabi defeated Rim-Sin, the last king of Larsa, and Babylon emerged as the dominant city of southern Mesopotamia. The Sumerians were submerged by the Semites and lost their identity as a people. In time their name was erased from the memory of man; the Sumerian language disappeared as a living, spoken tongue, though for centuries it continued to be the written language studied in schools.

The Sumerians firmly believed that when man died, his emasculated spirit descended to a dark, dreary nether world. The spirit and fame of this proud, vigorous people certainly suffered a remarkable eclipse after their empire fell. But what their minds created survives throughout the living corpus of present-day civilization: it appears in the form of a Biblical proverb, a statutory law, a heroic folktale, an Aesopic fable, a zodiacal sign, a Euclidean theorem, the weight of a coin, the degree of an angle. And in the cuneiform tablets which were the Sumerians' pre-eminent gift we have found the earliest intellectual record of man's strivings toward civilization.

EDITOR'S NOTE

The author wishes to thank the following individuals for their generous cooperation and help in the presentation of this article: F. G. Rainey, A. V. Kidder, Robert Dyson, Edmund I. Gordon, Jane Kohn, and the Board of Managers of the University Museum of the University of Pennsylvania.

19

The Decline of
the Harappans

by George F. Dales
May 1966

*While Egypt and Sumer prospered, a state of greater
size was swept away in South Asia. Aryan invaders
have traditionally received the blame; it now appears
that instead the Harappans were flooded out*

Four thousand years ago the world's first three civilizations were flourishing. The Sumerians of Mesopotamia and the Egyptians of the Nile valley are reasonably well known to us. The third civilization embraced an area more extensive than either Egypt or Mesopotamia, yet it is far less known. Its most impressive remains—the dead cities of Mohenjo-daro and Harappa in the Indus valley of what is now West Pakistan—were first excavated four decades ago [see "A Forgotten Empire of Antiquity," by Stuart Piggott; SCIENTIFIC AMERICAN, November, 1953]. Our knowledge of this remarkable culture of South Asia, which is called the Harappan civilization, has been limited until recently to what could be gleaned from archaeological findings at these two sites, mainly because the written records of the culture are scanty and not yet deciphered. New discoveries in both Pakistan and India, however, are now adding much to our understanding of certain events in Harappan times.

In the past few years many Harappan towns and villages have been discovered well outside the civilization's nucleus in the Indus basin, indicating that the Harappan state extended much farther than earlier investigators had realized. It is now known that Harappan authority reached westward at least to the modern border between Iran and Pakistan, that it touched the foothills of the Himalayas to the north, even extending to the headwaters of the Ganges, and that it stretched southward along the west coast of India as far as the Gulf of Cambay to the north of modern Bombay. The Harappan civilization thus controlled or dominated a triangle roughly 1,000 miles on a side [see illustration on next page]. A series of carbon-14 dates from Harappan sites

along the coast of India also shows that many of these southerly towns and trading posts had continued to be occupied much later than the sites in the Indus valley. This and other bits of unexplained evidence have raised doubts concerning a fundamental hypothesis about the Harappan civilization: that Harappa and Mohenjo-daro had been sacked, and the Harappan civilization liquidated or absorbed, by the Aryan invaders who presumably brought the Indo-European language and culture to prehistoric India sometime during the second millennium B.C.

With the intention of learning more about the life and death of Harappan civilization the University of Pennsylvania and the Pakistan Government Department of Archaeology agreed on a joint reopening of the Mohenjo-daro site during the winter of 1964–1965. The expedition undertook, as part of a three-year program, to determine the total depth of the site's deposits of human occupation, something earlier workers had been unable to establish because groundwater lies only 15 feet below the surface of the plain at Mohenjo-daro. Efforts were made to devise some means of excavating these flooded occupation levels and to analyze evidence at the site, in the form of abundant accumulations of water-deposited silt, that the city had more than once been exposed to major floods.

During its mature period, from a few centuries before to a few centuries after 2000 B.C., the city of Mohenjo-daro housed an estimated 40,000 inhabitants in an area about a mile square. Today its ruins consist of two parts; a western mound that contains the so-called citadel is separated by a broad gully from a much larger eastern mound that con-

tains the lower town [see illustration on page 193]. At the southwest corner of the lower-town mound an undisturbed area rises some 35 feet above the surrounding plain. In 1964 this area was selected for excavation in the hope of obtaining a sequence of stratified materials that could be correlated with the artifacts unearthed by earlier expeditions.

As a start it was decided to sink drill holes straddling the selected area to discover the depth of the earliest occupation levels. Core samples were collected at two-foot intervals; before the drills struck sterile soil 39 feet of core containing evidence of occupation had been raised to the surface. Thus the total depth of occupation in this part of Mohenjo-daro is 74 feet, about the equivalent of a seven-story building. Of the entire deposit, the deepest and therefore the earliest 24 feet (or almost a third) is still not available for study because of groundwater.

In the 1920's and 1930's, when the first digging was done at Mohenjo-daro, carbon-14 dating techniques were unknown and the only firm evidence of the city's antiquity came from the discovery of a few Harappan artifacts, principally stone seals, in ancient Mesopotamian sites. The Harappan seals found in reliably dated Mesopotamian strata belonged to a period extending from about 2350 B.C. to about 1800 B.C. The early investigators concluded that Mohenjo-daro and Harappan civilization in general had flourished during this same period. The carbon-14 dates now available for a number of Harappan and pre-Harappan sites tend to confirm this dating but also suggest that from 50 to 100 years might be added at each end of the period. When several new carbon samples collected from late levels at Mohenjo-daro in 1964–1965 are analyzed, they should establish the date when that city—and civilization in the southern Indus valley—met its end.

Before discussing why and how Harappan civilization declined, something should be said about its origins. No formative phase, or early stage, of Harappan culture has yet been positively identified in the archaeological record of South Asia, although current excavations in Pakistan and India are beginning to yield some clues. Numerous pre-Harappan cultures have been found in the hills and valleys of Baluchistan, to the west of the Indus valley. Pre-Harappan groups also lived in the Indus valley itself just before Harappan culture appeared there in mature form. The Baluchistan sites have strong ties with Afghanistan and the Near East,

but their relation to the origin and development of Harappan civilization is little understood. The same is true of the civilization's precursors in the Indus basin. At sites such as Amri, Kot-diji and Kalibangan materials belonging to the mature Harappan phase are found mixed with materials from late phases of the indigenous cultures. Such findings suggest that Harappan civilization arrived full-blown from some other area. At the same time earlier levels of these and other pre-Harappan Indus sites contain objects that are characteristic of Harappan civilization in its maturity. These findings argue either for an on-the-spot evolution from one culture to the other or, at the very least, for heavy borrowing from the local inhabitants by the Harappans when they first settled in the Indus valley. Perhaps the 24 feet of

waterlogged occupation layers at Mohenjo-daro, containing as they should a record of the city's earliest development, will help to illuminate this question of Harappan origins.

The problem of the decline and disappearance of Harappan civilization has been a matter of primary concern during the expedition's first two years of work. One of the discoveries made at Mohenjo-daro in the 1920's that is cited in support of the hypothesis that Aryan invaders destroyed the Harappan civilization was the presence of some 30 human skeletons in what appeared to be the upper levels of the site. The bodies had evidently been left where they fell rather than receiving burial; this seemed a dramatic archaeological confirmation of the postulated invasion and massacre. In 1964 the poorly preserved remains of five more bodies were unearthed in

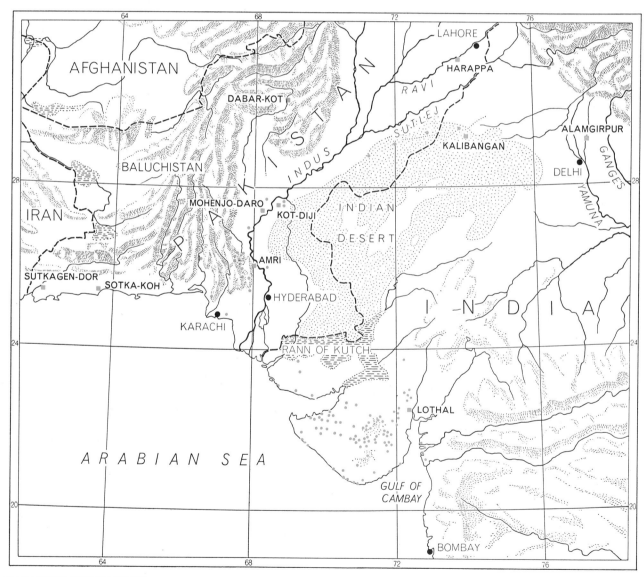

HARAPPAN CIVILIZATION at its maturity some 4,000 years ago controlled a triangular territory with sides roughly 1,000 miles long. The Indus valley was its central focus; Harappa, near modern Lahore, and Mohenjo-daro to the south were its great cities.

the upper levels of the excavation, only two to three feet below the surface of the mound. They lay in a narrow alley amid an accumulation of collapsed brick, broken pottery and ash. The period to which these dead belong is evidently late, but it has not yet been precisely determined. The fact that they had not had any normal kind of burial suggests that all five were the victims of some common disaster. Nonetheless, we are reluctant to believe that either the earlier discoveries or our own support the hypothesis of an Aryan invasion. For one thing, no one has any exact knowledge of the date when the Aryans first entered the Indus valley area; they have not yet been identified archaeologically. For another, the sole purpose served by the invasion hypothesis is to explain the demise of Harappan civilization. If evidence can be found that Mohenjo-daro declined for other reasons, the invasion hypothesis goes by the board. Such evidence, in the form of traces of catastrophic floods, is now being subjected to close scrutiny.

The presence of water-deposited silts at Mohenjo-daro had been recognized by early workers at the site as an indication that floods had played a role in the city's history, but no one suggested that the silts represented anything more significant than periodic brief overflows of the Indus River. Excavators who later worked at such sites to the south of Mohenjo-daro as Amri and Chanhu-daro found abundant evidence of flooding in these areas also. It was not until 1940, however, that anyone suggested a relation between the archaeological evidence of ancient floods and a number of topographic and geological anomalies of the Indus valley. In that year the Indian paleontologist M. R. Sahni noticed silt deposits perched many feet above the level of the Indus plain near the city of Hyderabad in what is now West Pakistan. This and other evidence suggested to him that the area's ancient floods had not been mere river overflows but events on a far larger scale. Major tectonic upheavals, Sahni proposed, might have blocked the Indus River from time to time; each such stoppage would have caused the gradual formation of a huge upstream lake that might then have persisted for decades.

Sahni's suggestion went virtually unnoticed until 1960. By that time two totally independent lines of research had led to the identical conclusion: natural disasters must have played a major

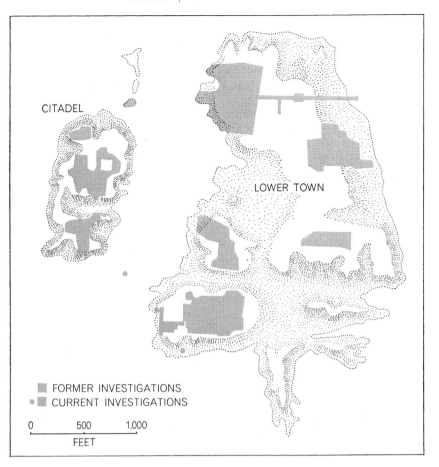

URBAN AREA of Mohenjo-daro is divided into the citadel district to the west and a larger district, called the lower town, to the east. The part of the lower town that was excavated in 1964 and the location of three test borings are shown in color. In this part of the site the culture-bearing strata are 72 feet thick; 24 feet of the accumulation is under water.

role in the decline of Harappan civilization. In that year the University Museum undertook an archaeological survey of the Arabian Sea coast of West Pakistan. The field party discovered settlements of the Harappan era that had clearly been seaports but were now located as far as 30 miles inland. These displaced ports made it evident that the coastline in this part of Pakistan had risen considerably during the past 4,000 years, with the initial rise apparently having occurred during the Harappan period. In the same year Robert L. Raikes, a hydrologist, was conducting extensive surveys in southern Baluchistan and the lower Indus valley. Raikes's keen antiquarian interests led him to investigate the possibility that ancient topographic changes in the area might well be related to the decline of Harappan civilization. The mutual desire to combine archaeological evidence with the findings of another discipline led to a joining of forces. Raikes is now working with the Mohenjo-daro expedition as engineering consultant and is

in charge of geological and hydrological investigations.

Just as Sahni had been puzzled by the silts near Hyderabad, so Raikes in 1964 sought an explanation for the thick silt deposits that are preserved in the ruins of Mohenjo-daro at points as high as 30 feet above ground level. The 1964 test borings that revealed the thickness of the underlying archaeological strata at the site showed that silt deposits also existed below the surface of the plain. When the layers above ground are added to those below, the silts sandwiched between the city's successive occupation levels span a vertical distance of 70 feet. A better explanation than occasional floods is obviously needed to account for such a multilevel accumulation.

Raikes's preliminary research not only suggests that the dam-and-lake hypothesis proposed 25 years ago by Sahni is tenable but also singles out an area near Sehwan, some 90 miles downstream from Mohenjo-daro, as the most probable area of tectonic disturbance

EXCAVATORS' HANDICAP at Mohenjo-daro is the presence of groundwater near the surface of the plain. This cut was made to uncover the bottom of the city wall (brickwork at rear). The work was halted by flooding at a depth of only 15 feet below the plain level.

affecting the city. Both at Mohenjo-daro and at smaller sites between the city and Sehwan the silt deposits are of the kind characteristic of still-water conditions in a lake rather than the kind deposited by the fast-moving waters of a flooded river. Moreover, there is abundant geological evidence of rock faulting on a large scale near Sehwan. The faulting by itself could have raised a natural dam and turned the upstream portion of the Indus into a slow-filling lake. More probably, however, the same disturbances that caused the faulting were accompanied by massive extrusions of mud, aided by the pressure of accumulated underground gases. Such mud extrusions are not uncommon in Pakistan even today; for example, a number of mud islands abruptly appeared off the Arabian Sea coast in 1945.

Let us assume that some such barrier was thrown up near Sehwan. Thereafter the normal discharge of the Indus would not have reached the sea but instead would have accumulated in a steadily growing reservoir [*see illustration at right*]. As the rising waters encroached on the valley's villages and towns, many small settlements undoubtedly disappeared below the surface and were completely obliterated by silt. When the waters approached such a major population center as Mohenjo-daro, however, it seems logical to suppose that efforts were made to protect the city. The archaeological evidence strongly suggests that large-scale community projects were indeed undertaken at Mohenjo-daro for this purpose. As an example, massive mud-brick platforms were erected and faced with fired brick, apparently with the objective of raising the level of the city safely above the lake waters. One such embankment, partially excavated by the expedition in 1964, is some 70 feet wide and well over 25 feet high [*see top illustration on following page*].

Eventually the waters accumulating behind the natural dam would have risen until they had spilled over it and begun to cut it away. Thereafter the Indus would have resumed its normal flow to the sea and re-erosion of the silt-covered floodplain would have begun. After each immersion the inhabitants of Mohenjo-daro found it necessary to rebuild or reinforce most of the city's buildings. Although they usually rebuilt directly on top of the older foundations and walls, they eventually encountered serious problems of decay and sinking. The ruins today dramatical-

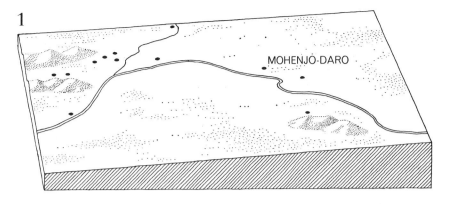

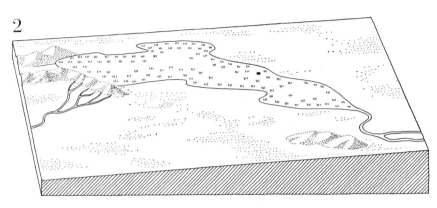

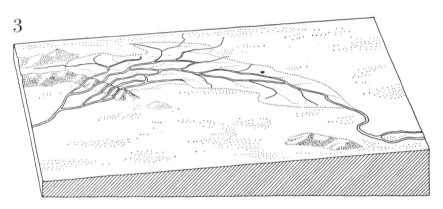

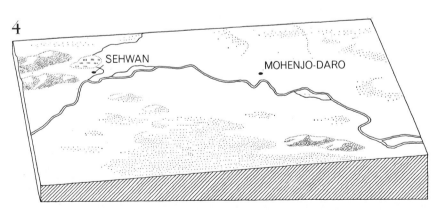

PERIODIC FLOODING of Mohenjo-daro and other Harappan settlements in the Indus River valley was apparently caused by geologic disturbances in the vicinity of modern Sehwan. In *1* the Indus follows an unhindered course to the sea (*south is at left, north at right*). In *2* a massive mud extrusion or a rock fault dams the river and produces a shallow, marshy lake upstream, flooding Mohenjo-daro. In *3* the lake waters have topped the barrier; as it erodes, the lake empties. In *4* the cycle is complete and the valley is habitable again.

FLOOD COUNTERMEASURES taken at Mohenjo-daro included the construction of massive brick embankments to keep the level of the city above water. A pit (*center*) was dug down through 25 feet of unfired brick in one such embankment without reaching bottom.

FLOOD DAMAGE at Mohenjo-daro is evidenced by slumping brick masonry (*center*), which presumably reflects erosion of the city's unfired brick foundations during their prolonged immersion in lake water. The Harappans simply leveled masonry and built on top of it.

ly illustrate the problems they faced [*see bottom illustration on opposite page*].

Both the multiple layers of silt at Mohenjo-daro and the evidence of multilevel reconstruction suggest that the city was flooded in this prolonged and damaging fashion no less than five times and perhaps more. At present it is impossible to estimate just how long each cycle of lake intrusion and withdrawal may have lasted, but it seems doubtful that the duration of any one cycle would have exceeded 100 years.

Could such a series of natural catastrophes, rather than the Aryan invasion, have brought about the collapse of Harappan civilization? The city of Harappa itself and lesser sites in the Indus valley to the north of Mohenjodaro do not seem to have ever suffered significant flooding. Instead they give the appearance of having been abruptly abandoned, after which they stood empty for centuries. Such a pattern is certainly compatible with the invasion hypothesis. It is also compatible with a situation in which the Harappan state's weakened heartland to the south was unable to send help to the inhabitants of the northern frontier when they were threatened. The people who presented the threat could quite well have been hill raiders rather than Aryan invaders. An archaeological fact must also be taken into account in any effort to reconstruct the Harappan demise: The northern Indus sites show no evidence of a decline in material prosperity before their abandonment but quite the opposite is true of Mohenjodaro and other southern sites. What does this contrast signify?

The mature phase of Harappan civilization at Mohenjo-daro appears to have degenerated into a well-defined late phase that in turn fades into a squatter phase. Both the materials and style of later artifacts and the quality of later architecture demonstrate a gradual process of degeneration. The traditional Harappan painted pottery of the mature phase, with its intricate black-on-red designs, is replaced in the late phase by plain unpainted ware. In contrast to the typical seals of the mature phase, carved out of soapstone and superbly engraved with animal figures in negative relief, the late-phase seals are not made of soapstone and bear only a few simple geometric designs. The deftly executed and spirited animal figurines of the mature phase are replaced by much cruder effigies. Even the buildings erected during the squatter phase reflect the same

degeneration: they are jerry-built and often made of broken or secondhand bricks. These examples of diminishing prosperity in the south, or at least of a debasement in the Harappan civilization's standard of values, suggest an associated breakdown in the efficiency of state administration. Perhaps not only Harappan prosperity but also the Harappan spirit was being mired in an unrelenting sequence of invading water and engulfing silt.

What was the final fate of the Harappans? Findings at more than 80 Harappan sites recently identified in the Gujarat area of India provide a partial answer. A majority of the Indian sites belong to the late phase of Harappan civilization, but the culture had also been present in force in this area during its mature phase. The seaport at Lothal, for example, contains the largest structure of fired brick erected anywhere in the Harappan realm; it is identified by its excavator as a docking basin, ingeniously designed so that the ships within it remained afloat even at low tide.

With the onset of the late phase of Harappan civilization the Gujarat sites present a sad picture of gradual

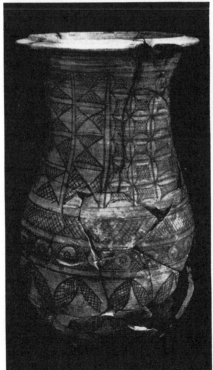

HARAPPAN DECLINE is reflected in the lowered standards of workmanship characteristic of the late Harappan phase. A skillfully carved stone stamp seal of the mature Harappan phase (*top left*) is contrasted with a simple geometric one (*top right*), typical of the late phase at Mohenjo-daro. A similar contrast is seen between a polychrome painted pot of the mature phase (*bottom left*) and an unpainted pot from late-phase levels (*bottom right*).

HARAPPAN ARTISTRY is exemplified by this miniature terra-cotta mask, one and a half inches wide, found at Mohenjo-daro in 1964. Typical of mature Harappan workmanship, the mask has a boldly outlined human face topped by the ears and horns of some animal.

degeneration. Sophisticated Harappan traits are watered down by a mingling with impoverished local cultures until what was once distinctively Harappan is diluted to the point of nonexistence. No urban centers rise along the Gulf of Cambay, no more soapstone seals are carved, no more clay figurines are modeled. Trade with the civilized centers of the Near East, once the *raison d'être* for these Indian coastal ports, comes to a stop. The Harappan script, with its 400 or so still undeciphered symbols, disappears.

These findings are compatible with a hypothesis that envisions the disastrous sequence of floods at Mohenjo-daro and elsewhere in the southern Indus valley as the stimulus that drove the Harappans from the heartland of the far-flung state to take refuge in the Gujarat area. Suddenly crowded with refugees and deprived of support from the once prosperous realm that had fostered them, the Harappan trading towns on the southern frontier could have done little else than gradually merge with the countryside they had formerly dominated. On the basis of present evidence it seems probable that the Harappans, to borrow a figure of speech from T. S. Eliot, met their end not with an Aryan bang but with an Indus expatriate's whimper.

20

A Forgotten Civilization
of the Persian Gulf

by P. V. Glob and T. G. Bibby
October 1960

*On the island of Bahrain lie the grave mounds and
buried cities of a culture contemporary with those of
Sumer and ancient India. Recent excavations indicate
that it was a link between the two*

Bahrain Island, halfway down the Persian Gulf from the delta of the Tigris and Euphrates rivers, has been known to archeologists and grave robbers as an island of the dead. The yellow sand of the island is covered with uncounted large grave mounds—an esti- mated 100,000 of them. They rise in such weird profusion that they give the impression of some natural cataclysm, as though a boiling, bubbling wasteland had suddenly solidified at the dawn of time. Yet all is the work of man: each of the mounds covers a stone chamber (often two chambers one above the other), and each contains a human burial.

The wonder of the grave mounds be- came a mystery when several archeo- logical expeditions came to the island after the turn of the century and found

GRAVE MOUNDS in this photograph are some of the estimated 100,000 that lie on Bahrain Island. Each of the mounds covers one or two stone chambers. The chambers contain human burials and objects of gold, copper and ivory that are more than 3,000 years old.

LARGE MOUND in this photograph is about 35 feet high. Most of the large mounds lie at the edge of the desert. Their size probably explains why they were robbed centuries ago.

of smaller settlements and an extensive temple-complex, all dating to the period of the grave mounds and representing a hitherto unknown civilization. From this auspicious beginning, the work has continued on an expanding scale for the past seven years. While excavations have yielded an increasingly complete revelation of the center in Bahrain, reconnaissance has extended the outer marches of this civilization ever farther to the north and east along the curving coastline of Arabia. In the 1960 season the expedition consisted of 27 Scandinavian archeologists and was operating over a front of 600 miles, from Kuwait at the head of the Persian Gulf to Abu Dhabi and Buraimi in the east. Bahrain has proved to be the legendary Dilmun referred to in the cuneiform texts of Sumer, the bridge between that primary seat of the urban revolution and the civilization of the Indus Valley in what is now Pakistan.

That we were the vanguard of one of the largest archeological expeditions ever to operate in the Middle East was not to be guessed when we landed at Moharraq airport on the northern island of the Bahrain archipelago and negotiated for the ancient station wagon that was to take us on our reconnaissance of the main island. Bahrain itself is a small island about twice the size of Manhattan. It is widest in the north, where most of the grave mounds lie, and tapers in the south to a sandy spit pointing to the head of the deep bay that lies between the peninsula of Qatar and the Arabian mainland, clearly visible on the western horizon. Along the north and northwestern coastal strip of Bahrain lie extensive plantations of date palms, interspersed with fields of alfalfa that provide fodder for humped Indian cattle, for goats and donkeys. The rest of Bahrain consists of open, windswept desert, plains of gravel and eroded limestone buttes, with the 440-foot Jebel Dukhan —the Mountain of Smoke—rising in the center. Of the 150,000 Arabic-speaking inhabitants of the archipelago, a third live in the capital city of Manama on the northeastern coast, a close-packed town of narrow streets, slender minarets and tall, windowless, whitewashed merchants' palaces. Another third live on the northern island of Moharraq, and the remainder in the villages strung out along the coasts. Here, in houses of interwoven palm fronds, the villagers live a life that can have changed little

no trace of towns or cities. Inevitably the expeditions tended to concentrate on the excavation of the larger mounds. These proved to have been already visited by robbers in remote antiquity. But the gold, copper and ivory objects that still remained here and there in the massive tomb-chambers bore witness to the wealth they once contained, and indicated that the graves were at least as old as the Bronze Age—earlier than 1000 B.C. The fact that no settlements were discovered gave rise to the theory that Bahrain was solely a burial island, a cemetery for peoples dwelling on the mainland of Arabia.

This theory had an essential weakness: The island has a plentiful water supply and a soil that is productive where it is watered, while nearby Arabia is sandy and waterless. Accordingly in 1953 the Prehistoric Museum of Aarhus in Denmark dispatched a small expedition, comprising the two authors of this article, to Bahrain. Our objective was to reconnoiter the island as a whole and to resolve the mystery of the grave mounds by locating, if we could, the settlements of their builders.

This limited objective was achieved in the course of the first season's work. We discovered one large city, a number

over the centuries, working in the date and vegetable gardens, tending the fish traps that line the tidal channels around the coast and in the summer months sailing to the oyster banks to dive for pearls.

Pearling, however, is a dying occupation. A new source of wealth has come to Bahrain, the first state in the Persian Gulf in which oil was discovered. Now in increasing numbers the new generation is leaving its fish traps and gardens to work in the machine shops and offices of the oil company and at the huge refinery that dominates the east coast. In the center of the island, north of Jebel Dukhan, in a town of pastel-colored bungalows and green gardens, live the American and European oilmen and their families, in an area that 30 years ago was desert.

It was in this desert that the first traces of prehistoric settlements were discovered. These settlements, however, dated back to a time long before the burial mounds. Where the wind had exposed the ancient surface of the desert lay hundreds of chipped flakes of flint. They marked the chipping floors and settlements of men of the Stone Age, and they followed closely an ancient coast-line now lying some two miles inland. A small number of finely chipped barbed and tanged arrowheads and toothed flint sickle-blades belonging to the first agriculturalists of the Neolithic period turned up among these artifacts, but the vast majority were the points and scrapers of the hunters of the Middle Paleolithic. These evidenced clear relationship with the early Stone Age cultures of northwestern India. The work in this realm of Middle East archeology has since been advanced with the finding on the Qatar peninsula of a succession of artifacts that lead back to the hand axes of 100,000 years ago. But these works of primitive, perhaps pre-*sapiens*, culture were scarcely clues to the mystery of the grave mounds.

The first month's wandering over the island also resulted, however, in the discovery of a large number of settlement sites: sand-covered ruins with scraps of pottery of many different types. Clearly it was necessary to determine whether the grave mounds contained the same types of pottery. We accordingly excavated two grave mounds and explored the slab-roofed burial chambers within. These are of a shape unknown outside Bahrain, with two alcoves at the western end giving the chamber a T-shaped plan. While both proved to have been robbed, they produced, in addition to copper spearheads and a drinking cup formed of an ostrich eggshell, a small quantity of distinctive red pottery.

With this encouragement we began to dig at a site where a large number of squared stone blocks, lying on the surface, argued an important building below the ground. A small underground well-chamber was found, with a flight of steps leading down to the wellhead, formed of a single square block pierced by a hole. Two decapitated statues of seated rams, which originally had stood at the head of the stairs, showed that this site was pre-Islamic. Further work was stopped, however, by water from underground and by the discovery in the meantime of a site of much greater importance.

This was a large mound near the village of Barbar on the northwestern coast. There a large block of hewn stone, projecting above the surface, tempted investigation. A trial trench laid bare a stone-flagged court surrounded by the lowest courses of a wall of cut limestone. In the center of this court the trench exposed part of a double circle of curved blocks. A widening of the trench showed these to be a plinth that must have borne statues or cult objects. To the east of the plinth two stone slabs stood upright,

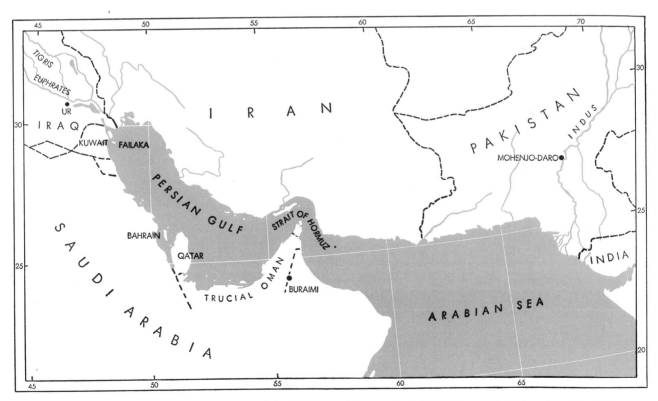

ANCIENT SITES are located on this modern map of the Middle East. Bahrain Island lies halfway down the Persian Gulf from the joint mouth of the Tigris and Euphrates rivers. Cuneiform texts describe the island as being some two days' sail from Mesopotamia.

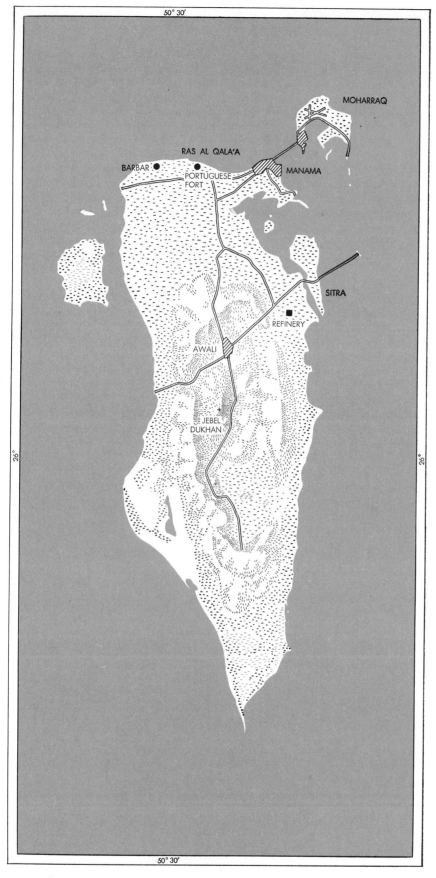

BAHRAIN ISLAND is about twice the size of Manhattan. Most of the grave mounds lie in the northern part of the island. The cross at center marks the 440-foot Jebel Dukhan (Mountain of Smoke). Shaded areas are modern towns; double lines represent modern roads.

with a recess in the upper edge to take a seat top, and before them was a square libation altar with a hollowed top, served by a stone-lined drain passing through the walls. To the north a square pit in the flags of the courtyard proved to contain a wealth of objects: lapis-lazuli beads and pendants, alabaster jars and objects of copper, including a figure of a naked and shaven priest in an attitude of prayer. We had uncovered the holy of holies of a temple. The statuette evidenced unmistakable Sumerian affinities—secure evidence for an early date. Moreover, several of the lapis-lazuli pendants were of a type found in the cities of the Indus Valley.

Now, after seven seasons of work on the temple of Barbar, the central area has been completely cleared. The square temple has been shown to stand upon a terrace supported by walls of finely cut and fitted limestone. A ramp leads down to the east to an oval enclosure full of charcoal from extensive and repeated burnings and containing stone foundations, perhaps blocks on which animals were sacrificed. To the west a flight of steps leads down from the terrace to a small tank or bathing pool. The temple is thus reminiscent in its layout of the temples of Early Dynastic Sumer, but, with its bathing pool, it also recalls the ritual baths of the Indus Valley cities. We have found the structure to be only the final stage of three successive building phases, each representing additions to the terrace and to the temple above it.

A wealth of small objects has been discovered within the complex—axes and spears of copper, a magnificent bull's head that calls to mind those that adorned the harps in the Early Dynastic royal graves at Ur of the Chaldees and eight circular soapstone seals. These seals are of a type well known to archeologists and much discussed. Among the thousands of cylindrical seals found in Mesopotamia there are a mere 17 of these round seals. They were not native to Mesopotamia, and appeared to date to the period between 2300 and 2000 B.C. Several bore inscriptions in the unknown language of the Indus Valley civilization. Moreover, three examples of the same type of seal had actually been found in the prehistoric Indus Valley city of Mohenjo-Daro. But they were obviously not native to the Indus Valley, where large square seals, found by the hundreds, had been shown to be the native type. It was now apparent to us that the round seals were native to Bahrain. The temples at Barbar could thus be placed in the third millennium B.C.; they belonged to a people who traded with both Mesopotamia and India and had a culture distinct from both.

The temples of Barbar have also yielded a large quantity of pottery. It is of a distinctive type—round-bellied jars of a red ware, decorated with horizontal ridges and often bearing a short spout. Further excavation of several more grave mounds with the distinctive T-shaped chambers has produced jars of precisely the same type. The link between the grave mounds and the temple-complex at Barbar is thus established beyond doubt.

Still another large site, discovered during the first season, has revealed the same Barbar pottery, and has at the same time greatly extended our knowledge of this forgotten civilization. Some miles to the east of Barbar, at a bend in the coast known as Ras al-Qala'a, a huge low mound is crowned by the ruins of a fort built by the Portuguese during their 100-year domination of the Gulf in the 16th century. The excavations of the first year showed this mound to be composed of the debris and ruins of a large city. The work of the subsequent years has laid bare a large area (though small in relation to the 200,000 square yards covered by the mound), and has shown that here lie seven cities, one buried below the other. The city second from the bottom has yielded the red-ridged pottery and round stamp-seals characteristic of the Barbar period. In the same levels are ruins of stone houses and a rectangular layout of streets, all surrounded by a massive wall of hewn stone, 14 feet thick. The city that lies below the Barbar city also yields round stamp-seals. But these are more primitive, with designs resembling more closely those of the Indus Valley cities than those found in Mesopotamia. The pottery, too, is related, but bears ridges pressed into a chainlike pattern.

The five successive cities that overlie the two third-millennium cities give a broad panorama of the history of Bahrain almost up to our own day. After the great days of the third millennium there comes a clean break in the style of pottery and other artifacts. It would seem that a different people now occupies the island. In many ways they are poorer and less artistic, and they seem to have deserted part of the city. And yet it is to their time that the most magnificent phase in the construction of a colossal building apparently belongs. This building was discovered at Ras al-Qala'a during the closing weeks of the first campaign. Built of squared stones a yard in length and more, it still stands

CLOSE-UP OF A MOUND shows the ruins of the circular stone walls that ring it. The stone-lined entrance shaft at top center leads to two T-shaped burial chambers within.

BURIAL CHAMBERS within the mounds are roofed with slabs of stone and sealed with large rocks. Although robbed, chambers contained spearheads, shell cups and pottery.

to a monumental height of 16 feet, with imposing doorways and sheer walls. Begun perhaps at the close of the Barbar period, it was completed and occupied by the new invaders. Some time in the second millennium this third city was destroyed and left desolate.

After a lapse of years a new people with new fashions of pottery and implements reoccupied the site. The ruins of the immense building were now cleaned out, repaired and partially rebuilt of inferior materials, apparently as a temple to a snake goddess. In the huge entrance hall two mighty square pillars had originally borne a roof. But in this period the hall was roofless; one pillar had disappeared, and of the other only the bottom block, a yard square and two feet high, still stood like an altar. In front of this block we found 14 offerings in pottery bowls deposited in shallow holes in the floor. In seven of the bowls lay the skeletons of snakes, some up to five feet in length. With the skeletons in

some cases were beads, while one of the offerings consisted entirely of a necklace of 26 beads of agate, amethyst, glass and porcelain, held by a silver clasp. Clearly these gifts of snakes and jewelry were either the offerings of women or were offerings to a female deity (or, most probably, both). They call to mind the snake goddess of fertility worshiped in the second and first millennia over a wide area, from India to Scandinavia, and best known from the Cretan statuettes of goddesses holding snakes.

Early in the first millennium the building was again abandoned, though it was for some time used as a burial vault. Its rooms now lay entirely below ground. Adults were buried in clay coffins, bathtub-shaped and painted with bitumen inside and out, while babies were buried curled up in large bowls. Most of these graves had been robbed, but in one lay a fine bronze wine-service, consisting of pitcher, bowl, strainer and ladle, together with an agate seal that securely dates the grave to about 700 B.C.

Outside the abandoned building the city extended its area, and its surface rose with the accumulation of rubbish and the demolition and rebuilding of houses. In these late levels we suddenly find sherds of black-painted pottery, the products of Athens in the fourth century B.C. Terra-cotta figures and a Greek name scratched on a potsherd show that not only Greek trade goods but also Greek art and speakers of Greek traveled the Persian Gulf before the time of Alexander the Great.

With the beginning of the Christian era and the fall of the successors of Alexander, the city of Ras al-Qala'a appears to have been once more deserted for some centuries. The two uppermost building levels of the city are Islamic, dated very neatly by Chinese pottery of the Sung and Ming dynasties to the 10th and the 16th centuries A.D. respectively. The last city is therefore contemporary with the 16th-century Portuguese fort that crowns the mound and within which the Danish archeological expe-

EXCAVATIONS AT BARBAR uncovered a stone-lined pool (*center*) similar to the ritual baths of the ancient cities of the Indus Valley. In the background is the terrace of a temple. The layout of the temple resembles that of Sumerian temples of the Early Dynas-

dition has pitched its camp these last five years.

It now seems clear that Bahrain was a center of urban life for at least 3,000 years before the Christian era. In the centuries around 2000 B.C. it was a place of considerable wealth and power. Its unique civilization was in close cultural contact with the Sumerians of Mesopotamia 150 miles up the Persian Gulf to the north and with the cities of the Indus Valley, 1,000 miles across land and sea to the east.

References to such a center of civilization turn up again and again in the extensive literature dug up in the cities of Mesopotamia over the past century. Commercial documents describe trading voyages down the Persian Gulf from the cities of Ur, Larsa, Lagash and Nippur. The historical accounts of the campaigns of the kings of Sumer, Babylon and Assyria tell of tribute and submission received from the countries of the "lower sea." Three lands down the Gulf are named with particular frequency: the

kingdoms of Dilmun, Makan and Meluhha. They are always named in that order, presumably the order of their distance from Mesopotamia.

Henry Rawlinson, the British colonial official and scholar who deciphered cuneiform more than a century ago, was also the first to suggest that Bahrain might be the site of Dilmun. He based his theory on the discovery on Bahrain of a cuneiform inscription naming the god Inzak, who is cited in the god lists of Mesopotamia as the chief god of Dilmun. With the discovery of the rich cities and temples of Bahrain this theory may now be regarded as confirmed. Dilmun is described in the cuneiform records of Mesopotamia as an island with abundant fresh water lying some two days' sail, with a following wind, from Mesopotamia. Ships are frequently recorded as sailing to Dilmun with cargoes of silver and woolen goods to be exchanged there for the products of Makan (copper and diorite) and those of

Meluhha (gold, ivory and precious woods). This would suggest that Meluhha was none other than the Indus Valley civilization, and that Makan must be sought between Bahrain and India. Dilmun is also named as supplying products of its own: dates and pearls. Clearly, however, Dilmun's main importance was as a clearing house for goods from farther east, the abode of merchants and shippers engaged in widespread commerce. This view agrees closely with the new archeological evidence.

But Dilmun was more than this. The Sumerian poems and epics of gods and heroes tell of another Dilmun, a land that before the creation of man was the abode of the gods, the home of immortality, a paradise of gardens and fresh water in which neither sickness nor old age was known. It was to Dilmun that Zius-udra, the sole survivor of the Deluge, retired when the waters subsided and he had been granted immortality. And it was to Dilmun that the greatest hero of ancient Sumer, Gilgamesh, came

tic Period. Another view of this temple appears on next page. EXCAVATIONS AT RAS AL-QALA'A unearthed the ancient water closet in center foreground. Dating back to first millennium B.C., water closet was complete with tank and running water.

in his vain quest for immortality. But of that golden age of Dilmun no traces have yet been found in the record.

In order to follow the ancient trade routes to the east and to the west the Danish archeologists have extended their research far beyond Bahrain to cover 600 miles off the coast of Arabia from Kuwait to the Trucial Oman on the Strait of Hormuz, the eastern entrance to the Gulf. Near Kuwait three seasons' work on the little island of Failaka, a

three-hour sail from the coast, has uncovered two adjacent sites of unusual importance. One is an outpost of the Dilmun culture, a small but very rich settlement, producing the typical ridged red pottery so well known from the Barbar temples of Bahrain, as well as fragments of soapstone bowls carved with figures of animals and men, amulets bearing cuneiform inscriptions, and almost 200 round seals identical with those of the Barbar period of Bahrain. The

other site, a fort, was built almost 2,000 years later by veterans of the army of Alexander the Great on their return from India. In and near it have been found Rhodian wine jars and molds for casting statuettes of Greek goddesses and even of the divine Alexander himself. And the campaign just completed has laid bare a pillared temple of Greek style. Standing before it is a slab that bears a long Greek inscription giving the instructions issued by the Greek king for

WALL OF TERRACE of the latest of the ancient temples at Barbar (*bottom*) masked the wall of the earlier terrace and its stone staircase (*top*). Three pierced stone blocks at extreme upper left were possibly tethering poles for animals awaiting sacrifice.

the foundation of this colony so far from the Greek homeland.

But perhaps the greatest perspectives are opened by the work that has now been going on for two years in the Trucial Oman. There, on a little island off the coast, and again at the oasis of Buraimi, three days' camel journey into the interior, groups of grave mounds have been found. The graves are of a completely new and imposing type, with perpendicular circular walls built with stones cut to fit the curve and standing to above the height of a man. Squeezing through tiny "porthole" entrances, one finds within cross walls supporting arched roofs. Unlike the single burials of the Bahrain mounds, these burial chambers each contains up to 50 skeletons, lying in disorder as they were successively pushed aside to make room for more bodies. Among them lie thousands of beads and a wealth of finely made painted pottery. This pottery resembles the pottery found in the Dilmun levels of Bahrain closely enough to determine that the burial vaults are of the same date as the Dilmun civilization. But it resembles even more closely the pottery of the Kulli culture of India, which is believed to have preceded the Indus Valley civilization. In this new culture, with its unique burial practices, we may be touching the fringe of the next great civilization toward the east, the kingdom of Makan.

GREEK TEMPLE at Kuwait, 250 miles north of Bahrain, was built at the order of Alexander the Great. A stone slab found in front of the temple contains a long inscription in Greek giving the instructions issued by Alexander for the founding of a Greek colony.

21   An Early City in Iran

by C. C. and Martha Lamberg-Karlovsky
June 1971

Tepe Yahyā, midway between Mesopotamia and India, was a busy center of trade 5,500 years ago. An outpost of Mesopotamian urban culture, it played a key role in the spread of civilization from west to east

The kingdom of Elam and its somewhat better-known neighbor, Sumer, were the two earliest urban states to arise in the Mesopotamian area during the fourth millennium B.C. Archaeological findings now show that the Elamite realm also included territory at least 500 miles to the east. For more than 10 centuries, starting about 3400 B.C., the hill country of southeastern Iran some 60 miles from the Arabian Sea was the site of a second center of Elamite urban culture.

Today all that is left of the city that stood halfway between the Euphrates and the Indus is a great mound of earth located some 4,500 feet above sea level in the Soghun Valley, 150 miles south of the city of Kerman in the province of the same name. Known locally as Tepe Yahyā, the mound is 60 feet high and 600 feet in diameter. Its record of occupation begins with a 6,500-year-old Neolithic village and ends with a citadel of the Sassanian dynasty that ruled Persia early in the Christian Era. Intermediate levels in the mound testify to the connections between this eastern Elamite city and the traditional centers of the kingdom in the west.

Such a long archaeological sequence has much value for the study of man's cultural development from farmer to city dweller, but three unexpected elements make Tepe Yahyā a site of even greater significance. First, writing tablets made of clay, recovered from one of the lower levels in the mound, have been shown by carbon-14 analysis of associated organic material to date back to 3560 B.C. (±110 years). The tablets are inscribed with writing of the kind known as proto-Elamite. Proto-Elamite inscriptions and early Sumerian ones are the earliest known Mesopotamian writings, which are the oldest known anywhere. The Tepe Yahyā tablets are unique in that they are the first of their kind that can be assigned an absolute date. It comes as a surprise to find these examples of writing—as early as the earliest known—in a place that is so far away from Mesopotamia.

The second surprise is evidence that Elamite trade with neighboring Sumer in an unusual commodity—steatite, the easily worked rock also known as soapstone—formed a major part of the commerce at Tepe Yahyā. Unlike Sumer, which was surrounded by the featureless floodplains of lower Mesopotamia, Elam was a hill kingdom rich in natural resources. Elamite trade supplied the Sumerians with silver, copper, tin and lead, with precious gems and horses, and with commoner materials such as timber, obsidian, alabaster, diorite and soapstone. To find that the soapstone trade reached as far east as Tepe Yahyā adds a new dimension to our knowledge of fourth-millennium commerce.

Third, the discovery of Tepe Yahyā has greatly enlarged the known extent of ancient Elam, which was hazily perceived at best. Susa, the most famous Elamite city, lies not far from such famous Sumerian centers as Ur and Eridu. As for other Elamite cities named in inscriptions (Awan, for example, or Madaktu), their location remains a mystery. To discover a prosperous Elamite city as far east of Mesopotamia as Tepe Yahyā is both a surprise and something of a revelation. It suggests how urban civilization, which arose in lower Mesopotamia, made its way east to the valley of the Indus (in what is now West Pakistan).

The British explorer-archaeologist Sir Aurel Stein was the first to recognize that southeastern Iran is a region with important prehistoric remains. Two sites that Stein probed briefly in the 1930's—Tal-i-Iblis near Kerman and Bampur in Persian Baluchistan—have recently been excavated, the first by Joseph R. Caldwell of the University of Georgia and the second by Beatrice de Cardi of the Council for British Archaeology. Although it is the largest mound in southeastern Iran, Tepe Yahyā remained unknown until the summer of 1967, when our reconnaissance group from the Peabody Museum at Harvard University discovered it during an archaeological survey of the region.

We have now completed three seasons of excavation at Tepe Yahyā in coopera-

LARGE EARTH MOUND, over a third of a mile in circumference, was raised to a

tion with the Iran Archaeological Service and have established a sequence of six principal occupation periods. The site was inhabited almost continuously from the middle of the fifth millennium B.C. until about A.D. 400. Following the end of the Elamite period at Tepe Yahyā, about 2200 B.C., there is a 1,000-year gap in the record that is still unexplained but finds parallels at major sites elsewhere in Iran. Tepe Yahyā remained uninhabited until 1000 B.C., when the site was resettled by people of an Iron Age culture.

Our main work at Tepe Yahyā began in the summer of 1968 with the digging of a series of excavations, each 30 feet square, from the top of the mound to the bottom [see illustration below]. Small test trenches were then made within the series of level squares. During our second and third season the excavations were extended by means of further horizontal exposures on the top of the mound and to the west of the main explorations. In addition we opened a stepped trench 12 feet wide on the opposite face of the mound as a check on the sequences we had already exposed.

The earliest remains of human occupation at Tepe Yahyā, which rest on virgin soil in a number of places, consist of five superimposed levels of mud-brick construction. We have assigned them to a single cultural interval—Period VI—that is shown by carbon-14 analysis to lie in the middle of the fifth millennium B.C. The structures of Period VI seem to be a series of square storage areas that measure about five feet on a side. Most of them have no doorways; they were probably entered through a hole in the roof. The walls are built either of sun-dried mud bricks that were formed by hand or of hand-daubed mud [see top illustration on page 213]. Fragments of reed matting and timber found on the floors of the rooms are traces of fallen roofs.

The tools of Period VI include implements made of bone and flint. Many of the flints are very small; they include little blades that were set in a bone handle to make a sickle. The most common kind of pottery is a coarse, hand-shaped ware; the clay was "tempered" by the addition of chaff. The pots are made in the form of bowls and large storage jars and are decorated with a red wash or painted with red meanders. Toward the end of Period VI a few pieces of finer pottery appear: a buff ware with a smooth, slip-finished surface and a red ware with decorations painted in black.

Human burials, all of infants, were found under the floor in a few of the structures. The limbs of the bodies had been tightly gathered to the trunk before burial, and accompanying the bodies are unbroken coarse-ware bowls. In one room a small human figurine was found face down on the floor, resting on a collection of flint and bone tools. The sculpture is 11 inches long and was carved out of dark green soapstone [see illustration on next page]. The carving clearly delineates a female figure. Its elongated form and the presence of a hole at the top of the head, however, suggest a dual symbol that combines male and female characteristics.

The Neolithic culture of Period VI evidently included the practice of agriculture and animal husbandry. Identifiable animal bones include those of wild gazelles and of cattle, sheep and goats. Camel bones are also present, but it is not clear whether or not they indicate that the animal had been domesticated at this early date. The domesticated plants include a variety of cereal grains. In the Tepe Yahyā area today raising crops involves irrigation; whether or not this was the case in Neolithic times is also unclear. At any rate the Neolithic occupation of the mound continued until about 3800 B.C.

The transition from Period VI to the Early Bronze Age culture that followed

height of 60 feet over a 5,000-year period as new settlements were built on the rubble of earlier ones. Located in southeastern Iran and known locally as Tepe Yahyā, the site was first occupied by a Neolithic community in the middle of the fifth millennium B.C.

NEOLITHIC FIGURINE was found in one of the storerooms in the earliest structure at Tepe Yahyā, associated with tools made of flint and bone. The sculpture was apparently intended to be a dual representation: a female figure imposed on a stylized phallic shape.

occurred without any break in continuity. The structures of Period V contain coarse-ware pottery of the earlier type. The finer, painted pottery becomes commoner and includes some new varieties. One of these, with a surface finish of red slip, has a decorative geometric pattern of repeated chevrons painted in black. We have named this distinctive black-on-red pottery Yahyā ware, and we call the material culture of Period V the Yahyā culture.

The commonest examples of Yahyā ware are beakers. These frequently have a potter's mark on the base, and we have so far identified nine individual marks. Evidence that outside contact and trade formed part of the fabric of Early Bronze Age life at Tepe Yahyā comes from the discovery at Tal-i-Iblis, a site nearly 100 miles closer to Kerman, of almost identical painted pottery bearing similar potter's marks. There is other evidence of regional contacts. Yahyā ware shows a general similarity to the painted pottery at sites elsewhere in southeastern Iran, and a black-on-buff ware at Tepe Yahyā closely resembles pottery from sites well to the west, such as Bakun. Moreover, the Period V levels at Tepe Yahyā abound in imported materials. There are tools made of obsidian, beads made of ivory, carnelian and turquoise, and various objects made of alabaster, marble and mother-of-pearl. One particularly handsome figure is a stylized representation of a ram, seven inches long, carved out of alabaster [see top illustration on page 216]. No local sources are known for any of these materials.

Although the architecture of Period V demonstrates a continuity with the preceding Neolithic period, the individual structures are larger than before. Several of them measure eight by 11½ feet in area and are clearly residential in character. Some rooms include a hearth and chimney. In the early levels the walls are still built of hand-formed mud bricks. Bricks formed in molds appear in the middle of Period V, which carbon-14 analyses show to have been around 3660 B.C. (±140 years).

The bronze implements of Period V, like much of the earliest bronze in the world, were produced not by alloying but by utilizing copper ores that contained "impurities." This was the case in early Sumer, where the ore, imported from Oman on the Arabian peninsula, contained a high natural percentage of nickel. Early bronzesmiths elsewhere smelted copper ores that were naturally rich in arsenic. Chisels, awls, pins and spatulas at Tepe Yahyā are made of such an arsenical bronze.

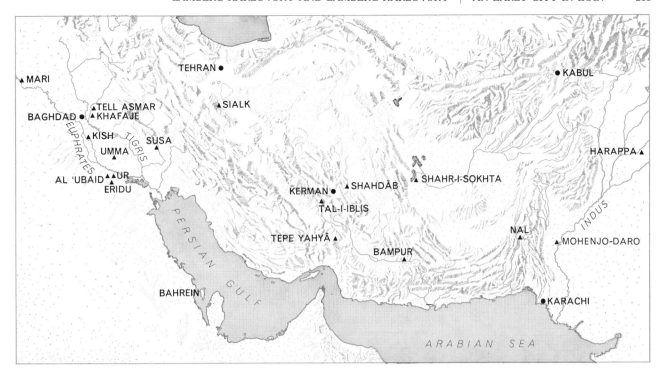

FIRST CITIES arose in the kingdom of Sumer in lower Mesopotamia (*left*). The earliest known forms of writing appeared in Sumer and in nearby Elam at cities such as Susa and Sialk. The discovery of proto-Elamite writing at Tepe Yahyā (*center*), which is 500 miles to the east, suggests that trade between the region and the early cities of Mesopotamia led to the rise of cities in this part of ancient Persia in the fourth millennium B.C. and to the later development of the urban Harappan civilization in the Indus region.

Six artifacts from the site have been analyzed by R. F. Tylecote and H. McKerrell of the University of Newcastle upon Tyne. They found that the bronze had been produced by smelting, which shows that the metalworkers of Period V were able to obtain the high temperatures needed to smelt copper ores into molten metal. The final shapes were not made by casting, however, but by hot and cold forging, a more primitive technique. One of the articles, a chisel, proved to contain 3.7 percent arsenic, which leads us to believe that the metalworkers consciously selected for smelting ores with a high arsenic content. This finding is further testimony in support of trade at Tepe Yahyā; none of the copper deposits native to the region could have been used to make arsenical bronze.

With the beginning of Period IV, around 3500 B.C., the appearance of writing at Tepe Yahyā allows the city to be identified as a proto-Elamite settlement. Much of the pottery representative of the first two phases of this period, IV-C and IV-B, is typical of the preceding Yahyā culture in both shape and decoration. Although there is plentiful evidence of external contact, the transition to Period IV at Tepe Yahyā, like the one that preceded it, occurred without any break in continuity. There is no need at Tepe Yahyā to conjure up that hackneyed instrument of cultural change: a new people arriving with luggage labeled "Proto-Elamite."

Architecture, however, was considerably transformed. The site ceased to be a residential area and became an administrative one. A large structure we have unearthed at the IV-C level of the mound is carefully oriented so that its walls run north-south and east-west. The walls consist of three courses of mold-formed brick in a new size. The earlier mold-formed bricks had been six by six by 12 inches; the new ones were 9½ by 9½ by 4¾ inches—a third wider and less than half as thick. So far we have identified five of an undetermined number of rooms within the large structure, although we have fully cleared only part of one room. Both the structure and the partially excavated room continue toward the center of the mound; the size of each remains to be determined.

The part of the room that has been cleared measures about 10 by 20 feet. Its contents strongly suggest a commercial function. Among the objects in the room are bowls with beveled rims made of a coarse ware. The vessels have counterparts at numerous sites in Mesopotamia. They are believed to have served as standard measures. Three large storage jars, which proved to be empty, were also found in the room; near them were some 24 "sealings": jar stoppers made of clay and marked with a seal impression. The seals used to mark the sealings were cylindrical; the designs resemble those on cylinder seals found at Susa, the Elamite capital in the Mesopotamian area. The finding creates the possibility that goods from Susa were reaching Tepe Yahyā early in Period IV.

Lying on the floor of the room were 84 blank clay tablets and six others that bore inscriptions. The tablets are all the same shape; they are made of unbaked dark brown clay, are convex in profile and measure 1⅛ by two inches. The six inscribed tablets bear a total of 17 lines of proto-Elamite writing. The inscriptions were impressed in the soft clay with a stylus; they read from right to left along the main axis of the tablet and from top to bottom. When an inscription continues from one side of a tablet to the other, the writer rotated the tablet on its main axis so that the bottom line of the obverse inscription and the top line of the reverse inscription lie opposite each other.

The Tepe Yahyā inscriptions are being deciphered now. Preliminary examination indicates that they are records or receipts dealing with goods. The fact that inscribed and otherwise identical blank tablets were found in the same room is strong evidence that the writing was done on the spot. Therefore the goods they describe must have been either entering or leaving the administrative area.

Until the discovery at Tepe Yahyā the only other proto-Elamite tablets known were from Susa or from Sialk in northwestern Iran. Susa yielded nearly 1,500 such tablets, Sialk only 19. Proto-Elamite writing has been found recently at Shahdāb, a site north of Kerman that is being excavated by the Iran Archaeological Service. The writing there is not on tablets but consists of brief inscriptions, with a maximum of seven signs, incised on pottery.

A second change in architectural style is evident in the single IV-B structure examined so far. It is a building, nine by 24 feet in area, that is oriented without reference to north-south and east-west. It is built of bricks of a still newer size and shape. They are oblong rather than square, and are either 14 or 17 inches long; the other two dimensions remained the same. The structure is subdivided into two main rooms and a few smaller rooms that contain large storage bins built of unbaked clay. Its walls are only one brick thick, and their inside surfaces are covered with plaster.

Storage vessels in one of the main

rooms still held several pounds of grain. The grain was charred, which together with the fact that the matting on the floor and the bricks in the wall were burned indicates that the building was destroyed by fire. Amid the debris on the floors were cylinder seals and, for the first time at Tepe Yahyā, stamp seals as well.

Some bronze tools of the IV-B period have also been discovered. Needles and chisels, unearthed in association with soapstone artifacts, were probably used to work the soapstone. A bronze dagger some seven inches long was found by Tylecote and McKerrell to have been made by forging smelted metal, as were the bronze tools of Period V. Analysis showed that the dagger, unlike the earlier artifacts of arsenical bronze, was an alloy comprising 3 percent tin. Tin is not found in this part of Iran, which means that either the dagger itself, the tin contained in it or an ingot of tin-alloyed bronze must have been imported to Tepe Yahyā.

The proof that writing was known at Tepe Yahyā as early as it was known anywhere is a discovery of major importance to prehistory. Perhaps next in

importance, however, is the abundant evidence suggesting a unique economic role for the city beginning late in the fourth millennium B.C. The IV-B phase at Tepe Yahyā is known from carbon-14 analyses to have extended from near the end of the fourth millennium through the first two centuries of the third millennium. During that time the city was a major supplier of soapstone artifacts.

Objects made of soapstone, ranging from simple beads to ornate bowls and all very much alike in appearance, are found in Bronze Age sites as far apart as Mohenjo-Daro, the famous center of Harappan culture on the Indus, and Mari on the upper Euphrates 1,500 miles away. Mesopotamia, however, was a region poor in natural resources, soapstone included. The Harappans of the Indus also seem to have lacked local supplies of several desired materials. How were the exotic substances to be obtained? Sumerian and Akkadian texts locate the sources of certain luxury imports in terms of place-names that are without meaning today: Dilmun, Maluhha and Magan.

Investigations by Danish workers on the island of Bahrein in the Persian Gulf have essentially confirmed the belief that the island is ancient Dilmun. There is also a degree of agreement that the area or place known as Maluhha lay somewhere in the valley of the Indus. Even before we began our work at Tepe Yahyā it had been suggested that the area known as Magan was somewhere in southeastern Iran. Our excavations have considerably strengthened this hypothesis. A fragmentary Sumerian text reads: "May the land Magan [bring] you mighty copper, the strength of ... diorite, 'u-' stone, 'shumash' stone." Could either of the untranslated names of stones stand for soapstone? Were Tepe Yahyā and its hinterland a center of the trade? Let us examine the evidence from the site.

More soapstone has been found at Tepe Yahyā than at any other single site in the Middle East. The total is more than 1,000 fragments, unfinished pieces and intact objects; the majority of them belong to Period IV-B. Among the intact pieces are beads, buttons, cylinder seals, figurines and bowls. Unworked blocks of soapstone, vessels that are partially hollowed out and unfinished seals and beads are proof that Tepe Yahyā was a manufacturing site and not merely a transshipment point.

Some of the soapstone bowls are plain, but others are elaborately decorated with carvings. The decorations include geometric and curvilinear designs, animals and human figures. Among the decora-

TWO CYLINDER SEALS from the level at Tepe Yahyā overlying the first proto-Elamite settlement appear at left in these photographs next to the impressions they produce. The seal designs, which show pairs of human figures with supernatural attributes, are generally similar to the designs on seals of Mesopotamian origin but appear to be of local workmanship.

EARLIEST STRUCTURE at Tepe Yahyā is a storage area consisting of small units measuring five feet on a side. Few of the units have doorways; apparently they were entered through a hole in the roof. The walls were built either of sun-dried mud bricks, formed by hand rather than in molds, or simply of hand-daubed mud. White circle (*left*) shows where female figurine was found.

TWO ELAMITE BUILDINGS at Tepe Yahyā left the traces seen in this photograph. The walls of the earlier building (*left*) were built sometime around 3500 B.C. of mold-formed mud bricks 9½ inches on a side. The walls run from north to south and from east to west. The walls of the later structure (*right*) are not oriented in these directions. It was built sometime after 3000 B.C. of oblong mold-formed mud bricks of two lengths. Both structures seem to have been administrative rather than residential. The earlier one contained storage pots and measuring bowls. Near one angle of its walls a pile of 84 unused writing tablets is visible.

tions are examples of every major motif represented on the numerous soapstone bowls unearthed at Bronze Age sites in Mesopotamia and the Indus valley. Moreover, motifs found on pottery unearthed at sites such as Bampur, to the east of Tepe Yahyā, and Umm-an-Nai on the Persian Gulf are repeated on soapstone bowls from IV-B levels.

During our 1970 season we located what was probably one of the sources of Tepe Yahyā soapstone. An outcrop of the rock in the Ashin Mountains some 20 miles from the mound shows evidence of strip-mining in the past. This is unlikely to have been the only source. Soapstone deposits are often associated with deposits of asbestos and chromite. There is a chromite mine only 10 miles from Tepe Yahyā, and we have noted veins of asbestos in stones unearthed during our excavation of the mound. Reconnaissance in the mountains to the north might locate additional soapstone exposures.

Taking into consideration the large quantities of soapstone found at the site, the evidence that many of the soapstone articles were manufactured locally, the availability of raw material nearby and the presence in both Mesopotamia and Harappan territory of soapstone bowls that repeat motifs found at Tepe Yahyā, it is hard to avoid the conclusion that the city was a major producer of soapstone and a center of trade in the material. Before turning to the broader significance of such commercial activity in this geographically remote area, we shall briefly describe the remaining occupation periods at Tepe Yahyā.

At present there is little to report concerning the final phase of Period IV, which drew to a close about 2200 B.C. It is then that the break occurs in the continuity at Tepe Yahyā. The Iron Age reoccupation of the site, which lasted roughly from 1000 to 500 B.C., comprises Period III. It is evidenced by a series of living floors and by pottery that shows strong parallels to wares and shapes produced during the same period in northwestern Iran. We have not yet uncovered a major structure belonging to Period III; both the nature of the culture and Tepe Yahyā's relations with its Iron Age neighbors remain unclarified.

Period II at Tepe Yahyā, which consists of more than 200 years of Achaemenian occupation, was a time of large-scale construction. The building material remained mud brick, but we have yet to uncover a complete structure. The appearance of the two large rooms excavated thus far suggests, however, that the site had once more become at least partly residential.

A subsequent 600 years or so of Parthian and Sassanian occupation, representing Period I, is the final period of urban civilization at Tepe Yahyā. We have uncovered suggestions of large-scale architecture, including courtyards and part of a massive mud-brick platform made by laying four courses of brick one on the other. By Sassanian times (early in the third century) the accumulated debris of thousands of years had raised the mound to an imposing height; the structure that has been partly exposed probably was a citadel standing on the summit.

Most of the Sassanian pottery consists

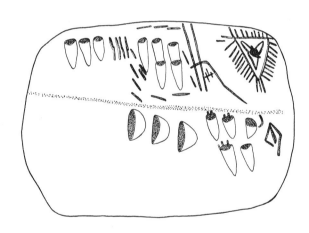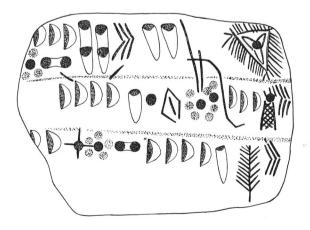

INSCRIBED TABLETS from Tepe Yahyā (*photographs*) are shown next to drawings that reproduce the written symbols. Only six inscribed tablets have been found so far. The inscriptions are in proto-Elamite, written from right to left across the length of the tablet by pressing the blunt or sharp end of a stylus into the soft clay. Similar written tablets have been unearthed at Susa and Sialk.

of coarse, thick-walled storage jars. An abundance of beads and several small glass and pottery bottles, perhaps containers for perfume, suggest a degree of prosperity during Period I. The presence of iron and bronze swords, axes and arrowheads adds a military flavor. A single work of art, a small clay figurine, represents a warrior with a distinctive headdress [*see bottom illustration on next page*]. Thereafter, from sometime in the fifth century on, Tepe Yahyā was occupied only by occasional squatters or transient nomads. The few scattered surface finds are of early Islamic age; none of the visitors lingered or built anything of substance.

What role did Elamite Tepe Yahyā play in the transmission of the urban tradition from west to east? The city's position suggests that Elamite culture, which is now revealed as being far more widespread than was realized previously, was instrumental in the contact between the first urban civilization in Mesopotamia and the civilization that subsequently arose in the Indus valley. It appears that the Elamites of eastern Persia may have accomplished much more than that. To assess this possibility it is necessary to examine the evidence for direct contact, as distinct from trade through middlemen, between Mesopotamia and the Indus valley.

A small number of artifacts that are possibly or certainly of Harappan origin have been found at sites in Mesopotamia. Because much of the archaeological work there was done as long as a century ago, it is not surprising that both the age and the original location of many of these artifacts can only be roughly estimated. Nonetheless, Mesopotamia has yielded six stamp seals, one cylinder seal and a single clay sealing, all of the Harappan type, that are evidence of some kind of contact between the two civilizations. Certain seals are engraved with Harappan writing. On others the writing is combined with animal figures that are indisputably Harappan in style: a "unicorn," an elephant, a rhinoceros. Evidence of contact, yes. But was the contact direct or indirect?

The single Indus sealing found in Mesopotamia was discovered by the French archaeologist G. Contenau at Umma in southern Iraq during the 1920's. It suggests the arrival there of freight from Harappan territory that had been identified with the sender's personal mark before shipment. The seven seals, however, are evidence of a more equivocal kind. Mesopotamian contact with the Indus evidently did not resemble the later trade

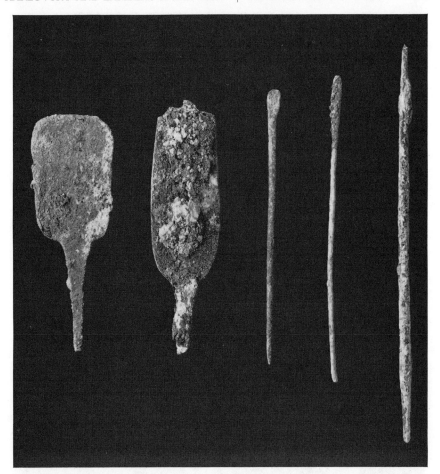

BRONZE OBJECTS contemporaneous with peak of work and trade in soapstone at Tepe Yahyā include two chisels (*left*) and three needle-like forms; the longest object measures 6½ inches. The bronze was not produced by alloying but by utilizing copper that naturally included significant amounts of arsenic. The enriched ores were obtained through trade.

SOAPSTONE BOWLS, many of them elaborately decorated, were among the numerous objects made at Tepe Yahyā and traded eastward and westward during the first half of the third millennium B.C. Fragments of bowls with decorations like the ones on these bowl fragments from Tepe Yahyā have been found from Mesopotamia to the Indus valley.

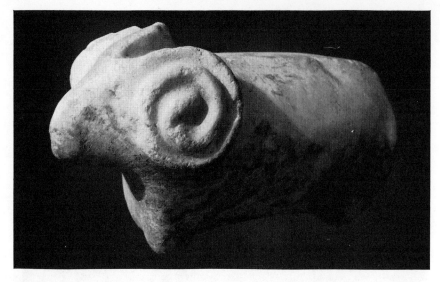

FIGURINE OF A RAM carved out of alabaster is one of the numerous articles made from imported materials that are found at Tepe Yahyā at the time of its first urban settlement about 3800 B.C. Evidences of trade between the city and outlying areas include, in addition to alabaster, mother-of-pearl from the Persian Gulf, marble, turquoise and carnelian.

FIGURINE OF A WARRIOR modeled in clay is from the final period of occupation at Tepe Yahyā, when a Sassanian military outpost stood on the top of the mound from sometime in the third century B.C. to about A.D. 400. Thereafter only nomads visited the dead city.

between Mesopotamia and, say, the Hittite realm to the west. In that instance Assyrian trading colonies were housed within special quarters of such Hittite strongholds as Kültepe and Hattusha [see the article "An Assyrian Trading Outpost," by Tahsin Özgüç, beginning on page 234]. There is simply no good evidence that Mesopotamians ever visited the Indus to set up residence and trade or that Harappans did the reverse.

What, then, were the seals of Harappan traders doing in Mesopotamia? What was the function of the three unearthed at Ur, the two at Kish and the two at Tell Asmar? So far there is no persuasive answer to these questions. It is tempting to look on these seals not as credentials but as souvenirs of indirect trade contact; all of them are handsome objects. At the same time another equally puzzling question presents itself. Some objects of Indus origin have been found in Mesopotamia. Why has nothing of any kind from Mesopotamia been found at any Indus site?

Evidence of direct trade contact between the two civilizations thus remains almost entirely absent. Other kinds of trade, however, are equally well known. One of the oldest and most widespread is simple exchange, which can interpose any number of witting or unwitting intermediaries between two principals. Exchange is notable for presenting the archaeologist with difficulties of interpretation; intangibles such as style and function are likely to travel along with the goods.

A system of exchange that involves a single intermediary seems to provide the theoretical model that best approximates the situation at Tepe Yahyā. Such a system is known as "central place" trade; we suggest that Tepe Yahyā was just such a central place in southeastern Persia during Elamite times.

A central place can lie outside the sphere of influence of either principal and at the same time produce goods or control natural resources desired by both. In addition to (or even instead of) exporting its own products, a central place can transship goods produced by either principal. Bahrein—ancient Dilmun—provides a good example of a central place whose prosperity was based on the transshipment of goods bound for Mesopotamia. Whether or not transshipment was important at Tepe Yahyā, the city's basic central-place role in Elamite times was clearly that of a producer manufacturing and exporting articles made of soapstone.

The names of the Mesopotamian sites that contain soapstone bowls identical in shape and decorative motif with those we unearthed at Tepe Yahyā read like an archaeologist's checklist: Adab, Mari, Tell Asmar, Tell Aqrab, Khafaje, Nippur, Telloh, Kish, Al 'Ubaid and Ur. Bowls of Tepe Yahyā style have also been found at Mohenjo-Daro on the Indus and at Kulli-Damb in Pakistani Baluchistan. In addition to bevel-rim bowls of the Uruk type at Tepe Yahyā as evidence of contact with the west, the mound has yielded Nal ware, a kind of Indus painted pottery that predates the rise of Harappan civilization, as evidence of contact with the east.

Tepe Yahyā was not, however, the only central place in eastern Persia. It seems rather to have been one of several that comprised a local loose Elamite federation astride the middle ground between the two civilizations. Shahr-i-Sokhta, a site 250 miles northeast of Tepe Yahyā, appears to have been another central place, exporting local alabaster and transshipping lapis lazuli from Afghanistan. The links between Tepe Yahyā and other possible central places in the region such as Tal-i-Iblis, Shahdāb and Bampur—mainly demonstrated by similarities in pottery—have already been mentioned.

How did this remote Elamite domain, which in the case of Tepe Yahyā predates the appearance of Harappan civilization by at least three centuries, influence developments in the Indus valley? In spite of exciting new evidence that trade networks existed as long ago as the early Neolithic, a strong tendency exists to view trade exclusively as an ex post facto by-product of urbanism. Trade, however, has certainly also been one of the major stimuli leading to urban civilization. This, it seems to us, was exactly the situation in ancient Kerman and Persian Baluchistan.

We suggest that trade between resource-poor Mesopotamia and the population of this distant part of Persia provided the economic base necessary for the urban development of centers such as Tepe Yahyā during the fourth millennium B.C. It can further be suggested that, once an urban Elamite domain was established there, its trade with the region farther to the east provided much of the stimulus that culminated during the third millennium B.C. with the rise of Harappan civilization. Sir Mortimer Wheeler has declared that "the idea of civilization" crossed from Mesopotamia to the Indus. It seems to us that the Elamite central places midway between the two river basins deserve the credit for the crossing.

22

The Tombs of
the First Pharaohs

by Walter B. Emery
July 1957

*Before the kings of Egypt made pyramids, they were
buried in great brick-lined pits topped by rectangular
buildings. These structures provide clues as to how
civilization came to the Valley of the Nile*

When the famous British archaeologist Flinders Petrie published his *History of Egypt* in 1894, he devoted only 10 pages of it to the period before 2680 B.C. Yet by that time there had already been three dynasties of Egyptian kings. Egyptologists had learned much about the succeeding 27 dynasties by archaeological excavation, but their knowledge of the first pharaohs was based only on the lists of kings compiled by later Egyptians and on the writings of Greek and Roman historians. Indeed, some authorities believed that these kings were figures of myth and legend rather than men who really lived. But at the turn of the century the pick of the excavator revealed many monuments of the First Dynasty, and the shadowy figures of the first pharaohs stepped forth onto the stage of history to tell their story of the rise of civilization in the valley of the Nile.

The most important of these discoveries was made in 1895 at Abydos, a site on the Nile 300 miles south of Cairo. Here the French Egyptologist Emile-Clément Amélineau discovered a group of graves consisting of great pits lined with brick. In 1899 Petrie began to work at Abydos, and in two years of brilliant research he established its tombs as monuments of the kings of the First and Second Dynasties. He was also able to identify the royal owner of each tomb and to establish the order of his succession. Originally each brick-lined pit was roofed with timber and surmounted with a superstructure. In all cases this part of the building has disappeared, and no indication of its precise form exists. We do know, however, that because the tombs are so close to one another the superstructures cannot have covered an area

much larger than the pits themselves. Each tomb was surrounded by numerous graves which contained the bodies of slaves sacrificed to continue their service to the king in the afterworld.

Petrie believed that the kings of the First Dynasty were actually buried at Abydos, and until recently there was no reason to doubt this conclusion. Later excavations strongly suggest, however, that the kings were buried not at Abydos but at Sakkara, far down the Nile [*see map on page 220*]. Sakkara, the vast cemetery of ancient Memphis, is best known as the site of a great stepped pyramid of the Third Dynasty. At its north end are the remains of tombs which had long been recognized as perhaps even older than this pyramid. But it was not until 1912 that any really serious research was undertaken at North Sakkara. The late J. E. Quibell, then Chief Inspector of the Egyptian Department of Antiquities, excavated for two seasons and proved the existence of First Dynasty tombs far better preserved than those at Abydos.

The site was still not considered especially promising because it had been systematically ravaged by tomb-robbers for more than 5,000 years, and so after the interruption of Quibell's work by World War I the site lay untouched until 1930. Then his successor, the late C. M. Firth, resumed the excavations. Firth cleared several more First Dynasty tombs, the most notable of which was known as 3035. The paneled exterior and burial pit of this great structure were excavated, but its interior was left untouched. This was because it was believed that the interior of the superstructures of such monuments was a solid network of brick walls filled with rubble. The excavation of Tomb 3035

was not very productive, for the burial chamber had been plundered and replundered in ancient times. Nonetheless Firth was able to establish that the tomb had been built during the reign of Udimu, fifth king of the First Dynasty. Firth

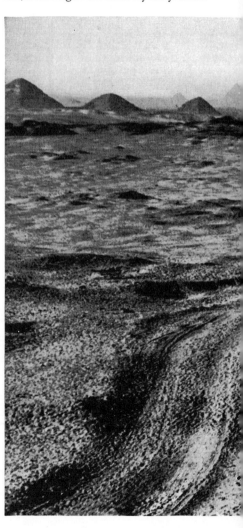

EXCAVATED TOMBS of the pharaohs of
the First Dynasty are on the right side of

died suddenly in 1932, and once again the exploration of North Sakkara was interrupted.

In 1935, when the Director General of the Department of Antiquities instructed me to reclear the tombs, I also turned my attention to Tomb 3035. In order to determine certain details of its construction I cut rather ruthlessly into the big brick superstructure and found that it was not just a solid mass of brickwork and rubble but was divided up into a series of 45 storerooms, many of which had escaped the attention of the ancient tomb-robbers. In these storerooms we found a great collection of funerary equipment—food, tools, weapons, games and drinking vessels—lying where they had been placed 5,000 years before. Inscriptions on the clay seals of jars led us to believe that the tomb belonged to a great noble named Hemaka, vizier of the pharaoh Udimu. This was the greatest single discovery of First Dynasty material that had been made up

to that time. Its importance was at once appreciated by the Egyptian Government and I was given permission to explore the whole area systematically.

Digging continued from 1935 until the beginning of World War II; one great tomb after another was cleared, each showing that civilization during the period of the First Dynasty was far more advanced than we had supposed. Tombs contemporaneous with the kings Hor-Aha, Zer, Udimu, Enezib and Ka-a were discovered—all much larger and more elaborate in design than their counterparts at Abydos. We knew that these kings originated at This near Abydos, but that they conquered the lower Nile Valley and established their capital at Memphis. Thus it seemed possible and even probable that the tombs at Sakkara were their actual burial places, and that the structures at Abydos were empty monuments. Only further excavation could confirm this theory, but at the outbreak of the war the work was shut down. With the exception of

a short season in 1946, nothing further was done at North Sakkara until 1952. In that year an arrangement was made whereby the Egypt Exploration Society reopened the excavations on behalf of the Department of Antiquities. The clearance is still in progress.

In 1952 we discovered a tomb which probably belonged to Uadji, the third pharaoh of the First Dynasty; in the following year we excavated another which we ascribed to Ka-a, the last king of the dynasty. A third large tomb was cleared in 1955, and although its ownership could not be established it supplies conclusive evidence that all the burials almost certainly belonged to the kings, queens and princes of the First Dynasty.

These big tombs of the First Dynasty have the same fundamental design: a large pit cut in the ground, within which were built the burial chamber and subsidiary rooms [see drawings on pages 222 and 223]. Here were stored the owner's most precious possessions. This

this photograph of the area around North Sakkara, 15 miles from Cairo. In the distance at the far left are three pyramids of the Fifth Dynasty. Beyond them are the three famous pyramids built by the Fourth Dynasty kings Khufu (Cheops), Khafra and Menkaura.

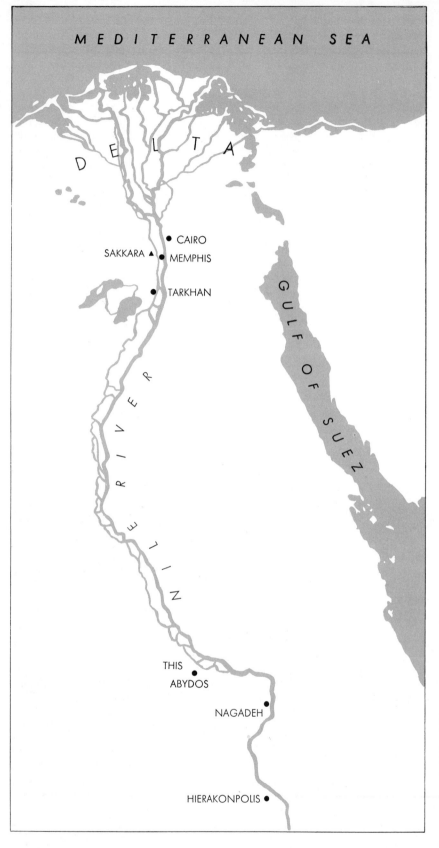

MEDITERRANEAN SEA

DELTA

CAIRO
SAKKARA ▲ ● MEMPHIS

● TARKHAN

NILE RIVER

GULF OF SUEZ

THIS ●
ABYDOS

NAGADEH ●

HIERAKONPOLIS ●

SITES mentioned in this article are located on a map of the Nile Valley. The pharaohs of the First Dynasty originated at This but later established their capital at Memphis. It was once thought that they were buried at Abydos, but it now appears that their graves are at Sakkara. Tarkhan, Nagadeh and Hierakonpolis are other sites of the First Dynasty.

substructure was covered by a large rectangular superstructure of brick, enclosing chambers in which were stored reserve supplies for the use of the deceased in afterlife. This was only the general scheme of the funerary edifice; refinements and developments occurred in rapid succession throughout the 250-odd years of the dynasty. The developments were confined principally to the substructure; the superstructure increased in size but remained largely unchanged. These great buildings, made only of unbaked brick, were undoubtedly dummy copies of the actual palaces of the kings. Although they now stand only five feet above their foundations, there is evidence that they originally rose to a height of not less than 30 feet. The elaborate recess-paneling of their exteriors was gaily painted with geometrical designs simulating the colored matting which adorned the interior walls of buildings at that time.

Although the burial chambers were ravaged and, in many cases, set afire by plunderers, we can reconstruct them with considerable certainty. The deceased lay slightly bent on his right side within a great wooden sarcophagus measuring about 10 by six feet. Outside the sarcophagus were furniture, games for the amusement of the deceased, and his last meal, served in vessels of alabaster, diorite, schist and pottery. These meals were of an elaborate character, consisting of soup, ribs of beef, pigeon, quail, fish, fruit, bread and cake. We found such a meal remarkably preserved in a tomb of the early Second Dynasty, and from fragments found with burials of the First Dynasty we have every reason to suppose that the same rich repast was left during the earlier period. Other rooms in the substructure were devoted to the storage of wine and food, furniture, clothing, games, tools and weapons of flint and copper. Similar objects were stored in the chambers of the superstructure: hundreds of great wine jars, furniture inlaid with ivory, toilet implements, agricultural equipment—all the appurtenances of a well-organized and highly developed civilization.

The principal evolution in the design of the substructure was the introduction of a stairway entrance which enabled the architect to build the whole funerary edifice before the burial. Before this innovation had been introduced the superstructure was built after the burial—obviously an unsatisfactory arrangement. At the end of the First Dynasty a small funerary temple was built at the north side of the tomb; both tomb and temple

SUPERSTRUCTURE of a First Dynasty tomb is exposed by excavation. The recessed walls of the superstructure originally stood at least 30 feet high and were painted with geometrical designs. This is probably the tomb of Queen Meryt-Nit of the First Dynasty.

CLAY MODEL of an ancient Egyptian estate is excavated beside the tomb of Hor-Aha, the first king of the First Dynasty. Such models may have been small-scale copies of the royal estates, presumably to be re-created for the use of their owners in the afterlife.

were enclosed by walls with an entrance to the east. In this final evolution of the First Dynasty tomb we have the prototype of the pyramid complex of later dynasties.

We still have much to learn about the earliest First Dynasty tombs, which are perhaps the oldest examples of monumental architecture in the world. They are not entirely what they seem. In the course of our excavations we have often been puzzled to discover stairways and passages which lead nowhere. For a time we were inclined to dismiss these mysterious features as the result of alterations in the architect's plans. Now we know that the tombs were built in two distinct stages. First they were raised to serve some unknown purpose; then, after this purpose was fulfilled, they were altered so that they could serve

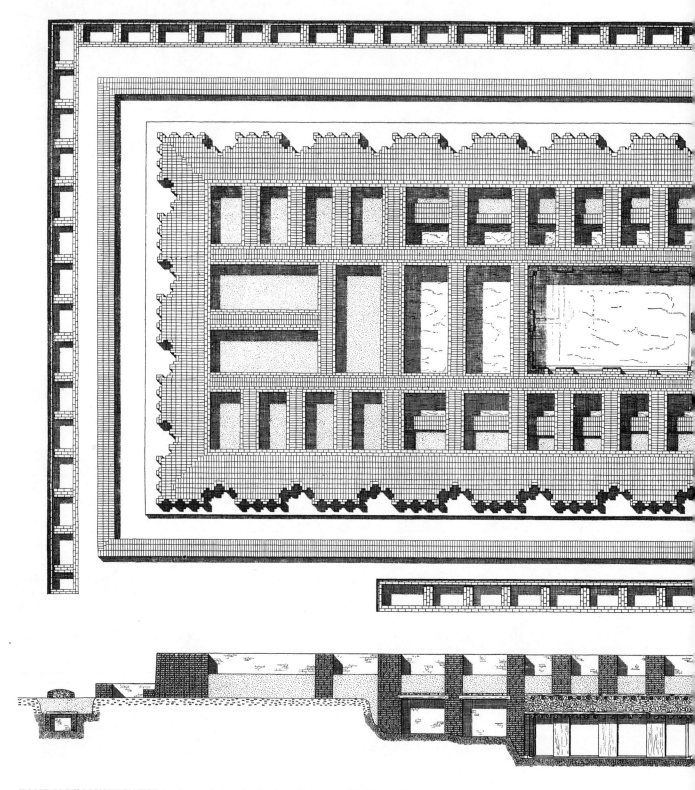

TOMB IS RECONSTRUCTED in plan and elevation by these drawings. This is Tomb 3504 at Sakkara. It is dated to the reign of Uadji, third king of the First Dynasty. The tomb is roughly 200 feet long and 100 feet wide. In the center is the burial chamber. Around

their final function as a house of the dead. We are still entirely ignorant as to the purpose of the original structure, and we can only hope that further excavation will give us the answer to this fascinating question.

The complete funerary installation consisted not only of the tomb, but also of surrounding graves of retainers sacrificed to accompany the king in death as in life. These small graves are of great interest, for we often find objects buried with the dead retainer which indicate his occupation: paint pots with the art-ist, model ships with the shipmaster, varieties of pottery with the potter, and so on. Around the tombs we frequently find the remains of gardens with rows of trees and plants. Near one tomb is a clay model of an estate with houses, granaries and fields. It is tempting to see in this model an exact copy of the royal estate, to be re-created in the next world for the service of its dead owner. Beside the tomb of Udimu are the remains of a wooden ship to carry the pharaoh with the celestial gods in their voyage across the heavens. This vessel, which was 50 feet long, was built 400 years before the recently discovered ship of Cheops.

There are still other sites of the First Dynasty awaiting excavation. It is thus a little early to come to any conclusion regarding the origin of civilization in the Nile Valley. Enough has been disclosed, however, to show that a highly developed culture existed in Egypt by 3000 B.C. In assessing this culture we must remember that we do so on evidence which has survived 5,000 years of destruction by nature and man. But even in their ruined state the magnificent monuments of Sakkara, Abydos and other sites show that they were built by a people with an advanced knowledge of architecture and a mastery of construction in both brick and stone. The scattered contents of their tombs show that they had a well-developed written language, a knowledge of the preparation of papyrus and a great talent for the manufacture of stone vessels, to which they brought a beauty of design that is not excelled today. They also made an almost unlimited range of stone and copper tools, from saws to the finest needles. Their decorative objects of wood, ivory and gold are masterly, and their manufacture of leather, textiles and rope was of a high standard. Above all they had great artistic ability: the motifs of painting and sculpture that were characteristic of Egypt for 3,000 years had already appeared.

This advanced civilization appears suddenly in the early years of the third millennium B.C.; it seems to have little or no background in the Nile Valley. Yet the Valley had been inhabited for a long period before the First Dynasty. Excavation has indicated that during this period burial customs developed little; the passage of time is marked only by changes in the design of pottery and other objects. The people of the period had an advanced neolithic culture which certainly made a contribution to the later Egyptian civilization. In my opinion, however, their culture does not pro-

it are many rooms for the storage of food and other goods. The long rows of small chambers on three sides of the tomb are the graves of retainers sacrificed to accompany the king.

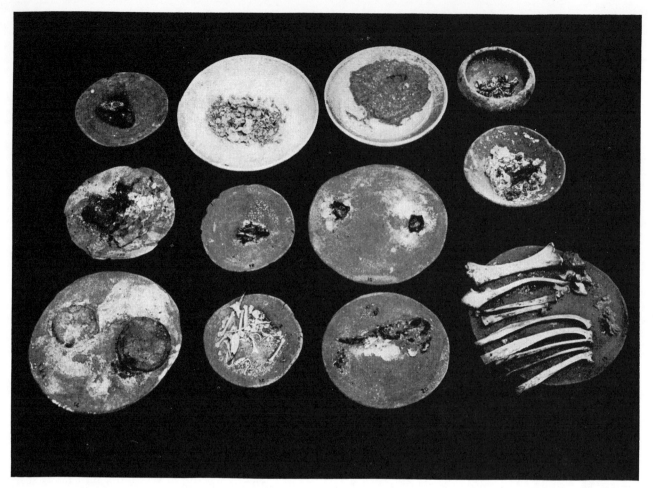

FUNERARY MEAL found in a tomb of the early Second Dynasty is in a remarkable state of preservation, considering that it was set out some 5,000 years ago. Fragments found in tombs of the First Dynasty indicate that similar meals were buried with its pharaohs.

vide a complete foundation for the Egypt of the pharaohs. It is of course possible that the architecture of the First Dynasty was the product of a superior people inhabiting the delta of the Nile, where constant flooding and agriculture has destroyed all remains of the period before the pharaohs. Since there is no evidence for or against this theory, it must remain speculative. In any case I feel it is unlikely that such a civilization could develop independently in the marshlands of the delta and suddenly impose itself on the upper Nile Valley. It is significant that during the First Dynasty only the nobles and officials were buried in monumental tombs. The mass of the people were buried in graves consisting of shallow pits with no superstructure beyond a circular mound of earth. The body lay in a huddled position on its left side; except for the objects in it such a grave had little to distinguish it from those of the period before the First Dynasty. By the end of the Second Dynasty we find the mass of the people had adopted the burial customs of their betters: the design of their tombs was the same in almost every detail except size. All this plainly suggests the existence of a superior culture which gradually imposed its burial customs on the conquered indigenes.

If we accept the theory that the civilization of the pharaohs was brought to the Nile Valley by a new people, we must ask: Who were they and where did they come from? The British historian Reginald Engelbach suggested a horde invasion, and there is evidence to suggest something of the sort. We must not overlook, however, the possibility of gradual infiltration over a long period. The monumental architecture of the First Dynasty has been compared to that of the Jemdet Nasr period in Mesopotamia, and I think the similarity is beyond dispute. But there are also great differences, so a direct connection between the Euphrates and the Nile at that time is still a matter of doubt. Thus the problem of how the civilization of the pharaohs originated remains unsolved. It is to be hoped that the further work of the Egypt Exploration Society will contribute to its solution.

Life in Mycenaean Greece

by John Chadwick
October 1972

When Pylos and Knossos were burned some 3,000 years ago, the notes written on clay by palace scribes were preserved by baking. These jottings provide a glimpse of how the Greeks lived before classical times

"Rowers bound for Pleuron.... Female slaves of the priestess on account of sacred gold.... Smiths with an allotment of bronze.... Masons who are to build.... Thus the woodcutters will contribute.... Thus Phygepris saw when the King appointed Augeas to be *damokoros*.... The private estate of Amaryntas...." These are some of the more striking phrases we can read on clay tablets written by the earliest literate inhabitants of Greece. What motivated their literacy? Why did the Greeks, long before they borrowed the Phoenician alphabet, adopt a clumsy and complex form of syllabic writing based on the Cretan system? The answer is simple: They needed to keep accounts.

No man willingly keeps accounts. So long as he can, he carries the figures in his head and guesses. A small farm can be run adequately, if not very efficiently, by an illiterate farmer. But if a number of small farms are united in a big one, and even more urgently if a number of tiny principalities are united in a small kingdom, the need for an accounting system arises and an expert who knows how to keep adequate records must be employed.

Although we can only guess at the details, small kingdoms seem to have begun to grow up in Greece around the 16th century B.C. All we can say for certain is that, at some time before the beginning of the 14th century B.C., the growth of these small states created the conditions that require bookkeeping. The requirement was met by borrowing a system of notation from nearby Crete, which was then the home of an alien and more advanced civilization. The Cretan system of writing, which we call Linear A, was crude but it was adequate for keeping rough accounts. The Greeks adopted and modified it. Using some 90 Cretan signs, they wrote down for the first time the sounds of their own language, syllable by syllable. The notation on the tablets these prehistoric Greeks left behind them we call Linear B. It seems safe to assume that by the 14th and 13th centuries B.C. every major Greek palace had a large staff of trained clerks who meticulously recorded in Linear B every transaction that concerned the palace stores.

It is an unlucky chance that once a method of recording accounts had been devised its users never chose to employ the system for any other purpose. Indeed, it seems very odd to us who are literate that other literate men never jotted down a private thought, never carved their name on a durable object and never even ordered that their name be engraved on their tomb. The fault lies as much in the script as in its users. The system at their disposal was slow and complicated and its meanings were often ambiguous. It was adequate for the headings of lists, such as the ones quoted above, and it was admirably suited for recording the numbers in a flock of sheep. But it was hardly suitable for a letter, much less a line or two of verse. All things considered, it may be that the attitude of the Greek kings toward their bookkeepers resembled the one attributed, apocryphally no doubt, to the American delegates at an international conference in the far-off days when the language of all such proceedings was French. Asked how, when none of them understood French, they could follow what was going on, one of them replied: "Aw, we've got secretaries."

This much at least is certain. Every Linear B tablet thus far uncovered by the patient work of archaeologists is a piece of the bureaucratic machinery that kept the prehistoric Greek economy operating. So far as the entire corpus of inscriptions is concerned, it is as if we had salvaged the contents of a few wastebaskets at four different state capitals. I call these collections wastebaskets rather than archives advisedly; there is good reason to believe that what we have unearthed are not the permanent palace ledgers at all. Instead they seem to be temporary records, notes written for immediate use and kept on file only until the end of the current year. Moreover, the notes are incomplete; the various series to which they belong have not been preserved intact. To make things harder for us, the individual tablets have not escaped damage, both at the time when the buildings that housed them were destroyed by fire and during the more than 30 centuries they were buried.

Even in those instances where the records happen to be complete, we cannot hope to translate them perfectly. They are not elegantly phrased reports but abbreviated jottings of economic data. To the writers the only matters of importance were the tallies; all the rest consisted of rough headings designed to ensure that the writer, or perhaps another clerk in the same office, remembered what the figures referred to. To those of us who attempt to penetrate the minds of these prehistoric bureaucrats the task is as baffling as it is fascinating. Still, areas of meaning are little by little beginning to appear, and we can already give some account of the facts that underlie the fragmentary records.

Four significant sets of Linear B tablets are known. The first that was found is also the earliest. It was unearthed at Knossos in central Crete in a context that assigns it to the early part of the

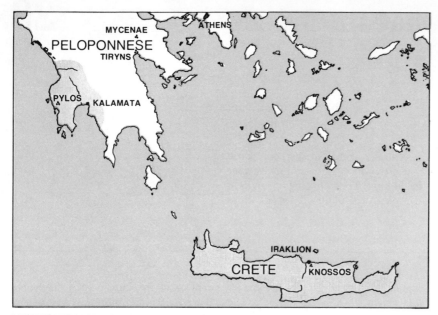

MYCENAEAN SITES where tablets with Linear B inscriptions have been unearthed in the greatest numbers are Knossos on the island of Crete and Pylos in southwestern Peloponnese. A few tablets have also been found at Thebes, north of Athens, and at two other sites: the ruins of Mycenae itself and of Tiryns, which may have been seaport for Mycenae.

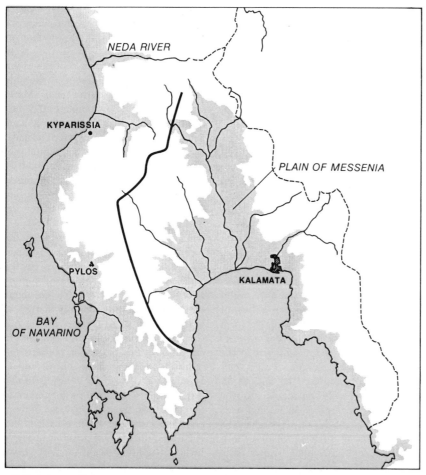

KINGDOM OF PYLOS consisted of two provinces. The western province, running along the coast, was separated from the eastern province by a mountain chain that probably provided a natural boundary (heavy line). The royal palace of Pylos was located in the western province, just north of the Bay of Navarino. The eastern province embraced the rich valley of Messenia; the southern frontier of the kingdom was probably near modern Kalamata. All areas lower than 200 meters in this map and the map on the opposite page are in gray.

14th century B.C. The second set of tablets was discovered at Pylos, in southwestern Greece; they are perhaps the most recent of any known, having been written late in the 13th century. Two very small collections of tablets fall between these extremes. One is from Thebes in Boeotia, about 30 miles northwest of Athens, and the other is from Mycenae in the northeastern part of the Peloponnese. There are now reports of fragments of tablets from Tiryns, which was probably the seaport for Mycenae, and clay jars bearing short, painted inscriptions in Linear B have been discovered at a number of Greek sites. Most of our conclusions concerning the earliest literate civilization in Greece are necessarily based on the relatively large collections of tablets at Pylos and Knossos. Regardless of the scarcity of the finds elsewhere, however, we are doubtless justified in believing that during this period of Greek prehistory a secretariat, busy recording economic statistics, was a fixture of every Greek state. The period itself is called by archaeologists the Mycenaean period after the famous site excavated by Heinrich Schliemann in the 19th century.

One feature common to the tablets from all the sites is the absence of any year date. Moreover, the tablets have an irritating tendency to refer to "this year" and "last year," which makes sense only if one assumes that they were meant to be scrapped at the year's end. An abstract of the rough information they contained was probably transferred to a "permanent" ledger at each year's end. By a fine irony the archives that housed these permanent records, evidently written in pen and ink on perishable material, appear to have been destroyed by the same catastrophic fires that baked the temporary records, jotted on raw clay, into hard pottery and thereby preserved them.

Although year dates are absent, we occasionally find month dates. For example, a month date is almost always present on tablets that record offerings to the gods. A typical superscription might be "In the month of Diwios." No day dates within the month are included. The names of five months are found in the collection of tablets at Knossos. Those at Pylos probably bear the names of three months; the identification of one of these, however, is uncertain.

If we knew at what point in the year the Greek calendar of the period began, we should be able to calculate the approximate date when each palace was

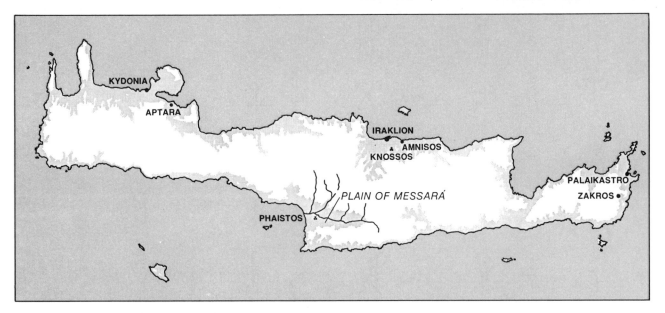

KINGDOM OF CRETE embraced the entire island but apparently did not include any overseas possessions. The mountainous interior of Crete minimized all but coastwise communications. Knossos, close to the coast, was thus a good location for the royal palace.

destroyed. The four natural points at which a year may begin are the solstices and the equinoxes, and we know that later Greek calendars favored starting with the autumnal equinox. Actually the Knossos and Pylos tablets do offer some clues to when the year began in Mycenaean times. For example, it cannot have begun with the vernal equinox because the Pylos tablets record nothing about the midsummer grain harvest and the Knossos tablets touch on harvest activities scarcely if at all. At the same time it is quite clear that at Knossos the spring shearing had been done and the wool clip had been gathered. This means that at least the month of April lay behind. Because the name of the current month may not have been recorded before the destruction of Knossos, a date for this event sometime during June appears plausible. This date in turn suggests that the Mycenaean year began with the winter solstice.

The Pylos tablets offer support for this hypothesis, particularly if they do record the names of three months. The third of these months seems to have been named "Sailing." Now, ancient navigators did not sail during the winter. Consequently a month that marked the start of the sailing season would come in early spring. Some confirmation of this conjecture is provided by other Pylos tablets, which contain numerous records of sheep but none of lambing or of shearing. This would accord well with a date in late March or early April for the destruction of Pylos. If the 1,400 tablets we have from Pylos indeed represent a mere three months' work by the palace clerks, we must deplore the fact that the burning of Pylos was not postponed until November.

That Knossos and Pylos were the seats of monarchies might be deduced merely from the size of the ruined palaces. The tablets confirm this (the Mycenaean word for "king" was *wanax*), but regrettably they fail to tell us the proper name of either monarch. The king's name was the kind of fact that would have been known to every inhabitant in each capital and therefore was not worth putting down in temporary records.

The tablets do reveal something of the organization below the ruler. There was a class of royal officers called "Followers," a term not unlike the European title "Count" in its original sense of "companion." At the local level there were other officials (and their deputies) who played a more restricted role. For example, these officials are directed to make contributions in bronze and gold. It seems likely that the local authorities were successors to the petty rulers, originally independent, whose principalities had been amalgamated into the royal kingdom.

How large were the kingdoms? In the case of Knossos this question is not hard to answer. Crete is a large island: some 160 miles long and up to 40 miles wide. It is also quite mountainous, with heights exceeding 7,000 feet. Apart from strips along the coast it has only one large level area: the fertile plain of Messará in the south-central part of the island [*see illustration above*]. Knossos

was situated a few miles inland from the northern coast, along which the island's lines of communication run, and thus it was well placed to administer the whole of Crete.

The size of the kingdom administered from Knossos is further documented by numerous place-names contained in the tablets. Eleven of the names are easily identifiable. They include Knossos itself; its port, Amnisos; the chief site in the Messará, Phaistos, and various other sites in the central sector. Two place-names belong to towns in the west of Crete: Kydonia (now Khania) and Aptara.

There is now reason to believe that two more names among the several on the Knossos tablets that are not yet geographically identified belong to sites in eastern Crete. This conclusion is the result of a remarkable feat of technology. The story is as follows. Two place-names appear both on the Knossos tablets and on pottery jars that have been unearthed at Thebes, the Boeotian site on the Greek mainland. H. W. Catling and A. Millett of the Ashmolean Museum in Oxford have analyzed the clay of these Theban jars. Its composition is not the same as that of other Theban clays, but it does match the material available from two contemporary sites in eastern Crete now known as Zákros and Palaikastro. The clay-analysis method is too new to give results that are beyond challenge, but the coincidence is at the least remarkable. In any event the general weight of evidence suggests that at this time,

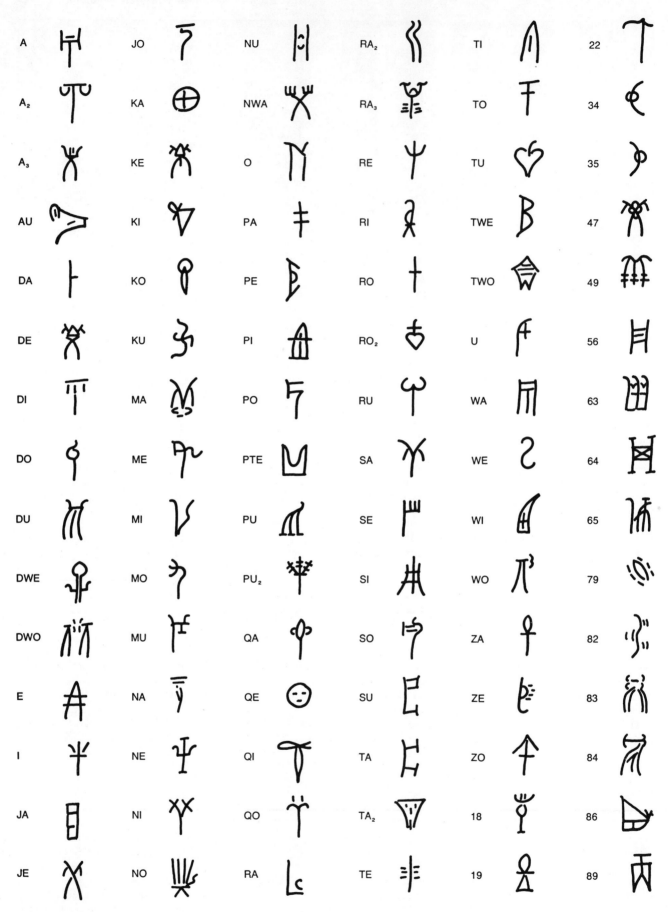

A	JO	NU	RA₂	TI	22	
A₂	KA	NWA	RA₃	TO	34	
A₃	KE	O	RE	TU	35	
AU	KI	PA	RI	TWE	47	
DA	KO	PE	RO	TWO	49	
DE	KU	PI	RO₂	U	56	
DI	MA	PO	RU	WA	63	
DO	ME	PTE	SA	WE	64	
DU	MI	PU	SE	WI	65	
DWE	MO	PU₂	SI	WO	79	
DWO	MU	QA	SO	ZA	82	
E	NA	QE	SU	ZE	83	
I	NE	QI	TA	ZO	84	
JA	NI	QO	TA₂	18	86	
JE	NO	RA	TE	19	89	

NINETY SIGNS comprise the Linear B syllabary. Seventeen are **not yet conclusively deciphered**; numerals appear beside them.

The vowel or vowel-consonant sounds of the other 73 signs are shown in alphabetical notation. Linear B also has 110 ideograms.

around 1375 B.C., the ruler at Knossos controlled the whole of Crete.

The Knossos tablets are lacking, however, in place-names that can be identified with Mycenaean sites outside the island, which suggests that the kingdom had no major overseas possessions. In this connection the sudden destruction that befell the palace at Knossos does not, in spite of earlier opinion, seem to have been the result of a foreign invasion. It appears increasingly possible that the kingdom was overthrown by a revolt originating on the island itself. Perhaps the rural population grew rebellious because it was weary of filling out endless reports for the benefit of the central administration.

In calculating the size of the domain ruled from Pylos we cannot apply the place-name method with much success. This mainland region seems to have changed more radically with respect to names during the interval separating the Mycenaean period from the classical period that followed it. Apart from Pylos itself, few of the place-names in the Pylos tablets can be located with any certainty. Even Pylos, although the name has been preserved down to the present, has twice been moved to a new location. It was shifted in classical times to a point on the north side of the Bay of Navarino and again in medieval times to its present location at the southern end of the bay.

Mycenaean Pylos was clearly a site well suited to the control of much of southwestern Peloponnese. The question is: How far did the kingdom's control extend to the north and east? We can start to answer this question by building up a picture of the relationships that existed between the place-names listed on the Pylos tablets, even though their locations are not known. This enables us to create a model of the kingdom's political organization and then see if the model can be fitted to the map. For example, we know that the kingdom was divided into two provinces and that the more distant of the two was located beyond some landmark visible from the palace. The outlook from the palace ruins today reveals a very evident mountain barrier that separates the strip of land along the west coast from the rich valley of Messenia to the east [see bottom illustration on page 226]. It therefore seems a reasonable assumption that the two provinces of Pylos, broadly speaking, probably corresponded to the western coastal region and to the valley beyond the mountains.

The area we shall call the Hither Province, that is, the coastal region, was subdivided into nine districts; each district included a main town. The tablets always enumerate the nine towns in the same order, and it can be shown that the order of enumeration runs from north to south. Where, then, was the northern boundary of the Hither Province? There are four clues. First, no place-name that can be identified is located more than 25 miles north of Pylos. Second, if the northern frontier had been more than 30 miles to the north, the palace itself would have been eccentrically located within the kingdom. Third, high mountains come close to the sea some 25 miles north of Pylos, providing a good natural line of defense. Fourth, there is archaeological evidence suggesting that this natural line of defense did form the kingdom's northern boundary. Indeed, no one would hesitate to accept this conclusion if it were not that Homer, recording events that had taken place 500 years before his time, placed the frontier of Pylos much farther to the north. Homer's geography, however, was clearly anachronistic if not entirely fictional, so that his evidence need not be taken too seriously.

As for the boundaries of the Further Province, the valley of Messenia is bordered on its eastern flank by another mountain range, the vast Taÿgetos, which includes peaks rising above 7,000 feet. This obstacle establishes a natural eastern frontier for the kingdom. What is less clear is just how far to the south the Further Province ran along the western shore of the Mani Peninsula, the central finger of the three south-pointing fingers of land that comprise the southern Peloponnese. Communications by land along the Mani coast have been notoriously difficult until recently. Adding this fact to the suggestion, contained in the Pylos tablets, that the Further Province had a short coastline, it seems logical to assume that the kingdom's southern boundary on the Mani coast lay somewhere near the modern town of Kalamata. If these frontiers of the Hither and Further provinces are the right ones, Pylos was a tidy kingdom that measured 50 miles at the most from north to south and about 30 miles from east to west.

The economic base of prehistoric Greek kingdoms such as Pylos must of course have been agricultural. In Mycenaean times currency was unknown, and we have no evidence that com-

WEIGHTS

1	=	30
1	=	4
1	=	12?
1	=	6?

DRY MEASURE

1	=	10
1	=	6
1	=	4

LIQUID MEASURE

1	=	3
1	=	6
1	=	4

TABLES OF EQUIVALENTS show signs used to record weights and volumes. The top unit in each table is the largest. For dry and liquid volumes these signs identified the commodity. Shown here are wheat and wine.

BROKEN TABLET seen reassembled here is an example of how contexts help to establish the identity between Mycenaean syllable sequences and words in classical Greek. This is the only tablet from Knossos that records horses in a context unconnected with chariots. A part of the tablet (*right*), obviously a tally, was found by the first excavator of Knossos, Sir Arthur Evans, but the part bearing four syllabic signs (*left*) was not studied until the 1950's. The two syllables on the top line read "i-qo," equivalent to the classical *hippoi*, or "horses." The two syllables on the bottom line read "o-no," which is equivalent to "asses."

modities had their relative value fixed in terms of any common unit. Trade must have been by barter. That exchanges of this kind did take place is suggested by some entries on the tablets.

The agricultural year was not far advanced when Pylos fell. One result of this is that the tablets do not give any clear indication of how the land was farmed. What deductions we can make about the crops in Pylos come from records of the rations issued by the palace. These records make it clear that the chief cereals were wheat and barley. The relative values of the two (rations of barley, a coarser grain, are nearly double those of wheat) suggest that the wheat grown in Pylos was not primitive emmer but the modern form *Triticum vulgare*.

Because no obvious equivalent to the Mycenaean volumetric system exists today it has not been easy to determine the exact quantities of the rations. By reference to similar values in other societies, however, one can estimate a range of magnitudes that ought to include the Mycenaean ones. The estimates can be further refined by a study of the containers the Mycenaeans used, because some of the vessels probably served as measures. For example, eight-tenths of a liter appears to be one standard Mycenaean unit of volume. Exactly which unit this is, however, remains uncertain. It could be twice as much or (less likely) four times as much as the smallest of the Mycenaean units of volume.

One Pylos tablet gives what is apparently an equation between 18 large units of olive oil and 38 storage jars; the figures allow us to cross-check the assumption that the Mycenaean minimum unit of volume was four-tenths of a liter. To judge from the tablet, the average capacity of a storage jar works out to 34 minimum units, or 13.6 liters if the minimum value is .4 liter. This

fits nicely with the fact that one kind of jar widely used for liquids in Mycenaean times ranged from 12 to 14 liters in capacity.

Using estimates like this, we reckon that the minimum daily ration for a slave was .64 liter of wheat or 1.2 liters of barley. Larger amounts were often provided, and the basic grain ration was supplemented with foodstuffs such as figs or olives. We know little of how the grain was prepared and cooked. It was evidently ground into meal with stone hand mills; the Pylos tablets refer to women assigned to this task. We do know that spices, among them coriander, fennel and mint, were used to season what must otherwise have been a rather uninteresting cereal diet. Wine was drunk, although in what quantities we cannot tell.

The management of livestock is rather better known. From Crete come very extensive records concerning sheep. J. T. Killen of the University of Cambridge has analyzed these records and deduces that some 100,000 sheep were under the direct control of the palace. There may also have been other flocks under private ownership. The sheep population consisted mainly of castrated males, kept for their wool; smaller breeding flocks served to provide replacements. The annual wool clip was carefully measured against a predicted norm. Any shortfall was duly recorded, but we are not told what the consequences of a deficiency were for the shepherd. The scale of wool production was considerable, although of course the yield per head was much smaller than it is with today's breeds of sheep.

An interesting series of tablets from Crete lists pairs of working oxen by name. The names are the equivalent, in Greek, of the descriptive names commonly given to animals. The important point here is that the names are Greek.

This indicates that Greek was the language of the peasantry in Crete and not, as has been suggested, exclusively the language of the palace.

At Pylos oxen are rarely mentioned, but an annual tribute of ox hides suggests that the cattle herds in the kingdom must have totaled at least 1,500 head. There is also evidence for large flocks of sheep and goats at Pylos. Records of pigs are few and list only small numbers.

Deer were hunted, possible for venison and certainly for skins. The hides of oxen, goats and pigs also were made into leather, some of which was used for footwear and some for straps. The native wild goat of Crete was hunted for its large horns. The horns seem to have been used to make composite bows; attaching a layer of horn to the wood gives a bow more power.

We do not read much about the husbandry of horses. At this time the domestic horse in Greece was quite small and not strong enough to make a good mount. Instead horses were used in pairs to draw two-wheeled chariots of light construction. It is most unlikely that the prehistoric Greeks used their chariots in mass military formations as did their contemporaries, the Hittites of Asia Minor. The plains almost everywhere in Greece are rather narrow and are usually intersected by watercourses, if not cluttered with olive trees and vines. As a result the light Mycenaean vehicles would rarely have been able to move freely cross-country except along well-built roads.

There is good archaeological evidence that an extensive Mycenaean road system did in fact exist. The primary function of the chariot must therefore have been road transportation, and indeed this is implied by later Greek tradition. The story of Oedipus' murder of his father is the first recorded instance of a fight developing out of a traffic incident; each driver, it will be remembered, refused to give way to the other. Even in the *Iliad* the chariot was mainly used to carry warriors in and out of battle. They dismounted to fight.

The wool clip of Crete was spun and woven. We have some of the records that enabled the ruler at Knossos to control the output of textile workshops all over Crete, and they suggest that a surplus of wool cloth was available for export. Pylos produced both wool and flax, a crop that is still grown on a considerable scale in this part of Greece. The palace seems to have assessed the local villages for a certain number of bales of prepared flax fiber; the flax was collected in depots, where a labor force of women made it into linen thread. There is mention of fine linen cloth, no doubt worn by the rich, but much of the linen may have gone into ropes and canvas. The canvas may have been used for sails and perhaps for padded armor. Craftsmen were employed to produce luxury goods other than fine linen. We have descriptions of ornate furniture, richly carved and inlaid with gold and ivory. A favorite material for ornament was a blue glass paste, an inexpensive substitute for lapis lazuli.

The principal metal was bronze. Although iron was known to the Mycenaeans, the techniques of working it were not. Bronze was made not only into tools and weapons but also, at least in the palaces, into cups, cauldrons and other vessels. Ordinary folk no doubt drank from and cooked in pottery. The main weapon was a heavy bronze slash-ing sword. A series of tablets listing such swords was found at Knossos near the king's private apartments, perhaps in the quarters of the royal bodyguard. Bronze body armor was also known but was not widely used.

There is evidence that at Pylos the working of bronze was a major industry. The ores required to make the alloy are not known to exist in quantity in southwestern Greece. The necessary raw materials must therefore have been imported from overseas, the copper doubtless from Cyprus and the tin probably from central or western Europe. Some of the bronzesmiths in Pylos may have originally been refugees who fled from Crete at the time of the Minoan collapse in the 15th century B.C. This is suggested by Pylos tablets that list tripod cauldrons "of Cretan work." Moreover, some smiths are listed as being "in the service of the Mistress." The Mistress is often mentioned in the tablets; the word must refer to the important female deity who is so often depicted in the religious scenes that appear in murals and vase paintings of the period. We know that in Crete groups of smiths had combined religion with craft, somewhat in the fashion of the guilds of Europe in medieval times. The excavations at Mycenae show that there too groups of craftsmen maintained shrines near their workshops.

The most curious aspect of the bronze metallurgy at Pylos is the large discrepancy between the number of smiths and the quantity of bronze issued to them. Making some allowance for the incomplete preservation of the Pylos tablets, we can estimate that there were nearly 400 smiths in the kingdom. If that number of smiths had been fully occupied, they should have been able to produce bronze objects in large quantities. The amounts of bronze they actually received from palace stores, however, are

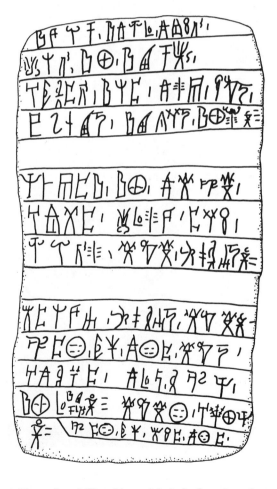

TWO TABLETS FROM PYLOS reflect the troubled last days of the kingdom in the late 13th century B.C. The tablet at left is a tally of the bronzesmiths at Akerewa, a town that was probably on the Bay of Navarino. Like the other Pylos bronzesmith tablets, it indicates underemployment, probably because there was a shortage of ores imported from abroad. The tablet at right is the first of a series concerning a coast-watcher force amounting to some five men per kilometer of shoreline, presumably deployed to bring news of any invasion from the sea. Introductory phrase reads "Thus the watchers are guarding the coastal regions." Soon afterward Pylos fell.

PLEA FOR DIVINE HELP comprises the text scribbled hastily on this clay tablet discovered in the palace ruins at Pylos in the Greek Peloponnese. Only the reverse of the tablet is shown; the syllabic system of writing used for the inscription is the one known as Linear B. The tablet lists sacrifices to 13 gods and goddesses of the Mycenaean pantheon. Each deity will receive a gold vessel; a man will be dedicated (and probably sacrificed) to each of the two chief gods and a woman to each of the eight chief goddesses.

remarkably small The total for all the smiths together is only about a ton. Some individuals received as little as 1.5 kilograms, and others are listed as receiving no bronze at all. In other words, the metallurgical labor force must have been partly unemployed and largely underemployed. Finally, there is evidence that the palace was calling on the principal local officials throughout the kingdom for the collection of bronze to be made into armaments (an interesting parallel to the British appeal for aluminum saucepans to be made into fighter planes during World War II).

All of this makes sense if we take two facts into account. First, in order to make bronze, Pylos had to import raw materials from abroad. Second, overseas travel must have been perilous just at this time. We know the second fact from Egyptian historical records that report major attacks on the Nile delta toward the end of the 13th century B.C. and at the beginning of the 12th century. The attackers, called by the Egyptians the "Sea Peoples," seem to have been an alliance of miscellaneous Mediterranean tribes who, by joining together, had assembled a powerful fleet.

A third fact is that Pylos was living in fear of attack from the sea. This is made clear by a remarkable series of tablets that describe a kind of coastal early-warning system: small units of guards spread out along the kingdom's seacoast. There is no reason to doubt that the king of Pylos expected the enemy to come by sea; the kingdom's natural defenses on its land frontiers made any attack from that quarter extremely difficult. The king's fears were fully justified. Soon afterward his palace went up in flames, and the absence of valuable objects among the artifacts unearthed at Pylos strongly suggests that the royal residence was looted before being put to the torch.

The evident shortage of the ores needed to make bronze at Pylos therefore ties in neatly with other evidence that the seas had become unsafe. The reason Mycenaean civilization collapsed is still unknown. The long popular theory that it was caused by a new wave of Greek invaders pressing down from the north is no longer tenable. All we are sure of is that nearly every major Mycenaean site so far excavated shows traces of fire and destruction around this date. Even at Mycenae itself a raid seems to have penetrated as far as the massive fortifications of the citadel, even if it did not actually breach them.

We can well imagine the scene at Pylos as news arrived of raiders scouring the shores of the Aegean. The king hastily organized his coastal-watch system. He must also have disposed his army so as best to block the approaches to the palace; Pylos, unlike Mycenae, had no fortifications. The tablets that speak of the coast-watchers also specify the whereabouts of 11 officers of the royal court. Although one function of these officers was liaison and communication, their disposition strongly suggests that each may have been accompanied by a regiment of the royal army. We can thus deduce that small forces were disposed to protect the north, south and east of the kingdom, while the main weight of defense was concentrated around the Bay of Navarino, by far the most likely place for an enemy landing.

Of course, divine help was also sought. A large, badly written tablet, bearing evidence of several false starts, changes of mind and simple errors, lists an offering to be made to an entire pantheon of deities [see illustration on page 232]. Some are the familiar Olympians of classical Greece: Zeus, Poseidon, Hermes and Hera. There are also names that later were entirely forgotten. The offering consists of 13 gold vessels and eight women and two men. This is surely too rich a treasure for any ordinary ceremony. Both the hasty writing and the fact that the tablet was never recopied in a more seemly fashion suggest that it was written only a short time before disaster struck. The ceremony must have been a last desperate attempt to secure the protection of heaven. The men and women were probably destined not to become slaves of the deities named but to be outright human sacrifices. In addition to numerous instances of this practice recorded in classical myth, there is now some archaeological evidence that such offerings were made in Mycenaean Greece under exceptional circumstances. Whether or not these 10 individuals actually fell victim to the priest's knife, the king's cry for help went unanswered. The palace was reduced to ruins and remained forgotten until it was brought to light by American excavators more than 3,000 years later.

FUNERARY MASK made of gold exemplifies the Mycenaean craftsmen's more elaborate work. The mask, presumably that of a chief, was discovered in a shaft grave at Mycenae.

234

SUMMIT OF CITY MOUND at Kültepe, which rises more than 60 feet above the level of the surrounding plain, is the open, treeless area in the bottom half of this photograph. The piles of rubble at the perimeter (*left center*) were left by early excavators who mistook the mound for the source of Assyrian cuneiform tablets. A recent excavation can be seen in progress in the foreground.

PRE-HITTITE ARTIFACTS found in the vicinity of Kültepe are characteristic of the indigenous art at the time of the Assyrian colonization of Anatolia. The three gold objects are a bowl, a cere-monial headdress and an ornamental pendant about four inches long. The pitcher (*left*), animal forms (*center*) and fruitstand (*right*) are all made of polished clay. Objects are not in same scale.

An Assyrian Trading Outpost

by Tahsin Özgüç
February 1963

*Clay tablets unearthed at the site of Kanesh in
Anatolia describe in detail an Assyrian merchants'
colony there, the headquarters of an extensive
commercial system that linked two ancient cultures*

Students of the ancient world once tended to think of each civilization as an isolated entity, a network of agricultural communities and administrative cities tied together by common cultural and political institutions and perhaps by rudimentary trade or some special common need such as an irrigation system. Sumer, Egypt, Assyria and the rest were conceived of as existing contemporaneously but more or less independently, or as succeeding each other in cycles of conquest or rebellion. In recent years a great deal of archaeological evidence has accumulated to show that this conception was incorrect, that man of the ancient civilizations was to a surprising degree a traveler and trader, and that civilizations influenced one another across deserts, mountains and seas. Most of the evidence has necessarily been indirect. Archaeologists investigating a site have found raw material that must have come from a distant place, an artifact of unmistakably foreign manufacture, a written reference to far-off peoples or a clear case of alien influence in indigenous works of art.

The site in central Turkey that my colleagues and I have been excavating for the past 14 years has provided more explicit and detailed evidence for such an interrelation of two ancient civilizations. What we have been studying is a commercial "colony," a foreign outpost in the central Anatolian city of Kanesh. Here, for 200 years from 1950 B.C. to 1750, two peoples with different languages and cultures lived together in a mutually advantageous commercial symbiosis. The local people were the native Hatti of Anatolia; the foreigners were Assyrian traders and businessmen from the plains of Mesopotamia far to the south. Their homes and artifacts and above all the thousands of clay tablets on which they recorded every detail of

their personal and business lives are providing us with a detailed picture of the complex politico-economic ties by which the Assyrians of Kanesh were linked to their homeland and to the local people and rulers.

The Assyrian colony in Kanesh was the culmination of many centuries of trade development. Since the plain of the Tigris and Euphrates is conspicuously deficient in mineral resources, the Mesopotamian cities were dependent from the beginning on imports for their metals. There are indications that as early as 3500 B.C. trade expeditions from the southernmost cities of Sumer were obtaining copper from the mountains of Urartu and central Anatolia, more than 1,000 miles to the north. A half-legendary text dating from a later period recalls a punitive expedition led by King Sargon the Great of Akkad against the Anatolian city of Purushanda, in the area of the "silver mountains," where the natives had been molesting itinerant Akkadian merchants. By the turn of the second millennium B.C. extensive foreign trade had become established as one of the primary features of Mesopotamian culture, and the most enterprising and successful businessmen of this period were the Assyrians.

Instead of relying on occasional expeditions, the Assyrians assured themselves of an adequate and dependable flow of raw materials by setting up permanent trade colonies at key locations throughout the principal ore-producing districts of central and eastern Anatolia. Regularly scheduled donkey caravans traveling over fixed trade routes connected these colonial outposts to the Assyrian capital of Assur [*see map on next two pages*]. Nine such colonies, or *karums*, are known to have existed in major cities of the indigenous Hatti between 1950 B.C. and 1750. Of eight of

these colonies only the names remain; their locations have not been discovered. Kanesh, the one colony that has been found, was the largest and was the controlling center of the whole network. The relation between the Assyrians and the Hatti and their rulers was for the most part harmonious. It was the rise to power of a new Indo-European ethnic group, the Hittites, that eventually put an end to the period of Assyrian colonization. But the Assyrians had left their mark. During their stay the indigenous Anatolian culture had become mixed with that of Mesopotamia. The amalgam became the basis of the ascendant Hittite civilization.

It is a curious fact that scholars knew a little about Kanesh and even suspected it was an Assyrian trading center long before Kanesh itself was uncovered. In 1881 clay tablets bearing Assyrian cuneiform inscriptions began to turn up in the shops of antique dealers in the modern Turkish city of Kayseri, 13 miles southwest of the site of Kanesh. They found a ready market among interested philologists and archaeologists, who could learn only that the tablets had been found by natives of the small village of Karahüyük. The village was near an ancient site known simply as Kültepe, or "ash mound": a hill rising more than 60 feet from the surrounding plain and covered by charred remains. When the French explorer Ernest Chantre undertook the first excavations of the mound in 1893, the villagers were unhelpfully reticent, and Chantre could not find the source of the tablets. Neither could a succession of scholars who followed him, until, in 1925, the Czech scholar Bedřich Hrozný had better luck. A friendly cook for his archaeological field party suggested that he look not on the mound but about 100 yards to the northeast. Hrozný dug there and came on the Assyrian merchants' quarter, the *karum* of Kanesh.

It is in the *karum* that our research under the auspices of the Turkish Historical Society and the Turkish Government's Department of Antiquities has been concentrated since 1948. We have found many thousands of clay tablets, and as we slowly decipher their wedge-shaped cuneiform characters the operations of the Assyrian trading system and the life of Kanesh emerge with increasing clarity.

The principal exports from Anatolia were, of course, metals. Gold, silver and precious stones made up most of the shipments to the markets of Assur. The Assyrians also traded locally in Anatolian copper, which the natives alloyed with tin to make bronze. Large quantities of tin, which was not available anywhere in Anatolia, constituted about 50 per cent of the imports. The Assyrians presumably obtained tin from some-

where in the Zagros Mountains east of Assyria, but their exact source of supply is not known. Textiles and clothing were the other major imports to Anatolia. In addition the Assyrians carried on a brisk local trade in hides, fleece, wool and rugs.

The trade was conducted both by direct barter and by exchange of currency. Gold was the principal capital of the commercial firms at Assur and was sometimes used as money, but silver provided the primary currency for trade with the natives. Both gold and silver were mined extensively in Anatolia, refined at the mines and shipped back to Assur. Within the native economy, on the other hand, copper was the medium of exchange.

The Assyrian merchants applied different terms in their dealings with the local people and among themselves. To their fellow merchants they extended credit more freely and at lower interest rates. In their transactions with the na-

tives they generally preferred cash payment, and when they made loans to Anatolians it was at a higher rate and for a shorter term. Imported manufactures sold in Anatolia at a 100 per cent markup on their price in Assur. The institution of collateral played an important role in trading contracts. A debt might be secured by every item of a man's property—including his wife and children.

As was their practice throughout Anatolia, the Assyrians did not attempt to interfere in any way with local politics. They managed their commercial activities and settled disputes among themselves through their own Assyrian institutions: local councils made up of officials appointed from Assur and other members elected by resident Assyrian traders for specific terms of office. Where commerce impinged on local politics their councils negotiated treaties or other agreements with the local princes.

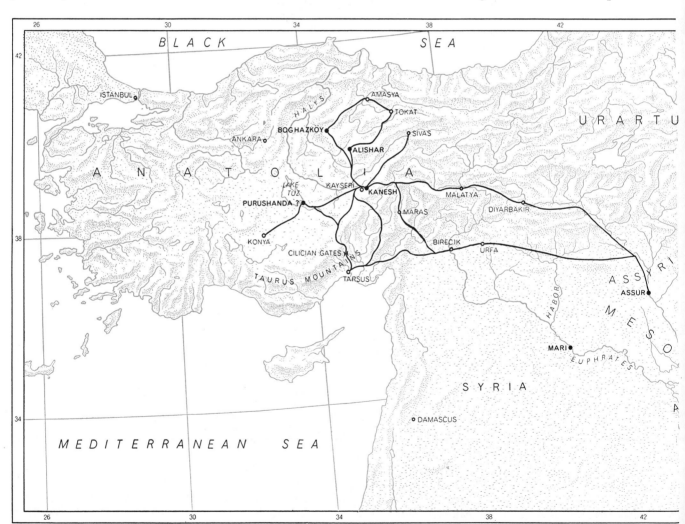

PRINCIPAL TRADE ROUTES traversed by the Assyrian merchants originated at Assur in northern Mesopotamia and terminated at the central Anatolian city of Kanesh. The northern route followed the upper Tigris River Valley and entered Kanesh from the east. The southern route skirted the edge of the North Syrian desert and ascended the Anatolian Plateau from three different

The dependence of the councils on the home government at Assur was effected by making them all subject to the *karum* at Kanesh, which was in turn directly connected to Assur, or, as it is usually referred to in the tablets, "the City."

Most of the major Anatolian cities of the period were ruled by local princes and princesses and were entirely autonomous. The Assyrian merchants paid taxes to the local prince on imports, exports and sales. In return the prince guaranteed the trade caravans safe passage through his territory. In the event of any change in local government, such as the accession of a new prince to the throne, an oath of confidence was asked from the council of the *karum*. The prince also acted as an arbitrator in cases of conflict between the Assyrians and his native subjects. For a certain fee the prince would provide storage space for merchandise in the cellar of his palace. We have found such cellar warehouses in both of the two palaces so far excavated on the Kültepe mound. In addition to his regular fee the prince also had the first option to buy any of the latest imports from Assur.

Most of the documents unearthed from the *karum* at Kanesh are of a purely commercial nature. They include business letters, contracts, bills of lading, memoranda about purchases and sales, and deeds between Assyrian traders. The local princes and even some of the common people learned to use the Assyrian script. We have found letters from one native to another, legal documents, lists of palace staffs and documents bearing on family relations that teach us something about the Hatti administrative system and civilization. In some cases the mention of proper names—local gods, people and places—provides a clue to the unwritten local language of the time.

More than most archaeological finds, some of the tablets give vivid insights into personal lives. One letter from a woman at home in Assur to her trader husband in Kanesh complains about her mother-in-law. Another woman left behind in Assyria writes to bemoan the fact that she does not have enough money to buy a sacrifice to a god. And we have one letter, apparently never dispatched, in which a woman whose mother-in-law is dying asks her sister-in-law to come to Kanesh to help. Encountered among vast stacks of commercial documents, these letters cut sharply through the centuries and remind one of the human beings behind the clay tablets and pottery shards.

The first Assyrian traders settled at Kanesh in about 1950 B.C. They established residence in a section of the city that lay like a crescent around the northeastern rim of the central mound, and it was this area that became the Assyrian *karum*. It is some 1,000 yards long, 700 yards wide and only a couple of yards above the level of the plain. Whereas the central city was populated from the Early Bronze Age until the end of the Roman era in the fourth century A.D., the *karum* was inhabited for but a short period of time. Only four distinct building levels are to be found there, the total thickness of which, from virgin soil to the floor of the latest level, is just under 28 feet. The two lowest levels, designated III and IV, antedate the Assyrian colonization and no written documents have yet been found there. It is Level II that introduces the documented historical era and the Assyrians, and it is here that we have unearthed the majority of the tablets—more than 14,000 of them.

The city of this era was divided into various quarters by squares and streets wide enough to allow the passage of carts. The residences of the Assyrian merchants were concentrated in the center and northern section of the *karum*, with local Anatolians in the southern part. Apparently the Assyrians preferred to stick together, but the boundaries between quarters were not distinct. The shops of craftsmen were grouped at the center of the community. We have found two-room buildings containing large amounts of crockery and kitchen equipment; these may have been restaurants. Other small buildings open to the street and outfitted with stone or wooden shelves seem to have been shops of some kind, but we do not yet know what they contained. Most of the residences were two stories high and had three or four rooms on each floor, grouped around a covered courtyard. In many cases small rooms filled with tablets and separated from the living quarters appear to have served as offices.

Unfortunately for the inhabitants but fortunately for the archaeologist, the history of Level II ended with a disastrous fire. The inhabitants departed in a hurry, leaving behind them the contents of their houses and workshops. Whatever resisted the flames remains to this day substantially as it was abandoned. The site was uninhabited for between 30 and 60 years, after which a new city was built on the ruins, apparently by a new generation of Assyrian merchants. The new city is designated I*b* to distinguish it from a slightly later, non-Assyrian level, I*a*. The houses of I*b* were larger and individual rooms were more spacious. Although we have found less evidence of business activity in the form of cuneiform records (only some 80 tablets have been unearthed so far), Level I*b* apparently represents a city at least as prosperous as its predecessor. Whereas the walls of houses in the earlier city had been built of mud brick on wooden frames, stone-wall construction now became more popular. The Assyrian merchants were still influential in the I*b* city, but more of the native merchants in the southern part of the city now lived in houses as large and well designed as those of the colonists.

The artifacts found in Levels II and I*b* reflect the remarkable degree to which the Assyrian colonists adopted the culture of their Hatti neighbors. Except for the clay tablets, with their cuneiform script and distinctly Meso-

directions. Auxiliary routes connected all the major trade centers of Anatolia to Kanesh. Open circles indicate modern cities.

potamian cylinder-seal impressions, all the artifacts of these levels are in the native style. If the tablets and their sealed envelopes had not been found, in fact, we might never have suspected the existence of the merchant colony.

It was during the colonial period that the ceramic art reached its highest de-

velopment in Anatolia. Some of the pottery was richly decorated, but the finest pieces depended for their beauty on purity of line and burnished monochrome finishes. Human and animal figures, drinking cups and small cosmetic boxes molded in the form of animals rank among the masterpieces of their kind.

The clay envelopes in which cuneiform tablets were enclosed were sealed with elaborate impressions made by carved stone cylinder seals [see bottom illustration on page 239]. The natives took over this ancient Mesopotamian device and developed it in their own distinctive style. In the locally made seals

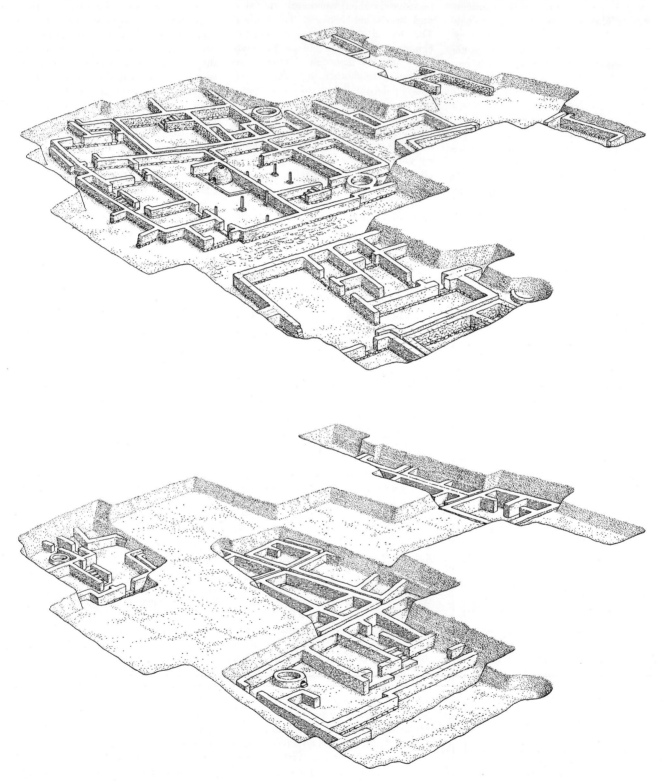

KARUM OF KANESH had four distinct building levels, two of which are shown in this schematic drawing of an excavation at the site. The houses of the earlier Level II (bottom), the settlement in which most of the clay tablets were found, were largely of mud-brick construction. Those of the later Level Ib (top) were more spacious and closer together, and many of them had stone walls.

BRONZE DAGGER from the mound of Kanesh bears the Assyrian words "Palace of Anitta, the King." Anitta ruled in the region toward the end of the Assyrian colonial period.

ivory. Both materials are native to North Syria. The ivory statuette is remarkably similar to the figures of naked goddesses discovered at Mari in North Syria and must have been an import from that area. Both of these figurines were found in the grave of a foreign merchant. They are in sharp contrast to the majority of the religious figures uncovered in Level I*b*, which are in the native style. Most of these are lead plaques showing the principal Anatolian goddess, with or without her family, in low relief. We have also found the stone molds from which the plaques were cast.

During the time when Level I*b* was occupied, major changes were taking place in Anatolia. Regional kings arose and began to extend their control over the feudal domains of the local princes. One of the rulers was Anitta, whose name appears on a bronze dagger unearthed in the remains of a palace on the mound of Kanesh. Anitta was king of the city of Kussara and apparently held dominion over Kanesh. Shortly after the reign of Anitta, during the first half of the 18th century B.C., invaders from the north—presumably Hittites—attacked and burned both the central city and the Level I*b* karum. Although a small city was built on the ruins and left its remains as level I*a* in the *karum* area, the fire marked the end of the Assyrian colony. With the consolidation of political power in the Hittite Old Kingdom, the immediate Assyrian influence in Anatolia was at an end.

The influence of Assyria in Anatolia nonetheless persisted. For more than a century the Anatolians had been in direct contact with the advanced culture of Mesopotamia, with a written lan-

processions of gods and scenes of the hunt and of battle are prominent; many of these themes were later developed into primary motifs of Hittite art.

Although the resident Assyrians apparently had little effect on Anatolian art forms aside from the cylinder seals, we have found a strong North Syrian influence, particularly in metal objects, pottery and small statues. Evidence of this influence is found in both imports and imitative native products. One of the most interesting imports is a hollow-shafted adz that is distinctly foreign to Anatolia and must have been brought in from the area of the Habor River [see map on pages 236 and 237]. This tool and many other metal objects found in specific strata at Kanesh and at Syrian sites

are useful for establishing archaeological synchronism. In both levels of the *karum* we have found clothing pins, axes, daggers and spearheads fashioned in bronze, silver or gold. None of these objects has been excavated at levels dating from either before or after the Assyrian colonization. The fact that they are not Assyrian but North Syrian indicates that the Kanesh *karum* maintained close relations not only with Assur but also with other neighboring lands. Some of them may not have been important items of trade but merely the personal effects of itinerant merchants passing through Kanesh.

Among the figurines of gods and goddesses, we have found two that are in a style alien to Anatolia. One is made of a glazed pottery and the other of

CYLINDER SEAL is shown at the right. At the left is its impress, made by rolling it over wet clay. Cylinder seals were characteristic Mesopotamian devices and were introduced into Anatolia by the Assyrians. This particular seal probably came from North Syria.

MODERN
VILLAGE

KARUM

5

5

INNER CITY

15

10

0

20

15

0

0

MAP OF SITE shows the central mound where the Hatti city of Kanesh was located and the outlying *karum* of the Assyrian merchants. The diagonally hatched areas around the perimeter of the mound were excavated by early archaeologists. The author's excavations on the mound and in the *karum* are outlined in black. Contour intervals are indicated in meters above the level of the plain.

CLAY TABLETS were often stored in large earthenware jars like this one, photographed as it was uncovered in the house of a merchant in Level II. The foot rule indicates scale.

guage and with a highly organized commercial system. Assyrian scribes served in the palaces of the Anatolian kings, and some of the local people learned enough of the written language to use it for commercial, legal and administrative purposes. The upper classes in particular came under the broadening influence of the Assyrians. They acquired a taste for the fashions and luxuries of Babylon and picked up administrative techniques and business acumen. Perhaps most important of all, this provincial people acquired from the Assyrians a sense of empire that later expressed itself in the powerful Hittite civilization, which dominated Asia Minor in the centuries that followed.

CLAY ENVELOPES in which the tablets were enclosed to be filed or dispatched were sealed with the writer's personal design, applied with a cylinder seal. Such a design is seen at the top of this envelope. The writing below may be an address or a summary of contents.

IV

EUROPEAN COMMUNITIES:
NEOLITHIC TO MEDIEVAL

EUROPEAN COMMUNITIES: IV
NEOLITHIC TO MEDIEVAL

INTRODUCTION

For several decades it has been the "informed wisdom" of the archaeological community working in the Old World that Europe attained a high level of civilization only in the latter part of the second millennium, that is, with the rise of Minoan and Mycenaean civilization. As is evident from the previous section, this is thousands of years after the rise of Egyptian, Mesopotamian, and Indus civilizations. Europe has been typically characterized as barbarian when compared to the urban communities of the third millennium in the Near East. In many cases, if not most, archaeologists argue that domestication, metallurgy, writing—in fact, the entire complex of a stratified urban society—was diffused from the Near East to Europe. The comparison of the "barbarians" of temperate Europe with the civilized world of the Aegean and Near East has long been a theme of Old World archaeology. Central concerns of this theme have addressed themselves to the following questions:

1. How did an agricultural subsistence economy diffuse from the Orient to Europe?
2. What was the nature of trade and interaction between the barbarian chiefdoms of temperate Europe and the East Mediterranean?
3. What was the nature of migratory movements brought about by Indo-European speaking pastoralist tribes at the end of the third millennium?
4. What were the relations between the civilized communities of classical Greek, Etruscan, and Roman communities and the more barbarian hordes of Europe?

Today we recognize that some of these questions are directed toward false issues, whereas others demand far more careful consideration than the assumption that Europe was more barbarous than the civilized Near East. The very use of such terms predetermine or prejudice our ability to deal objectively with the archaeological evidence.

The essays that follow address themselves to some specific communities in Europe. In their detail they point to the absurdity of classifying cultures as high or low in terms of social, economic, and technological innovations. Thus the essay by Hansjürgen Müller-Beck shows, in the neolithic Swiss lake dwellings, a successful adaptation to a specific environment, as distinctive from that of the Near Eastern neolithic as it is efficient.

The old saw that Europe was the recipient of technology obtained from the Near East through diffusion of a "higher" level of social complexity is directly challenged in Colin Renfrew's article, which is based on a reevaluation of radiocarbon dating. Although radiocarbon dates (or determinations, as the skeptics prefer to call them) are beginning to offer a relatively coherent pattern of absolute chronology, there are increasing concerns on the part of both archaeologists and physicists about the nature, care, and calibration of radiocarbon samples (Stuckenrath, 1965, Watkins, 1975). It has become clear that the assumption made by W. F. Libby and his collaborators, who developed the technique, that the carbon-14 content in the atmosphere has always been constant, cannot be upheld (Bucha and Neustupny, 1968). The half-life of carbon-14 has been changed to a newer and presumably more accurate one; that is, from 5568 to 5730 ± 40 years. Such a change makes radiocarbon dates based on the 5568-year half-life actually earlier than they were reported to be.

As if archaeologists were not already confounded by the challenge and changes in the radiocarbon system, physicists are now proposing major readjustments that they say will bring radiocarbon dates more into line with historical reality. Correction factors have been determined from inconsistencies between radiocarbon dates and tree-ring dates, and control measurements using dendrochronologically dated wood from giant sequoias and bristlecone pines have established several variations in the carbon-14 level. For the B.C. period the correction factors that should be applied to the standard radiocarbon dates grow progressively larger as one goes back in time, from plus 50 years at 300 B.C. to plus 650 years at 2700 B.C. For example, a published radiocarbon date of 1950 B.C. would have 400 years added to it and thus be altered to a more nearly correct date of 2350 B.C. The radiocarbon cycle, like all natural phenomena, deviates from the ideal; but until more sophisticated techniques of dating prehistoric materials are discovered, it remains the best timepiece for the prehistoric past. In spite of its real and alleged imperfections, it remains a vital tool for the construction of the archaeologists' absolute chronology and the establishment of cultural sequences.

The revolutionary impact of calibrating the radiocarbon dates and finding they are actually earlier than was first reported is dealt with in Renfrew's article. With the new calibrated dates, cultural and technological diffusion becomes an impossible explanation for certain developments (e.g., metallurgy) because, as Professor Renfrew argues, the new dates assign primacy for the invention to Europe. Thus if the new radiocarbon calibrations are correct, then the Tartaria tablets, reported on in the article by M. S. F. Hood, are 500 years older than the earliest evidence of Near Eastern writing. It is, however, still debatable whether the Tartaria tablets were found in their correct archaeological context (the Vinca-Tordos Culture, ca. 4000 B.C.) and whether the radiocarbon dates have correctly dated the context of the tablets. It is equally debatable whether the Tartaria tablets are related in script to the Near Eastern Uruk tablets. Although this is the most commonly held opinion, Professor Hood argues that they may belong to the later Aegean script of Eteo-Cretan. The argument, pending additional evidence, remains unresolved. One thing is clear: The calibrations of radiocarbon dates, for instance, the addition of 650 years to a reported date of 2700 B.C., has introduced the second radiocarbon revolution. It is far too early to agree positively with Renfrew that such a basic change in the formation of European cultures several centuries earlier than previously believed can be tolerated in the totality of our archaeological understanding. However, we can wholly agree with him that archaeologists have all too long accepted the alternative hypothesis about European prehistory: *Ex oriente lux.*

Because of recent work on its subject, Jacquetta Hawkes' paper on Stonehenge needs some comment. Hawkes sees Stonehenge in a humanist perspective as a monument exercising one's spiritual needs. In *Stonehenge Decoded*, Gerald Hawkins advanced the idea that Stonehenge was built for a singular purpose: The monumental stone structure was an astronomical observatory. The idea that Stonehenge was oriented in relation to the sun is at least a hundred years old, but Hawkins, an astronomer, suggested far more than this. His computer-assisted research on the stone alignments at Stonehenge seemed to show that the entire megalithic monument was built to predict important events in the heavens—solar and lunar eclipses, summer and winter solstices, and even more. The argument between Hawkins and his detractors can be followed in the pages of *Antiquity* from 1965 through 1967. The debate had all the elements of humanism vs. science and was perhaps not a question of who was right but a matter of how one perceives the past. Hawkes, whose article included here was written in 1953, could not accept Hawkins' "scientism," the reduction of Stonehenge to an astronomical observatory. She wrote a scathing rebuttal to his argument, "God and the Machine," which was published in *Antiquity*. Since then, current opinion has settled perhaps more in favor of Hawkins' view. Surely, Stonehenge appears to have been built to serve some astronomical function. Perhaps the most striking support of Hawkins' ideas came from a Scottish mathematician, Alexander Thom, who had, for years before Hawkins advanced his theory, been studying the alignments and measurements of the many megalithic structures that dot the landscape of England. He concluded, independently and most convincingly, that these stone structures of 2500 B.C. and earlier were carefully constructed in standardized measurements and were all aligned to serve as astronomical observatories. Their function seems undeniable.

The article by Martin Biddle represents one of the fastest growing concerns in the field—medieval archaeology. In the United States its counterpart is referred to as colonial archaeology. It has long been apparent that many of the major monuments of the world, as well as major cities, are directly beneath more recent constructions. Today excavations are being conducted beneath such major historical monuments as Winchester Cathedral in England and Notre Dame in Paris as well as in areas within the cities of London, Paris, Leningrad, Prague, Philadelphia, Williamsburg, Virginia, and Plymouth Plantation, Rhode Island, to mention a few. Excavations at these sites have yielded important information on the architectural predecessors of the monuments as well as the historical development of the cities. Such excavations are not only clear evidence of an archaeological interest in more recent times but a reflection of an even more recent interest in what has been termed *cultural resource management*. Archaeological sites are a limited resource, which is being rapidly depleted through the growth of cities, industrial development, the expansion of road systems, and so on. The rate of growth in both the developed and the developing countries threatens to destroy the archaeological resources throughout the world. Recognition of this fact has led to a concerted effort on the part of numerous governments to protect their archaeological sites through a directed program of cultural resource management. The preservation and conservation of archaeological sites is being complemented by an increasing concern for the preservation and analysis of archaeological objects.

The article by Maddin, Muhly, and Wheeler attempts to answer a seemingly direct, straightforward question: How did the Iron Age begin? The complexity of the question is revealed in the thoughtful essay, but is the question really answered? I leave it to the reader to decide.

REFERENCES

Bucha, U. and Neustupny, E. 1968. "Changing the Earth's Magnetic Field and Radiocarbon Dating," *Nature*, July 15.

Hawkes, J. 1967. "God and the Machine," *Antiquity*, vol. 61, no. 163, pp. 174–180.

Hawkins, G. 1965. *Stonehenge Decoded*. Doubleday, New York.

Stuckenrath, R., Jr. 1965. "On the Care and Feeding of Radiocarbon Dates," *Archaeology*, vol. 18, no. 4, pp. 277 *et seq.*

Thom, A. 1971. *Megalithic Lunar Observatories*. Clarendon Press, Oxford.

Watkins, T. 1975. *Radiocarbon: Calibrations and Prehistory*. Edinburgh University Press, Edinburgh.

25 Prehistoric Swiss Lake Dwellers

by Hansjürgen Müller-Beck
December 1961

For a century it has been widely accepted that the early Swiss built their houses on stilts over a lake. New excavations at the Lake of Burgäschi have shown that this quaint picture is mythical

Nearly everyone has heard about the lake dwellers of prehistoric Switzerland, who are said to have built their houses on stilts out over the water. There they were, in the land of the Alps, living like South Sea Islanders!

One man is primarily responsible for this rather romantic idea. In 1854 Ferdinand Keller, a reputable Swiss archaeologist, reported on a field of upright wooden pilings extending a few inches above the shore of the Lake of Zurich and exposed to view by a fall in the water level. Ethnologists had recently described whole villages in the Pacific islands that were built over water, the houses standing on platforms supported by logs driven into the water bed. With this image in mind, Keller proceeded to enlarge on the Zurich pilings. In prehistoric times, he wrote, Switzerland had been inhabited by people who lived in villages built on platforms over lakes [*see top illustration on opposite page*]. The statement found such immediate and widespread support that it was passed on virtually unaltered for nearly 100 years, not only in popular books on archaeology but in professional works as well. Tourists visiting southern Germany can still explore a life-size reconstruction of a pile dwelling that gives them a vivid and "authentic" view of this peculiar culture.

Nonetheless there is increasing evidence that Keller was wrong and that his less well-known colleague, Albert Jahn, was closer to the truth. Four years before Keller published his views Jahn had written about another pile field, this one a few yards off the shore of the Lake of Bienne and completely submerged beneath its waters. Like Keller, Jahn believed that the pilings had once served as part of a settlement. In Jahn's opinion, however, they had provided foundations for houses standing on the ground. The lake, he suggested, had advanced in the intervening centuries; where there now was water there had once been shore.

But Keller's hypothesis was not only more attractive; it also seemed to be supported by an abundance of evidence. Everyone interested in archaeology and ethnology was familiar with the pictures of South Sea island villages in travel books. What was more natural than to assume that prehistoric people should have lived like contemporary preliterate ones? Pile fields were discovered in great numbers as a result of the irrigation projects carried out in Switzerland between 1860 and 1880. Keller's pile field on the shore was an exception; in virtually every other case the upright logs were found in areas previously covered by lake water.

Keller's hypothesis was in fact just as speculative as Jahn's. But speculation was about all that archaeology could offer at the time. The methods of geological investigation then in use could not accurately determine dates for the construction of the pile fields. No one knew how to read the evidence in the layers of soil, lake sediment and rubble in which the piles stood. Such "culture layers" usually represent the floors of ancient dwellings; in Keller's interpretation they were made up of the refuse thrown into the lake from the platforms of the pile dwellings. But the techniques of archaeology did not yet allow detailed examination of the pile fields without such disturbance of the evidence they contained as to render almost worthless any judgment that might be made. Not until the 1920's, when systematic excavations were undertaken in a group of pile fields in southwestern Germany, did it become possible to make a genuinely scientific appraisal of the situation.

From that time on the Keller hypothesis was thrown open to serious question, and the "pile-dwelling problem," as it is called, became the subject of lively debate among archaeologists. As techniques of investigation were refined, it became clear that Jahn's view conformed far better to the facts than Keller's. By now it is widely agreed that the pile dwellers of prehistory lived on the shores of lakes, not on platforms over their waters.

My own concern with the pile-dwelling problem dates back to 1957, when, under the auspices of the Bern Historical Museum, I began excavations on the shores of the Lake of Burgäschi, in the Swiss midlands. This is a small lake, with a diameter of only about a third of a mile. Nevertheless, four separate and distinct Neolithic settlements have been found on its shores. One, excavated in the 19th century, was so badly disrupted that its archaeological value was completely destroyed. Two others have been only partially excavated in more recent times. The fourth, on the south shore of the lake, was the object of our investigation. We have studied it in detail and, although a final report of the findings will not be completed until 1963, the major outlines are clear. Our work has served two important purposes. It has helped to fill in the picture of Neolithic life in Europe north of the Alps and it has contributed significantly to a solution of the pile-dwelling problem.

Our first view of the south site was of a reedy shore behind which, at a distance of from five to 10 yards, begins the growth of bushes and trees that gradually deepens into true forest. A few piles protrude from the lake bed near the shore, but none reach as high as the sur-

PREHISTORIC SWISS PILE DWELLINGS were thought to have stood on platforms over lakes, like villages in certain Pacific islands. This drawing is based on a reconstruction that was proposed in 1854 by Ferdinand Keller, who originated the notion.

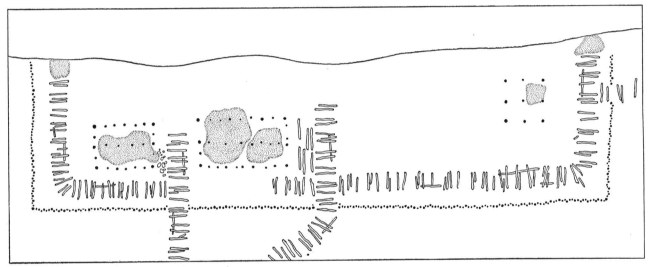

PILES AT BURGÄSCHI, found on lake shore, are shown as dots on this schematic representation of the top layer of the excavation. Shapes with irregular outlines are mounds of loam and rubble. Strips are remains of corduroy log road of the settlement.

PILE DWELLINGS at excavation site stood on the lake shore, as this reconstruction shows. Piles were driven into the ground to support houses and roads of the settlement. Pile dwellings here, among the most primitive excavated, date from Neolithic period.

face of the water. Nor are any visible along the beach; all are hidden beneath the layers of topsoil and lake sediments that have been laid down during the thousands of years since the area was occupied. Under these layers we found piles in profusion, more than 3,000 of them. Most are the trunks of alder, ash and young oak trees, and they measure from about three to seven and a half feet in length and from five to six inches in diameter. Originally set in the ground in a vertical position, they are now tilted at an angle, with their upper ends pointing out toward the lake. The logs that formed the roads of the settlement are still lying in the horizontal position in which they were originally placed. In addition to the piles, our excavations revealed parts of the walls and roofs of buildings and the mounds of loam, branches and rubble that served as their floors. What is more, we have uncovered artifacts and other remains that have helped us visualize the culture of the people.

Radiocarbon measurements show that the pile dwellers lived at the south site in the first quarter of the third millennium B.C. and remained there approximately 100 years. When they arrived, they found a broad and treeless strip of land that was ideal for cultivation. The lake, of moderate size when it was formed in the last ice age, had been gradually retreating, leaving on its shores mollusk shells and the deposits of carbon and lime that form around the roots of water plants. The soil cover was still too light to permit trees to take root and grow, but it was quite heavy enough for the demands of primitive agriculture, and its mineral-rich substratum was a guarantee of fertility.

If this stretch of virgin land was ideal for farming, it had serious drawbacks as a living place. The subsoil was wet and far too weak to hold the weight of houses. Structures built on it would have sagged and tilted within a short time if the builders had not found ways to secure the foundations. To make floors for their houses the settlers employed the older mesolithic technique of putting down layers of rubble, branches and soft earth, which they pounded into a smooth, firm surface. They then secured the underpinning of these floors by driving piles through the sediment down to the underlying gravel of bedrock.

Only a small fraction of the upright logs we uncovered at Burgäschi had formed part of the framework of the rectangular houses. By far the greatest number were anchor posts, driven into the ground to provide a firm base for the houses, for their loam floors and for the corduroy log roads of the settlement. But the anchor posts that were sunk when the settlers first arrived do not seem to have been adequate to support the community for the entire span of its occupancy. Whether the lake level rose with the passage of time or whether the buildings gradually sank into the wet ground despite the anchor posts is not known. In any event, it is clear that the settlement was often in need of repair. The floors sank in the middle as the earth beneath them gave way. For a while they could be leveled by the addition of new layers of rubble, branches and loam, and for as long as this expedient served, the houses were safe. But eventually more drastic action became necessary and the entire settlement had to be moved a few feet back from the lake, onto drier land. Each time the move was made, new anchor posts were sunk to support the new constructions. The piles that represent building foundations are disposed in overlapping layers, one behind and beneath another, in much the same manner as roofing tiles. Each layer is evidence of a new move back from the shore.

It was from the last layer, closest to the surface and consequently easiest to distinguish from the others, that we were able to reconstruct the appearance of the settlement during its final stage [see middle and bottom illustrations on preceding page]. At that time the entire settlement measured about 50 yards long by 10 yards wide. Among the piles we found were those that represented the remains of the palisade fence that enclosed this area on all but its lake side. Both outside and inside the settlement were a number of piles that had served as anchor posts. These supported two corduroy log roads, the remains of which we also found. The roads ran through two openings in the fence on the inland side and branched to lead to the fronts of the houses and to traverse the inner boundaries of the settlement. The fence had still a third opening, on the narrow side of the settlement near the shore. The road through this opening was only lightly reinforced, secured by fewer anchor pilings than the others.

Inside the settlement were three struc-

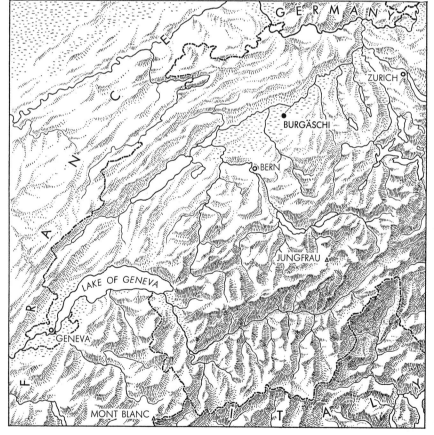

BURGÄSCHI is shown as black dot on this map of Switzerland. Lake of Zurich (*upper right*) is site of early discovery leading to idea that pile dwellings were built over lakes.

EXCAVATION AT SOUTH SITE revealed loam floors of houses and piles supporting them. Seen here is part of the floor of the larger house. Four-meter rule shows its size. Light area around floor is chalk, which lies immediately under the culture layer.

WOODEN HOE was found resting on chalk layer after excavation of the culture layer. The wet subsoil of the lake shore at Burgäschi acted as a barrier to air and so preserved logs and wooden implements of the settlement in good condition for more than 4,000 years.

tures. One, on the eastern side, was very small. There is no evidence that it had walls; only posts seem to have supported its roof. From this fact and from the fact that its loam floor was rather thin, we deduce that it was not used as a dwelling but for some other purpose. It may have been a granary, a working place or possibly an enclosure for small domestic animals.

The two larger structures were obviously dwelling places. The roof of the smaller of them was partially preserved, as were parts of the walls of both and the logs that served as their framework. This evidence makes the structure of the houses clear. They had pointed gable roofs, made of grass and reed. The unplastered walls were made of wickerwork and well-finished board about half an inch thick. On each of the thick loam floors was a fireplace, the position of which seems to have been changed several times. The doors of the houses faced away from the prevailing wind and gave on the corduroy roads that led outside the settlement. Since the walls were no more than three feet high, the houses must have been close and dark. But they were adequate as shelters against the night and bad weather.

The construction of the houses thus

IMPLEMENTS found at Burgäschi, seen here about half-size, showed differences in care of workmanship that were probably intentional. The arrow (a), with a wooden shaft and a

combined common primitive techniques with an innovation dictated by the peculiarities of the lakeside terrain. As far back as 5000 B.C. men were using branches and loam to form a thick flooring for the crude, dome-shaped huts they built on the shores of lakes. By 4000 B.C. the inhabitants of southern

Europe knew how to construct a rectangular house with a gabled roof and a framework of logs driven into the ground. The people who lived at the south site combined these two old principles and so produced a new kind of structure. Their gabled houses had log frames and loam floors and were secured by pilings driven deep into the ground.

This principle of supporting houses on pilings is still in use in coastal towns all over the world. One of its earliest known expressions is to be found at our excavation. The settlements that date from later times give evidence for the evolution of more refined techniques [see illustration at bottom of these two pages]. The settlement at the south site is primitive even in relation to its own period. In other parts of Europe fixed flooring was

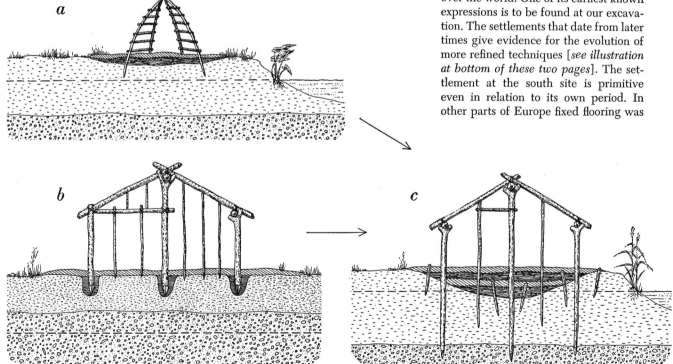

EVOLUTION OF SWISS PILE DWELLINGS is outlined in these drawings. In 5000 B.C. floors of mound-shaped lake-shore huts were reinforced with loam and rubble (a). By 4000 B.C. gabled rec-   tangular houses with framework of posts driven into the ground were built in southern Europe (b). At Burgäschi, occupied approximately 1,000 years later, these techniques were combined to

stone head, is the first such weapon discovered at a Neolithic site in Switzerland. The bone blade set in unworked wood (b) is highly

polished. The cylindrical vessel (c) is made of well-finished wood. The ax (d) has a stone blade and a broken wooden shaft.

already in use. By the time of the Copper Age and the Bronze Age the pile dwellers of Switzerland knew of it too. By then they also had metal tools with which to work wood. Their lake-shore settlements were constructed with wooden floors and supported by piles driven into the earth at one end and at the other into wooden plates, called ground plates, that served as the base for the flooring.

It is even possible that in time the pile dwellers learned to raise their houses slightly above the ground, as houses are today elevated in coastal communities in order to prevent the floor boards from rotting quickly. Since the ground level at different sites dating from the Copper Age and Bronze Age has not yet been fixed, it has not been determined

whether or not the more sophisticated pile dwellings elsewhere in Switzerland really reflect this refinement. Such a construction, if it was used, may sound reminiscent of the Keller hypothesis. Actually it has nothing to do with it. Keller had in mind entire settlements built on platforms over lakes. The present view is that the pile dwellers lived on the shores of lakes in houses with foundations reinforced by pilings.

The sealed, wet layers of clay, loam and lake sediments that preserved the piles at the south site also preserved other evidence of the life and culture of its people. Within the boundaries of the settlement was a layer of buried rubble, and scattered profusely through this culture layer were artifacts and objects of all kinds. There were the bones of ani-

mals, more than 80 per cent of them the bones of such wild species as deer, aurochs, boar, fox, beaver and bear. The remainder represent the remains of domesticated species such as pig, goat, sheep and dog. From this it is clear that although the settlers were stockbreeders, the hunting tradition was still strong. There were also flax and grains of cereal, as well as hazelnuts, berry seeds and mushrooms. This again is evidence that, whereas the settlers knew how to raise crops, they still obtained a good part of their food supply by the more primitive methods of gathering.

In these respects the people here were less advanced than contemporaneous peoples in Switzerland and other sections of Europe north of the Alps who

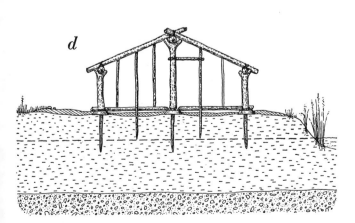

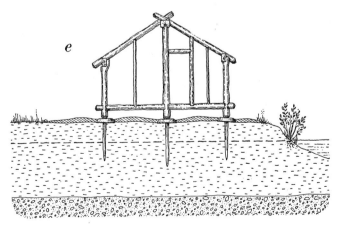

produce gabled rectangular houses with loam floors supported by underground pilings (c). By about 2000 B.C. wooden floors were in use and lake-shore houses were supported by pilings driven into

the ground through wooden plates beneath the floors (d). It is possible that in later times pile dwellings may have been elevated a little above the ground, as they are in coastal towns today (e).

were joined with them in the same pottery tradition. Our work uncovered hundreds of crudely shaped, unornamented ceramic pots of a type called Cortaillod, after the site on the Lake of Neuchâtel where they were first found. Other people who made this ware were primarily farmers and stockbreeders; the hunting and gathering component of their culture was far less important.

We uncovered many other artifacts: stone hatchets and knife blades, flint arrowheads, bone chisels and awls, harpoons and drinking cups made of deer horn. Among the most interesting of our finds were wooden implements, preserved for more than 4,000 years in the wet, airless ground. There were handles of hatchets, knives and sickles; clubs, mallets, short lances and drills used to make fire. There was also the shaft of an arrow with a stone arrowhead still fixed on it.

Perhaps the most interesting find was a string of copper beads, which had been placed near the wall of the smaller of the two houses. The beads, graduated in size and strung on thin cord, were made of a material rare in this part of Europe during the Neolithic period. Copper ore was commonly found much farther south, east and west. The beads are a strong argument for the beginning of trade that was to link the hinterlands of the Alps with the high civilizations of the Mediterranean.

We found some human teeth but no human bone at all. This is somewhat unusual for an agricultural Neolithic settlement, where archaeologists generally recover both the skeletons of buried dead and isolated bones often considered to be evidences of cannibalism. Our failure to find any human bone is another indication of the strength of the hunting tradition among these people. Hunters are rarely cannibals, and they seldom bury their dead. They leave the bodies in the open air, where scavenging and decomposition cause all traces of them to disappear.

From the size of the settlement and from what we know about the size of hunting groups we deduce that the entire community at the south site consisted of no more than two or three families, perhaps three generations in lineal descent. There may have been as many as 40 people; the number of animal bones we found suggests that the food supply was adequate for a group of this size. But it is more likely that the total population was between 20 and 30.

In such small groups social organization is generally loose, and the evidence suggests that the members of this community lived together on a basis of equality, with people coming and going as they chose. The separate entrances in the fence that surrounded the settlement and the separate roads to the houses within it would not have been found in a larger community, where relatively tight regulations usually govern the behavior of its members.

Yet such tight social organization was already operative in many parts of the world. The great temples and pyramids of Egypt are contemporaneous with the tiny settlement we excavated. Beyond the Alps and across the Mediterranean a complex culture was reaching a zenith at the same time that the modest culture of the pile dwellers was beginning to emerge. Switzerland, in a sense, was a backwater, but it was a corner of the world in which people could enjoy social individuality, a quality of life that has not been suppressed in this part of Europe even for a short time up to the present day.

The singular innovation in engineering that gives the pile dwellers their name was to provide the stuff of scientific controversy more than four millennia later on. That controversy has given impetus to fruitful investigation into the prehistory of Europe.

CLAY POTS were found at Burgäschi by the hundreds. All were crudely shaped and undecorated. Such ware, called Cortaillod, is the most common type found at excavations of Neolithic sites in Switzerland.

COPPER BEADS found at Burgäschi indicate the beginnings of trade with southwestern Europe. Copper ore was very rare in sections north of the Alps during the Neolithic period.

Carbon 14 and
the Prehistory of Europe

by Colin Renfrew
October 1971

*Tree-ring measurements have shown that early
carbon-14 dates are off by as much as 700 years.
As a result the view that cultural advances diffused
into Europe from the east is no longer tenable*

Our knowledge of European prehistory is currently being revolutionized. The immediate cause of the revolution is a recently discovered discrepancy between the actual ages of many archaeological sites and the ages that have been attributed to them on the basis of carbon-14 analysis. Some sites are as much as seven centuries older than they had been thought to be. This revelation has destroyed the intricate system of interlocking chronologies that provided the foundation for a major edifice of archaeological scholarship: the theory of cultural diffusion.

For more than a century a basic assumption of prehistorians has been that most of the major cultural advances in ancient Europe came about as the result of influences from the great early civilizations of Egypt and Mesopotamia. For example, megalithic tombs in western

Europe feature single slabs that weigh several tons. The prevailing view of their origin was that the technical skills and religious motivation needed for their construction had come from the eastern Mediterranean, first reaching Spain and Portugal and then France, Britain and Scandinavia. To take another example, it was generally supposed that the knowledge of copper metallurgy had been transmitted by Mediterranean intermediaries to the Iberian peninsula and to the Balkans from its place of origin in the Near East. The revolution in chronology shows, however, that the megalithic tombs of western Europe and the copper metallurgy of the Balkans are actually older than their supposed Mediterranean prototypes.

When the scholars of a century ago wanted to date the monuments and objects of prehistoric Europe, they had

little to help them. C. J. Thomsen, a Danish student of antiquities, had established a "three ages" frame of reference in 1836; structures and objects were roughly classified as Stone Age (at first there was no distinction between Paleolithic and Neolithic), Bronze Age or Iron Age. To assign such things an age in years was a matter of little more than guesswork.

Prehistoric finds are of course by their nature unaccompanied by written records. The only possible recourse was to work from the known to the unknown: to try to move outward toward the unlettered periphery from the historical civilizations of Egypt and Mesopotamia, where written records were available. For example, the historical chronology of Egypt, based on ancient written records, can be extended with considerable confidence back to 1900 B.C. because

MEGALITHIC MONUMENT near Essé in Brittany is typical of the massive stone structures that were raised in France as long ago as the fifth millennium B.C. Called "Fairies' Rock," it is made of 42 large slabs of schist, some weighing more than 40 tons. Because of the great effort that must have been required to raise such monuments, scholars traditionally refused to credit the barbarian cultures of prehistoric Europe with their construction and instead attributed them to influences from civilized eastern Mediterranean.

the records noted astronomical events. The Egyptian "king lists" can then be used, although with far less confidence, to build up a chronology that goes back another 11 centuries to 3000 B.C.

The need to establish a link with Egypt in order to date the prehistoric cultures of Europe went naturally with the widespread assumption that, among prehistoric sites in general, the more sophisticated ones were of Near Eastern origin anyway. In 1887, when the brothers Henri and Louis Siret published the results of their excavations in the cemeteries and settlements of "Copper Age" (late Neolithic) Spain, they reported finding stone tombs, some roofed with handsome corbeled stonework and others of massive megalithic construction. In the tombs there were sometimes human figurines carved in stone, and daggers and simple tools made of copper. That these structures and objects had evolved locally did not seem likely; an origin in the eastern Mediterranean—in Egypt or the Aegean—was claimed for all their more exotic features.

In the first years of this century this method of building up relationships and using contacts with the early civilized world to establish a relative chronology was put on a systematic basis by the Swedish archaeologist Oskar Montelius. In 1903 Montelius published an account of his "typological method," where the development of particular types of tools or weapons within a given area was reconstructed and the sequence was then compared with those of neighboring areas. Adjacent regions could thus be linked in a systematic manner, until a chain of links was built up stretching from the Atlantic across Europe to Egypt and Mesopotamia. It was still assumed that most of the innovations had come from the Near East, and that the farther from the "hearthlands" of civilization they were found, the longer it would have taken them to diffuse there.

Some diffusionist scholars went to extremes. In the 1920's Sir Grafton Smith argued the view that nearly all the innovations in the civilizations around the world could be traced back to Egypt. In this hyperdiffusionist theory the high cultures of the Far East and even the early civilizations of Central America and South America had supposedly stemmed from Egypt. Today very few continue to suppose that the essential ingredients of civilization were disseminated from Egypt to the rest of the world, perhaps in papyrus boats. There were, of course, scholars whose views lay at the other extreme, such as the German ultranationalist Gustaf Kossinna, whose chauvinist writings fell into a predictable pattern. For these men the truly great advances and fundamental discoveries always seem to have been made in the land of their birth. The *Herrenvolk* fantasies of Aryan supremacy in the Nazi era were rooted in Kossinna's theory of Nordic primacy.

Appalled by both of these extremes, the British prehistorian V. Gordon Childe tried to steer a middle course. In *The Dawn of European Civilisation*, published in 1925, Childe rejected Smith's fantasy that the ancient Egyptians were responsible for all the significant advances in prehistoric Europe. Working in the same framework as Montelius but with a detailed and sympathetic consideration of the prehistoric cultures of each region, he built up a picture in terms of what one colleague, Glyn E. Daniel, has termed "modified diffusionism."

Childe saw two main paths whereby a chronological link could be established between Europe and the Near East. First there were the Spanish "Copper Age" finds. Earlier writers had likened the megalithic tombs of Spain, particularly those with corbeled vaults, to the great tholos tombs of Mycenae, which were built around 1500 B.C. Childe saw that the Mycenaean tombs were too recent to have served as a model, and he suggested instead a link between the Spanish tombs and the round tombs of Bronze Age Crete, which had been built

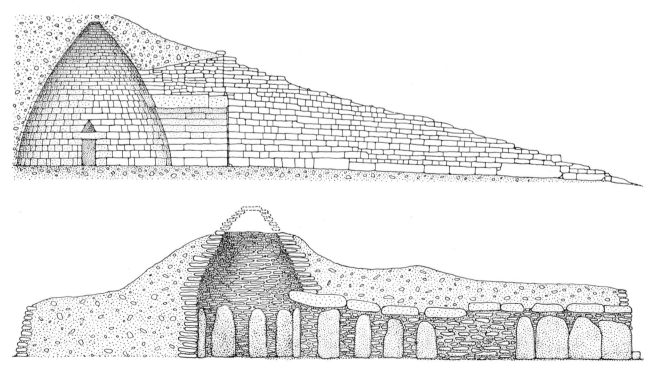

TWO SIMILAR STRUCTURES with corbeled domes are the famous "Treasury of Atreus," a Mycenaean tomb built around 1500 B.C. (*top*), and a megalithic passage grave, Île Longue in Brittany, which is probably some 6,000 years old (*bottom*). Unaware of the true age of the French passage graves, the prehistorian V. Gordon Childe nonetheless dismissed the notion that they were inspired by a civilization as recent as Mycenae. He suggested that they were probably modeled on earlier Minoan tombs built around 2500 B.C.

about 2500 B.C. As subsequent work provided more detail, it was even suggested that colonists from the Aegean had set up settlements in Spain and Portugal. With them they would have brought their knowledge of architecture, their custom of collective burial, their belief in a "mother goddess" and their skill in metallurgy. The fortifications at one or two of these early Iberian sites resemble those at the settlement of Chalandriani on the Aegean island of Syros [see bottom illustration at right].

It was on this basis that the earliest megalithic tombs of the Iberian peninsula were assigned an age of around 2500 B.C. The similar French and British tombs, some of which also have stone vaults, were assigned to times a little later in the third millennium.

Similar logic was used in assigning dates to the striking stone temples of Malta. Sculptured slabs in some of the island's temples are handsomely decorated with spirals. These spirals resemble decorations from Crete and Greece of the period from 1800 to 1600 B.C. The Maltese temples were therefore assumed to date from that time or a little later.

Childe's second path for chronological links between western Europe and the Near East was the Danube. Artifacts of the late Neolithic period found at Vinča in Yugoslavia were compared by him to material from the early Bronze Age "cities" at Troy. The Trojan finds can be dated to within a few centuries of 2700 B.C. It was concluded that metallurgy had arisen in the Balkans as a result of contacts with Troy. This view was strengthened by certain similarities between the clay sculptures found at Vinča and various artistic products of the early Bronze Age Aegean.

These twin foundations for the prehistoric chronology of Europe have been accepted by most archaeologists since Childe's day. The appearance of metallurgy and of other striking cultural and artistic abilities in the Balkans, and of monumental architecture on the Iberian peninsula, were explained as the result of contacts with the Aegean. Such skills make their appearance in the Aegean around 2500 B.C., a point in time that is established by finds of datable Egyptian imports in Crete and of somewhat later Cretan exports in datable contexts in Egypt. The chronology of Crete and the southern Aegean is soundly based on the chronology of Egypt and has not been affected by the current revolution.

It should be noted that, as Childe himself pointed out, these conclusions rested on two basic assumptions. First, it

TWO SIMILAR SPIRALS are the decorations on a stele from a Mycenaean shaft grave (top) and decorations at temple of Tarxien in Malta (bottom). Mycenaean spirals were carved about 1650 B.C. Maltese ones were held on grounds of resemblance to be same age.

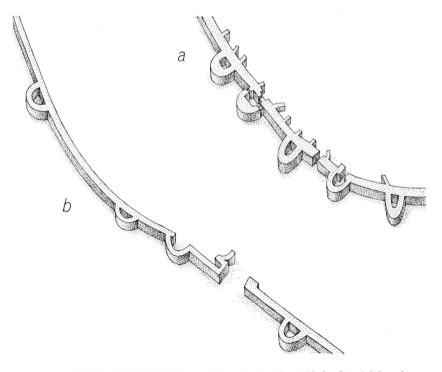

TWO SIMILAR FORTIFICATIONS are the bastioned walls at Chalandriani (a), a site on the Aegean island of Syros, and the walls of Los Millares (b), a "Copper Age" site near Málaga in Spain. The likeness was once attributed to the work of Aegean colonists in Spain.

was assumed that "parallel" developments in different regions—the appearance of metallurgy or the beginning of monumental tomb architecture—were not entirely independent innovations. Second, it was assumed that if the developments had indeed diffused from one region to another, the ancient civilizations of the Near East were the innovators and the barbarians of Europe were the beneficiaries. Childe realized that these assumptions could be questioned, but in the absence of any independent dating method the only way prehistoric Europe could be dated at all was to relate it to the dated civilizations of the Near East. In practice this meant full acceptance of the assumptions. As Childe remarked of his work, "the sole unifying theme was the irradiation of European barbarism by Oriental civilization."

The discovery of carbon-14 dating in 1949 offered, in principle at least, the possibility of establishing a sound absolute chronology without the need for the assumptions that Childe had had to make. Even without carbon-14 dating, however, some of the arguments of the modified diffusionist school were susceptible to criticism. For example, there are no megalithic tombs in the Aegean, so that some special pleading is needed to argue a Near Eastern origin for those of western Europe. Again, detailed studies in the Aegean area show that the resemblances between the pottery and fig-urines of the Iberian peninsula and those of Greece, the supposed homeland of the "colonists," are not as close as had been supposed. Nor are the Balkan Neolithic finds really very closely related to the Aegean ones from which they were supposedly derived. There was certainly room for doubt about some of the details in the attractive and coherent picture that diffusionist theory had built up.

Although the introduction of carbon-14 dating did not disrupt the diffusionist picture or the chronology based on it, the dates did produce a few anomalies. A decade ago there were already hints that something was wrong. The carbon-14 method, originated by Willard F. Libby, ingeniously exploits the production of atoms of this heavy isotope of carbon in the upper atmosphere. The carbon-14 atoms are produced by the absorption of neutrons by atoms of nitrogen 14. The neutrons in turn are produced by the impact of cosmic ray particles on various atoms in the atmosphere. Carbon 14 is radioactive, and like all radioactive elements it decays in a regular way. Its half-life was originally estimated by Libby to be some 5,568 years.

The manufacture of the radioactive isotope by cosmic radiation and its diminution through decay sets up a balance so that the proportion of carbon 14 to carbon 12, the much more abundant nonradioactive isotope, is approximately constant. The atoms of the radioactive isotope in the atmosphere, like the atoms of normal carbon, combine with oxygen to form carbon dioxide. This substance is taken up by plants through photosynthesis and by animals feeding on the plants, and in that way all living things come to have the two kinds of carbon in the same proportion in their tissues while they are alive. At death, however, the cycle is broken: the organisms no longer take up any fresh carbon and the proportion of the two isotopes steadily changes as the radioactive isotope decays. Assuming that the proportion of the two isotopes in the atmosphere has always been constant, one can measure how much carbon 14 is left in plant or animal remains (in charcoal, say, or bone) and, knowing the half-life of the radioactive isotope, can calculate how long the decay process has been going on and therefore how old the sample is.

This, put rather simply, is the principle of the dating method. In practice it is complicated by the very small number of carbon-14 atoms in the atmosphere and in living things compared with the number of carbon-12 atoms: approximately one per million million. The proportion is of course further reduced in dead organic material as the rare isotope decays, making accurate measurement a delicate task. Nonetheless, samples from archaeological sites began to yield coherent and consistent dates soon after 1949. In general the carbon-14 dates in Europe tallied fairly well with those built up by the "typological method"

BRISTLECONE-PINE CALIBRATION worked out by Hans E. Suess of the University of California at San Diego makes it possible to correct carbon-14 dates. The dates running across the top and the lines on which they rest refer to carbon-14 dates in carbon-14 years; the dates running across the bottom and the lines on which they rest refer to bristlecone-pine dates in calendar years. The colback to about 2500 B.C. The great surprise was how early the Neolithic period, defined by the appearance of farming villages, began everywhere. Instead of yielding the expected dates of around 4000 or 4500 B.C., the earliest villages in the Near East proved to date back to as early as 8000 B.C.

These dates for the early Neolithic period were most important. Indeed, their impact on prehistoric archaeology can be regarded as the first carbon-14 revolution. The sharp increases in age did not, however, actually disrupt the diffusionist picture. Farming developments in the Near East remained in general earlier than those in Europe. The pattern did not change nor did the Near East lose its primacy; it was just that all the dates were earlier than had been expected. Everyone had always been aware that, for the period before 3000 B.C., which is when the Egyptian chronology begins, all dates were guesswork. What the first carbon-14 dates demonstrated was that the guesses had not been bold enough.

Thus the first carbon-14 revolution did not seriously challenge the relationships that had previously been established in terms of relative chronology between the different areas of Europe and the Near East. Even with respect to the crucial period after 3000 B.C., for which the Egyptian historical chronology provided a framework of absolute rather than relative dating, the new dates seemed to harmonize fairly well with the traditional ones. Just three troublesome problems hinted that all was not yet well. First, whereas many of the early carbon-14 dates for the megalithic tombs in western Europe fell around 2500 B.C., which fitted in with Childe's traditional chronology, the dates in France were somewhat earlier. In Brittany, for example, the dates of several corbeled tombs were earlier than 3000 B.C. This did not agree with the established picture of megalithic tombs diffusing from Spain to France sometime after 2500 B.C. Most scholars simply assumed that the French laboratories producing these dates were no better than they ought to be, and that the anomaly would probably disappear when more dates were available.

Second, the dates for the Balkan Neolithic were far too early. Sites related to the Vinča culture gave carbon-14 readings as early as 4000 B.C. This implied that not only copper metallurgy but also the attractive little sculptures of the Balkans were more than a millennium older than their supposed Aegean prototypes. Clearly something was wrong. Some archaeologists, led by Vladimir Milojčić, argued that the entire carbon-14 method was in error. Others felt that some special factor was making the Balkan dates too early, since the dates in other regions, with the exception of Brittany, seemed to be in harmony with the historical dates for the third millennium B.C.

Third, the dates for Egypt were too late. In retrospect this now seems highly significant. Egyptian objects historically dated to the period between 3000 and 2000 B.C. consistently yielded carbon-14 dates that placed them several centuries later. With the early inaccuracies and uncertainties of the carbon-14 method these divergences could at first be dismissed as random errors, but as more dates accumulated such an excuse was no longer possible. The archaeologists kept on using their historical dates and did not bother too much about the problems raised by the new method.

The physicists were more concerned, but they supposed, to use Libby's words, "that the Egyptian historical dates beyond 4000 years ago may be somewhat too old, perhaps five centuries too old at 5000 years ago, with decrease in error to [zero] at 4000 years ago.... It is noteworthy that the earliest astronomical fix is at 4000 years ago, that all older dates have errors and that these errors are more or less cumulative with time before 4000 years ago." For once, however, the archaeologists were right. The discrepancy was to be set at the door of the physicist rather than the Egyptologist. The consequences were dramatic.

Remote as it may seem from European archaeology, it was the venerable pine trees in the White Mountains of

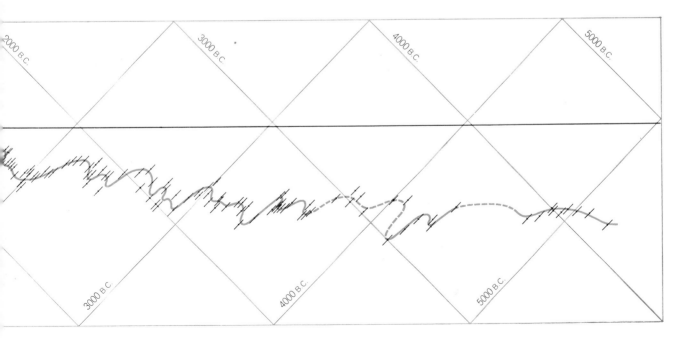

ored curve, which follows many individual measurements, shows how the carbon-14 dates go off with time. To calibrate a carbon-14 date, say 2000 B.C., one follows the line for that date until it meets the colored curve. At that point a diagonal is drawn parallel to the bristlecone-pine lines and the date is read off on the bristlecone-pine scale. The corrected date would be about 2500 B.C.

YEARS B.C. | EGYPT | AEGEAN | BALKANS | ITALY | MALTA

YEARS B.C.	EGYPT	AEGEAN	BALKANS	ITALY	MALTA
1500 —	DYNASTY XVIII	MYCENAE			TARXIEN CEME
		MIDDLE BRONZE AGE	FÜZESABONY	POLADA	
2000 —		EARLY BRONZE AGE			
			NAGYREV		
2500 —	PYRAMIDS	LERNA III			TARXIEN
3000 —	DYNASTY I	TROY I		REMEDELLO	
		EARLY HELLADIC I			GGANTIJA
3500 —	GERZEAN	FINAL NEOLITHIC	LATE GUMELNITSA	LAGOZZA	ZEBBUG
4000 —		LATE NEOLITHIC		CHIOZZA	
4500 —	AMRATIAN		LATE VINČA		RED SKORB.
		EARLY VINČA			

REVISED CHRONOLOGY, taking the Suess calibration into account, destroys the basis for the diffusionist theory of European prehistory. Colored area at left marks the portion of Egyptian and Aegean chronology that is related to historical records. Colored

California that brought about the revolution in Old World prehistory. These trees have provided a reliable check of the carbon-14 method and have produced significant modifications. By 1960 one major assumption of the method was already coming into question. This was that the rate of production of carbon 14 in the atmosphere, and hence its proportion in all living things, had been constant over the past 40,000 years. The assumption was first really checked when Eric H. Willis, Henrik Tauber and Karl Otto Münnich analyzed samples of wood from the stump of a giant sequoia that could be dated exactly by counting its annual growth rings. Although the carbon-14 dates and the tree-ring dates agreed to within 100 years all the way back to A.D. 650, some minor but real fluctuations were observed. This suggested that there had been definite small changes in the rate of carbon-14 production in the past.

It was obviously desirable to check back to even earlier periods. Fortunately the fantastically long life of the California bristlecone pine (*Pinus aristata*) was known to the late Edmund Schulman of the Laboratory of Tree-Ring Research at the University of Arizona. Bristlecone pines as old as 4,600 years had been authenticated. Since Schulman's death the study of the trees has been energetically pursued by Charles Wesley Ferguson of the same laboratory. With ring sequences from many bristlecones, Ferguson has succeeded in building up a continuous absolute chronology

reaching back nearly 8,200 years. The compilation of such a chronology, with due provision for multiple growth rings and missing rings, is a formidable task. Ferguson and his colleagues have developed computer programs for the comparison and matching of the ring sequence of different trees. This admirably systematic work has been the indispensable foundation of the second carbon-14 revolution.

Ferguson supplied wood samples whose absolute age had been determined by ring-counting to three independent carbon-14 laboratories: one at the University of Arizona, one at the University of Pennsylvania and one at the University of California at San Diego. The carbon-14 determinations, which in general agree fairly well with one another, reveal major discrepancies between previously accepted carbon-14 dates and actual dates. At San Diego, Hans E. Suess has analyzed more than 300 such samples and has built up an impressively clear and coherent picture of these discrepancies.

The divergence between the carbon-14 and tree-ring dates is not serious after 1500 B.C. Before that time the difference becomes progressively larger and amounts to as much as 700 years by 2500 B.C. The carbon-14 dates are all too young, but Suess's analysis can be used to correct them [see illustration on preceding two pages].

One problem that has emerged is that, in addition to a large first-order divergence, Suess's calibration curve shows

smaller second-order fluctuations or "kinks." Sometimes the rate of carbon-14 production has fluctuated so rapidly that samples of different ages show an identical concentration of carbon 14 in spite of the fact that the older sample allowed more time for radioactive decay. This means that a given carbon-14 date can very well correspond to several different calendar dates.

The reasons for the fluctuations are not yet known with certainty, but the Czechoslovakian geophysicist V. Bucha has shown that there is a striking correlation between the divergence in dates and past changes in the strength of the earth's magnetic field. The first-order variation is probably due to the fact that as the strength of the earth's field changed it deflected more or fewer cosmic rays before they could enter the atmosphere. There are strong indications that the second-order fluctuations are correlated with the level of solar activity. Both the low-energy particles of the "solar wind" and the high-energy particles that are the solar component of the cosmic radiation may affect the cosmic ray flux in the vicinity of the earth. Climatic changes may also have influenced the concentration of carbon 14 in the atmosphere.

To the archaeologist, however, the reliability of the tree-ring calibration is more important than its physical basis. Libby's principle of simultaneity, which states that the atmospheric level of carbon 14 at a given time is uniform all

IBERIA	FRANCE	BRITISH ISLES	NORTH EUROPE
EL ARGAR		MIDDLE BRONZE AGE	BRONZE HORIZON III
	EARLY BRONZE AGE	STONEHENGE III	HORIZON II
			HORIZON I
BEAKER	BEAKER		
	SEINE-OISE-MARNE CULTURE	STONEHENGE I	MIDDLE NEOLITHIC (PASSAGE GRAVES)
OS MILLARES		NEW GRANGE	
ALMERIAN	LATE PASSAGE GRAVE	NEOLITHIC	TRICHTERBECKER "A"
RLY ALMERIAN			ERTEBØLLE
	EARLY CHASSEY	EARLY NEOLITHIC	

area at right indicates periods when megalithic monuments were built in the European areas named. Lines and names in color show "connections" now proved to be impossible.

over the world, has been in large measure substantiated. Tests of nuclear weapons have shown that atmospheric mixing is rapid and that irregularities in composition are smoothed out after a few years. The California calibration should therefore hold for Europe. There is no need to assume that tree growth or tree rings are similar on the two continents, only that the atmospheric level of carbon 14 is the same at a given time.

There remains the question of whether some special factor in the bristlecone pine itself might be causing the discrepancies. For example, the diffusion of recent sap across the old tree rings and its retention in them might affect the reading if the sap were not removed by laboratory cleaning procedures. Studies are now in progress to determine if this is a significant factor; present indications are that it is not. Even if it is, it would be difficult to see why the discrepancy between carbon-14 dates and calendar dates should be large only before 1500 B.C.

The general opinion, as reflected in the discussions at the Twelfth Nobel Symposium at Uppsala in 1969, is that the discrepancy is real. Suess's calibration curve is the best now available, although corrections and modifications can be expected. It is particularly satisfying that when the carbon-14 dates for Egypt are calibrated, they agree far better with the Egyptian historical calendar. Further work is now in progress at the University of California at Los Angeles and at the British Museum on

Egyptian samples specially collected for the project, so that a further check of the extent to which the calibrated carbon-14 dates and the historical chronology are in harmony will soon be available.

The revision of carbon-14 dates for prehistoric Europe has a disastrous effect on the traditional diffusionist chronology. The significant point is not so much that the European dates in the third millennium are all several centuries earlier than was supposed but that the dates for Egypt do not change. Prehistorians have always used the historical dates for Egypt because they seemed more accurate than the carbon-14 dates. They have been proved correct; the calibrated carbon-14 dates for Egypt agree far better with the historical chronology than the uncalibrated ones did. Hence the Egyptian historical calendar, and with it the conventional Egyptian chronology, remains unchanged. The same is true for the Near East in general and for Crete and the southern Aegean. The carbon-14 dates for the Aegean formerly seemed too young; they too agree better after calibration.

For the rest of Europe this is not true. Over the past decade prehistorians in Europe have increasingly been using carbon-14 dates to build up a chronology of the third millennium B.C. Except in Brittany and the Balkans, this chronology had seemed to work fairly well. The dates had still allowed the megalithic tombs of Spain to have been built around 2500 B.C. There was no direct contradiction between the diffusionist

picture and the uncalibrated carbon-14 chronology.

All that is now changed. A carbon-14 date of about 2350 B.C. for the walls and tombs at Los Millares in Spain must now be set around 2900 B.C. This makes the structures older than their supposed prototypes in the Aegean. Whereas the carbon-14 inconsistency in western Europe was formerly limited to Brittany, it now applies to the entire area. In almost every region where megalithic tombs are found the calibrated carbon-14 dates substantially predate 2500 B.C. The view of megalithic culture as an import from the Near East no longer works.

The same thing seems to be happening in Malta, although there are still too few carbon-14 dates to be certain. A date of 1930 B.C. for the period *after* the temples now becomes about 2200 B.C. Clearly the spirals in the temples cannot be the result of Aegean influence around 1800 B.C.

The Balkans are affected too. The figurines of the Vinča culture now have dates earlier than 4500 B.C.; to associate them with the Aegean of the third millennium becomes ludicrous. The revision of dates also shows that in the Balkans there was a flourishing tradition of copper metallurgy, including such useful artifacts as tools with shaft holes, before metal production was well under way in the Aegean.

Similar changes are seen all over Europe. Stonehenge was until recently considered by many to be the work of skilled craftsmen or architects who had come to Britain from Mycenaean Greece around 1500 B.C. The monument is now seen to be several centuries older, and Mycenaean influence is clearly out of the question.

All is not confusion, however. As we have seen, the chronology of Egypt, the Near East, Crete and the Aegean is not materially changed in the third millennium B.C. Although the actual dates are altered in the rest of Europe, when we compare areas dated solely by carbon 14 the relationships between them are not changed. The great hiatus comes when we compare areas that have calibrated carbon-14 dates with areas that are dated by historical means. The hiatus may be likened to a geological fault; the chronological "fault line" extends across the Mediterranean and southern Europe.

On each side of the fault line the relationships and the successions of cultures remain unaltered. The two sides have shifted, however, *en bloc* in relation to each other, as the geological stra-

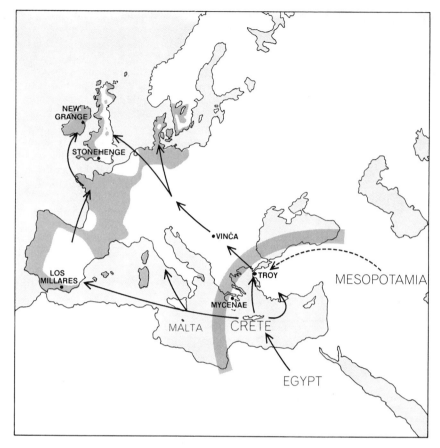

CHRONOLOGICAL "FAULT LINE" (*curved bar*) **divides all Europe except the Aegean from the Near East. Arrows above the fault line are supposed chronological links now discredited. Areas of Europe that contain megalithic chamber tombs are in color at left.**

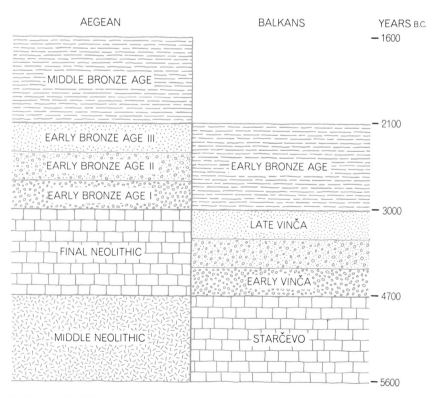

FAULT-LINE SLIPPAGE is shown schematically as it affects the chronological connection between the barbarian Balkans and the civilized Aegean. Strata with the same markings were once thought to be contemporary. Estimated Balkan dates, however, were too recent.

ta on two sides of a fault might. As a result much of what Montelius and Childe wrote about relationships and relative chronologies within continental Europe still stands. It is only the absolute chronology in calendar years and certain key links—between Spain and the Aegean and between the Balkans and the Aegean—that are ruptured. The dates for Europe as a whole have moved back in time, and the old diffusionist view of links connecting Europe and the Near East is no longer tenable.

The really important effect of tree-ring calibration is not that it changes the dates for prehistoric Europe by a few centuries. What matters is that it transforms our picture of what happened in prehistoric Europe and of how Europe developed. No longer can the essential theme of European prehistory be Childe's "irradiation of European barbarism by Oriental civilization." Indeed, the very early dates for some of the achievements of the prehistoric inhabitants of Europe make the term barbarism quite inappropriate.

Now it is clear that megalithic chamber tombs were being built in Brittany earlier than 4000 B.C., a millennium before monumental funerary architecture first appears in the eastern Mediterranean and 1,500 years before the raising of the pyramids. The origins of these European burial customs and monuments have to be sought not in the Near East but in Europe itself. The temples of Malta must likewise be viewed as remarkable, indeed unique, local creations: the oldest freestanding stone monuments in the world.

Even metallurgy may have been independently invented in the Balkans, and possibly in Spain as well. Certainly it was flourishing in the Balkans earlier than it was in Greece. The possibility remains, however, that the art of metalworking was learned from the Near East, where it was known even earlier than in the Balkans.

The central moral is inescapable. In the past we have completely undervalued the originality and the creativity of the inhabitants of prehistoric Europe. It was a mistake, as we now can see, always to seek in the Near East an explanation for the changes taking place in Europe. Diffusion has been overplayed. Of course, contact between prehistoric cultures often allowed ideas and innovations to pass between them. Furthermore, evidence might easily emerge for occasional contacts between western or southern Europe and the Near East in very early times. This, however, is not an adequate model for the explanation of culture change. Nor is there any case for turning the tables on the old diffusionists by suggesting that the early monuments and innovations in Europe inspired the pyramids of Egypt or other achievements in the Near East. That would merely be to reverse the arrows on the diffusionist map, and to miss the real lesson of the new dating.

The initial impact of the carbon-14 revolution will be to lead archaeologists to revise their dates for prehistoric Europe. This is the basic factual contribution that the tree-ring calibration has to make, although inevitably it will be some years before we can develop a definitive and reliable calibrated chronology for the entire area. The more profound impact, however, will be on the kind of explanation that prehistorians will accept in elucidating cultural change. A greater reluctance to swallow "influences" or "contacts" as sufficient explanations in themselves, without a much more detailed analysis of the actual mechanisms involved, is to be expected. This is in keeping with much current archaeological thinking. Today social and economic processes are increasingly seen as more important subjects for study than the similarities among artifacts.

When the textbooks are rewritten, as they will have to be, it is not only the European dates that will be altered. A shift in the basic nature of archaeological reasoning is necessary. Indeed, it is already taking place in Europe and in other parts of the world. This is the key change that tree-ring calibration, however uncertain some of its details remain, has helped to bring about.

ANCIENT PINE, its trunk scarred and its branches twisted, is one of the many trees of the bristlecone species (*Pinus aristata*) that grow in the White Mountains of California. An analysis of this tree's growth rings proves it to be more than 4,500 years old. Using this and other specimens, Charles Wesley Ferguson and his co-workers at the University of Arizona have built up a continuous tree-ring chronology with a span of more than 8,000 years.

27 The Tartaria Tablets

by M. S. F. Hood
May 1968

Three inscribed tablets found in Romania may be 1,000 years older than the oldest examples of writing from Mesopotamia. They are probably not that old, but they do illuminate the contacts between ancient cultures

The earliest known writing appears on clay tablets uncovered at Uruk, a Sumerian city that flourished in Mesopotamia during that region's early Bronze Age. The tablets are known to be a little more than 5,000 years old. Prehistorians were surprised, therefore, when what appears to be much earlier writing was found a few years ago in the ruins of a Neolithic village in the Balkans. The Neolithic find, consisting of three small clay tablets, was made at Tartaria in the Transylvanian region of Romania. On the widely accepted basis of carbon-14 dating, the Tartaria tablets could be more than 1,000 years older than the oldest Sumerian ones. This was not the only surprise at Tartaria. Some of the signs incised on the Tartaria tablets proved to be almost identical with Sumerian ones of the period around 3000 B.C. The Tartaria tablets also looked much like the written records produced in Crete around 2000 B.C., when the ear-liest archives uncovered at Knossos were established. The Tartaria discovery obviously raises a number of puzzling questions.

The least troublesome questions concern the distance between the Balkans on the one hand and Crete and Mesopotamia on the other. It is now established beyond doubt that in Neolithic times the Near East and other areas around the Mediterranean were criss-crossed by trade routes over which the volcanic glass obsidian, for example, was carried hundreds of miles from mine to toolmaker [see the article "Obsidian and the Origins of Trade," by J. E. Dixon, J. R. Cann and Colin Renfrew, beginning on page 108]. Other materials may have moved over these routes, and written records could easily have been among them.

The questions that arise because of the differences in age between Neolithic Tartaria, early Bronze Age Sumer and late Bronze Age Crete are much more troublesome. Are the Tartaria tablets in fact older than the earliest writing at Uruk? Could writing have first been invented in Neolithic Europe? Was this key element in civilization disseminated from Europe to the Near East, in contradistinction to the usually accepted view that the movement was in the opposite direction? Assuming that such was the case, how can one account for the arrival of writing in distant Mesopotamia perhaps 1,000 years before archives first appear in comparatively nearby Crete? These are only a few of the questions one might ask.

I hope to show that reasonably satisfactory answers can be given to most of such questions, if not all of them. First, however, the reader will need to be acquainted with the Tartaria site and its

SUMERIAN WRITING of the period around 3000 B.C. covers a clay tablet found at Jemdet Nasr in Mesopotamia. Several parallels exist between Sumerian writing and the inscriptions on tablets found at Tartaria in Romania (*see illustration on opposite page*). The Tartaria site belongs to the Neolithic period and thus the tablets have been thought to be older than the earliest Sumerian writing. The Jemdet Nasr tablet is reproduced by permission of the Keeper of the Department of Antiquities, Ashmolean Museum, University of Oxford.

contents, and with some facts about Balkan archaeology and about early writing in general. Tartaria is a town some 70 miles south of the city of Cluj; it lies on the Maros River near a part of Transylvania that was famous in classical times for its rich gold deposits. The Tartaria site is a mound some 250 yards long and 100 yards wide. It was first excavated in 1942 and 1943 but the war forced a halt; digging began again, under the direction of N. Vlassa of the Cluj Institute of History and Archaeology, only in 1961.

The main reason for excavating the Tartaria mound was that it was an undisturbed site and might provide a much-needed key to a more famous Neolithic site nearby: the mound at Tordos. This was one of the first Neolithic sites to be studied in Europe; excavations had been made there off and on since 1874. The most recent excavation had been undertaken in 1910. Soon afterward a nearby stream shifted its course and washed away most of the mound. Not all the digging had been up to modern standards, and it was hoped that a clear stratigraphic record from Tartaria would enable prehistorians to put the large number of artifacts from Tordos in their proper chronological sequence.

The culture represented at both Tordos and Tartaria is called Vinca after a major Neolithic village site in Yugoslavia, 120 miles southwest of the two mounds in Romania. The Vinca people were farmers who built simple huts with a framework of wooden posts and walls woven from thin branches and daubed with clay. When such a dwelling fell into disrepair or was destroyed, the villagers built a new hut on top of the leveled wreckage of the old one. Settlement mounds thus rose in the Balkans in the same way as did the *hüyüks* of Asia Minor and the *tepes* and *tells* of the Near East. The mound at Vinca is more than 30 feet high and has many successive building levels. The Tartaria mound is only six feet high but four periods of occupation can be distinguished.

The Vinca culture evidently lasted a long time, perhaps for 1,000 years or more. It is traditionally classified as a Neolithic culture, that is to say, a culture in which metal and its uses were unknown. In actuality two main phases of the culture can be distinguished, and throughout the later phase the Vinca farmers possessed axes and other tools made of copper, as well as axes and adzes made of polished stone and knives and arrowheads made of chipped flint and obsidian. Traces of copper have also been found in strata belonging to the

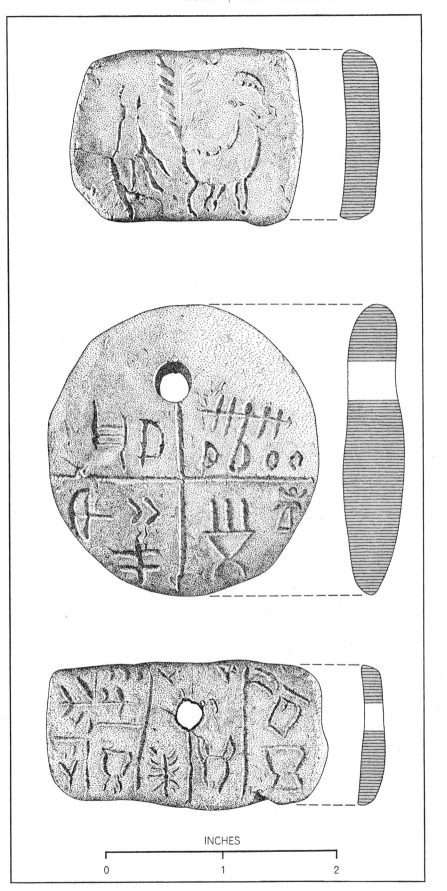

INCHES

0   1   2

THREE INSCRIBED TABLETS, found at the bottom of an ash-filled pit at Tartaria, are reproduced slightly larger than actual size. The tablets are marked on one face only. Many of the marks resemble the signs used for numerals and for syllables in Sumerian writing.

earlier phase of the Vinca culture; these traces are thought to be the remains of imported metal ornaments rather than objects made locally.

Of the upper three occupation levels at Tartaria, the lower two belong to the later phase of the Vinca culture and the uppermost to a still later period. The lowest level at the site belongs to the earlier Vinca phase. Vlassa and his co-workers discovered that a pit had been dug down below the lowest level, apparently during the time when that level was occupied. The pit was filled with ashes. In a small heap at its bottom the diggers found 26 clay figurines, two stone figurines, a seashell bracelet and the three inscribed tablets. Nearby were the disjointed and scorched bones of an adult human. The pit had evidently been used for a ritual, perhaps a sacrifice involving some form of cannibalism, and the tablets may owe their preservation to their having been baked in the same

fire that scorched the bones and filled the pit with ashes.

The Tartaria tablets are small. Two of them are rectangular; they are respectively two inches and two and a half inches across, an inch high and a quarter of an inch thick. The third tablet is a roundel, or disk; it is two and a quarter inches in diameter and is thicker than the other tablets [see illustration on preceding page]. The tablets are inscribed on only one face. The roundel and the larger of the rectangles have a hole in them through which a string may have been passed; they are also incised with signs that appear to be more than simple pictographs. The third tablet seems to be exclusively pictographic; at its right side is the figure of a goat, in the middle what may be the branch of a tree or an ear of grain, and at the left another animal, perhaps a second goat.

Most of the signs on the roundel resemble symbols the early Sumerians

incised in clay to record numerals or syllables. Their closest Sumerian counterparts are signs written during a period around 3000 B.C. This fact was noted by Vlassa at the time the tablets were discovered and was subsequently confirmed by the late Adam Falkenstein of the University of Heidelberg, the principal student of the written records of Uruk. Tablets that bear writing of this period, known as the Jemdet Nasr phase, have been unearthed both at the city of Uruk and at the lesser site of Jemdet Nasr itself. Among the more striking resemblances are the following.

To write the number 10 the Sumerians at that time held a round stick upright and pressed its end straight into the clay, making a circular mark. They represented two other numbers by pressing the end of the stick into the clay at an angle, making a semicircular mark: a small semicircle represented the number one, a large semicircle the number 60.

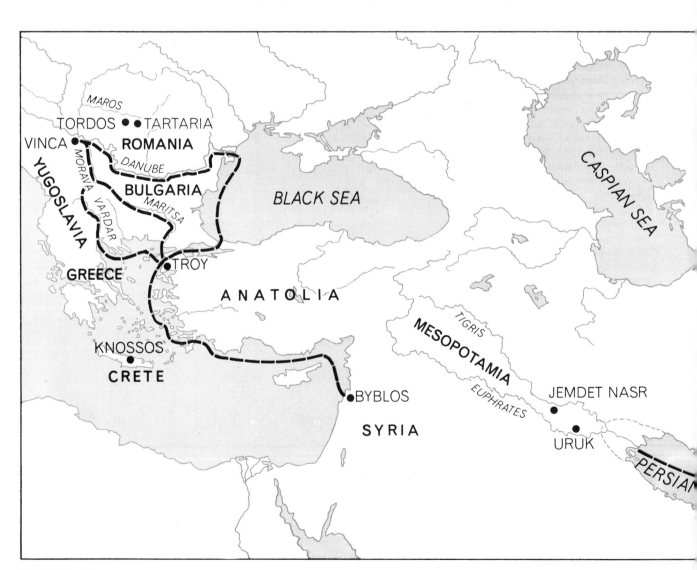

ANCIENT WORLD, from the Indus to the Danube, may have been familiar to the merchant voyagers of the Near East. In the latter

half of the third millennium B.C. the Mesopotamian monarch Sargon of Akkad conquered Syria and also raided into eastern Anatolia. In

The Tartaria roundel is incised with similar circles and semicircles in two sizes, rendered in outline rather than punched into the clay.

To denote the syllables *En-Gi*, the name of a god, the Sumerians linked one sign, a long line crossed by a number of short dashes, with another, a grid with several parallel bars. A sign resembling each of the Sumerian ones appears on the Tartaria roundel, although they are incised separately rather than together. Perhaps the most striking resemblance is a candelabrum-shaped sign in the lower right quadrant of the roundel. A sign just like it is very common on the tablets from Jemdet Nasr. A number of other parallels between the Jemdet Nasr and the Tartaria signs can be noted [see *bottom illustration on page 269*].

The parallels are not limited to signs alone. For example, the Sumerians incised their tablets with horizontal and vertical lines to separate one group of signs from another. There are similar dividing lines on the Tartaria roundel and the larger rectangle. In addition, on the Sumerian tablets a single word sign or a pair of signs is regularly found within a marked-off space along with signs that represent numbers. Two of the four divisions of the Tartaria roundel contain similar combinations. Finally, the Sumerians usually wrote on rectangular tablets.

There are differences as well as parallels. Rectangular Sumerian tablets with holes in them have been found, but they are extremely rare. Moreover, although most of the Tartaria signs are comparable to Sumerian signs, and some are strikingly comparable, they are by no means always identical with them.

Some of the differences between the Tartaria tablets and early Sumerian writing are points of resemblance with respect to the early written records of Crete. The earliest known Cretan tablets, including rectangles and roundels, often have string holes [see *top illustration on page 269*]. At least four signs on the Tartaria tablets resemble signs on the tablets found in the 1900's by Sir Arthur Evans in the part of the palace at Knossos that he named the Hieroglyphic Deposit. Since then similar tablets have been found in the ruins of the palace at Phaistos in southern Crete and at Mallia, east of Knossos.

There are also differences between the Tartaria tablets and those of Crete. A few of the earliest Cretan tablets, for instance, have lines that mark off groups of signs, but the practice was evidently becoming obsolete and most tablets have no lines. Every Tartaria sign that has a Cretan equivalent also has a Sumerian one, but some signs with Sumerian equivalents have no Cretan counterparts.

The Jemdet Nasr phase of Sumerian history is dated around 3000 B.C. In Crete, where the earliest evidence of writing is in the form of stone seals engraved with signs and of clay impressions made with seals, no sign-bearing seal is yet known that can be dated more than a century or so before 2000 B.C. The oldest written tablets discovered so far do not appear until later; the tablets in the Hieroglyphic Deposit at Knossos, for example, may not have been made until 1700 B.C. The early forms of Sumerian and Cretan writing may therefore have been separated in time by as much as 1,300 years. They have a minimum separation of some 900 years.

A number of carbon-14 dates from Neolithic sites in the Balkans indicate that the Vinca culture rose well before 4000 B.C. and perhaps even before 5000. This means that the Tartaria tablets could be a good deal more than 1,000 years older than their Sumerian counterparts and more than 2,000 years older than the Cretan ones. Is it possible somehow to bring these dates into line?

One way to do so is to deny that the Tartaria tablets are from the earlier phase of the Vinca culture. One might suggest that the pit where they were found had been dug down not from the lowest level of the Tartaria mound but from somewhere higher up. The pit's contents could then be given a considerably later date. But the excavation was a careful one, and Vlassa certainly got the impression that the pit had been dug down from the mound's lowest level. Vlassa's position is independently supported by the opinion of most experts that the figurines found in the pit are characteristic of the earlier phase of the

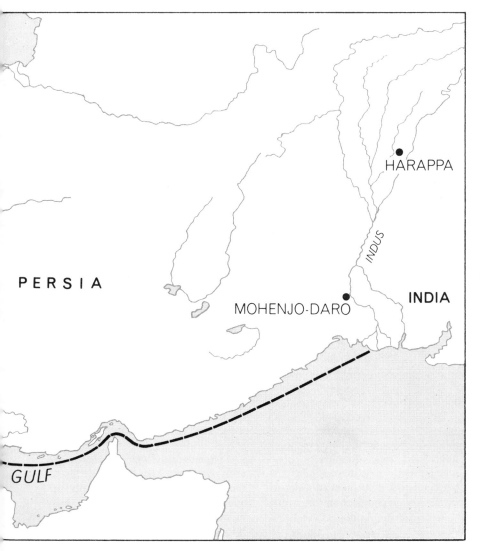

his successors' day traders visited the Indus delta (*right*). The author suggests that Syrian traders may have traveled beyond Troy to the middle Danube (*left*) in even earlier times.

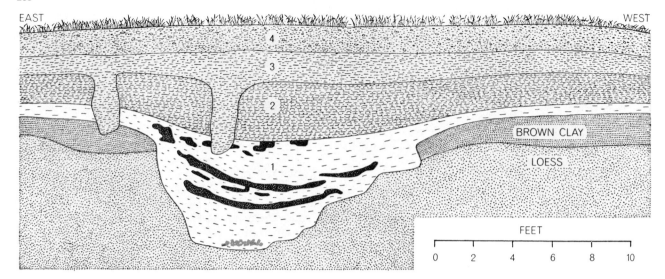

EAST   WEST

4

3

2

BROWN CLAY

LOESS

1

FEET

0   2   4   6   8   10

TARTARIA MOUND is seen in cross section. The three upper strata represent the later phase of the Vinca culture and a period thereafter. Two small pits had been dug down from the surface of the third level. The lowest stratum belongs to the earlier Vinca phase; here a large pit had been dug down into the underlying loess. It contained the tablets, human bones and other remains.

Vinca culture and not of the later phase, although this view is not held unanimously.

If we accept the Tartaria tablets as being from an authentically early period, what other ways are there to explain the puzzle? One would be to deny that the tablets had any real connection with early Sumerian writing, but the resemblances are so strong that such an argument is difficult to accept. Another way would be to challenge the validity of the carbon-14 dates obtained from Neolithic sites in the Balkans. This does not, of course, mean doubting the scientific principles of carbon-14 dating. The many carbon-14 dates for Neolithic cultures in central and eastern Europe are reasonably consistent and also in good agreement with the sequence of relative chronology suggested independently by archaeological correlations. There may nonetheless be room for thinking that the entire sequence of carbon-14 dates obtained for Neolithic Europe north of the Mediterranean is both too early and too long.

It has been suggested that carbon-14 dates may vary slightly in relation to latitude. Perhaps the variations due to latitude were greater in the Neolithic period than is now supposed. Perhaps factors of climate, or other factors that are not yet understood, have drastically influenced the carbon-14 dates for certain areas during early periods. Whatever the truth of the matter, once it is agreed that the Tartaria tablets' connection with Sumerian writing is authentic, and that they were written during the earlier phase of the Vinca culture, I find one conclusion inescapable. This is that the Vinca culture must have arisen some

1,500 years later than its carbon-14 dates suggest, that is, later than 3000 B.C.

One way to escape even this conclusion is to propose that the art of writing originated in the Balkans. But the origin of writing in Sumer can be traced with considerable precision from pictographic beginnings just before the Jemdet Nasr phase through the comparatively advanced writing of Jemdet Nasr—part ideographic and part phonetic—to the cuneiform of later Sumerian times. In contrast, the Tartaria tablets are a unique phenomenon in Balkan prehistory. They appear for an instant in time, boldly outlined against a barbaric background, and are succeeded by long ages of continuing barbarism that harbor no further suggestion of an acquaintance with writing. It seems impossible that the Balkan Neolithic was the milieu in which man first achieved literacy.

Let us assume, then, that the carbon-14 record is sufficiently wrong to allow setting the date of the Tartaria tablets at some time after 3000 B.C. It still remains to be shown how Sumerian writing of that period could have reached the wilds of eastern Europe. To consider the journey one step at a time, one can start by seeking an explanation for the similarity between Sumerian writing and the early archival writing of Crete.

Syria and Lebanon are clearly potential intermediaries between Sumer and Crete. At Byblos, Lebanon's ancient seaport, the large clay jars that were used for burials in the period that precedes the Jemdet Nasr phase in Sumer are stamped with groups of signs. The signs have been interpreted as a rudimentary form of writing at the pictographic stage,

the same stage that had then been reached by the Sumerians. If the signs stamped on the Byblos jars represent writing, it is plausible to suppose that the idea had come from Mesopotamia.

No formal writing of the kind indicated by collections of tablets is known in Syria before about 2000 B.C. Long before that, however, Syrians scratched marks on their pottery, apparently so that the owners could tell which pots were theirs. The practice is first evident in Syria at the time of the Jemdet Nasr phase in Sumer, when writing had become comparatively advanced. The Syrian owners' marks are not true writing, but they may reflect some acquaintance with the art. Certainly Syria and Mesopotamia had close relations during this period: cylinder seals of the Jemdet Nasr type, as well as the impressions made by them, are found in Syrian sites. It is conceivable that, in addition to owners' marks, Syrians at this time had a system of writing inspired by the Sumerian example and using many of the same signs.

The Jemdet Nasr phase was the last in which the Sumerians wrote on their tablets by scratching signs in the soft clay. In the Early Dynastic period that followed all tablets are written in cuneiform, a system that uses a special, wedge-shaped implement to mark the clay. If, as I suggest, a system of writing in the Jemdet Nasr style was then known in Syria, it could have continued in use there for some time after cuneiform was adopted in Mesopotamia. Such a development could have enabled Syria to transmit a system of writing with incised signs to Crete even a long time after incised writing had vanished from its original home. Such a hypothesis helps to solve one of our dating difficulties; it means that neither the early writing of Crete nor the Tartaria tablets need to be contemporaneous with the Jemdet Nasr phase in Mesopotamia.

Looking at the other end of the line for connections that would tie the Balkans to the Mediterranean, we readily find a geographic one. Only a short distance from Vinca down the Danube the main stream is joined by the north-flowing Morava River. Traveling southward along the valley of the Morava one crosses easily into the valley of the south-flowing Vardar River and can follow that route to the shores of the Aegean Sea. Exotic elements in the Vinca culture reflect this propinquity. It has even been suggested that the Vinca people, or at least some of them, came to the Danube from Macedonia and before that from Asia Minor beyond the Dardanelles. This is open to question, but in some respects the Vinca culture certainly resembles a simplified and barbarized form of Macedonian culture, which in turn is a simplified version of the early cultures of Troy in Asia Minor.

Many of the vases made by Vinca potters have shapes that are basically akin to Trojan ones. Pots with dark, polished surfaces, often decorated with incisions filled with a white paste, are common both in the first settlement at Troy and in the earlier phase of the Vinca culture. Vinca wares also show affinities with later pottery at Troy. In particular, pot lids strikingly decorated with representations of the human face are found in the lowest level and above at Vinca. They are not unlike the face-decorated pot lids found at Troy in the second settlement (Troy II) and later.

Even more compelling evidence of influences from Asia Minor in the Vinca culture is found in the numerous signs the Vinca people scratched on their pots, presumably as owners' marks. There are comparable marks—in many cases identical ones—on Trojan pots and spindle whorls dating from the period of Troy II and later. During this period similar marks appear in other parts of western Asia Minor, scratched or painted on pots. Within the area of the Vinca culture, owners' marks are particularly abundant at Tordos; the signs were usually incised on the bottom of a pot or low on the side before firing. Most Tordos pots that carry such marks have only one, but some have two or more.

Several of the marks used by both Trojan and Vinca potters are identical with signs that appear in the earliest Sumerian writing. Because the signs are

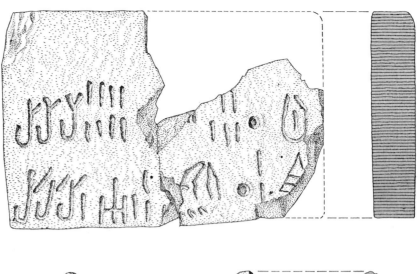

CRETAN WRITING that appears on the tablets found in the ruins at Knossos includes a few signs that resemble inscriptions on the Tartaria tablets. Other points of resemblance include tablets rectangular in shape (*top*), circular in shape (*bottom*) and with string holes.

JEMDET NASR PHASE	KNOSSOS HIEROGLYPHIC DEPOSIT	TARTARIA TABLETS

PARALLELS are apparent between the signs used in Sumerian writing of about 3000 B.C. (*left*), those of Cretan writing 1,000 years later (*center*) and the marks incised on the Tartaria tablets (*right*). Here only the Tartaria inscriptions are shown at a common scale.

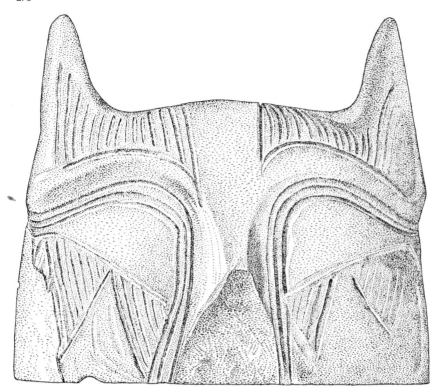

DECORATED POT LID from the lower levels of the Vinca mound, a Neolithic village site in Yugoslavia, shows a representation of a human face, a motif evidently derived from Asia.

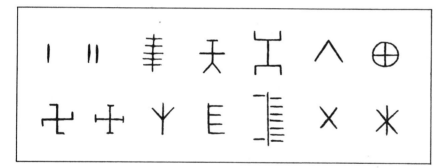

OWNERS' MARKS were placed on the sides or bottoms of pots by the potters of the Vinca culture. Pottery marked in this fashion is particularly abundant in the Tordos mound, a Neolithic site in the Transylvanian region of Romania only a few miles from Tartaria.

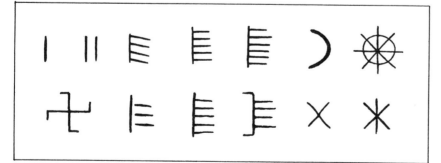

SIMILAR MARKS appear on the pottery and the spindle whorls unearthed from the second settlement and later levels at Troy, as well as elsewhere in western Asia Minor. The ones illustrated here are all from Troy II finds. Some are identical both with owners' marks of the Vinca culture and with signs that appear in early Sumerian writing. The author suggests that Trojan and Vincan marks, like the Tartaria ones, were brought from the Near East. This would mean that the Vinca culture is much younger than has generally been supposed.

simple ones, this coincidence has usually been explained away as an example of independent invention. In the light of the Tartaria discovery another interpretation suggests itself. Might not some of the signs, if not most of them, have been copied from the early writing of the Near East?

The traits that Troy and Vinca have in common imply that the Vinca culture could not have arisen much before the time of Troy II. Carbon-14 analysis of material from sites in western Asia Minor places Troy II some centuries after 2600 B.C., but the carbon-14 dates are not for Troy itself or for sites in the city's immediate neighborhood. On the basis of other criteria dates have been proposed for Troy II that range from 2600 to 2100 B.C. If one accepts a date of 2300 to 2200 B.C. for the start of Troy II, the Tartaria tablets need not have been made until as late as the turn of the second millennium B.C. Such a date would make the tablets not much older than the comparable tablets in Crete.

It is not hard to imagine how Trojan owners' marks could have reached the potters of Tordos. But how were the Trojan potters able to borrow the signs from Mesopotamia in the first place? Again Syria seems a probable intermediary. The people of Troy II evidently had many contacts with Cilicia, the southeastern coastal region of Asia Minor that borders Syria on the west. Cilician vase shapes were copied at Troy, and the "fast" potter's wheel, which was first used at Troy early in the Troy II period, may have been an import from Cilicia. The arrival of Mesopotamian influences in the Balkans by way of Syria, Cilicia and Troy is therefore far from impossible. Syrian and Cilician merchants may actually have had direct commercial contacts with the Balkans as early as the time of Troy II. When copper and bronze tools, weapons and ornaments came into general use in the Balkans, they were largely Syrian (ultimately Mesopotamian) types. The reader will recall that copper tools were present during the later phase of the Vinca culture and that traces of imported copper also appear in earlier Vinca strata.

What could have drawn Near Eastern goods, and perhaps Near Eastern traders as well, to the Balkans? It may have been mineral riches. The treasures of gold and silver unearthed from the ruins of Troy II attest to the city's wealth. Much of the Trojan jewelry is comparable in design and craftsmanship to Syrian and Mesopotamian work; some of it resembles the jewelry found in the royal tombs of Ur in Mesopotamia. Whence came the gold for these Trojan treasures? Perhaps from western Asia Minor, where the "golden Pactolus" runs to the sea. Some, however, may have reached Troy from gold-rich Transylvania.

Gold is not the only metal that could have enticed merchants to the middle Danube and beyond. Deposits of cinnabar, the ore that yields mercury, are found near Vinca. Tin, important in bronze metallurgy, can be had in the Erz Mountains to the northwest in what is now Czechoslovakia. The journey from the Aegean to Vinca by way of the Vardar valley is not a difficult one. Traders from the south could also have sailed through the Dardanelles into the Black Sea and entered the Danube at its mouth. Still a third route is along the valley of the Maritsa River, through present-day Bulgaria.

Near Eastern merchants traveled great distances in those days, as is shown by the records of the dynasty founded by Sargon of Akkad soon after 2400 B.C. Sargon himself conquered Syria and appears to have campaigned far into eastern Asia Minor. In the opposite direction Akkadian merchants sailed the length of the Persian Gulf and beyond to trade with the remote civilization of the Indus valley. Romania is no farther, as the crow flies, from Mesopotamia than the Indus is. Even the distances of the two voyages—to Vinca from some port in Syria by way of the Danube, and to the Indus from the head of the Persian Gulf—are roughly comparable. In my opinion it is within the context of some such trade contact that the Tartaria tablets and their analogies with the early writing of Sumer and Crete can best be explained.

The ritual setting in which the Tartaria tablets were found provides a second possible context. It is just barely conceivable that magicians or priests of the Vinca culture were familiar with the art of writing, but even such familiarity is not necessary to the hypothesis. The culture's relatively elaborate ritual equipment seems to be of Near Eastern derivation. The furnishings include little three- and four-footed clay altars and an abundance of figurines such as the ones found at Tartaria. Both the altars and the figurines have analogies in the Aegean world to the south. A large ritual jar from an early level at Vinca is incised with a design that seems to represent the façade of a shrine; it is comparable to the shrine façades depicted

on Sumerian seals of the Jemdet Nasr period and later. One can imagine archaic Sumerian writing as a part of some religious complex that eventually reached the Balkans from the Near East.

There is even a kind of backward precedent for such an event. Twice in later history systems of writing reached this part of Europe in the train of an imported religion. The first time, in the fourth century A.D., a Gothic bishop, Ulfilas, invented an alphabet so that his barbarous tribesmen could read the Bible in their own language. The second time, in the ninth century A.D., two Greek missionaries, Cyril and Methodius, invented the alphabet that won the Slavs of Moravia and Bohemia to Christianity. It is not impossible that missionaries of an even older religion carried the

first example of writing to the Balkans thousands of years earlier.

But do the Tartaria tablets actually bear writing? Probably not. The tablets appear to be of local clay, which favors their having been made on the spot and not imported. The close resemblance of their signs to Sumerian ones, however, favors their having been copied from some other document available to the copyist on the spot. It seems quite possible that they are merely an uncomprehending imitation of more civilized peoples' written records. Certainly the language in which they are written, if it is one, is unknown. Perhaps the Tartaria tablets are nothing more than a pretense by some unlettered barbarian to command the magic embodied in an art he had witnessed but did not understand.

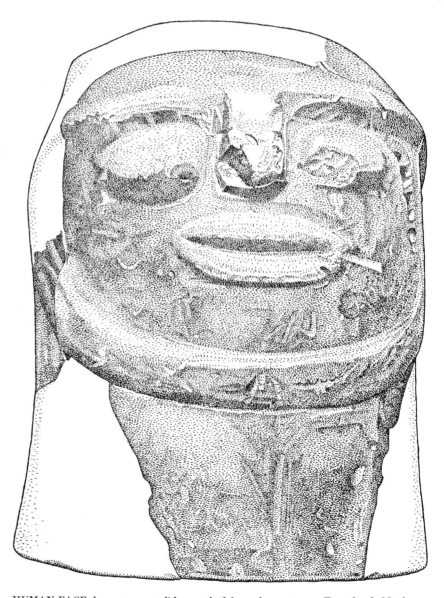

HUMAN FACE decorates a pot lid unearthed from the stratum at Troy that holds the remains of the city's second settlement. Other affinities between the pottery of the Vinca culture and of Troy include pots with similar shapes, polished surfaces and incised decorations.

28

Stonehenge

by Jacquetta Hawkes
June 1953

*The strange monument is often attributed to the
Druids of 2,000 years ago, but radiocarbon dating
supports the view that it was started by a savage but
aspiring people 2,000 years before that*

THE GREAT prehistoric sanctuary of Stonehenge stands among the sweeping curves of the chalk downland of Salisbury Plain. Not very many miles away on a more northern stretch of the Wiltshire downs is Avebury—another most remarkable though less famous stone circle. Around both Avebury and Stonehenge cluster vast numbers of burial mounds, many of them the graves of wealthy Bronze Age chieftains whose presence there is proof of the fame and sanctity of these circles in ancient times.

The architecture of Stonehenge is arresting in its strangeness. Nowhere in the world is there anything quite comparable to this temple, built not of masonry but of colossal rectangular blocks of stone. Plainly it is the handiwork of a people more barbaric than any of historic times, yet the careful shaping of the huge monoliths, the use of horizontal lintel stones, and above all the coherence of the whole as a work of architecture set it far above the usual megalithic building of prehistoric western Europe.

It is no wonder, then, that for the past thousand years Stonehenge has been so famous as to attract countless visitors and speculation of every kind. Among the many famous men who went there were Inigo Jones, Samuel Pepys, John Evelyn and William Wordsworth—indeed Wordsworth has enriched its literature with poetry of the first rank. James I knew it and was curious about its origin; Charles II, when he was sheltering at nearby Amesbury after the battle of Worcester, spent a day there counting and measuring the stones to pass the time and forget his anxieties.

Today more than ever Stonehenge attracts its visitors. Summer tourists go there in thousands, leaving buses and cars to buy tickets at a Ministry of Works kiosk and approaching this holy place of their forebears along a path flanked by neat waste-paper baskets. Even in these conditions, once inside the circle visitors surrender to the power of its stones. In spite of our familiarity with architecture on a vastly greater scale, there is something about these massive, weather-beaten monoliths which awes modern men with thoughts of a savage, primitive, yet mightily aspiring world.

We know that immediately after the Norman Conquest Stonehenge was rec-

HEEL STONE is seen from within the circles of Stonehenge. Sir Norman Lockyer tried to date the monument by computing that on Midsummer Day (June 24) in 1680 B.C. the sun rose directly over the Heel Stone.

ognized as one of the wonders of Britain. The fanciful 12th-century historian Geoffrey of Monmouth suggested that the stones had been fetched to Salisbury Plain from Ireland by the wizard Merlin in the days of Ambrosius, the uncle of King Arthur. Subsequently, he said, the circles were used as the burial place of Ambrosius and his brother, Uther Pendragon, Arthur's father.

This tale was believed all through medieval times and was repeated with variations by writers in Latin, French and English. By the 16th-century Renaissance scholarship was harshly and sometimes mockingly questioning Geoffrey of Monmouth and the whole glorious but improbable Arthurian legend. But the new scholars and antiquaries hardly knew whom to put in Merlin's place as the founder of Stonehenge. During the 16th, 17th and 18th centuries this baffling inheritance from the past was attributed to the Romans, Danes, Phoenicians and Druids. Most of these theorists recognized it as a temple, but one school of thought (the Danish) identified it as a crowning place of kings.

TODAY we are inclined to smile at all these notions; we can supply dates and attach archaeological labels that look convincing enough. The truth is, however, that we still have not explained the unique architecture of Stonehenge. Stone circles are a special feature of prehistoric Britain. They are found all the way from the south of England to the extreme north of Scotland, where there are fine examples in the Orkneys. Some of them are circles of free-standing stones; others are enclosed by a circular bank and ditch. These circles are all assumed to be holy places, and all can be said to have some relationship with Stonehenge. But how inferior they are! Even Avebury cannot compare with the architectural grandeur of Stonehenge.

It is not surprising that Avebury and Stonehenge, the two most imposing circles in Britain, should both be situated on the Wiltshire downs. As geographers have often pointed out, this region forms the hub of the uplands system of southern England, and it was on these uplands that prehistoric settlement was most strongly concentrated. Throughout almost the whole of prehistoric times the English lowlands were made largely uninhabitable and impassable by the heavy growth of oak forest. The early farmers sought the chalk and limestone hills, where the thin, light soil could readily be cleared to improve pasturage and make room for their small grain plots.

On the broad chalk plateau of Salisbury Plain and the adjacent Marlborough Downs many lines of hills converge—the Cotswolds and their northern prolongation up to Yorkshire, the Chilterns, North and South Downs, Dorset Downs and Mendips. The plateau there-

fore early achieved the dominance usual to centers of communication. Not only were the pastoral tribesmen of this area sufficiently prosperous to be able to afford the prodigious expenditure of labor needed to build Stonehenge and Avebury, but they were able to build them in places accessible to the whole of England south of the Pennines. They may have been able to draw labor or tribute from such a wide area, but whether or not this was the case we can be reasonably confident that the sanctuaries served as rallying points. At the most important seasonal festivals tribesmen must surely have traveled to them along the ridgeways of all the radiating hills. There is interesting evidence for such a gathering of peoples in the occurrence of grave goods of a kind characteristic of the north of England in at least one of the barrow burials lying close to Stonehenge.

LIKE MANY Gothic cathedrals, Stonehenge is a composite structure in which feature was added to feature through the centuries. This structure includes several important parts in addition to the circles of standing stones which are what most people mean when they speak of Stonehenge. Before going on to discuss the history of the monument it will be well first to describe its parts [see diagram on page 278].

To the north of the sanctuary, stretches the great length of the Cursus, a very narrow embanked enclosure some 1¾ miles long. It owes its odd name to the 18th-century antiquary William Stukeley, who liked to fancy that it served as a course for chariot racing. It is easy to laugh at Stukeley's fantasy, but the actual purpose of this and the few other enclosures of the kind in southern England remains unexplained. What is of particular interest for an understanding of Stonehenge itself lies in a recent discovery made at the west end of the Cursus, at the point where the side banks appear to terminate against a long burial mound. In this area excavation and field survey discovered a strong concentration of chippings from the Blue Stones which now form a part of the sanctuary itself. It has therefore been suggested that these stones, known from other evidence to have been present in the area before they were erected in their present sockets, originally stood here at the west end of the Cursus.

The other important outlying earthwork associated with Stonehenge is the Avenue, which can be assumed to have been the main ceremonial approach to the sanctuary. It consists of two parallel lines of bank and ditch about 70 feet apart which, from the northeast side of the circles, run almost dead straight for 1,800 feet, then swing eastward and curve gradually toward the River Avon. The banks and ditches are now so nearly

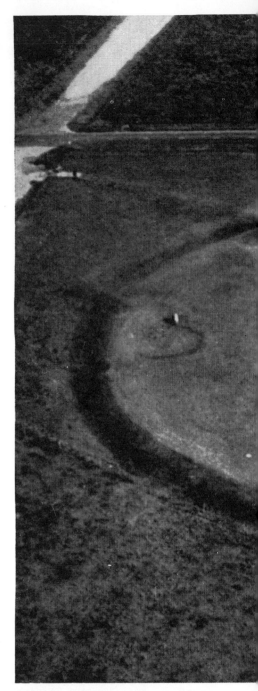

AERIAL VIEW of the monument shows how its stones are encircled

level as to be clearly visible only from the air.

A circular embankment about 320 feet in diameter encloses the sanctuary itself. Such an enclosing bank and ditch is the feature which is held to distinguish a "henge" from an ordinary freestanding stone circle. Immediately inside the bank is a ring of pits, named the Aubrey Holes after their 17-century discoverer. They are 56 in number and all roughly circular. Cremation burials, without urns and normally without grave goods, were found in many Aubrey Holes and also in a quadrant of the ditch and bank.

Between the Aubrey Holes and the

by a bank and a ditch. The small white circles within the bank mark those Aubrey Holes which have been excavated. At the upper right is the Avenue, which runs straight for 1,800 feet and then curves toward the Avon.

stone circles are two more rings of pits, long known to archaeology as the Y and Z Holes; the individual pits are oval and about six feet long.

AFTER THIS account of the earthworks and ceremonial pits associated with the monument, we can leave these painfully unspectacular but historically important features and approach the stones themselves. Those that first catch the attention are the immense sarsens, great monoliths of sandstone. The nearest place from which blocks of this size could have been obtained apparently is the Avebury region, miles away, and the transport of the some 80 sarsens at Stonehenge, running up to 30 feet in length and weighing an average of 28 tons each, was a prodigious effort, especially as the journey necessitated the crossing of a broad, soft-bottomed and overgrown valley. Presumably they were dragged on rollers by men hauling on rawhide ropes.

The sarsen architecture of Stonehenge has two parts: an outer circle about 100 feet in diameter and an inner horseshoe formed of five gateways. The circle originally had 30 columns, united by a continuous lintel of smaller blocks laid over their tops. The stones are all roughly squared, and the lintel stones are secured onto the uprights by tenons and sockets, and to one another by mortise joints. The chopping out of two tenons on the top of each upright and of the rails of the mortise joints is a remarkable achievement for masons working only with clumsy stone mauls. The largest sarsens of all are found in the inner horseshoe, which measures 44 feet across and 50 feet along the axial line. Its colossal central gateway is more than 25 feet high.

THE SARSEN peristyle and horseshoe setting astound us by their size and the unparalleled precision of their masonry; they please the eye, too, by their soft gray color and the richness of texture produced by the weathering of the sandstone. Yet it is the other element of this extraordinary monument that can claim the most fascinating and dramatic history. The plan of the outer circle and horseshoe of sarsens is repeated on a smaller scale by a circle and horseshoe of the so-called Blue Stones. These stones are very much smaller and they lack the architectural refinement of lintels. What is so astonishing about them is that they were made from rocks (mainly dolerites and rhyolites) which are found together only in the Presely Mountains in the extreme west of Wales.

It is equally astonishing whether one thinks of the immense physical difficulties of their transport from Wales to southern England or of the sanctity which must have resided in them to prompt prehistoric men to undertake such a feat.

The question of the route by which the stones were carried has been much disputed. Perhaps the most satisfactory view is that they came by sea (probably from Milford Haven in the west of Wales) to the mouth of the Bristol Avon and were then conveyed across Somerset and Wiltshire by a series of rivers

close enough together to require only short portages. This seems the easiest route—but even so the distance involved is well over 300 miles. Across the innermost tip of the Blue Stone horseshoe lies a single so-called Altar Stone. This supposed Altar Stone, which in fact may formerly have stood upright, is made of a variety of sandstone found near Milford Haven.

THE layout of the complicated sanctuary at once suggests different periods of construction for its parts. The enclosing embankment and the Aubrey

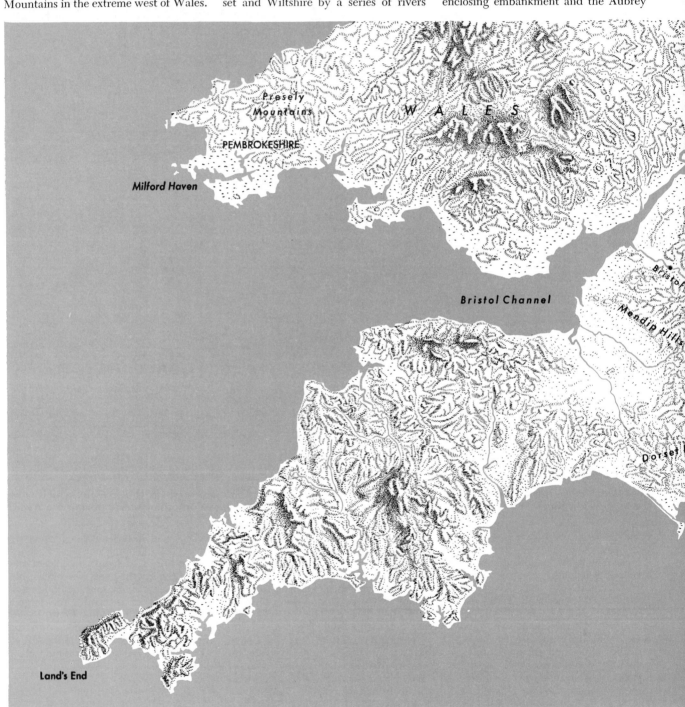

RELIEF MAP of southern England and Wales shows the geography which influenced the location of Stone-henge. When the monument was built, the English lowlands were covered with a thick oak forest; the early

Holes have one common center, while the stone structure is very precisely centered on a different point, a foot or two from the center of the earthwork. The axis of the stone complex as marked by the horseshoes falls exactly along the center line of the Avenue but considerably to one side of the entrance causeway through the earthwork. As for the Y and Z Holes, they are set in irregular arcs as though the distances had been measured not from a true center but by estimation from the outer sarsen circle.

Thus the plan suggests that the enclosure and Aubrey Holes are of one age, the stone structure and the Avenue of a second, and the Y and Z Holes of a third. Excavation and analysis of many kinds have proved this division to be correct, and furthermore that this order in fact represents their correct chronological sequence. They have also shown that the Cursus belongs to the earliest period, being approximately contemporary with the enclosure and Aubrey Holes.

ALTHOUGH many difficulties and uncertainties still remain, years of digging and research have at last made it possible to give a coherent account of the long history of Stonehenge. The first building period is now generally recognized as belonging to a late neolithic culture. These tribesmen dug the long entrenchments of the Cursus, the enclosure ditch with its single entrance and the ritual pits within. Just before or after the making of these very humble earthworks they transported the Blue Stones and Altar Stone from Wales. As these stones must already have been imbued with a most compelling religious value, it can be assumed that they had formed part of a sacred monument in Wales. They were set up at some spot

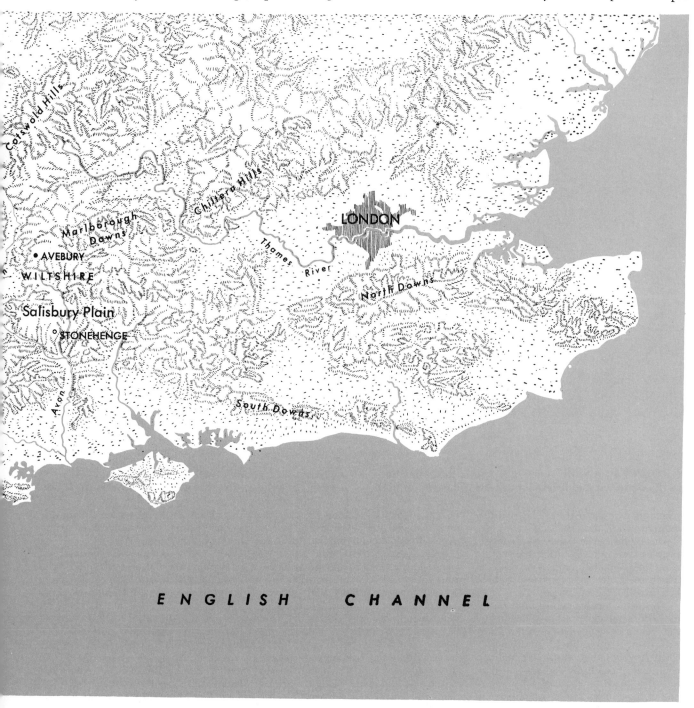

farmers thus sought the thinly covered chalk and limestone hills of Wiltshire. Some of the stones for the monument came from the Presely Mountains in Wales by way of the Bristol Channel or around Land's End.

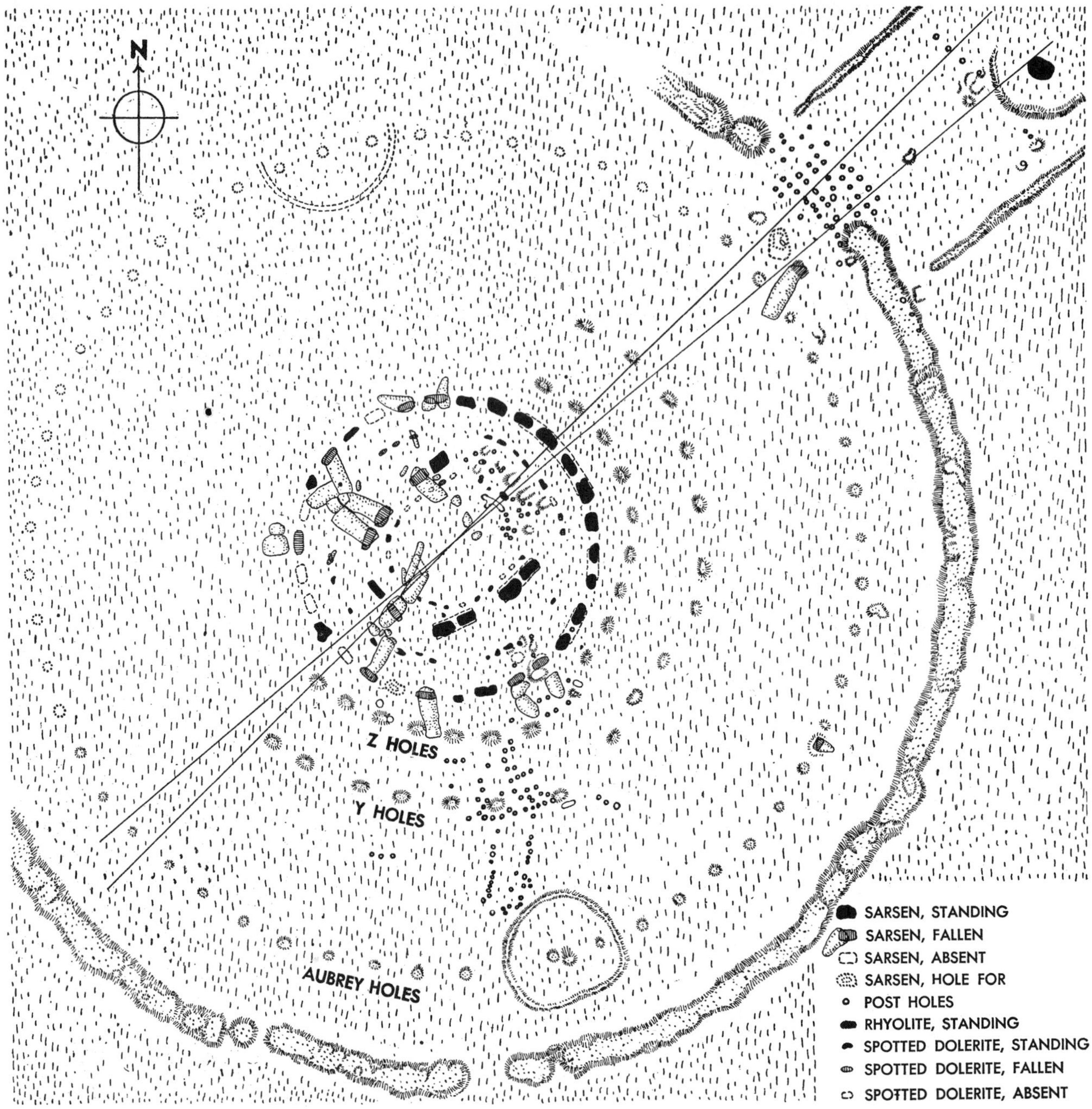

SARSEN, STANDING
SARSEN, FALLEN
SARSEN, ABSENT
SARSEN, HOLE FOR
POST HOLES
RHYOLITE, STANDING
SPOTTED DOLERITE, STANDING
SPOTTED DOLERITE, FALLEN
SPOTTED DOLERITE, ABSENT

GROUND PLAN of Stonehenge shows its stones both in their present and original positions. The axes of both the large and small horseshoes are aligned with the Avenue, but the main entrance to the enclosure is not.

which may or may not have been at the western end of the Cursus.

During this earliest phase the neolithic peoples were already using the monument for cremation burials—a practice which seems to have continued unbroken into the second phase.

This first Stonehenge has been dated by British archaeologists as belonging to the centuries immediately after 2000 B.C. It was exceedingly gratifying to them to have their historical findings confirmed recently by radiocarbon dating of a piece of charcoal taken from one of the Aubrey Holes, which gave a date of about 1845 B.C., with a possible margin of error of 275 years.

The second period of Stonehenge, the period of its greatness, appears to have followed upon the first with no greater break than is implied between the Romanesque and Gothic phases of a cathedral. The enormous sarsen blocks were dragged from the Marlborough Downs, given their final shaping with stone mauls and set in position; the Blue Stone monument was dismantled and its pieces reassembled to enhance the sanctity of the new building. At much the same time the Avenue was laid out as a ceremonial way. Cremation burials continued to be made inside the sacred area, while outside it the wealthy and powerful men and women of the tribe were buried with their gold, their scepters of office and other precious posses-

sions below the barrows which still ride so majestically upon many of the neighboring downs.

For the exact period and cultural background of the men of genius who designed this second Stonehenge there is no direct evidence. Certain elements which Stonehenge has in common with the relevant phase at Avebury suggest that this, like the more northern sanctuary, was built by beaker-using peoples who began to invade and settle in Britain in about 1800 B.C. On the other hand, it has been very tempting to assume that the building was done by the people of the Bronze Age Wessex culture, whose leaders lie buried in the richest of the associated barrow graves, and in whose time (about 1450 B.C.) the power and prosperity of the Salisbury Plain region was at its height.

AS FOR the uses for which this great building was raised, there is no possibility of doubting that it was a sacred place, and little need, except for the excessively cautious or scholastic, to refrain from calling it a temple. There is no question, either, that its orientation was dictated by the position of the midsummer sunrise. The axis of the second Stonehenge points to the spot where the sun would have risen at the summer solstice during the first half of the second millennium before Christ.

If in its second phase the monument reached its glory, in its third phase it must have presented a melancholy picture of decay. It would hardly be possible to claim anything better for a period represented by the Y and Z Holes, and possibly by a single inhumed burial! It is not known for what purpose these Y and Z Holes were dug, for they appear never to have held either posts or standing stones.

That they were dug after the stone circle was already tumbling into decay is clearly shown by at least one piece of evidence. One of the big sarsens of the outer stone circle has fallen across the Z circle, and there is no hole beneath the stone, although the spacing of the Z Holes indicates that one should have been there. It seems plain enough that it could not be dug because the stone already blocked the way.

Pieces of pottery found in the pits suggest that the Y and Z Holes date from the Celtic Iron Age, probably from about the second century B.C. If this is so, it is more than likely that they represent a very limited attempt to restore the use of the sanctuary after a long period of decay covering all the latter part of the Bronze Age. This Iron Age revival makes it permissible to say that perhaps by good luck Stukeley may not have been altogether wrong when he spread the idea, still too widely held, that Stonehenge was the handiwork of the Celtic priesthood of the Druids. Build it they most certainly did not, but they may conceivably have officiated there before the ancient sanctuary was abandoned and left to turn into a noble ruin.

AS WE have seen, the history of Stonehenge did not end with its abandonment. If we take a unified view of history, Stonehenge is no less important as a subject for countless chroniclers and many poets, as a place visited by Pepys and where Charles II whiled away an afternoon after the battle of Worcester, than it is as the greatest sanctuary of prehistoric Europe. Certainly we can say that if in the Bronze Age it was known throughout Britain, today it is famous all around the world.

VARIOUS ASPECTS of Stonehenge are shown by these photographs. The monument is seen from the east (*top*), southeast (*middle*) and northwest.

The Archaeology of Winchester

by Martin Biddle
May 1974

*This English cathedral city was faced with the loss of
its past as a result of urban redevelopment.
Excavation has now revealed the pattern of its
growth since its birth some 2,000 years ago*

How is a city born and how does it grow? If it is long dead, like Troy or royal Ur, archaeology can readily provide some of the answers. If the city is still very much alive, like Rome or London, the evidence is harder to obtain. Nonetheless, over the past 12 years an intensive archaeological campaign has uncovered the early periods and amplified the recorded history of one such city. The site was a major defended settlement during the latter part of the British Iron Age, was the island's fifth-largest town in Roman times, was a prosperous bishopric from the seventh century, was a royal seat until well after the Norman Conquest and is today one of England's leading cathedral cities, with a population of 33,000. The city is Winchester, and what more than a decade of urban archaeology has revealed about it is a fair indication of how much can be achieved elsewhere in the world when the work is begun before the past is irretrievably destroyed.

The River Itchen, the trout stream made famous by Izaak Walton in *The Compleat Angler*, rises in central Hampshire and flows south through a range of chalk downs on its way to Southampton Water, behind the Isle of Wight. Since remote antiquity the river valley and the grassy downs have provided natural lines of communication, the one north-south and the other east-west. At the point where the two routes cross and the alluvial valley floor is narrowest a spur of the chalk downs slopes more gently than elsewhere toward the riverbank.

A mile or so southeast of this spur the valley of the Itchen is commanded on its opposite eastern side by an Iron Age hill fort: St. Catharine's Hill [*see illustration on page 283*]. Built during the third or second century B.C. and enclosing an area of more than 20 acres, the defenses give evidence of having been recon-

structed several times before being burned in the first century B.C. By then a settlement had appeared on the western side of the valley, on the same chalk spur where Winchester would later lie. In about the middle of the first century B.C. the new settlement was formally defined by the construction of a rampart and ditch that enclosed an area of just over 40 acres, or nearly twice the area of the eastern hill fort. This enclosure was the dominant feature of the valley in the later Iron Age. It lay astride the east-west route and commanded the river crossing.

Although little is known of the interior of the western settlement, its central area seems to have been densely occupied. The economy of the inhabitants was based on agriculture, but there is also evidence for long-distance trade connections. Fragments of southern Italian wine amphoras of the first century B.C. have been found, and the enclosure and its immediate vicinity have produced nine large bronze Ptolemaic coins of the third century B.C. from Egypt. These, of course, may have been imported for the value of their metal long after the time when they were first minted.

The size of the western enclosure is impressive, but there is not yet enough evidence to suggest that it contained an urban or even a proto-urban community. Moreover, the settlement appears to have been a false start; there is a break of as much as 100 years in its habitation. When the area was reoccupied soon after the Roman conquest of Britain in A.D. 43, the settlement was on the valley floor near the river, outside and downhill from the Iron Age enclosure.

Much of what we know about the growth of the settlement in Roman times is the result of emergency excavations first undertaken in 1961, when

preparations were being made for the building of a new hotel in the center of the city. The rescue excavation soon revealed two facts. The first was the immense and virtually untapped wealth of Winchester's archaeological record. The second was the rate at which that record would be destroyed by the modern developments then planned for the decade ahead.

The city today is an important administrative, judicial, military, ecclesiastical and business center. The pressures generated by these urban functions find expression in plans for new roads and buildings, all potentially destructive of the buried remains of the city's past. A special body, the Winchester Excavations Committee, was set up in 1962 to deal with the problem of investigating and recording the archaeological evidence before its destruction. During the next 10 years the committee administered the largest program of urban excavation yet undertaken in Britain (or elsewhere in Europe for that matter). For seven years the work has been a joint Anglo-American venture, done in collaboration with the University of North Carolina and Duke University and supported by government and foundation funds from both sides of the Atlantic.

The project had from the start the principal objective of studying the origin and changing character of the urban community throughout its entire existence, from the first permanent settlement down to the emergence of the modern city in the reign of Victoria. The city itself was to be the subject, rather than any one period or aspect of its past. We hoped to try to grasp the totality of the urban phenomenon and the interaction of the city and its setting, both at distinct moments in time and between one period of its development and another.

The project involved not only rescue

excavations on threatened sites but also excavations on unthreatened ones, some of them large enterprises that yielded information essential to any balanced concept of the city's evolution. The project also required the integrated utilization of all the available evidence, whether it was from archaeology, from the natural sciences or from written records (in which the city is immensely rich from the 12th century on).

In 1968 the Winchester Research Unit was set up to prepare this large body of material for publication. A series of perhaps 12 volumes of *Winchester Studies* is planned. They will come from the Clarendon Press at Oxford and the University of North Carolina Press. The first volume will appear late this year or early in 1975.

The new Romano-British settlement on the Itchen was peopled not by Romans from Italy but by Romanized Celts. Their settlement may have grown up in a rather formless way at the junction of the new Roman roads that met close to the old river crossing. These roads, built shortly after the Roman conquest, were perhaps protected by a detachment of troops housed in a fort at or near their junction. If the fort ever existed, and the evidence is still unclear, its life was no more than 20 years. The development of

the civil settlement was in contrast rapid: by the end of the first century it had become a walled city with a chessboard street plan and public buildings. The earth-and-timber ramparts of the city defenses enclosed an area of more than 143 acres. Their line was followed by all subsequent walls of the city down to the end of the Middle Ages.

The size of the enclosed area made Winchester the fifth-largest city in Roman Britain. Two long-distance Roman roads formed the axes of the rectilinear street system that divided the city into *insulae,* or blocks. A central block was occupied by the forum and basilica, constructed by about A.D. 100 to house the judicial, administrative and principal commercial functions of the city. The city was now known as Venta Belgarum. As "Venta" may imply, it was the market center of its region, and as "Belgarum" indicates, that region was populated by the Celtic tribesmen known as the Belgae, from among whose principal landowners the city's chief citizens were drawn.

Little is known of the detailed development of Roman Winchester. At first its houses, even if they were provided with such amenities as glazed windows, painted walls, tiled roofs and mosaic

floors, were built of timber. Increasing prosperity in the later second century led to their being rebuilt in stone. About A.D. 200 the defenses, which must long have been out of repair, were totally remodeled. Within a generation the earth-and-timber perimeter was strengthened by the addition of a stone wall that was to stand for 1,500 years. The influence of the stone ramparts is still reflected in the traffic problems of the modern city.

The Romano-Britons left behind one common kind of archaeological evidence: the remains of their dead. In the Roman fashion the cemeteries lay along the roads outside the city gates. Here in the mid-fourth century, among the burials of the native population, is found the first clear evidence of the arrival of aliens at Winchester. Some graves, distinguished by the leather belts with bronze fittings they contained, are apparently those of soldiers. Their equipment is of a kind well known along Rome's frontiers on the Rhine and the Danube.

During the second half of the fourth century, following the barbarian ravaging of Britain in A.D. 367, the defenses of the island provinces were reorganized. An important element in the revised strategy was a system of "defense in depth," which was to be provided by walled towns. The towns' fortifications were strengthened by the addition of projecting towers, evidently to mount catapults that could rake attackers with arcs of intersecting fire. Winchester was included in the defense system. The maintenance and use of such artillery probably required the services of specialized troops; the alien element now recognized in burials of this period at Winchester and at other towns may well indicate the presence of such specialists. They were foreigners (perhaps Germans), either regular soldiers or mercenaries.

The movement of troops and even of entire peoples in the interests of frontier defense was a normal part of Roman policy. That policy was evidently continued even after the departure of the Roman administration of Britain at the beginning of the fifth century. In A.D. 410 the Emperor Honorius told the cities of Roman Britain to look after their own defense; this they did by continuing to hire mercenaries. The foreign levies now came not from the distant frontiers of the empire but from the barbarian shores around the North Sea, the traditional homeland of the Anglo-Saxon peoples.

The presence of Anglo-Saxons among the Romanized Celts of Winchester shortly after A.D. 400 is indicated by the

WINCHESTER LIES beside the River Itchen near the center of Hampshire, some 12 miles to the north of Southampton and 60 miles southwest of London, the city that eclipsed it.

presence of pottery identical with the pottery used in their home settlements along the lower reaches of the German rivers Weser and Elbe. Together with the evidence from the cemeteries, the pottery shows that the population of late Roman Winchester was already mixed and that before the end of Roman Britain the first forerunners of the English were already established in and around the city that was eventually to emerge as the capital of an English kingdom: Wessex.

It appears that urban life in Roman Winchester came slowly to an end during the fifth century. At every site of excavation the evidence of decay, the abandonment of buildings and the loss of streets is the same. No objects and only a little pottery of the period from A.D. 450 to 650 have been found. The ruined Roman city nonetheless remained an important focal point as Anglo-Saxon settlement of the region progressed, and this is indicated by two lines of evidence.

First, comparatively few Anglo-Saxon cemeteries of the pagan period from the fifth to the seventh century have been found in the county of Hampshire. The most striking cluster of these cemeteries lies in the immediate area of Winchester, outside the city walls to the east and west. Moreover, an early cemetery that was in use by A.D. 500 lies two miles upstream from the city. Unless the former Roman center was still a focus of some kind, why should these cemeteries, each of which presumably holds the burials of a farm or a small village, be concentrated in its vicinity?

Second, in about A.D. 648 Cenwalh, king of Wessex, founded a church dedicated to St. Peter and St. Paul inside the still standing Roman walls of Winchester. About a decade later this church became the see of the bishop of Wessex. Cenwalh had built the Winchester church not as a bishop's see but simply as a minster, that is, a church served by a group of priests and clerks not necessarily living under monastic rule. One may ask what function and what community this church in the center of a ruined city was intended to serve.

The Anglo-Saxon cemeteries suggest that from the late fifth century into the seventh Winchester was still an important place. (The Saxons transformed the name Venta into Wintancæster.) King Cenwalh's church may indicate the nature of that focus. Excavation of the seventh-century church has shown that it lies adjacent to the Roman forum. In the late Saxon period the Anglo-Saxon royal palace was immediately west of the church and was intimately associated

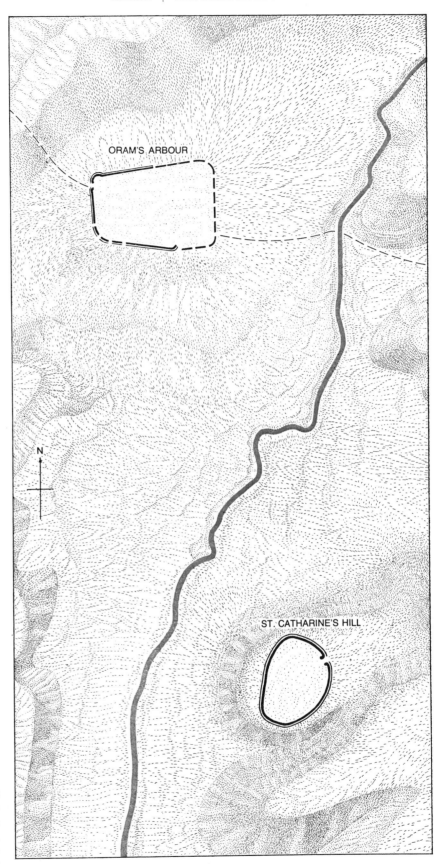

EARLIEST SETTLEMENTS in the Winchester area were two Iron Age defended enclosures. The earlier of the two (*bottom*), the hill fort now known as St. Catharine's Hill, was built in the third or second century B.C. By the time it was abandoned a second defense, twice the size of the first, had been constructed to the north on the opposite side of the river. Commanding the east-west route across the chalk downs, the new enclosure, now known as Oram's Arbour, has yielded pottery made in Italy and large bronze coins minted in Egypt. Both the route location and parts of earthworks shown at Oram's Arbour are hypothetical.

with it. The royal palace also lay close to the forum, in particular to the south end of the basilica, the principal public building of Roman Venta. The origins of the royal palace are unknown, and the site has not been excavated. The relationship of these structures may nonethe-

less support the following interpretation.

We know that the Germanic mercenaries serving in post-Roman Britain revolted against their native masters, thereby destroying the fabric of the life they had been engaged to protect. Power passed to the victorious rebels, who did

not entirely forget, even when they were augmented by successive waves of settlers from barbarian Europe, that they were in some sense heirs of Rome. Continental analogies, for example the towns of Trier and Cologne, show that the buildings that had been the seat of Ro-

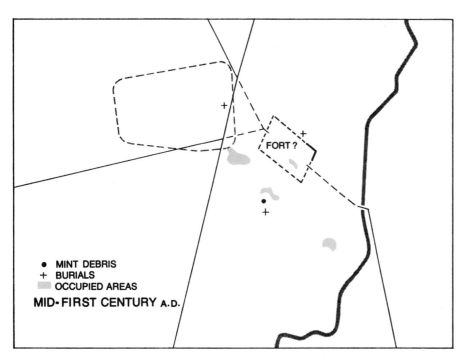

- MINT DEBRIS
+ BURIALS
  OCCUPIED AREAS
MID-FIRST CENTURY A.D.

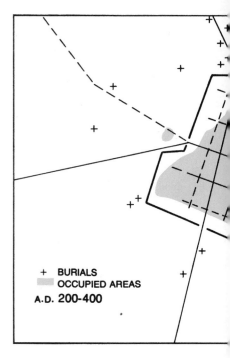

+ BURIALS
  OCCUPIED AREAS
A.D. 200-400

THREE MAJOR CYCLES of urban efflorescence at Winchester are illustrated on these two pages. The city's first roots were planted (*above*), perhaps in the form of a military post, to the east of the abandoned Iron Age enclosure (*light gray*) at the juncture of five Roman roads; this took place in the middle of the first century B.C. Broken lines indicate conjectural restoration.

VENTA BELGARUM, as the growing settlement was known in Roman times, was a fortified town with its streets comprising a rectangular

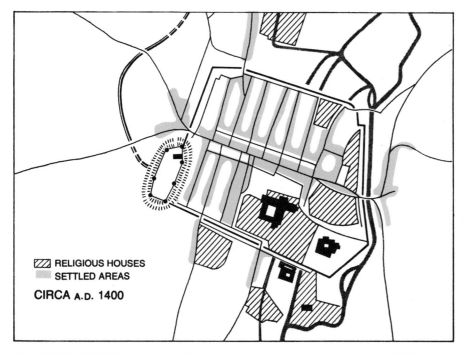

⧄ RELIGIOUS HOUSES
  SETTLED AREAS
CIRCA A.D. **1400**

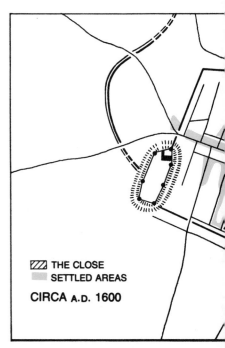

⧄ THE CLOSE
  SETTLED AREAS
CIRCA A.D. **1600**

MEDIEVAL REVIVAL, first under English and then under Norman rule, raised Winchester above its former eminence as a Roman town. As seen here, some two centuries after the Conquest it had already begun to diminish in importance in spite of the great new Norman cathedral that had obliterated Old Minster. Growth of city in this period is illustrated on next two pages.

SECOND SLUMP saw the city drop to 37th place among English towns by the 1520's. Winchester fell even lower after England's monasteries

man authority sometimes survived as the residences of the new rulers. The same may have happened at Winchester. Germanic peoples of Saxon origin were established in the Roman city before its collapse. To them authority over the city and its lands may have passed by conquest or by survival, and their leaders, later to be kings, may have taken up residence in or next to the basilica that was the symbol of that authority.

On that hypothesis the Anglo-Saxon cemeteries outside the walls would reflect the presence of this ruling element within the old walled city, and the founding of the church by a king of Wessex in the middle of the seventh century would represent the establishment of a chapel to serve the royal household. The lack of archaeological material from this period is negative evidence of a certain

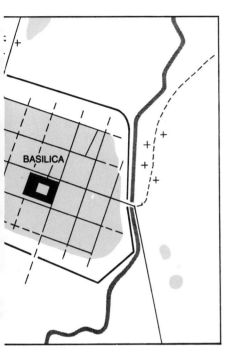

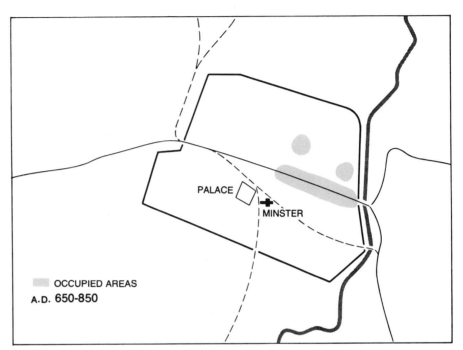

grid surrounding a central basilica and forum. In the third and fourth centuries A.D. it was the fifth-largest of the settlements in Roman Britain.

FIRST DECLINE came in the centuries after the end of Roman rule. By the sixth century only the wall and a single road bisecting the enclosed area remained of Venta Belgarum. For the next three centuries the town, called Wintancæster by the Saxons, may have sheltered a "king's hall" near the ruined basilica; the bishop's minster nearby could also have served as a royal chapel.

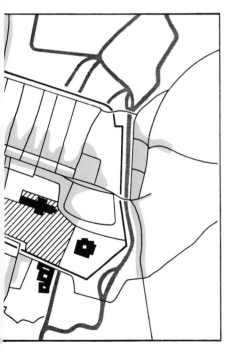

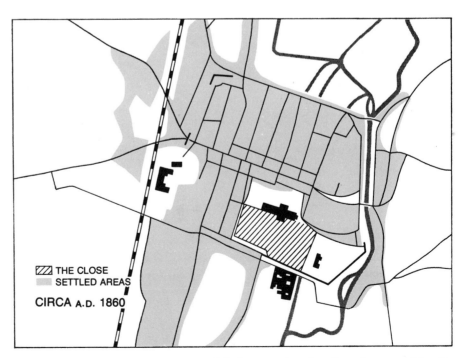

were dissolved during the 1530's. Depressed for 300 years thereafter, the cathedral city largely marked time until early in the 19th century.

VICTORIAN REVIVAL of Winchester included construction of a railway just west of the city, which now stretched beyond the bounds of its Roman walls although only slightly exceeding its maximum extent in medieval times. The southeast quadrant of the old walled area remained dominated by the cathedral and its "close." Just south stands Winchester College, a public school.

value: it shows that the greater part of the walled area was uninhabited. On the other hand, it has nothing to say about the Anglo-Saxon royal palace that has been buried under the cathedral graveyard for eight centuries and remains unexcavated.

With the founding of the church, which later became known as Old Minster, the city of Winchester entered a new phase. A few contemporary written records, an increasing amount of archaeological evidence and comparisons with other English and continental centers make it possible to present a less hypothetical picture of the character of the city in the two centuries following A.D. 648.

Within the walled area of Winchester four components become evident. One is the bishop's church and its community.

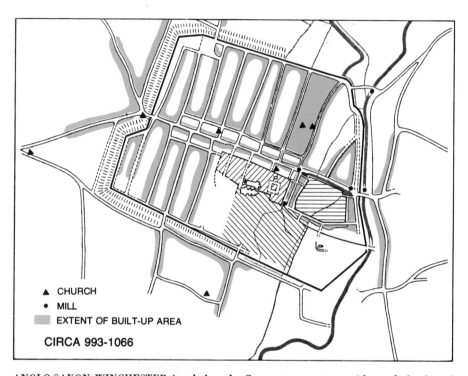

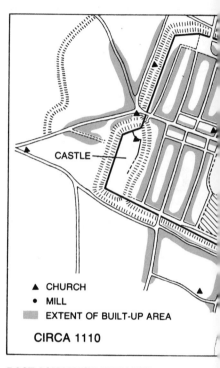

ANGLO-SAXON WINCHESTER just before the Conquest was a town with regularly aligned streets, elaborate defenses and many churches in addition to the Old and New Minsters and Nunnaminster. The illustration directly below shows the city's southeast quadrant in detail.

POST-CONQUEST DECADES were notable for Norman expansion. A new castle (*lower left*) enhanced the

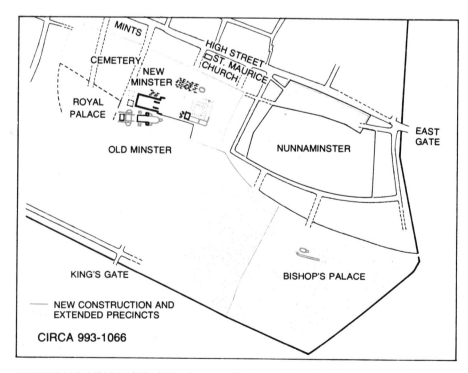

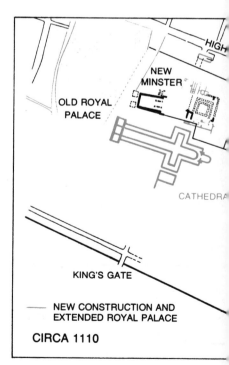

SOUTHEAST QUADRANT of Winchester at the close of the Anglo-Saxon era was the site of the royal palace, the bishop's palace and, in addition to lesser churches, the cathedral church or Old Minster, New Minster and Nunnaminster (nuns' church). Mints may have been located here.

NORMAN CHANGES doubled the size of the royal palace, rebuilt and extended the bishop's palace and also

Another is the royal residence; there is more circumstantial evidence for its existence during this period, when the church was the burial place of the Wessex kings. A third component is the presence of an unknown number of private residences; there is evidence of two such

residential complexes. Of one, only the name survives as a description of an area within the city's East Gate: Coitburi. Names of this type, the second element signifying a defensible enclosure, are known from early London. The other private residence has actually been ex-

cavated in part; its earliest feature is a small private cemetery of the seventh century, probably adjacent to the earliest buildings, which remain unexcavated. The area of the cemetery was eventually built up; the first structures here were of timber, and in about A.D. 800 a stone

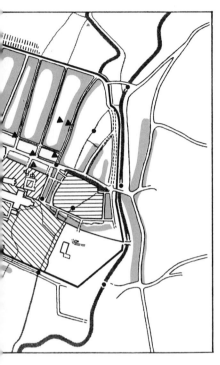

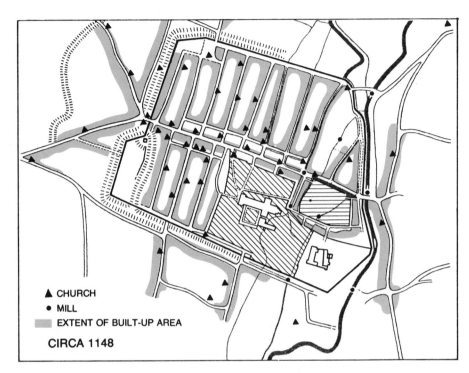

CHURCH
MILL
EXTENT OF BUILT-UP AREA
CIRCA 1148

defenses and a great new cathedral rose. As a Norman seat the city stood second among English towns.

NORMAN APOGEE at Winchester came in the 12th century, when the city's churches numbered more than 50. Winchester's decline began that same century with a loss of close contact with the court. The trend was accelerated by removal of the royal treasury to London during the 1180's.

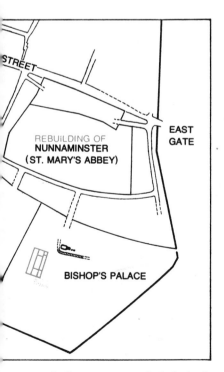

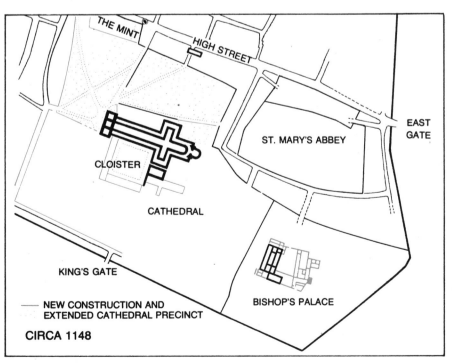

NEW CONSTRUCTION AND EXTENDED CATHEDRAL PRECINCT
CIRCA 1148

raised a great new cathedral. At the time of completion the cathedral was the longest church in all England.

CATHEDRAL PRECINCT had extended over the sites of the royal palace and New Minster by 1148. Nunnaminster, now called St. Mary's Abbey, was rebuilt once again. The bishop's palace, one of the greatest houses of its age, had by now almost reached its ultimate dimensions.

house was built [*see illustration on opposite page*]. Its remains contain evidence for the working and assaying of gold. The wealth of the burials in the private cemetery (one contained a necklace with gold and garnet pendants and 27 silver rings), the construction of a stone building and the working of precious metal all suggest occupants of high social status.

The fourth component is more problematical. It seems likely that the royal, ecclesiastical and private residences must have been supported by some service population, perhaps in the form of a developing street market along the eastern part of High Street, in the area known by about A.D. 900 as *ceapstræt*, or market street. As extensive excavations have shown, much of the walled area of the city was certainly uninhabited at this time, but contemporary records and the archaeological evidence both indicate that some of the walled acres were used for the grazing of livestock and the raising of crops.

The existence of these four components does not make Winchester an urban community at this time; there is no evidence of industry, of a dense population, of trade or of a full social hierarchy. Indeed, only the higher levels of society

seem to be present. Comparisons with Anglo-Saxon Hamwih (modern Southampton), some 12 miles downstream, are instructive. At Winchester we have a royal residence and royal burials, a bishop and his church, the homes (two at least) of subjects of substance and just possibly a mint. Southampton had a mint but no other obvious marks of social greatness. At this time, however, Southampton had a substantial population, much industrial activity and the elements of a regular street plan. Moreover, there is evidence of long-range trade. In contrast, none of these is found in Winchester.

Here are two different kinds of settlement: the old royal and ceremonial center, limited in its extent and functions, and the complementary port and industrial settlement emerging as a true town at the head of a superb natural harbor. Now, Anglo-Saxon kings had many residences, and the primitive apparatus of government moved with the king as he journeyed among his estates. Winchester therefore was not at this time a capital any more than it was an urban community. It was, however, one of the more important royal residences, perhaps because of its church and the city's close association with the royal house.

Beginning toward the close of the

eighth century England was subjected to a series of Viking attacks that steadily increased in severity. By the middle of the ninth century these had evolved into a phase of extensive Scandinavian settlement. Alone among the English kingdoms Wessex survived. After the Battle of Edington in 878 and the Treaty of Wedmore in the same year King Alfred, who ruled Wessex from 871 to 899, set about bolstering the defenses of his kingdom. Alfred's strategy was based on a series of "burhs," or fortified places, so located that no part of Wessex was more than 20 miles from one of them. The burhs were of several kinds: simple forts, refurbished Roman fortresses, newly created towns and former Roman towns that had been refortified and replanned. Winchester was in the last category.

The Roman defenses of the city were brought back into commission and the city gates repaired or rebuilt. Within the walls a new street system was laid out along the axis of the main east-west street; this street had survived in modified form from the Roman period. The other new streets, however, had no connection with the Roman pattern, which had long since vanished. The elements of the new pattern—the east-west High Street, the back streets parallel to it and the intersecting north-south streets—

ROW OF SMALL DWELLINGS, built in the 13th century, lies exposed by excavation. Only the earth floors and the clay sills of walls have survived. Medieval records place cloth-finishing works in this area; the cottages may have housed workers in the industry.

have remained in use with minor changes down to the present. A fourth element, a street running around the entire city inside the wall and providing direct access to the city's perimeter defenses in time of war, is partly lost today. As its original function became unnecessary it was built on in many places.

The ninth-century street plan shows that the entire walled area of the Roman city—143 acres—was brought back into use by the end of the century. Similar street systems can be seen in many of the other burhs set up by Alfred, and there can be no doubt that they represent a deliberate intent to establish urban communities; this English episode of organized town foundation is without parallel in early medieval Europe. The blocks formed by the new streets seem to have represented land apportioned for permanent settlement. In such places military effectiveness was to be secured by economic success.

N ot all Alfred's burhs were successful, but Winchester never looked back. By the 960's the privacy of its monasteries had to be protected against a rising tide of urban life. Before the end of the century several city streets were named after the trades practiced in them. There was a Tanner Street, a Fleshmonger Street, a Shieldmaker Street and later a Shoemaker Street (to give their names in modern English), and suburbs were growing outside each of the city's five gates.

The southeastern quarter of Winchester gave the city its unique character. Here, 100 years before the Norman Conquest, was the most remarkable group of royal and ecclesiastical buildings in Anglo-Saxon England. Edward the Elder (899–924) founded New Minster and Nunnaminster, that is, a "nuns' minster." In the reign of King Edgar (959–975), Old Minster, New Minster and Nunnaminster were reformed and reconstructed. The bishop's palace was established in the same quarter of the city at about the same time, and between 971 and 994 Old Minster was entirely rebuilt. By this time written evidence at last confirms the existence of the royal palace immediately east of the cathedral.

It was in these buildings toward the end of the Anglo-Saxon period that the apparatus of a centralized English state began to emerge. By the reign of Cnut, or Canute (king of both England and Denmark from 1016 to 1035), Winchester had become the permanent repository of the king's treasure. The time of Edward the Confessor (1042–1066) may have seen the emergence of an embryo

ANGLO-SAXON HOUSE, some 23 feet square, may have been built around A.D. 800. The four corners and the doorway incorporate masonry, much of it taken from Roman buildings, but the walls are mainly courses of flint rubble. The two graves (*right*) continue under wall; antedating the house construction, they form part of a cemetery of seventh century.

financial and secretarial administration. The cathedral continued its ancient association with the ruling house: Cnut was buried in it in 1035 and Edward was crowned there at Easter, 1043, thus formalizing his accession the preceding year. Even before the Norman Conquest the custom seems to have been established of the king of England's wearing his crown in Winchester Cathedral at Easter, the most important feast of the Christian year.

No other place in England and few places in all Europe played such a central role in the life of a state during the 11th century. Yet Winchester was not the largest city in the realm. It was perhaps fourth in size and economic power, being surpassed by London, York and Lincoln in that order. Yet it was emerging as a kind of national capital, a distinction that was destined to pass to Westminster and London in the century that followed.

Victorious at Hastings on October 14, 1066, William the Conqueror seized Winchester without opposition in November, opening the way for the surrender of London and his coronation in Westminster Abbey on Christmas Day. The effects of the Conquest on Winchester were as complex as they were considerable. In the larger buildings, in the composition of the upper levels of urban society and in social fashion there were profound changes. In administration, in

the bulk of the population and in the basic fabric of the houses and the streetscape there was essential continuity. If for many in Winchester the immediate dislocation caused by the Conquest and the appropriation of land for new buildings was serious, the massive Norman financial investment in major public works during the remainder of the century and the presence of royal officials, barons and magnates of the newly rich Anglo-Norman aristocracy ensured for the city a rapid recovery and a clear improvement in its wealth and status.

By about 1100 the ancient role of Winchester as a royal center had been given new emphasis. In February, 1067, a Norman castle had been begun at the point where the Roman defenses at the southwest corner of the city formed a salient. In about 1070 the Anglo-Saxon royal palace was extended northward to High Street and doubled in area, the additional space being required for the construction of the Conqueror's hall and palace. East of the palace the total rebuilding of Old Minster was begun in 1079. The eastern part of the new cathedral was dedicated 14 years later, in 1093, and the entire project was completed in 30 or 40 years.

The Norman cathedral demonstrated most clearly, as perhaps its builders had intended, not only the eminent role of the city but also the finality of the Norman acquisition of the Anglo-Saxon

SITE OF OLD MINSTER, the principal cathedral church of the Anglo-Saxon kingdom of Wessex, is seen under excavation (*left*) in this aerial photograph. The excavation lies to the north of the cathedral built by the Normans following their conquest of England.

MORE THAN 1,100 REINTERRED SKELETONS were found near the west end of the cathedral. In digging foundations for the Norman cathedral the builders disturbed many burials. In filling the trench dug to gather stone from Old Minster for use in the new building they disposed of the disturbed remains. Skulls were placed toward west according to tradition, but other bones were jumbled.

state. The new cathedral was more than 500 feet long, making it larger than any other church in England or Normandy, longer than old St. Peter's or any of the churches on the pilgrims' route to Santiago de Compostela in Spain. Only the contemporary abbey church built by St. Hugh at Cluny in Burgundy was longer.

With the building of the castle, the rebuilding of the palace and the cathedral, the repair and reconstruction of New Minster and Nunnaminster (renamed St. Mary's Abbey), Winchester in about 1100 was a principal residence of the Norman kings, the seat of the royal administration and a center of great ecclesiastical importance. Englishmen had yielded place to Normans in the houses along the most important streets of the city. The English had also adopted Norman fashions to such an extent that 70 percent of the citizens' names recorded in about 1110 were foreign, whereas only 15 percent had been before the Conquest. The English were nonetheless still prominent in affairs. Winchester's

mint was now second in importance only to London's, and the moneyers, whose ranks included the leading burgesses and property owners in the city, were almost all English.

Winchester probably reached its zenith in the early years of the 12th century. After 1104 Henry I abandoned the custom of the annual Easter crown-wearing at the cathedral, a practice that had been regularly observed by his predecessors. Royal interest shifted from the palace in the center of the city, in intimate contact with the cathedral, to the new castle on the hill beside the wall. By the 1130's the palace was no longer a royal residence; it may by then have passed to the bishop, whose role in city affairs was now increasing. At that time the rebuilding of the episcopal palace at Wolvesey in the southeastern corner of the city was undertaken. Successive kings also extended the period over which the bishops of Winchester might enjoy the profits of St. Giles Fair, held on

the hill east of the city. The three days originally granted by William Rufus in 1098 were increased to 16 days under Henry II. Although the fair was probably of pre-Conquest origin, its heyday came in the 13th century, when it was one of the most important fairs in England and was attended by traders from many parts of Europe.

In the civil war of 1141 Winchester was seriously damaged. The old royal palace was burned down, and St. Mary's and Hyde Abbey and many parish churches and private houses suffered severely when the city was sacked by the London contingent supporting the king. By that time London had been the largest and wealthiest city in England for some 200 years. Westminster had emerged as a royal residence in the 11th century and increased greatly in importance with the rebuilding of the Abbey by Edward the Confessor and his burial there in 1066. By the middle of the 12th century an increasing number of administrative functions were located at Westminster. Finally in the 1180's even the tradition of Winchester as the site of the royal treasury gave way, and the king's treasure was transferred to London.

The close link between Winchester and the crown was now severed. The castle remained an important royal residence, often embellished and often visited, but it was of no more importance than many another great house. The economy of the city held up during the rest of the 12th century, but there are signs of trouble in the 13th century, as first the western suburb and then the western neighborhood within the walls began to decline. Large areas of the city passed into religious hands. By the 14th century considerable tracts within the walls were no longer built up. A petition of 1440 cited the destruction of 11 streets, 17 parish churches and 987 houses as a result of pestilence and the withdrawal of trade. Where Winchester had occupied second place among English cities at the end of the 11th century, by 1200 it was sixth or lower. By 1334 it was 14th, by 1377 it was 29th and by 1527 it was 37th. Many of the city parishes were amalgamated in the early 16th century, but it was the suppression of the monasteries in 1536–1539 that wrought the greatest changes, removing three monastic communities, four friaries and several lesser institutions.

The built-up area of the city was by now confined to the central and eastern parts of High Street, to the adjacent areas of the side streets, to the main north-south street and to the eastern and southern suburbs. So it was to remain for three centuries. By the early 19th century a revival had begun, encouraged by the growing role of Winchester as a garrison town and by the advent of the railway in 1839.

Ancient Winchester now lies under the streets and buildings of an active and dynamic modern urban center. Reconstruction, redevelopment and the redesign of approach roads and internal streets are destroying the evidence of the city's past at a quantifiable rate. The pattern of the city's Roman-built defenses was effectively breached for the first time only in 1939. By 1950, 2 percent of the defenses had been destroyed and by 1965, 8 percent. By 1980 completion of the city's traffic plan will have raised this figure to 35 percent. A third of the 2,000-year-old defensive system will have been removed in 40 years. There are many similar examples.

In such a situation the raw material for the study of urban evolution has to be rescued now or not at all. Winchester

is exceptionally rich in written records, but they barely touch the first 1,000 years of the community's existence, its Iron Age and Roman cycles and its Anglo-Saxon rebirth. Historical data only become full during the time of Winchester's long medieval decline. This is a pattern that is repeated all over Europe. The basic evidence for the study of urban origins and growth, for the waxing and waning of our towns and cities, has not been recognized until the last moment before its destruction. In London not more than 15 years remain in which to undertake an inquiry that will never again be possible. The example of Winchester may show what can be won. It also shows how much may be lost.

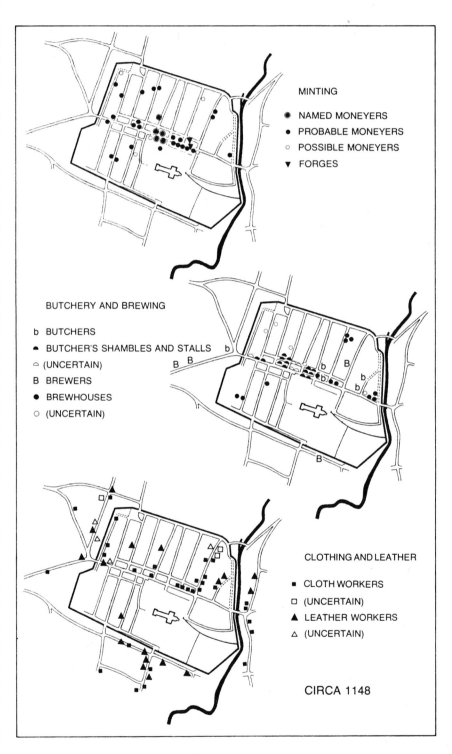

MINTING

● NAMED MONEYERS
• PROBABLE MONEYERS
○ POSSIBLE MONEYERS
▼ FORGES

BUTCHERY AND BREWING

b BUTCHERS
⌒ BUTCHER'S SHAMBLES AND STALLS
◠ (UNCERTAIN)
B BREWERS
● BREWHOUSES
○ (UNCERTAIN)

CLOTHING AND LEATHER

■ CLOTH WORKERS
□ (UNCERTAIN)
▲ LEATHER WORKERS
△ (UNCERTAIN)

CIRCA 1148

URBAN TRADES AND INDUSTRIES in mid-12th-century Winchester included victualing and manufacture in addition to the minting of coins. Five properties, four of them on High Street, were occupied by moneyers whose names appear in an 1148 survey. Another 27 properties are identifiable as probably or possibly moneyers', and two moneyers' forges are known.

How the Iron Age Began

by Robert Maddin, James D. Muhly and
Tamara S. Wheeler
October 1977

*Until almost the end of the second millennium B.C.
bronze was the utilitarian metal of the Mediterranean
world. Within a few centuries it was replaced by a
new kind of metal: "steeled" iron*

It is an old adage that necessity is the mother of invention. The many unanticipated inventions of modern times would seem to be counterexamples, but over the span of human history the adage probably has a certain rough justice. A current investigation in the history of technology is providing a case in point: the appearance some 3,000 years ago of a kind of steel as a substitute for bronze, which until then had been the dominant metal of the civilized world.

For some two millenniums, up to about 1200 B.C., the civilizations of the Old World had satisfied their needs for a utilitarian metal—for tools, weapons, armor and many other durable articles—with various types and alloys of copper, including bronze. Toward the end of that era, known loosely as the Bronze Age, the civilizations of the eastern Mediterranean suffered a series of disturbances. Exactly what caused these disturbances is not known, but one fact about the ensuing centuries has become clear: the use of bronze rapidly diminished and the use of iron—specifically "steeled," or carburized, iron—increased even more rapidly.

Various items of evidence, necessarily fragmentary but diverse enough to inspire a degree of confidence, suggest the speed of the transition. Iron was known as a workable metal during most if not all of the Bronze Age. Nevertheless, Bronze Age sites in the eastern Mediterranean and Southwest Asia representative of a 2,000-year span of history have yielded a total of fewer than 500 iron artifacts, most of them ornamental. The bronze artifacts recovered from the same sites are numbered in the scores of thousands.

Contrast this picture with the number of knives and weapons made from both metals that have been found at sites in Greece representative of the period between 1050 and 900 B.C. A. Snodgrass of the University of Cambridge tabulated the relative abundance of bronze and iron as follows: bronze knives none, iron knives more than 15; bronze swords none, iron swords more than 20; bronze spearheads eight, iron spearheads more than 30.

This distribution is remarkable on two counts. First, bronze articles of this kind can be made by casting, a quick and easy production method, whereas similar iron articles must be individually shaped by forging, a comparatively arduous process. Second, bronze, like its principal constituent, copper, is remarkably durable and can be scrapped and recast repeatedly. Why had the people at these sites substituted a complex process for a simple one? And what had become of the bronze articles they had made in earlier years?

Future archaeological investigation may reveal why bronze went into a decline. Among the causes could have been a breakdown of the trade in tin, the principal alloying ingredient in the articles of the later Bronze Age. With respect to the rapid rise of iron as a substitute metal the picture is a good deal clearer. Both archaeological investigations and studies of ancient inscriptions have in recent years substantiated much that was conjectural and revealed much that was entirely unknown. To present this information in context let us briefly describe copper and iron metallurgy as it was known in the last millenniums before the Christian Era.

Copper is found both as a metal (in lumps of "native" copper) and as an ore that must be heated to yield the metal. For the purposes of this discussion native copper can be ignored. The oldest copper-smelting sites known are at locations in Iran and Israel and date from the fifth and fourth millenniums B.C. Copper ores are found in modest abundance on Cyprus, in various parts of Turkey, in Iran and in Israel. The commonest ore is chalcopyrite, a complex copper iron sulfide that must be roasted in the open air to remove the sulfur before it can be smelted. Certain copper ores contain arsenic; when they are smelted they yield an arsenical copper alloy that can be characterized as "natural bronze."

The early metalworkers of the eastern Mediterranean commonly smelted copper by filling a stone furnace with alternating layers of charcoal and ore combined with a flux. The flux served the purpose of removing from the copper ore the constituents the metalworker did not want in his finished product. These constituents are collectively known as gangue (a word originally derived from the Greek for a vein of ore). In the hot furnace the flux tended to combine with the gangue and remove it from the metal. In many ores of the eastern Mediterranean the gangue was silica: any one of a number of silicon oxides. The appropriate flux for these ores was the iron oxide hematite; the heat of the furnace combined the silicon and iron oxides to form an iron silicate.

When the metalworker had filled his furnace, he ignited the charcoal. In some furnaces the heat of the fire was increased by the natural draft provided by a flue; in others air was forced into the top, sides or bottom of the furnace through clay pipes. As the charge in the furnace got hotter the charcoal was oxidized to carbon monoxide; the hot gas flowed upward through the mixture of ore and flux, chemically reducing both. Reduction took place at about 1,100 degrees Celsius, and the molten copper trickled down to form a puddle at the bottom of the furnace, leaving the gangue behind as a slag. The early metalworkers could not have accurately predicted or measured the furnace temperature; presumably if no puddle of copper appeared, they let the furnace cool off and started over again with a different charge or more draft.

If the ore happened to contain more than a few percent of arsenic what the metalworker found was a puddle of natural bronze. The bronze had the advantage of being harder than copper. Even if the puddle was merely soft pure copper, however, the cast metal could be made harder by hammering. Working the copper in this way made it possible for metalworkers to fashion reasonably durable copper articles during a pre-

Bronze-Age period that varied in its duration in different parts of the eastern Mediterranean and Southwest Asia.

Arsenical copper ores eventually came to be widely smelted because of the greater hardness of natural bronze. It was later discovered that copper combined with tin instead of arsenic was also hard. It may be that the toxicity of arsenic led to the replacement of arsenical bronze by tin bronze. In the eastern Mediterranean and Southwest Asia tin bronze first appeared around the beginning of the third millennium B.C.; by the early years of the second millennium the production of tin bronze had surpassed that of arsenical.

Late in the second millennium B.C. upheavals in the eastern Mediterranean, some of them attributed in Egyptian texts of the time to the activities of interlopers known collectively as the "Peoples of the Sea," led to the collapse of local authority in a number of areas. In the centuries that followed, described by students of the ancient world as a dark age, iron soon replaced bronze as the metal most commonly used for tools, weapons and other articles. Since bronze had been satisfactory for the same purposes for several thousand years and iron did not appear to be as useful, it must be inferred that iron was not suddenly adopted as a result of technical innovation but rather that bronze suddenly became scarce. The further inference is that the scarcity resulted from an interruption in the supply of tin and even of copper to the bronze smelters of the eastern Mediterranean. Where the tin had been coming from is not known. The source may have been such relatively nearby mining areas as the Balkans or the Eastern Desert of Egypt; it may even have been such distant areas as Cornwall or eastern Iran.

The early metalworkers produced iron from ores, mostly hematite and magnetite, by a smelting process much like the one used to produce copper. There was, however, an important difference. Iron does not melt at temperatures below 1,537 degrees C., and the highest temperature that could be reached in a primitive smelter appears to have been about 1,200 degrees. Smelting iron ore at that temperature yields not a puddle of metal but a spongy mass mixed with iron oxide and iron silicate. These nonmetallic substances, which collectively represent slag, arise from the combination of ferrous oxide and silica gangue in the reduction process.

The commonest of the nonmetallic substances is fayalite, which remains viscous at temperatures down to 1,177 degrees C. The metalworker therefore withdrew a mass of spongy iron from the furnace, reheated it in a forge and quite literally squeezed the fayalite out of it by hammering.

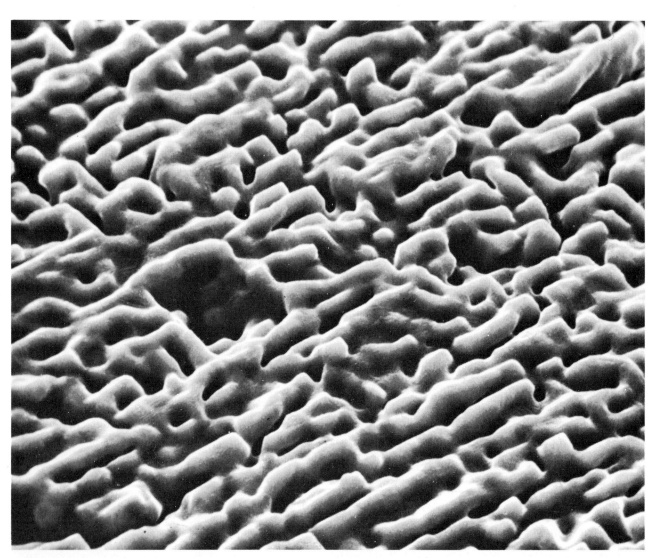

SPONGY STRUCTURE of bloomery iron is revealed in this scanning electron micrograph which shows a modern sample of iron that was smelted at a temperature below its melting point. To produce the sponge a very pure oxide of iron was reduced in an atmosphere of helium and carbon monoxide; the result is seen magnified 2,400 diameters. With a sample of ordinary iron ore the interstices of the sponge would be filled with slag, which could be expelled by hammering. The sample was prepared by Y. K. Rao of the University of Washington.

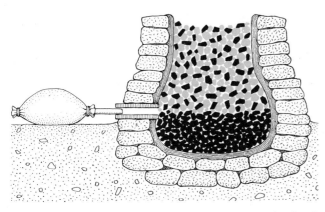

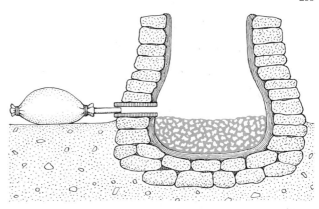

IRON SMELTER, seen here in a speculative reconstruction based on the remains of European Iron Age furnaces, was first filled with a mixed charge of ore, usually hematite or magnetite, and charcoal (*left*). The charge was ignited and the furnace temperature was raised to about 1,200 degrees Celsius by a draft. Because iron does not melt below 1,537 degrees C. the product of the smelting process (*right*) was the spongy mixture of nonmetallic wastes and iron (*color*) known as a bloom. The blacksmith reheated the bloom on a forge to above 1,170 degrees C., making the wastes viscous. The smith then removed the wastes from the iron by hammering. What remained was soft iron.

The hammering at the same time turned the porous iron "bloom" into a continuous network of iron grains interspersed with a few stringers of slag that had not been eliminated. The bloom was the blacksmith's raw material; the iron articles were made by heating and hammering the bloom further.

What the blacksmith had to work with was a poor substitute for bronze. Bloomery iron is a soft metal; its tensile strength is about 40,000 pounds per square inch, only slightly more than the strength of pure copper (about 32,000 p.s.i.). Work-hardening, that is, continued hammering, will bring the strength of iron up to almost 100,000 p.s.i. A bronze containing 11 percent tin, however, has a tensile strength after casting of some 60,000 p.s.i. and a strength after cold-working of as much as 120,000 p.s.i. Bronze was clearly a better material than bloomery iron for the manufacture of weapons and tools.

Bronze had other major advantages over iron. Since it melted at temperatures that the early metalworkers could attain, it was suited to casting. A bronze containing 11 percent tin begins to lose fluidity when it cools to 1,000 degrees C., and it is completely solid at 831 degrees. Since pure iron does not melt below 1,537 degrees, it could not be cast. When iron is alloyed with large amounts of carbon, say 4 percent, it can be made to melt at about 1,150 degrees. The resolidified metal, however, is very brittle. In any event iron was not cast before the middle of the first millennium B.C., when the process was pioneered by the Chinese in the Far East.

The casting methods used in the

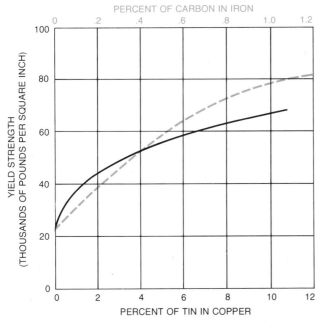

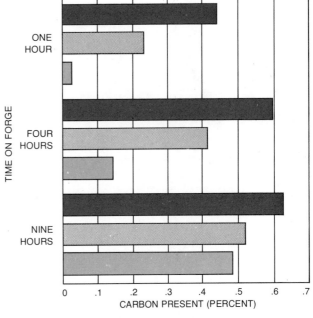

EFFECT OF STEELING, the carburization of bloomery iron by alloying the metal with carbon, is to strengthen the metal until its yield strength is substantially greater than the yield strength of bronze. The addition of 1 percent of tin to copper produces a bronze alloy (*black*) with a yield strength of 30,000 pounds per square inch and the addition of 5 percent tin produces a bronze alloy with a yield strength of 50,000 p.s.i. The addition of .4 percent carbon to iron produces a carburized alloy (*color*) with a yield strength of more than 50,000 p.s.i. An iron that contains 1 percent carbon, in turn, is more than 10,000 p.s.i. stronger than a bronze that contains as much as 8 percent tin.

CARBURIZATION OF IRON results from the diffusion of carbon into the iron from a charcoal fire. The diffusion rate depends on the heat of the fire and the length of time the iron is in the forge. At a temperature of 920 degrees C. the amount of carbon diffused to a depth of half a millimeter below the surface of the iron in an hour (*top bars*) is nearly .5 percent by weight (*black*) but only .02 percent of the carbon has penetrated to a depth of 1.5 mm. (*color*). As the middle and bottom bars show, prolonged exposure increases the percentage of carbon diffused to depths of one mm. (*gray*) and 1.5 mm. below the surface of the iron without greatly increasing percentage at .5 mm.

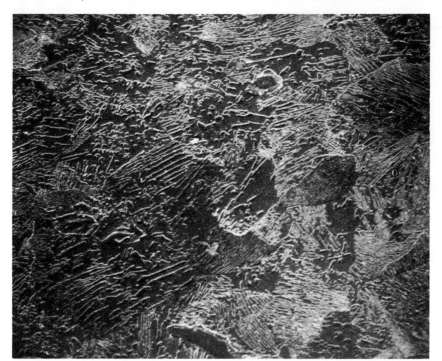

PEARLITE, a characteristic microstructure of carbon steels, has a layered pattern at high magnifications. This scanning electron micrograph enlarges the sample 1,250 diameters. It shows a gold-covered replica of the corroded surface of a steeled-iron blade found at a site in Israel: Tel Fara South. Although the iron is oxidized a relic pearlite microstructure is preserved. The blade was made available for study by the Institute of Archaeology of the University of London.

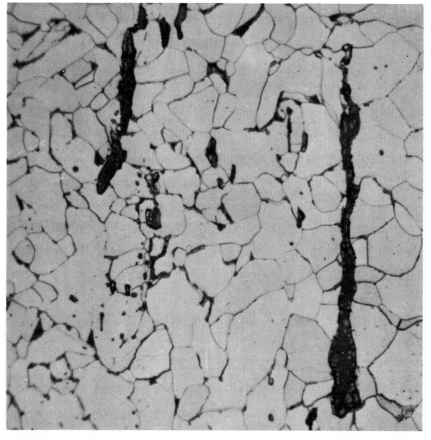

IRON SPIT from a site in Greece is seen in longitudinal section at a magnification of 200 diameters. The narrow dark areas are stringers: fragments of slag in the original iron bloom that were deformed but not expelled by the hammering preparatory to the forging of the spit. The iron artifact was made available for study by the staff of the Numismatic Museum in Athens.

Bronze Age, as indicated by actual molds that have survived or as inferred from written references, were remarkably diverse. There were one-piece, two-piece and multipiece molds made of earth, clay and stone. Some molds had cores, and the lost-wax process made it possible to cast the bronze in complex shapes and with elaborate surface decoration. Iron, except for the brittle high-carbon metal, was useless for any of these processes, which turned out not only utilitarian articles but also a great number of purely ornamental objects such as figurines and jewelry. Bronze had one further advantage. It corrodes slowly, and the characteristic green patina is considered decorative. Iron corrodes rapidly, and in the process often suffers considerable damage.

How, then, could iron become a satisfactory substitute for bronze as the second millennium B.C. drew to a close? The answer is that if bloomery iron is treated in a certain way, it can be transformed into an alloy that is for most purposes far superior to bronze. That treatment is steeling, and its initial discovery was probably accidental. What happened was as follows. When the blacksmith reheated the iron bloom in order to hammer out the slag, he did so with a charcoal fire in the forge. He needed to heat the bloom to 1,200 degrees C. to make the slag viscous, and he probably did not let the temperature go much below 800 degrees until the work was finished. The bloom was in direct contact with the white-hot charcoal and with the hot carbon monoxide evolved by its combustion. In that temperature range a small amount of carbon from both sources slowly diffused into the iron, in effect converting it into carbon steel down to a certain depth below the surface.

The time required for carbon to diffuse into iron follows simple physical laws. For example, if one plots carbon concentration and depth of penetration at a temperature of 950 degrees C., one finds that after nine hours the concentration at a depth of 1.5 millimeters below the surface is .5 percent. At higher temperatures the carbon atoms diffuse into the iron more rapidly; at 1,150 degrees C. after nine hours the concentration at the same depth can reach 2 percent.

In modern metallurgical terms carburized iron at a temperature higher than 910 degrees C. has the microstructure of the form of steel known as austenite. When the temperature falls below 727 degrees C., the austenite breaks down into two components. One is ferrite, or pure iron. The other is the iron carbide known as cementite. Called the eutectoid reaction, this two-phase breakdown gives rise to the microstructure of the form of steel known as pearlite: alternating layers of ferrite and

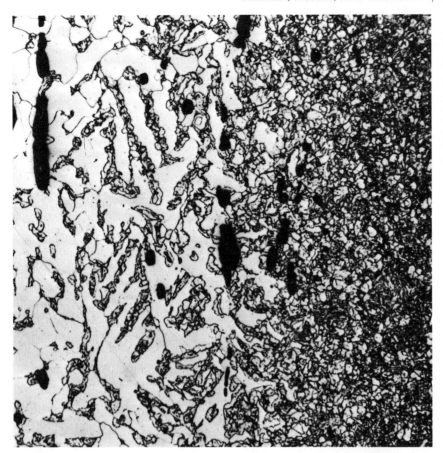

METALLURGICAL SKILL in the fourth century B.C. is indicated in this micrograph. Shown at a magnification of 300 diameters is a section of an adze blade unearthed at Al Mina, the ruins of a Greek trading colony on the coast of Turkey near Syria. The blacksmith who made the implement used a sheet of carburized iron for the working face of the adze but economized by using soft iron for the other face. The micrograph, showing the juncture between fine-grained steeled iron and coarse-grained uncarburized iron, is clear proof of the blacksmith's mastery.

cementite. Reflected in this microstructure is the proportion of carbon in the metal. If the iron is free of carbon, no pearlite will be present. If the alloy contains as much as .8 percent carbon, the microstructure that is formed will be 100 percent pearlite.

It is illuminating to compare the tensile strengths of carburized iron and bronze. A carbon content ranging from .2 to .3 percent gives the steeled iron a strength equal to that of unworked bronze: about 60,000 p.s.i. If the carbon content is raised to 1.2 percent, the steeled iron has a tensile strength of 140,000 p.s.i., which is somewhat greater than the strength of cold-worked bronze. If the blacksmith then cold-hammers the steeled iron, its tensile strength can be increased to 245,000 p.s.i., or more than twice the strength of cold-worked bronze.

The accidental discovery of steeling must have encouraged experimentation, because in due course the early blacksmiths could control the process well enough to develop properties in the metal appropriate to the function of the object they were making. It is possible that future metallurgical studies (and even some that are now in progress) will help to trace the progression from accidental steeling to purposeful steeling. For example, carbon can get into iron by pathways other than carburization. It can be trapped in the pores of the iron bloom; forging would then form the trapped carbon into stringers within the metal. In a polished metallographic section of such an accidentally steeled piece the stringers would appear as uneven streaks. Entirely accidental carburization through exposure to charcoal in the course of heating and forging, although more difficult to detect microscopically, should leave some trace. The carbon content would probably be low and the concentration would be uneven. It is incontrovertible proof of deliberate steeling, however, when one finds an iron object consisting of layers with dissimilar percentages of carbon. The blacksmith would have no reason to make such an object unless he understood the different properties of the different layers. The earliest-known object of this kind is an Egyptian iron knife that was probably made between 900 and 800 B.C.

On the basis of our research and that of others it seems evident that by the beginning of the 10th century B.C. blacksmiths were intentionally steeling iron. Very few iron artifacts of the 12th century B.C. or earlier have been metallurgically analyzed, so that the prevalence of steeling in that period remains uncertain. Nevertheless, a 12th-century knife from Idalion, a site on Cyprus, was certainly carburized to improve its hardness. A site on Mount Adir in northern Israel has yielded an iron pick in association with 12th-century pottery. One would hesitate to remove a sample from the pick for analysis, but it has been possible to test the tip of it for hardness. The readings averaged 38 on the Rockwell "C" scale of hardness. This is a reading characteristic of a modern hardened steel.

Unlike the Mount Adir pick, many of the ancient iron artifacts that have survived in eastern Mediterranean sites are badly corroded, a condition that complicates metallurgical study. Several techniques, however, make it possible to detect pearlite even in objects that are totally oxidized. In one such technique a polished surface is prepared for study under the microscope at magnifications greater than 1,000 diameters. Since the ferrite layers of the pearlite differ from the cementite layers in their chemical composition, it is sometimes possible to detect them even in iron oxide. An even more promising technique makes use of the scanning electron microscope. Here it is not the polished surface that is examined but a gold-plated thin-film replica of it. The ferrite layers are softer than the cementite ones, even in a corroded artifact, and they stand out clearly when the replica is tilted to accentuate the different levels of the two constituents. The presence of pearlite in an iron artifact is a clear indication that the artifact has been carburized.

After 900 B.C. the production of iron implements rapidly increased. Even though at this time tin again became available in the eastern Mediterranean, bronze did not replace iron. Sites dating from the 10th century B.C. to the sixth have yielded great hoards of iron implements. At Hasanlu in northwestern Iran a University of Pennsylvania expedition unearthed iron weapons numbering in the thousands. At Gordion, the capital of ancient Phrygia, another University of Pennsylvania expedition discovered one of the largest collections of iron artifacts ever found in the eastern Mediterranean. At Nimrud in Iraq, the excavations of Max Mallowan of the University of Oxford uncovered another major iron assemblage.

The evidence for the growing popularity of iron goes beyond archaeological finds. Neo-Assyrian and Neo-Babylonian writings reflect a world technologically quite different from that of the period before 900 B.C. References are made to iron axes, iron hoes, iron picks, iron saws, iron arrowheads, iron scissors, iron fetters and even iron furniture and iron lamps. Iron also became the metal of choice for knives and daggers. A passage from the corpus of Babylonian "wisdom literature" strikes a sour note to this effect: "A woman is a pitfall, a hole, a ditch, a woman is a sharp iron dagger that cuts a man's throat."

We have not yet mentioned a second process that significantly enhances the quality of carburized iron. This is quenching: quickly cooling a hot piece of metal by plunging it into water. An article of steeled iron that is left to cool by itself in the open air develops a microstructure of coarse pearlite. If the blacksmith instead waves the finished article in the air, accelerating the process of cooling, the pearlite microstructure is much finer. Even faster cooling by quenching can suppress the development of pearlite altogether; the steeled material has a quite different microstructure and is known as martensite. Martensite is significantly harder than pearlite, although it is quite brittle.

When one displays the results of quenching graphically, it appears that different rates of cooling—from the temperature of the furnace or forge, about 1,200 degrees C., to the temperature of transformation, about 700 degrees— give rise to different microstructures. In an iron containing .8 percent carbon, if the cooling period is approximately 60 seconds, coarse pearlite will form. To produce fine pearlite the cooling period should be only two or three seconds. To produce martensite the temperature must be reduced from the forge level to below 220 degrees C. in less than a second; only quenching can cool the material so quickly. One may assume that for small objects such as arrowheads hardness would be important and brittleness could be tolerated. If such small objects were made from iron with a .8 percent carbon content quick quenching would make them martensite. The same could have been accomplished with the surface layers of larger iron objects where hardness was important and brittleness could be tolerated, even though the interior of the object, being slower to lose heat, would remain pearlite.

It is not possible to estimate when the quenching process was invented; like steeling, it could easily have been discovered accidentally. One item of literary evidence, however, clearly indicates that blacksmiths of the eastern Mediterranean were familiar with the process in the eighth or seventh century B.C. The passage is in the ninth book of the *Odyssey*. Trapped in the cave of Polyphemus, the one-eyed giant, Odysseus and his men manage to get the giant drunk. They decide to blind him by snatching a

burning olive trunk out of a fire and thrusting it into his eye. Our translation follows Richmond Lattimore's:

"As when a man who works as a blacksmith plunges into cold water a great axe or adze which hisses aloud, 'doctoring' it, since this is the way that steel is made strong, even so Cyclops' eye sizzled about the beam of the olive."

The description could only have been written by someone who had watched a blacksmith quench hot iron and knew that the quenching was done to increase the hardness of the metal. It also suggests that quench-hardening was something of a novelty in the Greek world at that time. "'Doctoring' it" is a free rendering of the Greek word *pharmasso;* the

FOUR IRON IMPLEMENTS made in the Near East come from sites of late in the second millennium B.C. to late in the first millennium B.C. The largest (*a*) is a 39-centimeter pick from northern Isreal that was found in association with pottery of the 12th century B.C. Its tip, tested for hardness, yielded an average reading characteristic of a modern hardened steel. The chisel (*b*), from Al Mina, is almost 13 centimeters long; it was cleverly quenched to make its matrix hard without leaving its cutting edge brittle. The small adze (*c*), from Al Mina, is almost 12 centimeters long. It may have been made from the same bloom of iron as the chisel and perhaps by the same blacksmith. Its microstructure is shown in the illustration on page 61. The fourth tool (*d*), 25 centimeters long, comes from the ruins of Nimrud in northern Iraq. Under microscopic examination it shows the pearlite structure characteristic of carburized iron.

implication is that the iron was being treated in some magical way, as if by means of drug potions. Perhaps Homer was puzzled by the fact that whereas water softened or even dissolved many materials, it turned carburized iron into a metal harder than any that had been known before.

It is more difficult to obtain evidence of deliberate quenching than evidence of deliberate steeling. For one thing, water quenching could have been done simply to cool a forged object quickly, perhaps to be able to use it immediately or perhaps to avoid having too many hot objects around the smithy. For another, with an object of any size it is the outer layer that consists of martensite, and it is this layer that is most likely to have been removed by corrosion over the centuries. Nevertheless, some meager evidence of deliberate quenching exists. For example, so far 11 iron artifacts from Nimrud have been analyzed metallurgically. Although all are heavily corroded, five of them show possible indications of quenching. The rest show signs of some carburization but evidently were not quenched.

A third technique of ironworking arises directly from quenching. This is the process of tempering, a practice that reduces the brittleness induced by quenching. The early blacksmiths must have realized soon that quenching made their products brittle. The quenching would have left cracks along the edges of many articles, and users would have complained of breakage. Tempering, that is, reheating up to but not above the temperature of transformation (727 degrees C.), affects the iron carbide that quenching forces into the microstructure of iron so as to give rise to martensite. The carbide precipitates and then coalesces by diffusion. Both the exact temperature attained and the time that the article is held at that temperature determine the amount of iron carbide that coalesces and hence the final hardness and ductility of the metal. As ductility increases, hardness decreases.

For the blacksmiths of antiquity tempering was probably never done intentionally. There is no change in the color of the hot iron at the critical range of temperatures and thus no obvious way of gauging the correct heat in the forge. A method was developed early in the fourth century B.C., however, that surmounted the difficulty of achieving true tempering and at the same time produced carburized-iron tools that were both hard and durable. Our evidence for this statement is a stonecutter's chisel unearthed at the Greek trading colony of Al Mina, a site in coastal Turkey near the Syrian border. The chisel has a matrix composed largely of martensite but containing nodules of pearlite that increase in density toward the tip of the

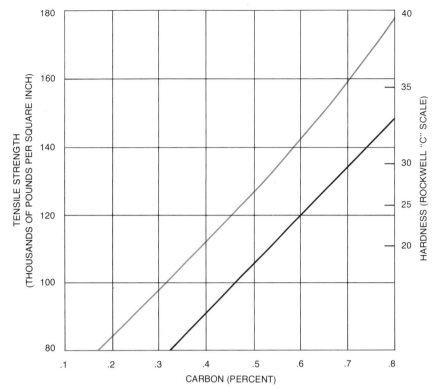

STRENGTH AND HARDNESS of carburized iron both increase as the percentage of carbon in the alloy rises. Degrees of hardness here are measured on the Rockwell "C" scale. If the speed of cooling is not rapid, the steel microstructure that develops is coarse pearlite (*black*). Regardless of its carbon content, coarse pearlite steel is less durable than fine pearlite steel (*color*).

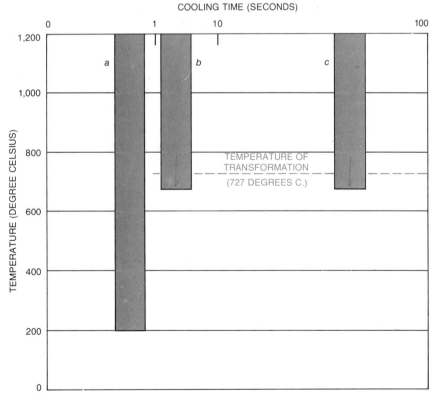

EFFECT OF QUENCHING on the microstructure of carburized iron is shown on this graph in terms of the length of time required to lower the temperature of the iron from its forging heat (about 1,200 degrees C.). If cooling requires less than one second (*a*), the microstructure that forms is martensite, tough but somewhat brittle. If up to three seconds is required, the resulting microstructure is fine pearlite (*b*). Cooling as quick as this calls for quenching. Prolonged cooling, in excess of 10 seconds, forms a third kind of microstructure: coarse pearlite (*c*).

tool, rather than toward the interior as one would expect. Laboratory experiments suggest that this reverse distribution was achieved by covering the tip of the tool with some kind of insulating material, such as clay, heating the piece and then quenching it. Clay would crack off as soon as the tool hit the water, but it would nonetheless slow the cooling rate enough to reduce the amount of martensite formed at the cutting end of the tool. It was evidently by some cheap and simple means such as this one that the blacksmith of Al Mina created a chisel with a strong body and a durable edge.

Another example of innovative smithing was found at Al Mina. Analysis of the elements present in an adze uncovered with the chisel suggests that both tools were made from the same bloom of iron and thus perhaps even made by the same smith. The adze was formed by hot-hammering two sheets of iron together. One sheet was carburized and the other was not. The combined sheets were forged into shape, and the finished adze was air-cooled rather than quenched. The blacksmith, if he was the same man who made the chisel, evidently appreciated the fact that a woodworking adze need not have as hard an edge as a stoneworking chisel. He adjusted the manufacturing process accordingly, probably at a net saving in time and effort. The moment when smiths were first able to control the ironworking process so that the properties of the products were suited to their end uses is clearly a significant one in the history of technology. Such a moment may well be what we see in the finds at Al Mina.

To sum up, by the beginning of the seventh century B.C. at the latest the blacksmiths of the eastern Mediterranean had mastered two of the processes that make iron a useful material for tools and weapons: carburizing and quenching. And by the beginning of the fourth century B.C. at the latest a method had been found to overcome the disadvantages of brittle steel while preserving the advantage of its hardness. The smiths' quest had involved hundreds of years of experimentation and uncountable hours at the furnace and the forge. All the craftsmen of antiquity—potters, masons, stonecutters, weavers, carpenters and smiths of bronze, copper and precious metals—shared the blacksmith's empirical approach to their work, but none of them faced as large a challenge as he did. To be made strong and durable iron needs sophisticated treatments. The blacksmith could not have understood, at least at first, why these treatments improved the iron, but his tenacity, pragmatic knowledge and skill in the centuries following the end of the second millennium B.C. enabled the peoples of the eastern Mediterranean to take the momentous step from the Bronze Age to the Iron Age.

INDEX